Views of Seventeenth-Century Vietnam
Christoforo Borri on Cochinchina & Samuel Baron on Tonkin

 Cornell University

Olga Dror and K. W. Taylor, editors and annotators

Views of Seventeenth-Century Vietnam

Christoforo Borri on Cochinchina & Samuel Baron on Tonkin

SOUTHEAST ASIA PROGRAM PUBLICATIONS
Southeast Asia Program
Cornell University
Ithaca, New York
2006

Cornell Southeast Asia Program Publications
640 Stewart Avenue, Ithaca, NY 14850-3857

Studies on Southeast Asia No. 41

Printed in the United States of America

ISBN-13: 978-0-8772-7771-2 hc / ISBN-10: 0-8772-7771-0 hc
ISBN-13: 978-0-8772-7741-5 pb / ISBN-10: 0-8772-7741-9 pb

Cover Design: Maureen Viele, Ithaca, NY

TABLE OF CONTENTS

Maps
    The World of Borri and Baron   9
    Cochinchina and Tonkin   10
    Cochinchina   11
    Tonkin   12
Preface   13
Introduction   15
    Cochinchina and Tonkin   15
    The Vietnamese Historical Context   20
    Phantasmatic Cochinchina, by Olga Dror   23
        False Start   24
        Looking for New Venues   28
        En route   29
        Mission: Impossible   31
        New Enemies, Friends, and Destinations   41
        Conquering Iberia: Success   44
        Conquering Iberia: Failure   48
        The Return of the Prodigal Son   50
        In a Crossfire   52
        A Layman of Two Religious Orders?   56
        Coda   57
        In Memoriam: Chacun À Son Goût   60
        Onward, Britannia!   64
        Long Live Vietnam!   67
    The Real Tonkin, by K. W. Taylor   74
        A Dutch Father   75
        Baron Goes Over to the English   76
        Adventures   78
        Against Tavernier   80
        Epilogue   82

A Collection of Voyages and Travels, Vol. II   85
An Account of Cochin-China, by R. F. Christopher Borri   89

An Account of Cochin-China, the First Part, of the Temporal State   91
   of the Kingdom of Cochin-China.
    Of the Name, Situation, and Extent of this Kingdom.   91
    Of the Climate, and Nature of the Country of Cochin-China.   95
    Of the Fruitfulness of the Country.   98
    Of the Elephants and Abadas, or Rhinocero's.   108

Of the Qualities, Customs, and Manners of the Cochin-Chinese;   113
   of their Way of Living, their Habit and Cures.
Of the Civil and Political Government of the Cochin-Chineses.   122
Of the Power of the King of Cochin-China, and of the Wars   127
   he has in his Kingdom.
Of the Trade and Ports of Cochin-China.   132

An Account of Cochin-China, the Second Part, Treating of the   137
   Spiritual State of Cochin-China.
Of the First entering of the Fathers of the Society of Jesus into that   137
   Kingdom: And of the two Churches built at Turon and Cacchian.
Of the Persecution the New Church of Cochin-China endur'd, at its   142
   first institution: and how I was Sent Thither to be Assisting to It,
   by my Superiors.
The Governor of Pulucambi Introduces the Fathers of the Society   147
   into his Province, Building them a House and Church.
Of the Governor of Pulucambi's Death.   151
How God Made Way for the Conversion of the Province of   156
   Pulucambi, by Means of the Noblest Persons in It.
How God Open'd Another Way to Christianity, Through the Means   162
   of the Learned People among the Heathens.
How God Open'd Another Way to Christianity, by Means   168
   of the Omsaiis, or Heathen Priests.
A Short Account of the Sects in Cochin-China.   171
How God Opened Another Way to the Conversion of the   176
   Meaner Sort by Miraculous Means.
Of the Churches and Christians of Faifo, Turon and Cacchiam.   179
Of the Kingdom of Tunchim.   181
The Conclusion.   184

A Collection of Voyages and Travels, Vol. VI   187
A Description of the Kingdom of Tonqueen, by S. Baron   189

Taverniere's Account of Tonqueen Animadverted On.   195
Of the Situation and Extent of Tonqueen.   200
Of the Nature and Productions of the Kingdom of Tonqueen.   205
Of the Riches, Trade, and Money of the Kingdom of Tonqueen.   210
Of the Strength of the Kingdom of Tonqueen.   212
Of the Manners of the People of Tonqueen.   214
Of the Marriages of the Tonqueenese.   218
Of the Visits and Pastimes of the Tonqueenese.   221
Of the Learned Men of Tonqueen.   228
Of the Physicians and Diseases of the Tonqueenese.   233
Of the Original Government, Law, and Policy of the Tonqueenese,   236
   with some Considerations Thereon.
Of the General of Tonqueen, His Family, Officers, and Court.   248
That There is No Such Manner of Coronation and Inthronization   256
   of their Kings, as is Related by M. Taverniere.

Of the Ceremony of the King's Blessing the Country, Vulgarly   259
  amongst them, Called Boua-dee-yaw, or, according to their
  Characters, Can-Ja.
Of the Theckydaw, or Purging the Country from all Malevolent Spirits.   262
Of the Funerals in General.   265
Of the Funeral Pomp of the Choua or General of Tonqueen.   270
Of the Sects, Idols, Worship, Superstition, and Pagodas or Temples   277
  of the Tonqueenese.

Bibliography   283

The World of Borri and Baron

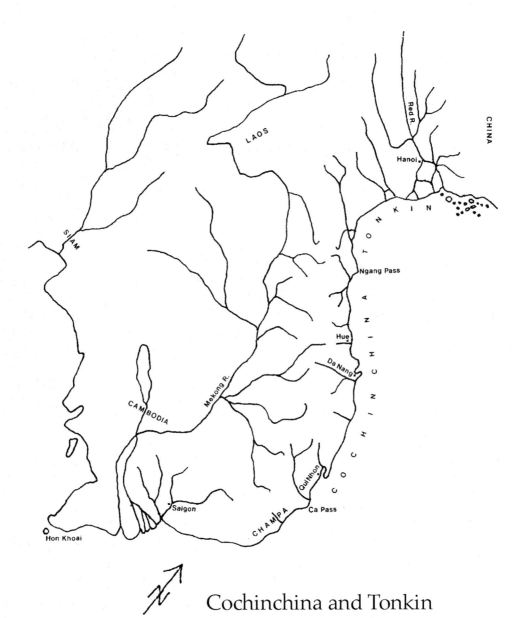

Cochinchina and Tonkin

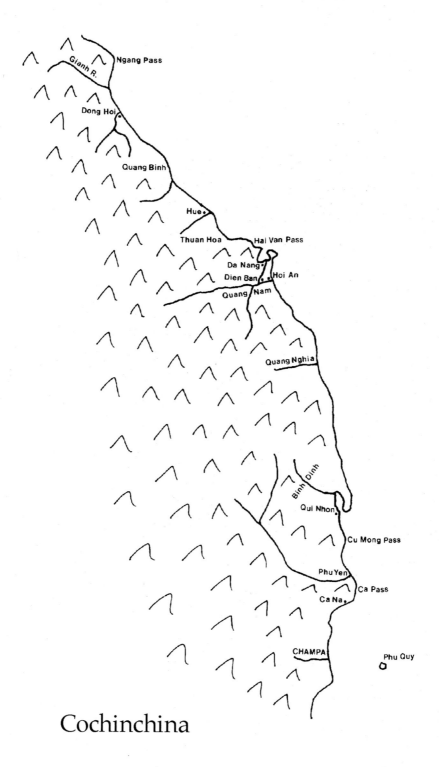

Ngang Pass

Gianh R.

Dong Hoi.

Quang Binh

Hue.

Thuan Hoa   Hai Van Pass

Da Nang.
Dien Ban.   Hoi An
Quang Nam

Quang Nghia

Binh Dinh

Qui Nhon.

Cu Mong Pass

Phu Yen
Ca Pass
Ca Na.

CHAMPA   Phu Quy

Cochinchina

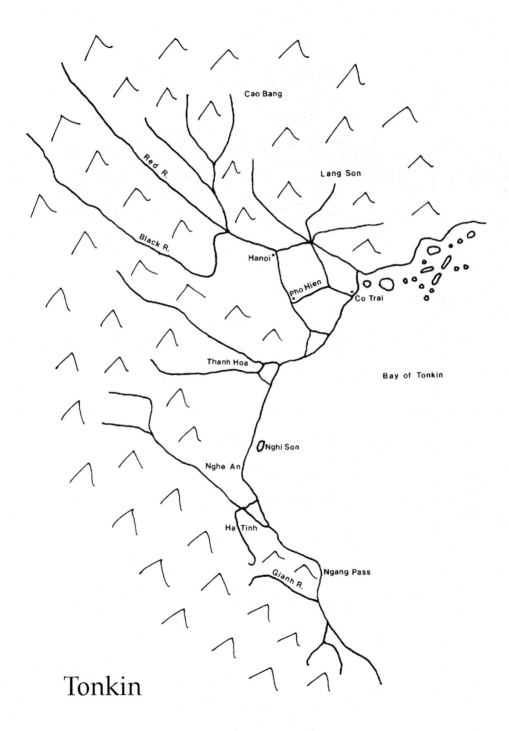

Tonkin

PREFACE

The idea for this volume came from a realization that although Vietnamese sources for the seventeenth century are few there is nevertheless a relative abundance of European accounts from that time, when Europeans first began to publish observations of the Vietnamese. European accounts, written by merchants, missionaries, travelers, and scientists, offer a wealth of detail and a diversity of perspectives. The selection of Christoforo[1] Borri and Samuel Baron was initially guided by three considerations. First, their accounts appeared in English translations prior to the nineteenth century, so they have a history of being read in the English language and in shaping an English-language vantage on the Vietnamese. Second, in the seventeenth century Vietnam was divided into two rival states, and we wanted to include an account written from each. Third, we wanted to represent the voices of the two main groups who experienced and wrote about life among the Vietnamese: merchants and missionaries. But beyond this, having looked carefully at the two authors and their accounts, we have become aware of how their writings reflect specific agendas, which will be discussed in the Introduction.

Although we have benefited enormously from our discussions about all aspects of both authors and both accounts, we divided our work, with Olga Dror completing the introduction and annotations for Christoforo Borri and Keith Taylor doing so for Samuel Baron. We express our gratitude to Deborah Homsher for her patient and professional editorial assistance and to Michael Dror for his help with proofreading.

NOTE ABOUT THE TRANSLATION: ( ) indicates material in parentheses in the original; { } indicates marginal notes in the original; [ ] indicates material added by the annotators. Old English spelling has been retained in many cases, but in some cases has been updated for ease of modern reading.

The map and illustrations from Samuel Baron reproduced in this volume were obtained by permission of the Division of Rare and Manuscript Collections, Carl A. Kroch Library, Cornell University.

---

[1] Although Borri's personal name is spelled variously in different sources, we follow the spelling used in the original 1631 edition of his book about Cochinchina.

INTRODUCTION

COCHINCHINA AND TONKIN

In the seventeenth century, Europeans encountered two Vietnamese-speaking kingdoms. They called the northern kingdom Tonkin (variously spelled Tonqueen, Tonking, Tunquin, Tunchim, etc.), derived from Vietnamese Đông Kinh, meaning "Eastern Capital," a name for Hanoi to distinguish it from the "Western Capital" that had been built at the beginning of the fifteenth century in a neighboring province.[1] This kingdom extended from the Chinese border south to include the modern province of Hà Tĩnh.

Europeans called the southern kingdom Cochinchina; its capital was eventually located at Hue. Several theories have been advanced to explain the name Cochin in Cochinchina. Some early European sources surmised that it derived from the vernacular appellation of the capital city of Tonkin, Kẻ Chợ ("marketplace"), corrupted into Cochi;[2] this theory cannot be sustained. About the same time, a Japanese scholar, Arai Hakuseki (1657–1725), proposed a theory by which Cochin (pronounced Koshi in Japanese) derived from Guangxi (pronounced Kosai in Japanese), but this idea has no discernible merit.[3] Early French colonial writers favored the idea that Cochin came from the expression Cổ Chiêm or its variant, Cổ Chàm, sometimes conflated with Kẻ Chàm ("Cham place"; transcribed Cachiam or some variant thereof in early European accounts), a Vietnamese expression for what is now the central coast of Vietnam, where the kingdoms of Champa once existed (the term means: "Old [i.e., pre-Vietnamese] Champa").[4] This conjecture has not survived.

It is now generally agreed that Cochin derived from Giao Chỉ, the name (pronounced Jiaozhi in Chinese, Koshi in Japanese) given by the ancient Chinese to northern Vietnam as early as 111 BCE.[5] As for the origin of Jiaozhi/Giao Chỉ, as is

---

[1] The "Western Capital" (Tây Kinh, variously Tây Đô) was a fortress built by the ruler Hồ Qúy Ly (r. 1400–1407) in his home province of Thanh Hóa.

[2] For this idea, from the sixteenth century, see: Fernão Vaz Dourado, in A. Kammerer, "La découverte de la Chine par les portugais au XVIe siècle et la cartographie des portulans," *T'oung Pao*, supplement to vol. XXXIX (1944): 260; and Giovanni Battista Ramusio, *Delle navigationi et viaggi* (Venetia: Giunti, 1554), 1:391, and, from the seventeenth century, see Alexander de Rhodes, *Histoire du royaume du Tonkin*, annot. J.-P. Duteil (Paris: Édition Kimé, 1999), p. 21.

[3] See N. Peri, "Essai sur les relations du Japon et de l'Indochine aux XVIe et XVIIe siècle," *Bulletin de l'Ecole Française d'Extrême-Orient* 23 (1923): 5-6, n. 2.

[4] E. Luro and E. Aymonier were cited for this theory at the turn of the twentieth century by Paul Pelliot; see P. Pelliot, "Le Fou Nan," *Bulletin de l'Ecole Française d'Extrême-Orient* 3 (1903): 299, n. 1. A. Bonifacy also favored this idea when annotating his translation of Borri; see Cristoforo Borri, *Relation de la nouvelle mission* in "Les Européens qui ont vu le vieux Hué: Cristoforo Borri," *Bulletin des Amis du Vieux Hué* 18,3-4 (July-December 1931): 286, n. 9.

[5] Pelliot, "Le Fou Nan," was apparently the first to propose this.

often the case with such terms, there is both a classical explanation based on ancient Chinese texts and an ethnographic explanation based on anecdote, but both have to do with feet. The term literally means "intertwined feet" and first appears in the *Liji* (Records of Rituals) to describe the habit among "southern barbarians" of sleeping in circular groups with heads out and feet together in the middle.[6] Europeans have been fond of explaining the term as a reference to a peculiarity in the anatomy of the inhabitants of northern Vietnam, whose large toes extend outward perpendicular to the foot, supposedly to help maintain balance while working in the mud of rice paddies.[7]

The term Giao Chỉ was used as an administrative designation for the Hanoi area throughout the centuries when northern Vietnam was a province of Chinese empires, until the tenth century. Giao Chỉ then became part of the title by which the Chinese Song dynasty enfeoffed Vietnamese kings from the mid-tenth to the mid-twelfth centuries. In the early fifteenth century, the Ming dynasty used the name during its twenty-year effort to reestablish provincial government in northern Vietnam. The Portuguese, arriving in Asia at the beginning of the sixteenth century, encountered the term and used it to refer to Vietnam at a time when the country was not yet divided into two kingdoms.[8]

Christoforo Borri, as we see in this volume, believed that the Portuguese obtained "Cochin" from the Japanese "Koshi," apparently because of the phonetic similarities of the names in Portuguese and Japanese. Alexandre de Rhodes was of the same opinion.[9] This was a plausible supposition for those who like Borri and de Rhodes witnessed the lively maritime relations between Japan and Cochinchina in the early seventeenth century. It was the beginning of the expansion of Japanese trade after the establishment of the Tokugawa peace in the early seventeenth century. In part because trade with China was constrained by coastal disorder, Cochinchina became Japan's major trading partner. The Japanese Shoguns regulated trade by issuing "vermilion seal certificates" to ships specifying where the ships were allowed to trade.[10] Between 1604 and 1622, when Borri departed Cochinchina, sixty-nine Japanese ships received certificates to trade in Cochinchinese ports; during the same time, forty-nine certificates were issued for Luzon, forty for Siam, twenty-eight for Cambodia, twenty-one for Macao, twenty for Tonkin, and five for Champa.[11] From this, we can see the importance to Japan of trade with Cochinchina. The main port city of Cochinchina, Hội An (called Faifo by Europeans), where Borri resided for a time, had a quarter especially reserved for the Japanese community.[12] De Rhodes notes the presence of Japanese merchants

---

[6] See K. W. Taylor, *The Birth of Vietnam* (Berkeley, CA: University of California Press, 1983), p. 26.

[7] For example, Gio. Filippo de Marini, *Relation nouvelle et curieuse des royaumes de Tunquin et de Lao*, tr. L.P.L.C.C. (Paris: Gervais Clouzier, 1666), p. 2.

[8] See L. Aurousseau, "Sur le nom de Cochinchine," *Bulletin de l'Ecole Française d'Extrême-Orient* 24 (1924): 564ff.

[9] De Rhodes, *Histoire du royaume du Tonkin*, p. 21.

[10] See Peri, "Essai sur les relations du Japon et de l'Indochine," pp. 2-3.

[11] See Robert L. Innes, "The Door Ajar: Japan's Foreign Trade in the Seventeenth Century" (PhD dissertation, University of Michigan, Ann Arbor, 1980), p. 58.

[12] See *Ancient Town of Hoi An: International Symposium Held in Da Nang on 22-23 March, 1990* (Hanoi: Foreign Languages Publishing House, 1991).

in Tonkin,[13] and several Japanese Christians assisted the early Jesuit missionaries in Cochinchina.

Nevertheless, there is overwhelming evidence that the Portuguese obtained the name from the Malays; the nasalization of the second syllable of Cochin has no possible origin in Japanese, while there is a strong tendency to nasalize this syllable in Malay.[14] Sixteenth-century Portuguese transcriptions of Cochinchina include: Quachymchyna, Concamchina, Cauchimchyna, Cachenchina, Cauchenchina, Cauchinchina, and Coccincina.[15] Tomé Pires and João Barros, two Portuguese who visited the area in the sixteenth century and wrote in 1515 and 1565, respectively, explicitly attribute the appellation to Malays. For example, we read in Tomé Pires's account, written before Cochinchina existed as a separate kingdom in the south, that: "In Malacca this country [i.e., Vietnam] is called Cauchy Chyna" and "The kingdom is between Champa and China"; furthermore, he explains that it is called Cauchy Chyna "on account of Cauchy Coulam."[16] The reference to Cauchy Coulam is to Cochin, a city-state on the Malabar coast of southwestern India where the first Portuguese fleet arrived in 1500 and founded the first European fort in India. Cochin is not far from Quilon (here transcribed Coulam; also transcribed elsewhere as Kollam). Quilon was the largest and richest kingdom in that region, according to Pires, "the greatest in Malabar in land and subjects."[17] Quilon was a seaport that had diplomatic relations with China as early as the fourteenth century. Pires is making the point that the term Cochinchina was meant to distinguish this place from the Cochin in India.

In fact, in 1502 and 1503, after the Portuguese had reached India but before they had taken Malacca, Cochinchina had already appeared on maps made in Genoa in the inverted form of Chinacochim.[18] There is no apparent explanation for this inversion, but it reminds us that the name had an existence even before Europeans had explored the South China Sea. In the thirteenth century, Marco Polo reported the existence of Caugigu, which modern scholars read as Chinese Jiaozhiguo (Vietnamese Giao Chỉ Quốc, "Kingdom of Giao Chỉ"), and an equivalent to this term appears in an early fourteenth-century Persian history of the Mongols.[19] Furthermore, by the thirteenth century, Arab geographers were using the term Kawci min Cin ("Giao Chỉ of China"), following a pattern they used for other places in the region of China, and L. Aurousseau conjectured that this is the source of the term in Malay, for the word "min" was typically abbreviated into a nasalized syllable when spoken to produce KawcimCin, which is a plausible explanation for the Portuguese transcriptions of Malay that nasalize the second syllable. While other names from the Arab geographers in the pattern of "_____

---

[13] De Rhodes, *Histoire du royaume du Tonkin*, p. 21.

[14] See Pelliot, "Le Fou Nan," and Pierre-Yves Manguin, *Les Portugais sur les côtes du Viêt-Nam et du Campa: Etude sur les routes maritimes et les relations commerciales, d'après les sources portugaises: XVI, XVII, XVIII siècles* (Paris: Ecole Française d'Extrême-Orient, 1972), p. 42, n. 2.

[15] Aurousseau, "Sur le nom de Cochinchine."

[16] See Armando Cortesão, trans., *The Suma Oriental of Tomé Pires: An Account of the East, from the Red Sea to Japan, Written in Malacca and India in 1512-1515* (London: The Hakluyt Society, 1944), pp. 114.

[17] Ibid., p. 80.

[18] Aurousseau, "Sur le nom de Cochinchine."

[19] Ibid., pp. 574-5.

min Cin" fell out of usage, this one did not because of the need to distinguish between the Cochin in India and the Cochin near China.[20]

Borri is the first to use the name Cochinchina to refer not to the Vietnamese polity as a whole but rather only to the southern realm. The nomenclature of Tonkin and Cochinchina to refer to northern and southern Vietnamese kingdoms appears to have originated with the Jesuits in the early seventeenth century,[21] for they were the first Europeans to pay close attention to this part of the world and to write about it.

In the early seventeenth century, Cochinchina extended from the Gianh River in the province of Quảng Bình to the pass on the southern border of Phù Yên province (Đèo Cả; Cape Varella of French geographers); by mid-century, this kingdom was expanding the range of its armies into the Mekong plain, and by the end of the century it had established a major administrative center at Saigon, which had been a Vietnamese outpost since the 1620s.

At that time, aside from sailors, Europeans in Asia were either Catholic missionaries or merchants. Christoforo Borri, an Italian Jesuit, was a missionary in Cochinchina from 1618 to 1622. Samuel Baron, born in Hanoi, probably in the late 1630s or early 1640s, of a European father and a Vietnamese mother, was active in Tonkin as a merchant in the 1670s and 1680s. Their accounts are among the earliest descriptions of what we now call Vietnam to appear in European languages.

In the eyes of seventeenth-century Europeans, Tonkin and Cochinchina were two countries with their own forms of government, economy, society, and culture. It was understood that the two countries were related by language, by historical memory among the educated, and by theoretical allegiance to a common but powerless monarch, but it was also understood that there was no meeting of minds between the northern and southern rulers, who were at war with each other for most of the century. Indeed, the border between the two countries was marked by fortified military encampments; the southerners had built a system of walls from the sea to the mountains at Đồng Hới to block northern armies.

What seventeenth-century Europeans saw as the Kingdom of Cochinchina had been relatively recently settled by Vietnamese-speakers. The most northerly parts of it, as far south as the vicinity of the modern city of Đà Nẵng, had been vulnerable to Vietnamese armies and immigrants at least since the early fifteenth century. In the 1470s, the Vietnamese permanently garrisoned the southern coast as far as what is now the southern border of Bình Định province (Đèo Cù Mông). When the Nguyễn clan gained ascendancy in these lands during the last half of the sixteenth century, Vietnamese speakers there were already viewing themselves as different from the "northerners."[22] By the end of the seventeenth century, the Nguyễn had defeated repeated invasions by the northern Vietnamese and had established military garrisons in the Mekong plain.

The accounts of Borri and Baron give sharply different views of the Cochinchinese and the Tonkinese. According to Borri, the Cochinchinese were well governed, friendly and easy-going, curious about other countries, welcoming to foreigners, good at trade and commerce, wealthy and prosperous, and their

---

[20] Ibid., pp. 577-9.

[21] Ibid., pp. 567-69.

[22] K. W. Taylor, "Nguyen Hoang and the Beginning of Viet Nam's Southward Expansion," in *Southeast Asia in the Early Modern Era*, ed. Anthony Reid (Ithaca, NY: Cornell University Press, 1993), pp. 42-65.

language was easy to learn. According to Baron, the Tonkinese were poorly governed, unfriendly and choleric, not curious about other countries, suspicious of foreigners, clumsy at trade, poor and hungry, and with a language difficult to learn. These accounts can be read as evidence of two different countries at that time in the territory of modern Vietnam. At the same time, we must remember that Borri and Baron were quite different people with different backgrounds, experiences, and agendas. Borri was a foreigner who resided among Vietnamese no more than five years. Baron was at home in Hanoi, where he was born and raised. Borri was European. Baron was Eurasian. Borri was a Catholic missionary. Baron was a Protestant merchant. Any use of their writings to document two separate Vietnams must also take into account their backgrounds, perspectives, and aims.

THE VIETNAMESE HISTORICAL CONTEXT

For nearly three centuries, from the collapse of the Lê dynasty at the beginning of the sixteenth century until the founding of the Nguyễn dynasty at the beginning of the nineteenth century, rival governments, most of the time at war with each other, ruled the Vietnamese. It appears that this was related to the southward movement of the Vietnamese into territories inhabited by Chams and Khmers and the inability of any single regime to maintain control of all Vietnamese speakers during that time of change.

The Lê dynasty was the first major dynasty not to come from the Red River plain. After less than a century in power, the Lê were overwhelmed by rivalries among clans in its home province of Thanh Hóa and a reaction to Thanh Hóa dominance of the Red River plain led by the Mạc, who in the 1520s proclaimed their own dynasty at Hanoi. During the rest of the sixteenth century, there was war between the Mạc, who came from the coast near a mouth of the Red River, and the Trịnh and Nguyễn clans of Thanh Hóa, who claimed to be fighting to restore the Lê. Vietnamese terms later applied to what Europeans called Tonkin and Cochinchina—that is Đàng Ngoài ("outside") for Tonkin and Đàng Trong ("inside") for Cochinchina—appeared at this time as the terms used by Lê partisans, both the Trịnh and the Nguyễn, to refer to themselves as the "inner" group that remained loyal to the Lê and to the Mạc as the "outer" group in rebellion against the legitimate dynasty.[23] It appears that in the seventeenth century this terminology acquired geographic as well as, if not instead of, political connotations, with a usage that appeared during the years of southern expansion and continues today among all Vietnamese, by which one goes "in" to the south and "out" to the north.[24]

In the 1470s, the Lê had extended Vietnamese rule into the south as far as Cù Mông Pass, on the southern border of what is now Bình Định province. The new territories thereby opened up for Vietnamese settlement became the base for a new political power in 1558, when the leader of the Nguyễn clan, seeking to avoid the rising power of his Trịnh ally, went south and established his headquarters in the region of Hue. In the 1590s, Nguyễn military forces assisted the Trịnh in driving the Mạc out of the Red River plain and into the upland province of Cao Bằng on the northern border, where they were protected by Ming China. However, within two decades, the Trịnh and Nguyễn were locked in a series of wars that lasted into the 1670s. Aside from a few years in the 1650s when Nguyễn forces occupied parts of what is now Hà Tĩnh province, these wars mainly consisted of Trịnh expeditions against the Nguyễn. By the 1630s, the Nguyễn began to construct a series of walls stretching from the mountains to the sea at Đồng Hới, which became the rock upon which all subsequent Trịnh attacks were broken. During this time, both the Trịnh and the Nguyễn claimed to be fighting on behalf of the Lê kings, who existed as virtual prisoners of the Trịnh in Hanoi. The Lê kings were called *vua*, the

---

[23] Roland Jacques, *Portuguese Pioneers of Vietnamese Linguistics* (Bangkok: Orchid Press, 2002), p. 15.

[24] K. W. Taylor, "Surface Orientations in Vietnam," *The Journal of Asian Studies* 57,4 (November 1998): 959.

Vietnamese word for "king," while the Trịnh and Nguyễn rulers were called *chúa*, the Vietnamese word for "lord" or "warlord."

The Trịnh-Nguyễn wars ended in relation to three factors. First, the rise of the Qing dynasty in China to replace the decrepit Ming had a calming effect on Vietnamese politics. The arrival of Qing forces on the border enabled the Trịnh to finally eliminate the Mạc, who had survived in Cao Bằng under the diplomatic protection of the Ming. But it also discouraged the Trịnh from continuing to channel its resources into warfare on its southern border. Second, the chronic lack of battlefield success eventually turned the focus of Trịnh government away from the frontier ambitions of Thanh Hóa warrior clans and toward administering the rice lands of the Red River plain. And third, Nguyễn success in continuing to expand the southern frontier and to accumulate wealth from foreign trade, even while concentrating resources to protect the northern border, made the aggressive Trịnh policy toward the south increasingly implausible.

In 1611, the Nguyễn pushed their border down to Cả Pass to include the modern province of Phú Yên. Champa thereafter became a subservient vassal kingdom. By the 1620s, the Khmer king had ceded the site of modern Saigon, which became a Nguyễn outpost. Thereafter, Nguyễn armies began to appear regularly in the Mekong plain to intervene in Khmer politics on behalf of various factions at the Khmer court. Later in the century, the Nguyễn settled large numbers of Ming loyalists fleeing the Qing conquest of China in the Mekong plain, and in the 1690s a permanent administrative headquarters was established at Saigon.

European merchants and missionaries first arrived among the Vietnamese during the era of the Trịnh-Nguyễn wars. The Portuguese had already been in the region for a century. They developed a strong relationship with the Nguyễn in trade and in military technology, particularly gunnery. Thus, in the second decade of the seventeenth century, the first missionaries to arrive among the Vietnamese came to Cochinchina on Portuguese boats. Among these first Europeans to live among the Vietnamese was Christophoro Borri. We read in his account about the warlike situation between the two Vietnamese states, even before the first battles took place. We also read about Nguyễn envoys on their way to Cambodia at the very beginning of Vietnamese involvement in the Mekong plain. Borri's account was written at the start of what would become a relatively successful Jesuit mission among Vietnamese in both Cochinchina and Tonkin. As we will see, he had interests other than gaining converts to the Christian religion, and these interests clearly shaped how he chose to remember his time in Cochinchina.

The Dutch East India Company established a relatively strong trading relationship with the Trịnh in the 1630s. The Trịnh were keen to involve the Dutch in their wars against the Nguyễn, and the rivalry between the Protestant Dutch and the Catholic Portuguese played into this situation. In the 1640s, the Dutch allowed some of their ships to be involved in Trịnh operations against the Nguyễn. Later efforts by the Dutch to establish relations with the Nguyễn were unsuccessful. Samuel Baron's father was deeply involved in Dutch affairs among the Vietnamese during this time, and Samuel Baron himself was born in Tonkin and apparently lived there through the 1650s. After his father sent him to Europe in 1659 and after his father's death in 1664, Baron went over to the English and reappeared in Asia in the 1670s and 1680s with the English East India Company.

The English attempted to establish trade with Tonkin beginning in 1672, but with virtually no success. By the time the English had arrived on the scene, the Trịnh-Nguyễn wars had ended and the Trịnh no longer saw any advantage in humoring Europeans. The English maintained a trading presence in Tonkin into the 1690s, but it was nothing but frustration for them. Failure to develop profitable trading relations colored the English view of Tonkin, and Baron's account expresses this frustration, emphasizing all the reasons that had become current among the English to explain the impossibility of conducting trade there. In contrast, half a century earlier, Borri's cheerful account of Cochinchina, affirming that the Vietnamese were wonderfully welcoming to Europeans and that trading with them could yield great profit, was immediately translated into English in the 1630s to promote English interest in establishing trading relations there.

Perhaps because the Vietnamese found themselves caught in a military and political impasse during the seventeenth century, there is very little that remains from them during that time in terms of literature or other unofficial writings. The voices of Borri and Baron offer unique points of entry into the Vietnamese scene of that era and at the same time carry us into their agendas, which, although not Vietnamese, reveal examples of early contact, interaction, and the exchange of information between Vietnamese and Europeans.

Phantasmatic Cochinchina[25]

In 1631, Father Christophoro Borri became the first European to publish an account of Cochinchina, indeed of any part of what is now Vietnam. Since then, his work, titled *Relatione della nuova missione delli PP. della Compagnia di Giesù, al Regno della Cocincina*[26] and referred to in this essay as the *Account*, has been translated into several languages and has become fascinating reading for the curious and an indispensable source for students and scholars studying seventeenth-century Vietnam. As the eighteenth-century English introduction to the *Account* published in this volume demonstrates, Borri was well qualified to write this work. An Italian Jesuit, one of the first missionaries among the Vietnamese, he spent five years in Cochinchina. The introduction affirms that he was fluent in the Vietnamese language, well traveled around the country, familiar with various classes of people, and that he wrote not as a visitor but as a resident of the country.[27]

This essay is a first step to look at Christoforo Borri beyond the *Account* and to consider how this might influence our understanding of his work.[28] Aside from the *Account*, information about Borri is scarce and controversial. We have notes about Borri and his works written by his contemporaries and by later generations of his fellow Jesuits, as well as by members of other religious orders, scientists, and scholars. But all of these notes are from people who evidently did not know Borri well, if at all. In addition, we have several letters from Borri to his friend Pietro della Valle, as cited in the latter's correspondence with various officials upon Borri's death, which were discovered in 1947 in the Archivio Vaticano and published by Angelo Mercati.[29] And there remains a letter from Borri to his superior, the General of the Society of Jesus, published by Mauricio Gomes dos Santos.[30] There are very few points on which the sources are in agreement with each other.

---

[25] I paraphrase the title of Panivong Norindr's book, *Phantasmatic Indochina*, on the French colonial effort to "exoticize" their colony; *Phantasmatic Indochina: French Colonial Ideology in Architecture, Film, and Literature* (Durham & London: Duke University Press, 1996).

[26] Rome: F. Catanio, 1631. All translations in this essay are mine, unless noted otherwise. I express my sincere gratitude to Daniel Bornstein and Andrew Kirkendall of Texas A&M University, who more than once lent me a hand in the intricacies of Italian and Portuguese texts, but who are not responsible for any mistakes, which always remain my own.

[27] Christopher Borri, "An Account of Cochin-China in Two Parts; The First Treats of the Temporal State of that Kingdom; The Second of the Spiritual," in Awnsham & John Churchill, eds., *A Collection of Voyages and Travels* (London: John Walthoe et al., 1732), vol. 2, p. 721.

[28] This essay is based only on published materials.

[29] Angelo Mercati, "Notizie sul gesuita Cristoforo Borri e su sue 'inventioni' da carte finora sconosciute di Pietro della Valle, il pellegrino" (Note on the Jesuit Cristoforo Borri and on His "Inventions" from Previously Unknown Letters of Pietro della Valle, a Traveler), *Acta*, 15 (3), 1953, pp. 25-46. These letters, according to Mercati, were kept at the Archivio della Valle-del Buffalo, an archive of one of the most noble Roman families, consisting of documents from the fourteenth to the mid-nineteenth century.

[30] Christoforo Borri, "Al molto Rev. Pre. Generale. Christoforo Borri sopra il libro che ho composto per stampare delli tre cieli" (To the Most Reverend General. Christophoro Borri on the Book Composed for Publication on the Three Heavens), Arquivo National da Torre do Tombo, Armários dos Jesuitas, fol. 314 r, 314 v, 315 r, 315 v, 316 r, 316 v, 317 r, 317v.

Borri appears as a tragic persona who, spending his life in different countries on different continents, created controversy wherever he went. He was despised by some and respected by others. The works on astronomy, cosmology and navigation to which he devoted his life have become lost amid the scientific, political, and religious developments of his time, never to be fully recovered and studied by following generations. If he is remembered today, it is mainly because of his *Account of Cochin-China*, describing this country and his missionary life there, which hardly constituted the main interest in his life.

False Start

Christoforo Borri was born in Milan in 1583. We do not know the exact date of his birth, only that he was from a noble family.[31] On September 16, 1601, he entered the Society of Jesus.[32] It is recorded that he "studied philosophy, four years of theology, three years of humanities, and two years of mathematics."[33] Mathematics and astronomy, which at that time were inseparable, became the focus of the young Jesuit's interest. In 1606, at the age of twenty-three, he began to teach mathematics at the Jesuit Collegio di Mondovi, in a small town in Piedmont, northern Italy. In 1609 he transferred to another Jesuit college, Collegio di Brera, in Milan.[34] The Collegio di Brera was a celebrated center of education not only in Lombardy but throughout all of northern Italy. Unlike the seemingly straightforward development of Borri's life during his first twenty-six years, the years that followed his appointment at Collegio di Brera, as depicted in surviving sources, present many mysteries that may never be unraveled.

The sixteenth and seventeenth centuries were a creative and turbulent era for astronomy. Geocentricity, the Ptolemaic idea of the structure of the universe, had dominated scientific and religious discourse for many centuries. According to this idea, the earth is at the center of the universe, which consists of heavens or celestial orbs (caelum or coelum), widely believed to be of solid matter. After 1543, when Copernicus published *De revolutionibus orbium coelestum* (On the Revolution of the Celestial Spheres), advocating a heliocentric universe, the geocentric system was seriously questioned. Tycho Brahe (1546-1601), a Danish astronomer, while maintaining the Ptolemaic geocentric structure of the universe, developed a theory that combined the views of Ptolemy and Copernicus; he proposed that all the planets except for the Earth revolve around the Sun, which revolves around the Earth. He furthermore denied the solidity of the celestial orbs or heavens, accepted by prevailing opinion at that time, and suggested instead that they were fluid or

---

Published in the Appendix (pp. 143-150) of D. Mauricio Gomes dos Santos, "Vicissitudes da obra do P. Cristóvão Borri," *Anáis* (Academia Portuguese da História) 3 (1951): 119-150.

[31] Otto Hartig, "Borrus (Borri, Burrus), Christopher," in Charles G. Herbermann, et al., *The Catholic Encyclopedia* vol. 2 (New York: Robert Appleton Company, 1907), p. 689.

[32] Angelo Mercati, "Notizie," p. 26, dos Santos, "Vicissitudes da obra," p. 119,

[33] Joseph Franz Schütte, S. J., *Monumenta historica japoniae I, Textus catalogorum japoniae, 1549-1654"* (Rome: Monumenta Historica Soc. Iesu, 1975), pp. 848, 849, 854, 884.

[34] L. Petech, "Borri, Cristoforo," in Alberto M. Ghisalberti, *Dizionario biografico degli italiani* (Rome: Istituto della Enciclopedia Italiana, 1971), 13:3-4. Schütte, *Monumenta historica*, pp. 424, 780-781, 1141.

liquid.[35] Brahe created a foundation for formulating laws of planetary motions, later developed by his assistant, the famous German astronomer, Johannes Kepler (1571-1630), who in 1604 discovered the phenomenon of the appearance of new stars. In 1609, Galileo Gallilei (1564-1642) built what he called an *occhiale*, later known as a telescope, which, along with his other discoveries and theories, provided an empirical foundation for Copernican theory and caused Galileo to be considered the father of modern astronomy. In this vibrant intellectual milieu of adventurous astronomers and mathematicians, Borri's curious mind was stirred. Following in the footsteps of Brahe, Borri developed a theory of three heavens: aerial of the planets, sidereal of the fixed stars, and the empyrean beyond it. These heavens, according to him, were liquid or tenuous.

Neither Copernicus nor Galileo (not to mention Brahe) endured the difficulties that befell Borri. The Church did not attack Copernicus's work until 1616, and even then allowed his work to be published with some passages deleted, yet without compromising his basic ideas. Until his heresy trial in 1633, Galileo continued to enjoy success and fame under the attentive but not forbidding eye of the Church, on the condition that he claimed his view only as a hypothesis and not as a proven fact. However, with ideas even less revolutionary than Copernicus or Galileo, Borri saw his promising career come to an abrupt end, and years of bitter disappointment followed for the young professor. He failed to survive in the Jesuit academic community of that time apparently because he lacked adequate skill in navigating the currents of factions and rivalries in the politics of his order.

Soon after his transfer to the Collegio di Brera, Borri found himself at odds with his superiors. We can only speculate about the reasons for this because available sources are scarce and unenlightening. One such source is Father Dominique Le Jeunehomme, from the Society of Jesus, who wrote in 1627 that Borri

> invented an opinion, concerning heavens as being liquid, of which there are only three, one which we call air, another for planets or stars, and the other empyreal. This is what displeased Rome so much, during the time of Father Aquaviva [then General of the Society of Jesus], so that he drew a penitence and a small rebuke [*il en tira une penitence, et un petit mot au bout*].[36]

For his part, Borri, in his letter to General Aquaviva's successor, General Mutius Vitelleschi, written around 1630 or 1631, described the episode differently, alleging that General Acquaviva,

> at the insistence of the old Fathers of our Province [Society of Jesus], ordered me therefore to leave my lectureship not to be charged by the world with new ways of thinking, with which certain new opinions that the Society produced in the theological field at that time the Pope particularly charged us.[37]

---

[35] Victor E. Thoren, "The Comet of 1577 and Tycho Brahe's System of the World," *Archives Internationales d'Histoire des Sciences* 29 (1979): 53-67.

[36] Dominique Le Jeunehomme, S. J., *Relation d'un voyage de la Flèche à Lisbonne en 1627*, (Poitiers: Oudin, 1864), p. 39, cited in Carlos Sommervogel, S. J., *Bibliothèque de la Compagnie de Jésu* (Paris: Alphonae Picard & Bruxelles: Oscar Schepens, 1890), vol. 1, col. 1822, under "Borri, Burrus, Christophe."

[37] Borri, "Al molto Rev. Pre. Generale," in dos Santos, "Vicissitudes da obra," p. 143.

Here, Borri explains his dismissal as an effort by the Jesuit order to demonstrate its submission to the Papacy by disciplining a member who appeared to show excessive zeal for "new ways of thinking."

Each letter cited above has to do with a rebuke: in Le Jeunehomme's letter, Borri is rebuked; in Borri's letter, he implicitly rebukes his superiors, notwithstanding the fact that later in the letter he talks about the patience and humility with which he endured the decision. But whom does he blame: the Pope, General Acquaviva, or those "old Fathers"? While General Acquaviva made the decision, Borri believed that he was prompted to do so by others. The Pope could hardly have known or cared about the young Lombardian teaching at a Jesuit college in Milan. Thus, those who prompted General Acquaviva were "the old Fathers." If we carefully read Borri's letter and familiarize ourselves with the development of his celestial theories, we see that it was his polemic with one of "the old Fathers" that colored his entire life and career. In this letter, written around two decades after his expulsion from the Collegio di Brera, he still argues against one of the "old Fathers" without naming him, while repeatedly referring to this man's book and his theory of eleven heavens. This father was almost certainly a German Jesuit, Christopher Clavius (1537-1612), who was one of the most celebrated scientists of the late sixteenth and early seventeenth centuries. He was the premier mathematician of the Jesuit Order and the most senior professor of astronomy and mathematics at the Collegio Romano in Rome, the main Jesuit college founded by Ignatius Loyola in 1551. The book against which Borri vehemently argued is Clavius's *In sphaeram Iohannis de Sacro Bosco commentarius*.[38] Father Clavius was an adherent of the Ptolemaic system, and one of the aspects of his work concerned the structure of heavens or orbs, the number of which he suggested was eleven.[39] Later he increased this number to twelve: "Beyond the eleven moving heavens," Clavius wrote, "theologians such as Strabo and Bede and all the rest affirm that there is another heaven, which they call the empyrean. It is not a heaven with stars, but rather is the happy seat and home of the angels and the blessed."[40]

Despite being a follower and a developer of the Ptolemaic system, and thus an opponent of the Copernican theory, Father Clavius had a relatively open mind, and he clearly proved this. In 1610, Galileo discovered three of Jupiter's largest satellites and observed different phases of Venus; both of these phenomena were incompatible with the Ptolemaic system. Galileo published his observations in Venice in the work titled *Siderius Nuncius* (Sidereal Messenger). The Jesuit order and other church officials requested the scholars of the Collegio Romano to confirm the performance of Galileo's invention, the telescope, and the accuracy of observations made with it. The mathematicians of the Collegio under the direction of Clavius confirmed Galileo's discoveries. In 1611, Father Clavius organized a

---

[38] Christopher Clavius, *In sphaeram Ioannis de Sacro Bosco commentarius* (Rome: Victorium Halianum, 1570). Thanks to Mariya Berezovska for help with Latin.

[39] Edward Grant, *Planets, Stars, and Orbs: The Medieval Cosmos, 1200-1687* (Cambridge: Cambridge University Press, 1994), p. 318.

[40] Clavius, *In sphaeram*, p. 24.

solemn convocation at the Collegio to honor Galileo with the attendance of numerous dignitaries, including scholars and high-ranking church officials.[41]

Considering the mutual respect and even friendship between Clavius and Galileo despite the seriousness of their difference of opinion, it is hard to imagine that Father Clavius would persecute Borri, who was by far more moderate than Galileo in his views. Moreover, the issue of the number of heavens and their composition were not as crucial as the issue of a geocentric versus a heliocentric system. On the number of heavens, there was no unity among medieval natural philosophers and astronomers, who, according to Edward Grant, "divided the celestial region into as few as eight and as many as eleven major units."[42] None was persecuted or even punished for his preferred number of heavens. As for the liquidity or tenuous substance of the heavens, this issue became relatively important, though not critical, later in the century after Galileo's trial in 1633, but it was not a particularly contentious topic before and during the second decade of the century. For example, in the 1570s, Cardinal Roberto Bellarmine (1542-1621), also a Jesuit and one of only thirty-three Doctors of the Church, had discussed the fluidity of heavens in his lectures at Louvain University (modern Belgium).[43]

On the other hand, General Aquaviva, in order to strengthen the position of his Order vis-à-vis the Pope, required the members of his Order not to deviate from the official doctrines, the main one in astronomy being the Ptolemaic system. As a junior member of the Society of Jesus, Borri had to comply. Perhaps he had an uncompromising nature, which did not allow him to assume the "hypothetic" stance suggested to Galileo. Perhaps because, unlike Galileo and many other astronomers, he was inside the Order, Borri found himself under special scrutiny and on the wrong side of ecclesiastical politics. It is likely that, rather than the "small rebuke" mentioned by Le Jeunehomme, Borri was in fact expelled from the Collegio di Brera, if only because Borri mentions this in the letter to his superior, General Vitelleschi, and would hardly be inclined to invent such an event.

We do not know a precise date for his departure from the school. Mauricio Gomes dos Santos, a modern Portuguese scholar, who based his research on Borri's aforementioned letter to General Vitelleschi as well as materials in Spanish and Portuguese archives, avoids dating this event but talks about scientific developments at the end of 1610 and in 1611 that Borri could not closely follow because he was out of the academic circle.[44] This implies that he dates Borri's expulsion prior to the end of 1610, that is, shortly after Borri's 1609 arrival in Milan. On the other hand, an Italian scholar, Ugo Baldini, dates Borri's departure as late as 1614, but although he cites Borri's 1631 letter to Vitelleschi in support, the letter does not give us the date. Baldini mentions that in 1612 Borri gave a public lecture in Milan, a copy of which is kept in Biblioteca Nazionale in Rome,[45] and this would

---

[41] Pasquale M. D'Elia, S. J., *Galileo in China*, trans. Rufus Suter and Matthew Sciascia (Cambridge, MA: Harvard University Press, 1960), p. 13.

[42] Edward Grant, "Celestial Orbs in the Latin Middle Ages," *Isis* 78,2 (1987): 160.

[43] Robert Bellarmine, "Whether by Its Nature the Sky Is Corruptible," in *The Louvain Lectures (Lectiones Lovanienses) of Bellarmine and the Autograph Copy of his 1616 Declaration of Galileo*, translated with introduction and annotations by Ugo Baldini and George V. Coyne, S. J. (Vatican: Specola Vaticana, 1984), pp. 8-9.

[44] Dos Santos, "Vicissitudes da obra," p. 121.

[45] In Rome there is a manuscript of his lecture titled "De astrologia universa tractatus" (Biblioteca Nazionale, ms. Fondo Gesuitico 587), noted in Ugo Baldini, *Saggi sulla cultura*

seem to extend Borri's period at the Collegio at least to 1612. In any case, Borri's departure from the Collegio certainly took place before January 1615, when General Acquaviva, who ordered Borri's expulsion, died.

Looking for New Venues

Being deprived of his post must have been very painful for Borri. Although he continued to hope that new scientific observations would sweep out old theories,[46] he was nevertheless outside academic circles and could no longer follow closely the activities of other scholars. Desperate to rejoin the scientific world, he looked for new opportunities to pursue his astronomic interests and his interest in magnetic observations and cartography. According to another seventeenth-century Jesuit, Valentin Estãncel (1621-1705), Borri was convinced that he had discovered a new way to determine longitude by the use of a magnetic needle (*agulha magnetica*), and he wanted to go to India to observe the behavior of the magnetic needle there. He hoped this would enable him to create a map for navigation on the basis of isogones, the lines connecting points of the Earth where the magnetic declination is the same.[47]

The issue of determining longitude was a very important issue for navigation. For many centuries, most navigation was conducted along coasts, and methods of determining longitude by surface orientation were developed. However, in the fifteenth and sixteenth centuries the development of navigation led to exploring new territories, and ships started to venture farther from coasts, which created a serious problem with their orientation at sea, as coastal markers could no longer serve as points of orientation. This was so important that in 1598 the King of Spain and Portugal, Philip III, offered, according to some sources, a prize of 50,000 cruzados to the first person to discover the solution to this problem.[48] According to another source, the prize was six thousand ducats of permanent revenue, supplemented by two million ducats of life-long revenue and a thousand ducats the winner would receive immediately. Fifty years later, the Dutch government announced a prize of 100,000 pounds for the same achievement.[49] The way to solve this seemed to lie either through the observation of the sun, moon, and stars, or by using magnetism. Among those who worked on this problem was Galileo. He relied on the former approach and in 1613 offered the Spanish crown his tables of eclipses for defining longitude. However, his method did not prove reliable.

Borri wanted to try a different approach based on magnetism. The technique seemed to involve the construction of a chart that mapped points of equal magnetic declination, the use of an azimuthal compass, and a technique for

---

della Compagnia di Gesù, secoli XVI-XVIII (Essays on the Culture of the Society of Jesus, XVI-XVII centuries) (Padova, Italy: CLEUP Edifice, 2000), p. 156, fn. 80 & p. 163, fn. 102.

[46] Borri, "Al molto Rev. Pre. Generale," in dos Santos, "Vicissitudes da obra," p. 143.

[47] Valentin Estancel, *Tiphys Lusitano* (Fuondo generale 2264, Biblioteca Nacional de Lisboa), cited in Joaquim de Carvalho, "Galileu e a cultura porgutuesa," *Biblos* XIX (1943): 447.

[48] Ibid., p. 448. The same information is also in Athanasius Kircher, *Magnes, sive de arte magnetica* (Rome: L. Girgnani, 1641), p. 502.

[49] Carvalho, "Galileu e a cultura porgutuesa," p. 406.

measuring the declination at any time of day.[50] By that time it was already known that the geographic north pole and the magnetic north pole are not the same. Borri apparently wanted to measure the angular declination from the magnetic to geographic north pole to determine longitude at sea. For this, he needed to conduct extensive observations. India, being on the opposite side of the Earth from the north magnetic pole, is located at a larger angle of magnetic declination than Europe. Consequently, magnetic measurements made in India could provide Borri with data unavailable in Europe.[51] In Goa, for example, the declination turned out to be between 16 degrees 40 minutes and 17 degrees, while in Naples it did not pass 30 minutes.[52]

At that time, Christian missionaries were rapidly developing their presence in Asia, where conducting astronomical research seemed to be especially promising. Missionaries such as Jesuits Matteo Ricci (1552-1610) and Niccolo Longobardi (1565?-1655), who arrived in China at the end of the sixteenth century and established their missions there at the beginning of the seventeenth century, reported the enormous interest of the Chinese in astronomy and mathematics and how their skills in these fields facilitated the Jesuit approach to the local society. Father Ricci wrote on May 12, 1605, from Beijing to Rome: "if the mathematician of whom I spoke came here, we could readily translate our tables into Chinese characters and rectify their year. This would give us great face, would open wider the gates of China, and would enable us to live more securely and freely."[53] Father Ricci's successors, Sabatino de Ursis and Niccolo Longobardi, also petitioned the Jesuit officials in Rome and the General in Charge of the Portuguese Province and Missions at Rome, Father Anthony Mascarenhas, to urgently send missionaries skilled in astronomy and mathematics.[54] Consequently, when Borri petitioned to be sent on a mission to Asia, his request was immediately granted.[55] His destination was China, but he had first to go to the Portuguese base at Goa, on the western coast of India, and from thence to Macao, the Portuguese base on the coast of China and the headquarters for the Jesuit missions in Asia.

En Route

The way was long and difficult. Lisbon was the sole port of embarkation for Portuguese Asia.[56] In the words of one scholar of that time:

[50] Michael John Gorman, "The Angel and the Compass: Athanasius Kircher's Geographical Project," in *Athanasius Kircher: The Last Man Who Knew Everything*, ed. Paula Findlen (New York, NY: Routledge, 2004), p. 244.

[51] I am indebted to Professor Peter Dear of Cornell University, whom I consulted on this issue as well as on the issue of the eleven heavens.

[52] Estancel, *Tiphys Lusitano*, in Carvalho, "Galileu e a cultura porgutuesa," pp. 442-443.

[53] Letter from August 22, 1608, from Beijing, in Tacchi Venturi, *Opere storiche del P. Matteo Ricci* (Macerata, 1913) II:367.

[54] D'Elia, *Galileo*, pp. 21-23.

[55] Dos Santos, "Vicissitudes da obra," p. 122.

[56] In February 1633, Pope Urban VIII issued a Bull allowing all religious to travel to the East Indies by any route to facilitate access to the missionaries' destinations. See Ludwig Freiher von Pastor, *The History of the Popes From the Close of the Middle Ages*, trans. Dom Ernest Graf, O. S. B., 2nd ed. (London: Routledge & Kegan Paul Ltd., 1955), vol. XXIX, p. 132.

... ships, when they left Lisbon at all, left only once a year, in March; and, after rounding the Cape of Good Hope, they arrived at Goa, if they arrived at all, only after six months of terrible crossing, if all went well, in September of the same year. Then in India the traveler had to halt at least until April of the following year when the monsoons would permit another ship to sail for the port of Macao, if all went well.[57]

Borri departed in April 1615.[58] If he took the usual route, he could arrive in Macao not earlier than 1617. October 1617 is also the first time when his name is listed among missionaries residing in Macao.[59] Apparently, upon his arrival in Macao, Borri, whose name was also spelled Borro in Italian, or even Burro, started to use, at least on certain occasions, the last name Brono, Bruno, or Bravo, "not to offend the Portuguese ears with the word *boro* which in their language does not sound good."[60] *Borro* in Portuguese means sheepskin or stupid, *burro* "ass," or *borra* "dregs, lees, sediment, rabble, or scum."[61] In the Latin texts, his name was usually transcribed as Borrus.

In Macao, according to Borri, Father Francisco Vieira, Apostolic Visitor to Japan and China,[62] approached him with a request to write a tractate to persuade the missionaries in China to abandon the opinion of eleven heavens and their hard or "incorruptible" nature, based on Aristotle, which was in conformity with Papal doctrine at that time, and instead to adopt ideas prevalent in China, which were proving to be "more viable than ours." While ideas about the celestial structure were changing in Europe, among the missionaries in China they remained fixed in the established doctrine. Matteo Ricci wrote about the Chinese celestial structure: "There is only one sky and it is empty, not solid."[63] The Jesuits in China, according to Joseph Needham, opposed the Chinese doctrine that posited the "floating of the heavenly bodies in infinite space, and the irony was that they did so just at a time when the best minds in Europe were breaking away from the closed Aristotelian system."[64]

Borri seemed to be nonplussed by Vieira's request because earlier he had advocated the idea of the fluidity of heavens and considered this to be a reason for his expulsion from the Collegio di Brera by General Acquaviva. The explanation given to Borri by Father Francisco Vieira provides us with a curious glimpse into

[57] D'Elia, *Galileo*, p. 19.

[58] Schütte, *Monumenta historica*, p. 1141; Petech, "Borri, Cristoforo," in Ghisalberti, *Dizionario*, p. 3.

[59] Schütte, *Monumenta historica*, p. 691.

[60] Pietro della Valle, *The Travels of Sig. Pietro della Valle, a Noble Roman, into East India and Arabia Deserta* (London: J. Macock, 1665), part 3, p. 81. Later cited in Sommervogel, *Bibliothèque* vol. 1, col. 1822, under "Borri, Burrus, Christophe," and from Sommervogel in other works, for example Schütte, *Monumenta historica*, p. 780.

[61] Petech, "Borri, Cristoforo," in Ghisalberti, *Dizionario*, p. 3.

[62] Schütte, *Monumenta historica*, p. 1323. Father Vieira (1556?-1619) arrived in Macao from India. He apparently arrived there simultaneously with Borri. Sommervogel, *Bibliothèque*, lists him but does not provide any information except for one work (vol. 8, col. 685, under "Vieira, François").

[63] Matteo Ricci's letters on October 28 and November 4, 1595, cited in Joseph Needham, *Chinese Astronomy and the Jesuit Mission: An Encounter of Cultures* (London: The China Society, 1958), p. 2.

[64] Ibid., pp. 1-2.

Jesuit policies towards new developments in general and the policies of Acquaviva in particular. In his letter to General Vitellescho, Borri conveyed Vieira's explanation and wrote:

> The reason why Father Claudio [Acquaviva] had prohibited to me such a doctrine [in Europe] is the same reason, as I was told, why [this doctrine] is to be held and taught in China; because this doctrine [of eleven heavens and their "incorruptibility"] is old to us in Europe, but there in China it is totally new and therefore the aforesaid new way of thought would chase us [out of China].[65]

What was "the same" reason that Borri refers to as explaining both Acquaviva's forbidding a doctrine of fluid heavens to Borri in Europe and his proposed advocacy of such a doctrine in China? Apparently, it was pragmatism. To safeguard the Order and to avert possible repercussions from above, General Acquaviva sacrificed Borri, a young and vulnerable scientist among the Jesuits. Similarly, it seems that Acquaviva regarded the missionary presence in China as more vital than any particular doctrine about the structure of the heavenly bodies, and he was willing to sacrifice the latter for the sake of the former. The irony of this, however, lay in the fact that it was Borri's lot to be requested to explain this to the Chinese mission. It is hard to imagine that Borri was enthusiastic about the task requested of him, and we have no evidence that he ever accomplished it.[66]

Mission: Impossible

If initially Borri was designated to join missionaries in China, this plan was changed. In 1616, a persecution arose at Nanking when several missionaries were arrested and expelled to Macao, "some of them in cages, while others managed to remain hidden among Chinese Catholics and secretly continued their Apostolic work."[67] Instead of China, Borri went to Cochinchina.

While some Portuguese and Spanish Dominicans and other missionaries penetrated to Cochinchina before the seventeenth century, it was the Jesuits who established the first mission there in 1615. It happened allegedly because of a Portuguese merchant, Ferdinando da Costa. Upon his return to Macao from a trip to Cochinchina, he related "what he had seen and the excellent likelihood there was of converting that kingdom. Immediately after this speech, Fr. Buzomi went and threw himself at the feet of his superior to ask a permission to go to this beautiful land to which God was calling him. His request was soon granted to him."[68] As the head of the mission, Father Francesco Buzomi[69] was joined by

---

[65] Borri "Al molto Rev. Pre. Generale." in dos Santos, "Vicissitudes da obra," p. 144.

[66] Petech, "Borri, Cristoforo," in Ghisalberti, *Dizionario*, p. 3.

[67] Pascal M. D'Elia, S. J., *The Catholic Missions in China* (Shanghai, China: The Commercial Press, 1954), p. 51.

[68] Alexandre de Rhodes, *Rhodes of Vietnam*, trans. Solange Hertz (Westminster, MD: The Newman Press, 1966), pp. 46-47. Also see on this Nguyễn Văn Tố and L. Cadière, *Lịch Sử Đạo Thiên Chúa ở Việt Nam* (History of Christianity in Vietnam) (Hue: Đại Việt Thiên Bản, 1944), p. 110.

[69] (1576-1639). Italian Jesuit born in Genoa and educated in Naples, joined the Society of Jesus in 1592 (Shütte, *Monumenta historica*, p. 1143). According to Alexandre de Rhodes, "He succeeded so well that although he found very few Christians on first arriving in

another Jesuit Father, Jacques Carvalho,[70] and three Brothers Coadjutors: Antonio Diaz, a Portugese, and two Japanese, Joseph and Paul. A year later, Father Carvalho departed for Japan, where he would become a martyr in 1624.[71] The mission proved to be viable, and within a short time there were three hundred neophytes. The officials from Macao decided to send Father Francisco de Pina to reinforce Father Buzomi.[72]

But soon troubles befell the Cochinchinese mission. Local religious leaders blamed the fathers for a drought afflicting the country. A church was burned down, and Father Buzomi fell seriously ill. In response to these events, the officials in Macao dispatched two new missionaries to Cochinchina: a Portuguese, Father Peter Marques,[73] and Christoforo Borri. Borri wrote that he "freely and affectionately embraced the opportunity to dedicate myself to God in the mission of Cochin-China." The two departed on a Portuguese boat. As a precaution, in order not to arouse suspicion among the Cochinchinese in a time of persecution, Father Marques was appointed the chaplain of the ship and Father Borri was disguised as a slave. They arrived in Cochinchina either at the end of 1617 or the beginning of 1618.[74]

When the ship entered the harbor, as Borri informs us, a fight between two sailors erupted. The locals were afraid to intervene, but Borri fearlessly separated the fighters. While this won him enormous respect from the Vietnamese, it also revealed to them his identity as a religious man, as they could not believe that a mere servant would be able to do this. Realizing this, Borri changed into his clerical

---

Cochinchina, he left at least 12,000 when he went to heaven to receive as many crowns as he had made new Christians." De Rhodes, *Rhodes of Vietnam*, p. 78.

[70] In Borri's original Italian, the name is spelled Diego Caravaglio (Borri, *Relatione*, p. 100). He was born in Portugal, in 1578, joined the Society of Jesus in 1594, and in 1600 departed on his mission to Asia. He propagated Christianity in Macao, Japan, and Cochinchina, where he arrived in 1615, and from whence he departed back to Japan in 1616. According to Charlevoix, *Le Christianisme au Japon 1542-1660* (Lille: L. Lefort, 1853), he died the way Borri describes, in Sendai, Japan, on February 22, 1624.

[71] L. - E. Louvet, *La Cochinchine religieuse*, vol. 1 (Paris: Challamel Aîné, 1855), p. 235.

[72] Henri Chappoulie, *Aux origins d'une église. Rome et les missions d'Indochine au XVII siècle*, vol. I (Paris: Bloud et Gay, 1943), p. 23. In the English translation used in this volume, Francesco de Pina's name is spelled as Francis de Pina. (1585?-1625) A Portuguese, he entered the Society of Jesus in 1605, and studied and preached in Macao, where he met Christoforo Borri. Father de Pina arrived in Cochinchina sometime in 1617 (Shütte, *Monumenta historica*, p. 1271). He was the first to master the language of the country and thus was very successful in conversion and establishing good rapport with local people. F. de Montézon and Ed. Estève, eds., *Mission de la Cochinchine et du Tonkin* (Paris: Charles Dounoil, 1858), p. 386. Alexandre de Rhodes initially studied Vietnamese under Father de Pina's guidance.

[73] Pedro Marques (1577-1657), a Portuguese Jesuit, who was appointed as the Superior of the Cochinchinese mission and is listed as such in the Catalogue of Cochinchinese missionaries: "Catalogo com supliment do primeiro e segundo rol dos Padres e Irmaons que estao no Collegio de Macao e Missao de Cochimchina sojeita a este mesmo Collegio, feito em Junho de 1618," in Shütte, *Monumenta historica*, p. 782. He returned to Macao in 1620 (Ibid., p. 1228). He later became Alexander de Rhodes's companion during his mission in Tonkin, where they arrived together in 1627. Borri fails to mention that Father Marques stayed in Cocinchina only for two or three years.

[74] Petech, "Borri, Cristoforo," in Ghisalberti, *Dizionario*, p. 3; and Otto Hartig, "Borrus (Borri, Burrus), Christopher," in Charles G. Herbermann, et al., *The Catholic Encyclopedia* (New York, NY: Robert Appleton Company, 1907), vol. 2, p. 689, respectively.

robes, disembarked, proclaimed his Christian faith, and said the mass, expecting the fate of a martyr. Fortunately for him, however, at this point a downpour intervened, ending the drought for which Father Buzomi had been blamed and persecuted. Thus, the local people viewed Borri's arrival as having caused the much-desired rain, and the missionaries accordingly benefited in popular esteem.[75]

Upon their arrival, Fathers Borri and Marques joined forces with Fathers Buzomi and de Pina. After a short stay in Đà Nẵng and a visit to Hội An, he, along with Fathers Buzomi and de Pina, at the invitation of the governor of Pulucambi (modern Bình Định province), departed for the provincial capital located at the modern city of Qui Nhơn. Father Marques stayed at Hội An to preach there since he was fluent in Japanese and there was a large Japanese community there. The missionaries seemed to be successful in Qui Nhơn until the governor, their protector, died. After that, their situation deteriorated as narrated in Borri's *Account*. Borri apparently stayed in Qui Nhơn for nearly all of his time in Cochinchina.

In 1622, Pope Gregory XV established in Rome the Congregation de Propaganda Fide (Congregation for the Propagation of the Faith). The Pope "declared that it was his desire to continue with greater energy and vigilance the work of training laborers for the rich harvest which his predecessors had inaugurated with so much zeal."[76] But Borri was not to be among these laborers. In that same year, Borri's missionary career came to an abrupt end and he left Cochinchina, again finding himself at odds with his Order. He became such an instant non-person among the Jesuit missionaries in Asia that Alexander de Rhodes (1591-1660), a French Jesuit and the most celebrated missionary of that time in Vietnam, who arrived in Cochinchina in 1624, only two years after Borri's departure, and who wrote several works on Vietnam and the missionaries there, never mentioned Borri either in discussing the work of his predecessors or in any other context.

Nowhere does Borri mention a reason for his departure from Cochinchina. He simply states matter-of-factly, after describing the churches in Cochinchina: "This was the state of affairs there, when I came away out of that country for Europe, which was in the year 1622."[77] Dos Santos speculates that the reason was a new persecution against the missionaries,[78] but there is no evidence to support this theory, not to mention that Borri would be unlikely to omit mention of any case of persecution. The official reason, as documented in the *Index Personarum* of the Society of Jesus at that time, was his poor health.[79] However, Borri seemed to be in good health while in Vietnam as we see from the list of the missionaries compiled every year for the Jesuit Order. Under the year 1620, we read, for example: "Father Christóvão Brono, native of Milan, thirty-seven years of age and in the Order for nineteen years, in good health."[80] While we cannot exclude the possibility that

---

[75] Borri in this volume, Part II, Chapter II, Section titled "The author in Cochin-China."

[76] Ludwig Freiher von Pastor, *The History of the Popes From the Close of the Middle Ages*, trans. Dom Ernest Graf, O. S. B., 2nd ed. (London: Routledge & Kegan Paul Ltd., 1955), vol. XVII, p. 132.

[77] Borri in this volume, Part II, Chapter X, Section titled "At Cacchiam."

[78] Dos Santos, "Vicissitudes da obra," p. 127.

[79] "[P]ropter infirmam salutem Macaum rediit" (on the account of infirm health [he] returned to Macao), "Index Personarum," Schütte, *Monumenta historica*, p. 1141.

[80] "Textus Catalogorum Japoniae," Schütte, *Monumenta historica*, p. 854.

Borri fell seriously ill between 1620 and 1622, this is unlikely considering that he makes no mention of this in his account, nor does this idea appear in any source other than the official explanation.

Evaluations of Borri's missionary activities are various. Caroli de Visch in his 1656 collection of the works of the Cistercian Order commended Borri for his "praiseworthy" activity in Cochinchina.[81] Filippo Argelati, a century after Borri's death, in his collection of works and short biographies of Milanese, employed the highest praise to describe Borri's missionary activity in Cochinchina, "where he exercised his apostolic duties with utmost fervor."[82]

Not so with one of Borri's fellow Jesuits. According to an Italian Jesuit, Father Daniello Bartoli (1608-85), who published a six-volume work on the history of his order, "there was not a small increase in the number of Christians" in Cochinchina. But all the glory for this, Bartoli believed, should go solely to Father Buzomi, who singlehandedly carried out their education and conversion. Bartoli insisted on attributing "no part [of this] to Father Christoforo Borri, who has been his [Father Buzomi's] companion, and who was recalled by his superiors to Macao; not because, as he wrote, to be put into the hand of physicians there, who would heal his body, because [his body] was not ailing; but to cure his soul, that is, to return it from anxiety to fervor of the spirit. When it turned out to be in vain, it was necessary to discharge him from India and to return him to Europe."[83]

A century later, another Jesuit, Julio Cesare Cordara (1704-1785), ascribes a very high value to Borri, characterizing him as "once the most praised among the evangelical laborers." According to Cordara, the reason that put an end to Borri's mission in Cochinchina was that "truly more anxious for the well-being of others rather than of his own, [he] has sinned, on account of which he seemed to have been removed from that mission and recalled to Europe."[84]

We will perhaps never discover what stands behind Bartoli's diagnosis of Borri's ailing soul nor Cordara's description of Borri's anxiety for others' well-being and who was right and wrong in their judgment of Borri's missionary merits. We can only try to reconstruct the situation there based on available materials, the most important of which are Borri's *Account* and a letter or a draft of a letter written by Borri's fellow missionary, Francisco de Pina, to his superior in Macao, Father Visitor Jerónimo Rodrigues Senior, in 1623, following Borri's departure from Cochinchina.[85] In this letter, de Pina does not mention Borri, but some details of his letter are instructive to understand Borri, his life in Cochinchina, and his *Account.*

---

[81] R. D. Caroli de Visch, *Bibliotheca scriptorum sacri ordinis cisterciensis* (Coloniae Agrippinae: Apud I656), p. 71, under "Chistophorus Borrus."

[82] Filippo Argelati, *Bibliotheca scriptorum mediolanensium* (Mediolani: In Aedibus Palatinis, 1745), vol. I, p. 239.

[83] Daniello Bartoli, *Dell'historia della Compagnie di Giesu, La Cina* (Rome: Nella Stamperia del Varese, 1663), III:707.

[84] Julio Cordara, *Historiae societatis Jesu* (Rome: Ex Typographia Antonii de Rubeis, 1750), p. 331. Thanks to Brian Ostrowski for this reference.

[85] The document was discovered by the French scholar, Roland Jacques, in the Biblioteca da Ajuda, Lisbon, the *Jesuítas na Ásia* collection, vol. 49/V7, fol. 413r-416r, translated in Roland Jacques, *Portuguese Pioneers of Vietnamese Linguistics Prior to 1650* (Bangkok: Orchid Press, 2002), pp. 40-45. Jacques discusses the authorship, addressee, and the dating of the letter on pp. 23-24.

As we already know, with Borri's arrival, the Cochinchinese mission consisted of four fathers: Buzomi, de Pina, Marques, and Borri himself. In addition, there was Brother Antonio Diaz.[86] Father Marques left the mission either in 1619 or 1620, but new figures soon arrived: Father António Fernández, who was occupied with the conversion of Japanese in Hội An,[87] and Father Manouel Fernández.[88] During this time, the mission, for the most part financially dependent upon Macao, was under severe financial restraints. This was the consequence of difficulties the Jesuit headquarters at Macao had in distributing money to the missions because of "the ever tighter closure of Japan to Portuguese business; the insecurities of navigation as Dutch ships were attacking everything that displayed the Portuguese flag; and the war waged by the Manchu against the Chinese dynasty, resulting in a volatile situation that had repercussions in Macao."[89] Consequently, the Cochinchinese mission was left almost without supplies. Borri mentions these difficulties only in *passim*, when he says that Father Buzomi departed for Hội An in an attempt to get some alms from the Portuguese. But the difficulties also surface in de Pina's complaint about the inability to provide churches with "images," or even with paper prints, and the effect of poverty on the missionaries' everyday life.

Talking about the missionary activities in Cochinchina in his *Account*, Borri most often employs the pronoun "we." This creates a sense of "brotherhood" in the portrayal of those few laboring in Cochinchina. However, this brotherhood crumbles in de Pina's letter. He hardly has a kind word for any of his fellow missionaries. De Pina envies Father Buzomi, who, alone in Pulucambi after Borri's departure, enjoys much more financial freedom than de Pina, being able to hire local assistants for his work. Father Buzomi, whom Alexander de Rhodes hailed as "the real apostle of Cochinchina, who spent himself there entirely, working for twenty years with a fortitude that couldn't be too highly praised,"[90] is accused by de Pina of a *laissez-faire*, if not outright sybaritic, attitude:

> At Pulo Cambi [Pulucambi], father Buzomi has two or three monks *ông sãi* who do all the work for him. Thus, if something happens, if there is something to be settled or important messages, he sends his interpreter, or then again one of the *ông sãi*; when the catechizing is finished, he retires, and they stay to either repeat or converse with the catechumens.[91]

---

[86] A Portuguese Jesuit (1585-?), listed among the Cochinchinese missionaries until 1623. Unlike Jesuit "fathers," his duty was to take care of the house. "Catálogo das Informaçõens Commuas dos Padres e Irmãos que estam na Missam de Cochinchina, feito no anno de 1620," in Shütte, *Monumenta historica*, p. 885.

[87] Also listed as António Rodríguez (1552-1630), a Portuguese Jesuit, the oldest in the mission. He arrived in Cochinchina in 1619 or 1620 and worked with Japanese Christians as he *sabe bem a lingoa de Japam e prega nella* (knows well the language of Japan and preaches in it). Ibid., p. 884.

[88] Also spelled (Emmanuel Fernandes). A Portuguese Jesuit (1584?-1634), entered the Society in 1601, studied in Macao, ordained in 1611, and remained in Macao occupying various positions at the Jesuit College until his departure to Cochinchina. Ibid., p. 1170, and Jacques, *Portuguese Pioneers*, p. 28.

[89] Jacques, *Portuguese Pioneers*, p. 87.

[90] de Rhodes, *Rhodes of Vietnam*, p. 46.

[91] De Pina's letter, cited in Jacques, *Portuguese Pioneers*, p. 45.

De Pina's life markedly differs from that of Father Buzomi's: "It is I who must catechize, go out to [meet] those who arrive or leave . . . Whenever something happens, if I don't go, no one else goes."[92] De Pina himself is stationed under the supervision of Father Manoel Fernández, who arrived there in January 1622 just before Borri's departure.

One of the main contentious points for Father de Pina, on which he criticizes his fellow-missionaries as undermining their effectiveness in propagating Christianity, is their inability to master the language. He apparently would not agree with Borri's statement about the easiness of the language, which allows a man to preach in a year.[93] The main target of de Pina's disdain is his Superior, Father Manoel Fernández. According to de Pina, after a year of study, "whether he [Father Fernández] says a word or not, that comes about to the same," and the locals "were stupefied that after a whole year he did not know more."[94] Nor is he more lenient toward his other colleague in the mission, António Fernández, who, according to him, also neglects his duties towards the Japanese Christians and does nothing but pray.[95]

But controversial issues, as revealed in de Pina's letter, go beyond finance and language. We can only surmise what arguments were dividing these people who found themselves bound to each other in a land they wanted to change but that none of them really knew. Yet, in de Pina's letter we see a shadow of the emerging Rites Controversy, at the core of which lay the attitude of missionaries towards local religious beliefs, practices, and terminology. Conflicts in the microcosm of the Jesuit mission in Cochinchina in the 1620s are an inkling of the larger conflict that eventually exploded at the beginning of the eighteenth century in the Rites Controversy and culminated in 1767 with the expulsion of Jesuits from all the missions and, shortly after, in the suppression of the Society itself. At issue was the Jesuits' flexibility and willingness to accept some local religious practices that offended the orthodox views of other orders. Father de Pina mentions numerous contentious debates that apparently hindered the missionaries' activities.[96] He does not elaborate on these debates, but elsewhere in the letter he addresses the issue of local young men, whom missionaries, not only in Cochinchina but elsewhere as well, would educate toward the goal of enabling them to preach. Along with their studies, these young men also performed domestic chores in the missions without remuneration.[97] As we can infer from de Pina's letter, the officials in Macao insisted on a policy of disengaging converts from their own culture, which led, among other things, to instructing local youths in only European, or Portuguese, script. Father de Pina, if reluctantly, complied with this requirement. However, as a result, he complained that young people "do not want to stay here with me, because I allow them to study only our own script; for this reason they want to go live in Pulo Cambi [Pulucambi] with father Buzomi, who allows them to study [their own script] and gives them a tutor; or they wish to study at their own

---

[92] Ibid., p. 45.

[93] Borri in this volume, Part II, "Conclusion."

[94] De Pina's letter, cited in Jacques, *Portuguese Pioneers*, p. 42.

[95] Ibid., p. 43.

[96] Ibid., p. 41.

[97] Jacques, *Portuguese Pioneers*, pp. 69-71.

homes."[98] Thus, Father Buzomi, working in the relative isolation of Qui Nhơn, at least in de Pina's description, did not honor the policy of Macao.

Even though de Pina wrote this letter in 1623, when Borri was already in Macao, we see that the controversies in the mission started earlier, and Borri could hardly have avoided them. If reading Borri's *Account* we cannot understand his position on the education of the locals, we definitely get some clues about his perception of the local religious life and his own position vis-à-vis it. First of all, Borri extracts Confucius and Confucianism from his description of religions, placing it in the Chapter "Of the Civil and Political Government of the Cochin-Chineses." Moreover, he seems to have sincere respect, if not admiration, for Confucian wisdom. He says that Confucian books are "full of erudition, of stories, of grave sentences, or proverbs, and such like things."[99] Thus, Borri, following the lead of Matteo Ricci and other Jesuits in China, was ready to secularize Confucius. This eventually became a central topic in the Rites Controversy when the other orders claimed that local people worshiped Confucius in the same manner as other "idols" and that Confucianism could not coexist with the monotheistic Judeo-Christian tradition.

Another crucial point of the Rites Controversy that augmented discord among the missionaries was the attitude towards ancestral rituals in general and of food sacrifice to the dead in particular. Borri's comments on these issues reveal, perhaps better than anything else, the dualism of his personality and his ambiguous view of mission work in Cochinchina. While his missionary half considers the idea of providing food for dead relatives foolish and vain and attempts to explain to the Vietnamese that the dead cannot consume this food, his scientific half appreciates the explanation of Vietnamese that this food was comprised of material and immaterial parts, of which the soul consumes only the latter. "Any wise man," says Borri, "may by this false answer discover the acuteness of the Cochin-Chinese philosophers, though they absolutely err as to the reality of the argument."[100] His mind can appreciate their logic even as his religious commitment rejects their argument.

As for Cochinchinese beliefs, he illuminates them in the chapter titled "A Short Account of the Sects in Cochin-China." In his description, which mainly dwells on Buddhism and Daoism, Borri demonstrates utter confusion in failing to distinguish clearly between the two. On the one hand, he perceives the reality of a fusion of Buddhist and Daoist practices that existed in Vietnam. However, on the other hand, he reveals a lack of comprehension of the basic doctrines of Buddhism and Daoism, the extent of which is surprising considering his relatively long residence there of five years. In this respect, we can surmise that Father Pina's attitude towards Borri in 1620 or 1621 would hardly differ from de Pina's derision of his Superior Father Manoel Fernández in 1623, when he compared him to a local youth, named Andrew, who served as interpreter for Father Fernández and could "understand at least the easiest [points]; however, in regard to questions concerning the sects and controversies he can't go very far because he is not [ready] any more than the Superior."[101] Father Fernández is criticized for not being

---

[98] De Pina's letter, cited in Jacques, *Portuguese Pioneers*, pp. 44-45.

[99] Borri in this volume, Part I, Chapter VI, Section titled "Learning."

[100] Borri in this volume, Part II, Chapter VIII, Section titled "Errors of Cochin-Chinese."

[101] De Pina's letter, cited in Jacques, *Portuguese Pioneers*, p. 43.

ready to discuss the sects after a year in the country; Father Borri was not ready after five years.

This raises a question: how arduous was Borri in performing his missionary activities and in studying Cochinchina and its natives? First, the issue of the utmost importance for Father de Pina: language acquisition. Borri never addresses the issue of why, taking into account his claim that the language was easy to master, after at least three years in Cochinchina, he had only "some knowledge of the Cochin-Chinese language," not sufficient to instruct "in the lofty mysteries" of the Christian religion,[102] and how it happened that after five years in the country, he mistranslated its Vietnamese name Annam, meaning "Pacified South," as "western country."[103] While Borri explains Father Buzomi's lack of language skill with reference to his old age,[104] he does not provide a similar excuse for himself. In any case, such an excuse would be hardly plausible since Father de Pina, who apparently did learn Vietnamese, was only three years younger than Borri.

The inevitable question comes up about Borri's contribution to the development of the Latinized script, *quốc ngữ*, on which Father de Pina scrupulously and ardently worked. Despite Borri's inadequate language ability in Vietnamese, his transcriptions of Vietnamese words opened a new venue in linguistics. His description of the language inspired a comparative analysis by Tommaso Campanella (1568-1639).[105] He referred to Borri when discussing non-flectic languages, such as Cochinchinese.[106] Borri was the first to publish alphabetic transcriptions of the Vietnamese language. However, according to Roland Jacques, Borri made no contribution to the development of the Vietnames alphabet, for his interests were far from linguistics.[107] Moreover, Jacques argues that Borri's case is irrelevant for even a representation of the patterns of writing in *quốc ngữ* despite the fact that the first published alphabetic transcriptions of the Vietnamese language appear in Borri's *Account*. He was writing in Italian for Italians, and the Vietnamese words and phrases that he incorporated into his *Account*, "show that the author had not mastered the transcription system elaborated by his own group, or at least did not follow its rules."[108]

Borri seemed to be not without ability for foreign languages, as, in addition to his native Italian, he was fluent in Latin and Portuguese, as his written works testify. Without any indication from him about the difficulties to be encountered in learning the language, it is logical to assume that he apparently did not devote

[102] Borri in this volume, Part II, Chapter V, Section titled "Conversion of a great lady."

[103] Borri in this volume, Part I, Chapter I, Section titled "Of the Name, Situation, and Extent of this Kingdom."

[104] Borri in this volume, Part II, Chapter I, Section titled "Churches erected": The officials in Macao decided to send to Father Buzomi "another father, that was younger, … that learning the language, he might afterwards preach without standing in need of an interpreter." On his arrival in Cochinchina, Buzomi was forty-one years old.

[105] An Italian philosopher and author of the famous *The City of the Sun*; in comparison with his tragic life, Borri's turbulent career looks pale and uneventful.

[106] Thommaso Campanella, *Philosophiae rationalis partes quinque: videlicet, grammatical, dialectica, rhetorica, poetica, historiographia, iuxta propria principia* (Paris: Apud Ioannem Du Bray, 1637-8), p. 52.

[107] Jacques, *Portuguese Pioneers*, p. 52. Jacques mistakenly allotted to Borri only three years in Cochinchina.

[108] Ibid., pp. 52-3.

enough time or effort to this. It is especially important to note that Borri, as he informs us, was sent to Cochinchina to learn the language in order to later go to Tonkin to establish a mission there.[109] Failing in mastering the language, he defied his superiors' plans for him and undoubtedly provided Father de Pina with a reason to disrespect him.

Moreover, when Borri describes conversions that took place during his tenure in Cochinchina, he is vague about his precise role in them. The titles of all four chapters on conversion relegate the merit for it solely to God through four different groups of people (Noblest Persons, Learned People, Heathen Priests, and Meaner Sort).[110] Most of the conversions occurred by "miraculous means." In addition to the "miraculous means," Father Buzomi was "labouring in all places to instruct, convert, and dispose the people to receive baptism."[111] Borri did not describe himself as "laboring" in places other than the city of Nuocman in the province of Pulucambi (Qui Nhơn), where he resided, along with Father Buzomi and Father de Pina, after the death of their protector and benefactor, the governor of Pulucambi, having spent three years without converting anyone. After these three "barren" years, the other two Fathers left, de Pina for Hội An, Buzomi for Đà Nẵng, to attempt to get "alms of the Portuguese there."[112] Borri, however, was left in Nuocman, "solitary and desolate," not being able to convert even when someone requesting conversion appeared on his doorstep. This person eventually played a very important role in many later conversions.[113] Borri had to wait until Father Buzomi returned with the interpreter. In his chapters on conversion, we trace his passive attitude. It seems that conversions took place at the initiative of local people as if by divine intervention rather than by any active role on the part of the missionaries.

For most of the time, Borri uses the pronoun "we," shielding or concealing his own role, which might be attributed to his modesty if not for one notable exception. In Chapter VI, "How God Open'd Another Way to Christianity, Through the Means of the Learned People Among the Heathens," he explains the benefits of his astronomical knowledge for conversion. Then and there the pronoun "I" appears, and we see Borri active and aware of his actions. Indeed, this concerns the area of his field of study: astronomy. Moreover, the mission benefited from his ability to predict the lunar eclipse of December 9, 1620, and the solar eclipse of May 22, 1621, which Borri describes with evident satisfaction in his *Account* as bringing him high esteem from the local astrologers. And after that everything sinks back to "we."

It is possible that the switch of the pronouns reveals to us Borri's real interest and raison d'être to be in Cochinchina or to be on any mission. Borri certainly had an experimental and scientific nature. For instance, having received some pieces of

---

[109] Borri in this volume, Part II, Chapter XI, Introductory passage.

[110] They are: "How God Made Way for the Conversion of the Province of Pulucambi, by Means of the Noblest Persons in It" (Chapter V), "How God Open'd Another Way to Christianity, Through the Means of the Learned People Among the Heathens" (Chapter VI), "How God Open'd Another Way to Christianity, by Means of the Omsaiis, or Heathen Priests" (Chapter VII), "How God Opened Another Way to the Conversion of the Meaner Sort by Miraculous Means" (Chapter IX).

[111] Borri in this volume, Part II, Chapter I, Section titled "Churches erected."

[112] Borri in this volume, Part II, Chapter V, Section titled "The fathers disperse."

[113] Ibid., Section titled "Conversion of a great lady."

a fragrant tree and curious about the strength of their fragrance, he buried them "for a trial" to see how far through the earth the fragrance could penetrate.[114] On another occasion, admiring the potency of herbal medicine applied by a local physician to cure Borri's accidental wound, he "caused the leg of a hen to be broke in several places" and then cured it with the same herb.[115] He mentions these small examples in his *Account*. What he does not mention there and what perhaps occupied a lot of his time are other experiments.

Athanasius Kircher (1602-1680), the foremost intellectual not only of the Jesuit Society but perhaps of his time, regarded as a brilliant mathematician and astronomer, worked on magnetic fields as Borri did. Kircher had a very high regard for Borri's thoroughness in his magnetic observations in Asia.[116] On top of this, Borri continued to develop his theory about the tenuousness of the heavens, for which he had paid with the loss of his tenure at the Collegio di Brera. Corroboration of this comes from Borri's aforementioned letter to General Mutius Vitelleschi, in which he argues about the precision of his observations of two comets in 1618 that "completely confirmed the tenuousness and corruptibility of the Heaven, which I already in Europe demonstrated for the sake of modern observations. This phenomenon was observed not only by myself but also by Father Giovani Vremano in China, and Father Manuel Dias in India," as well as by mathematicians in Europe. According to Borri, this gave "the unique proof of the truthfulness of observations, when it is found in different territories and countries, far from each other."[117] Despite all his troubles, the fluidity of three heavens had remained the baby of his mind, which he could not abandon.

His case of being both a scientist and a missionary was not unique, as Jesuits before and after him successfully combined these capacities. But while other Jesuits, like Matteo Ricci, were primarily missionaries for whom science was a means to achieve their ends, Borri seemed to be the reverse. Walking a tightrope between his duties and his interests in the very limited and interconnected microcosm of the Cochinchinese mission, Borri failed or did not want to negotiate his existence there as a missionary. Someone reported to Macao on Borri's activities, and he was recalled. The four other Jesuit Fathers at the time of Borri's departure were Buzomi, de Pina, António Fernández, and Manoel Fernández. The last one arrived only in January of 1622, just before Borri's departure, and hardly could be behind Borri's recall. In his *Account*, Borri never mentions Father António Fernández, who stayed with Father de Pina in Hội An, never seemed to meet Borri, and, according to de Pina, spent all his time in prayer. Thus, Borri was in contact only with Fathers Buzomi and de Pina. In general, the Head of the mission, at that time Father Buzomi, was the one to write an annual report on the mission. Borri resided with him. Borri's "hands off" attitude seems to have been similar to Father Buzomi's, and it is possible that Buzomi wanted someone more involved in the everyday work. However, although in his *Account* Borri identified Father de Pina as his great friend from the College in Macao,[118] it is very possible that de Pina was

---

[114] Borri in this volume, Part I, Chapter III, Section titled "Aquila, and Calamba, odoriferous wood."

[115] Borri in this volume, Part I, Chapter V, Section titled "Great cures."

[116] Kircher, *Magnes*, p. 502.

[117] Borri "Al molto Rev. Pre. Generale," in dos Santos, "Vicissitudes da obra," p. 144.

[118] Borri in this volume, Part II, Chapter II, Section titled "Charity of Japonese Christians."

dissatisfied with Borri, who fits the profile of a bad missionary as developed in de Pina's letter critiquing other missionaries. While there is not sufficient evidence to put a finger on either Buzomi or de Pina, one of them surely had a hand in Borri's recall to Europe, which perhaps was only timely.

New Enemies, Friends, and Destinations

From Cochinchina, Borri went to Macao, where he stayed for a year occupying a post of "Minister" in a Jesuit college. At that time, Macao, the Portuguese commercial base in eastern Asia, was a point of contention with the Dutch. The expansion of Dutch interests in Asia, especially after the establishment of the Dutch East India Company (Vereenigde Oostindische Compagnie, or VOC) in 1602, launched a bitter struggle between the Dutch and the Iberian countries, Spain and Portugal, relations with whom were already antagonistic as a result of the Netherlands' struggle for independence from Spain and its acceptance of Protestantism. By the 1620s, the Dutch became more and more active and successful in their attempt to establish dominance in the Asian trade and endeavored to seize Macao. At the end of May 1622, several Dutch boats shelled Macao and seized two junks loaded with Chinese merchandise, but after that they immediately retreated to Japan. However, the Dutch did not give up and sent a fleet under Admiral Cornelis Ryersen with 1,300 marines and soldiers, which attacked Macao on June 24, 1622. The Portuguese, under the command of Lopo Sarmento de Carvalho, reacted swiftly and decisively and repulsed the attackers, but the city was heavily affected.[119] Borri, as well as other Jesuits, played an active role in the defense of the place.[120] He "headed an improvised troop which vigorously repelled the attack."[121] Borri and other Jesuits "who had distinguished themselves in this brilliant yet unexpected victory, were granted by the Senate of Macao an honorary award for gallantry, dated October 14, 1623."[122]

At the end of the same year, Borri departed for Goa.[123] There, on April 10, 1623, he met Pietro della Valle (1586-1652), a rich Italian nobleman, widely educated, a globetrotter, fluent in several languages. Writing to an Italian friend, della Valle mentioned his encounter with Borri. He commented that Borri had changed his name due to its unpleasantness to Portuguese ears and praised Borri as "a great mathematician."[124] The two men became friendly. Father Borri shared Tycho Brahe's teaching with della Valle,[125] as well as his own scientific observations on the three heavens, which he had apparently put into written form by that time,

---

[119] Albert Kammerer, *La découverte de la Chine par les portugais au XVIème siècle et la cartographie des portulans* (Leiden: E. J. Brill, 1944), p. 127.

[120] Vu Khanh Tuong, "Les missions jésuites avant les missions étrangères au Vietnam (1515-1665)," PhD dissertation, Institute Catholique de Paris, 1956, vol. 1, p. 254.

[121] Jacques, *Portuguese Pioneers*, p. 80.

[122] The Lisbon Biblioteca da Ajuda, vol. 49/V5, fol. 511v-514v, cited in Jacques, *Portuguese Pioneers*, p. 80.

[123] Schütte, *Monumenta historica*, p. 1141.

[124] Mercati, "Notizie," p. 26, cites della Valle's letter. The English translation is Della Valle, *The Travels*, p. 81.

[125] Della Valle, *The Travels*, p. 84.

either in Cochinchina or in Macao or after arriving in Goa.[126] Borri evidently completely won his new acquaintance over to his side, and in 1624 Pietro della Valle translated Borri's work into Persian as *Risalah- i Padri Khristafarus Burris Isavi dar tufiq-i jadid dunya* (Compendium of a tractate of Father Christoforo Borri, S.J. on the new model of the universe according to Tycho Brahe and the other modern astronomers).[127] Borri proudly announced della Valle's translation in his letter to General Vitalleschi:

> On my way to Europe, through India, I met Signor Pietro della Valle, to whom, as he was curious, I communicated this doctrine, and he later communicated it to the sages of Persia, Armenia, and Arabia, all of whom, as he also confirmed, remained so satisfied with it, that they put it in front of any other opinion.[128]

Another issue that Borri shared with della Valle was his work on defining longitude, which the latter also found extremely interesting.[129] Even after the two men parted ways, they remained in contact, exchanging letters from which comes much of our information about Borri, whom della Valle called *mio grande amico* (my great friend).[130] After Borri's death, della Valle seemed to be the only person interested in his legacy.

According to *Monumenta historica,* Borri departed from Goa in 1623.[131] Della Valle, however, dates Borri's departure at the beginning of February 1624. He mentions that Borri departed on the same ship with Don Garcia de Silva y Figueroa (1614-1624).[132] Figueroa indeed sailed from Goa to Portugal on January 28, 1624,

---

[126] Two copies of this work, according to Sommervogel, are kept in the Vatican Library under the title *Compendium tractatus patris Christophori Bori iesuitae de nova mundi constitutione, iuxta systema Tichonis Brahae, aliorumque recentiorum mathematicorum, e lingua Latina in persicam translatum a Petro de Valle in urbe Goa, regia Lusitanorum in India, anno Christi 1624 et ab eodem nuncupatum Zaineddino Lari astronomo; apposite e regione interpretatione, quam idem Petrus de Valle Romae confecit anno 1631.* Sommervogel, vol. 1, col. 1822, under "Borri, Burrus, Christophe."

[127] In 1631, della Valle translated this work into Italian as *Compendio di un trattato del Padre Christoforo Borro giesuita della nuova costitutione del mondo secondo Tichone Brahe e gli altri astologi moderni* (Sommervogel, *Bibliothèque*, vol. 1, col. 1822, under "Borri, Burrus, Christophe").

[128] Borri "Al molto Rev. Pre. Generale," in dos Santos, "Vicissitudes da obra," p. 143.

[129] Della Valle, "Al Sig. Ingoli, 21 Maggio 1632," in Mercati, "Notizie," p. 29.

[130] Della Valle, "Lettera mia alla S. M. del Re di Portogallo," in Mercati, "Notizie," p. 41.

[131] Schütte, *Monumenta historica,* p. 1141.

[132] Della Valle, "Ricordi miei al Padre Fra Luys Coutinho. 24 Aprile 1642," in Mercati, "Notizie," p. 36. On page 218 of his *Travels,* Della Valle records an observation made on August 9, 1624, a day that falls after the date he indicated elsewhere for Borri's departure. He describes the observation as follows and seems to imply that Borri was present: "Two hours and forty minutes before Noon (if the Calculation and Observation of *Christoforo Borano* or *Boro* be true) the Sun was in the Zenith of *Goa,* and began to decline towards the South." Della Valle, *The Travels,* p. 218. However, this statement does not necessarily imply that Borri was physically present there on that day and had not made his calculation before his departure. The difference in dating (February or January 28) is insignificant. The document where della Valle mentioned Borri's departure was written eighteen years after the fact. In his *Travels,* della Valle dates the departure of the ship on January 31, 1624. It was the same ship that della Valle identifies as the only ship that departed Goa for Portugal that year. Della Valle, *The Travels,* p. 205.

and died of scurvy on July 22, 1624, off the Azores,[133] which are located off the coast of Portugal. Assuming that a trip from Goa to Lisbon would take roughly the same amount of time as it usually took to travel from Lisbon to Goa—that is six months—these dates are correct.

As with so many other points in Borri's life, his departure from Asia is obscured by a veil of mystery, produced by the existence of his manuscript known as *Informatione del P. Christoforo Borro giesuita a S. S.* [Sua Santità] *d'una nuova India per portar in quella con sua autorità apostolica mandar a piantare, e propagare la santa fede à petitione della Santa Congregatione de Cardinali de propaganda fide* (Information of Father Christoforo Borro, Jesuit, to His Holiness on a New India in Order to Bring, Plant, and Propagate There with His Apostolic Power the Holy Faith, through a Petition to the Sacred Congregation of Cardinals for the Propagation of the Faith)[134] and of another manuscript, or the same one under a different title: *Relazione a Sua Santità delle cose dell'India orientale, del Gaippone, della Cina, dell'Etiopia, dell'Isola di San Lorenzo, del Regno di Monomotapa, e della terra incognita australe* (Account to His Holiness about East India, Japan, China, Ethiopia, Madagascar, the Kingdom of Zambeze, and the Southern Unknown Land).[135] Dos Santos suggests that after his departure from Goa, Borri actually traveled to all these countries to collect ethnographic information and the data for his navigational research.[136] The Jesuit Dominique Le Jeunehomme, whom we have previously mentioned, appears to indirectly corroborate this information when he writes, in 1627, that Borri wandered extensively in different lands and in different seas, all over the Orient and Africa.[137] If Borri indeed traveled to all these places, the period between Goa and Portugal would be his only chance to do so, as the rest of his life seems to be better illuminated and uninterrupted by such long, unaccountable gaps in information. But neither in Borri's published works, nor in della Valle's letters, nor in any other place, can any evidence of such a detour be found.

We do not know the exact date, nor even the exact year, of Borri's arrival in Portugal. Dos Santos found the first mention of Borri's arrival in a letter dated June 8, 1627, describing Borri as still "weak from the fatigue of the voyage but already teaching a course on astronomy." From this, dos Santos surmises that Borri arrived in Portugal the previous year, that is, 1626.[138] The first letter that we have from Borri in Portugal is the one reported by Pietro della Valle. It is dated September 21, 1626.[139] However, the fact that della Valle himself did not return to Rome from his

---

[133] Luis Gil, "The Embassy of Don Garcia de Silva y Figueroa to Shah Abbas (1614-1624)," Abstract of the paper presented at the Conference of the Iranian Heritage Foundation, London, "Iran and the World in the Safavid Age" (September 2002), http://www.iranheritage.com/safavidconference/soas/abstract24.htm

[134] Archivio di Propaganda Fide, Scritture antiche, 190, f. 19-26, as indicated by Dr. Schmidlin "Die ersten Madagascarmissionen im Lichte der Propagandamaterialien" (The First Madagascar Missions in the Light of Propaganda Material), *Zeitschrift für Missionswissenschaft und Religionswissenschaft*, vol. XII (1922), p. 198.

[135] This work is mentioned in de Visch, *Bibliotheca scriptorum sacri oridinis cisterciensis*, p. 71, under "Christophorus Borrus"; in Argelati, *Bibliotheca scriptorum mediolanensium*, p. 239; in Sommervogel, *Bibliothèque*, vol. 1, col. 1822, under "Borri, Burrus, Christophe."

[136] Dos Santos, "Vicissitudes da obra," p, 128,

[137] Le Jeunehomme, *Relation d'un voyage*, cited in Sommervogel, *Bibliothèque*, vol. 1, col. 1822, under "Borri, Burrus, Christophe."

[138] Dos Santos, "Vicissitudes da obra," p. 129.

[139] Della Valle, "Ricordi miei," in Mercati, "Notizie," p. 36.

travels until March 1626 might explain the interval in their correspondence. Another source dated Borri's arrival in Portugal by 1625, but there is no supporting evidence for this.[140] But perhaps the best source for dating his return to Europe is Borri himself. Praising Cochinchinese medicine in his *Account*, he admitted bringing with him "a small cask of *rhubarb*, which was extraordinary good there, and when I came into *Europe*, having spent two years by the way, I found it so changed, that I scarce knew it myself."[141] Thus, by his own account, having departed Cochinchina in 1622, Borri arrived in Portugal by 1624 at the latest, apparently without visiting all these places but passing, or briefly stopping at, Madagascar, Ethiopia, and Zambeze on his way to Europe.

Why did he not stay longer in Goa? And why did he not go directly to Italy? Did he hasten to Iberia in hopes of claiming the aforementioned reward offered by the Spanish monarch? As has been pointed out, during his years in Asia, Borri apparently had made significant progress on his magnetic observations and in drawing maps based on them. If he indeed achieved some results, he would want to make them known and find practical applications for them. Spain and Portugal, which at that time were unified under the single crown of Philip IV,[142] would be appropriate locations for such an effort. Even though in decline compared with the two previous centuries, these two countries still were major naval powers, especially if we talk about the Catholic world, to which Borri belonged. In the Iberian countries Borri hoped to find more interest in his inventions than in his homeland of Italy.

Conquering Iberia: Success

Upon his arrival in Portugal, Borri lost no time rejoining the European academic world. He lectured on astronomy at the Universidade de Coimbra, a famous Jesuit institution in Portugal. At that time, one of the lecturers there passed away and the University, experiencing a lack of faculty members, offered the position to Borri, which he accepted.[143] He continued to work in two main directions: the celestial theory, as he discusses in his letter to General Vitelleschi, and the application of magnetic observations to navigation, as della Valle reports, referring to Borri's letters to him.

After all his fiascos in promulgating his theory in Italy and elsewhere, Borri endeavored to resuscitate his theory of the three heavens. He approached his colleagues in various fields, such as Arts, Philosophy, Theology, and Scriptures, at the Universidade de Coimbra, and all of them, according to Borri, supported him and repudiated the theory of the hardness and the incorruptibility of the heavens. Not only did they unanimously support him, but they also officially reported their support of his views to the head of the college.[144] Borri's colleagues were no less enthusiastic about his work on longitude at sea and advised him to go to Lisbon to make it known to the Viceroy, and through him, to the king himself.

---

[140] Schütte, *Monumenta historica*, p. 1141.

[141] Borri in this volume, Part I, Chapter V, Section titled "Great cures."

[142] Lived 1605-1665, King of Spain as Philip IV from 1621 to 1665 and King of Portugal as Philip III from 1621 to 1640.

[143] Dos Santos, "Vicissitudes da obra," p. 129.

[144] Borri, "Al molto Rev. Pre. Generale," in dos Santos, "Vicissitudes da obra," p. 129.

And so, Borri moved to Lisbon. In 1628, he was teaching at the Colégio de Santo Antão. Many of his colleagues there were interested in new theories.[145] Moreover, in Lisbon there was a broader circle of scientists among whom were not only Portuguese but also many foreigners who came to Lisbon either to settle down or to await their departure for Asia.[146] Borri was the only one there to teach on celestial spheres, and in his lectures he introduced the heliocentric system,[147] with which he essentially disagreed. The Colégio de Santo Antão, while having rather open-minded faculty members, was a Jesuit college and discussions could not trespass the limits imposed by the Order. Borri's introduction of the heliocentric system in his lectures was somewhat daring, for after 1616 the Copernican system had become a more restricted subject for discussion. At the same time, he continued to develop the three-heaven theory. The evidence of Borri's relentless work can be found in his notes titled *Nova astronomia, na qual se refuta a antiga da multidão de 12 ceos* (New Astronomy in which the Ancient Multitude of the 12 Heavens Is Refuted).[148] At the Colégio, his attitude, ideas, and writings passed as exciting and innovative, while in fact they hardly deserved such a status, as Borri introduced few novel ideas into the theories of his predecessors, in particular, Tycho Brahe.[149]

At the Colégio, Borri also taught a course on the Art of Navigation, the fruit of his long deliberations and observations, and he wrote a manuscript entitled *Arte de navegar*, which he signed as: "Father Master Cristóvão Bruno, from the Colégio de Santo Antão from this city of Lisbon, on March 19, 1628."[150] This manuscript has had a history almost as complex as its author's. Borri wrote it in Portuguese. This limited the circle of potential readers outside Portugal. Father Le Jeunehomme, the one who reported that the consequence of Borri's early work on three heavens in Milan was "a small rebuke," was apparently commissioned to translate this manuscript into Latin. According to him, Borri "found a means to identify the distances of longitude from east to west[151] and a new way for better navigation, which is in grand vogue here [in Portugal]."[152] In fact, in *Arte de navegar*, Borri wrote that he was not talking about an "invention but *aperfeiçoamento* [improvement] of the old idea of using a clock to determine longitude." He suggested a construction consisting of an hour-glass (*uma ampulheta*) with the duration of at least six hours, and perhaps of twelve or twenty-four, and with a division of the intervals between the hour-marks into fifteen parts, corresponding

---

[145] This can be supported by the analysis of works published and courses taught by the faculty members at Coimbra and S. Antao. See for example M. G. da Costa, "Inéditos de filosofia em Portugal," *Revista Portuguesa de Filosofia*, 5,1 (1949): 37-77.

[146] For a list of foreign and Portuguese professors who taught at the College see Baldini, *Saggi sulla cultura*, p. 146, fn. 53.

[147] Ibid., pp. 159 & 160, fn. 94.

[148] Biblioteca da Universidade de Coimbra, ms. 44, fols. 65 and after, cited in dos Santos, "Vicissitudes da obra," p. 135. By the time that Borri wrote this work, the idea of twelve heavens had replaced the idea of eleven heavens.

[149] Baldini, *Saggi sulla cultura*, p. 163.

[150] Biblioteca da Universidade de Coimbra, ms. 44, fol. 1 r, cited in dos Santos, "Vicissitudes da obra," p. 131.

[151] Father Le Jeunehomme makes a mistake as Borri's theory is explicitly built on determining longitude from West to East, not in the opposite direction.

[152] Cited in Sommervogel, *Bibliothèque*, vol. 1, col. 1822, under "Borri, Burrus, Christophe."

to the fifteen degrees that the sun goes in an hour. It was to be used with an astrolabe, which would help to measure degrees between the shore and the big mast. According to the modern Portuguese scientist Joaquim de Carvalho, theoretically, this improvement was admissible as the determination of longitude would be essentially relegated to the issue of time; in practice, however, maintenance of correct time turned out to be precarious and costly, at least for long voyages.[153]

Le Jeunehomme reports that Borri tried to publish the book in Rome, but because it was in Portuguese "our fathers encouraged me to turn this book into Latin, because everybody thinks that this book would have a wider distribution than in Portugal; perhaps I will be occupied with that this year."[154] We do not know whether Le Jeunehomme completed the translation as the only extant copy of this book is still in Portuguese and was published in 1940, since its significance, according to Caravalho, was not recognized until the twentieth century.[155]

Simultaneously with his hourglass-based solution, Borri continued working on the magnetic method defining longitude, the study he started in Milan and was so eager to try in India. In a manuscript, Borri presented another "invention to navigate from West to East, based on vacillations of the magnetic needle [*fuxumbrio*] and tracing the respective lengths through points of equal declination," *tractus chalyboclytici*, as he designated them, upside down.[156] This manuscript is titled *Regimento que o P. Christovam Bruno da Comp. de Jesus, por ordem de S. M., dá aos pilotos das náos da India para fazerem as experiências sobre a invenção de navegar de lest a oest* (Regulation of Father Christoforo Borri of the Society of Jesus by Order of His Majesty to the Pilots of the Boats for India to Make a Test of the Invention for Navigation from West to East).[157] We will discuss the fate of this manuscript below.

Borri seized the opportunity of being in Lisbon to present his work to the Royal Council, and della Valle cites Borri's letter to him dated March 17, 1629, as follows:

> My business of the invention from the West to the East has already been examined, and approved in this Royal Council of Portugal, where all the sages and intellectuals [skilled] in this issue from the entire kingdom assemble together with the Pilots. And later it was approved by the Council in Madrid. Finally, the King commanded that this March an armada of three ships and six galleons under the Viceroy would be dispatched to India navigated by this my invention. Necessary instruments for all the ships have already been made at royal expense, and the Pilots have been instructed and obligated to comply with the invention, etc.[158]

In December of the same year, according to della Valle, Borri wrote to him from Madrid, where he was summoned by the king to his court and where he three

---

[153] Carvalho, "Galileu e a cultura porgutuesa," p. 405. On how to use it see Ibid., pp. 429-432.

[154] Cited in Sommervogel, *Bibliothèque*, vol. 1, col. 1822, under "Borri, Burrus, Christophe."

[155] Carvalho, "Galileu e a cultura porgutuesa," p. 406.

[156] João Andrade Corvo, "Linhas isogónicas no século XVI" (Isogone Lines in the Sixteenth Century), in his *Roteiro de Lisboa a Goa* (Pilgrim from Lisboa to Goa) (Lisbon, 1882), p. 393, cited in Carvalho, "Galileu e a cultura porgutuesa," p. 434.

[157] See Ibid., p. 405.

[158] Della Valle, ""Ricordi miei," in Mercati, "Notizie," p. 37.

times demonstrated his invention in three councils of various people. Borri continues:

> the King ordered that there would be the last council to determine the prize; and in this he ordered to give me maintenance and the cost of the publication of the book on this issue, also the King ordered to tell me he wanted to see the invention. Two crowns of Portugal and Castille, were fighting over me: this one wanted me to return to Lisbon to supervise their navigation; that one wanted me [to go] to Seville in order to apply the same invention to their Navy of the West Indies, including the Philippines, etc.[159]

His next letter was from Barcelona, dated July 20, 1630:

> After my invention of the graduation of longitude from East to West (*sic*)[160] was approved with universal applause at the Court; the King and the Count di Olivares[161] wanted to nominate me to be Bishop of Macao; but our Portuguese Fathers blocked it as I was a foreigner, and also those in the Royal Council decreed that the King order me to Seville to instruct these Pilots of the West Indies and to provide them with the instruments necessary to put in practice the new art for these seas.

But Borri did not want to share with Spain what he already implemented in Portugal the previous year. So, as he writes to della Valle,

> to be true, as well as to be more desired, I went to the King and the Count di Olivares and told them that it was already too late for me to go to Seville for this year because the fleet was to depart in several days and to introduce all the new instruments etc. I would at all times need three months; and so I asked the King for a permission to go to Rome, which he gave me, but with a condition that I would return in time to dispatch the fleet next year; and with this I departed and arrived at the port of Barcelona, from which I will shortly depart for Rome.[162]

In Madrid, Borri not only found admirers of his navigational inventions in the Royal Council, but also fervent supporters of his celestial theory at the Colégio Imperial de Madrid, a Jesuit institution, which at that time was under the patronage of the Empress Maria, and thus titled "Imperial College." As Borri reported to General Vitelleschi, French, German, Flemish, and Scottish mathematicians there approved his theory.[163] And he desperately needed their

---

[159] Ibid.

[160] I believe that Pietro della Valle, like Father Le Jeunehomme, erred in citing Borri's letter as about the "graduation of longitude from East to West" when it should be from "West to East."

[161] Gaspar de Guzmán y Pimentel, Count-Duke of Olivares (1587-1645), was the *valido*, that is, the favorite, closest associate, and powerful minister of Philip IV. See also, J. H. Elliot, *The Count-Duke of Olivares: The Statesman in an Age of Decline* (New Haven, CT, and London: Yale University Press, 1986).

[162] Della Valle, "Ricordi miei," in Mercati, "Notizie," p. 38.

[163] Borri, "Al Molto Rev. Pre. Generale," in dos Santos, "Vicissitudes da obra," p. 147.

approval as he was determined to publish his theory on the celestial structure, on which he continued to work despite difficulties with publishers. Eventually, he turned his *Nova astronomia* into a final product titled *De tribus coelis aereo, sydereo, empyreo*. The body of the work was printed in Lisbon, in 1629, as is seen from the imprint inside the book: "Em Lisboa. Por Matias Rodrigues. Anno de 1629." But the book did not come out until later, as it had not received official approval, which was finally given in February 1630 by the censor, Dr. Jorge Cabral. He required that the title page read *Collecta Astronomica ex doctrina P. Christophori Borri Mediolanensis, ex Societate Jesu*, thus obscuring the disputed question of *tribus coelis* (three heavens).[164] In his struggle for the book, Borri tried to drum up all the support he could and that is why the support from the Colégio Imperial de Madrid was vital. The book eventually saw the light in 1631, as we read on the front page "Vlysipone. Apud Mathiam Rodrigues. Anno M.DC.XXXI." It contains six parts and argues against both the Copernican and the Ptolemaic systems. It discusses the movement of the planets and the composition of heavens. It attributes the movement of the celestial bodies to angels.[165] The last part of the book is on the creation of heavens. It follows the Book of Genesis and, according to Lynn Thorndike, a science professor from Columbia University, this part was compiled to appease the religious authorities.[166]

Conquering Iberia: Failure

Borri portrays himself as a victor successfully playing on the aspirations of Spain and Portugal, which, according to him, fought over him. He further implies that the reason for his departure from the hospitable Spanish monarchy is his own loyalty to Portugal, which first gave him a comfortable and supporting refuge. But other voices bring this thesis into doubt. It is questionable whether his successes as reported to Pietro della Valle were so complete and cloudless. According to Athanasius Kircher, Borri is the one to whom the invention of the magnetic declination was attributed. As evidence for this, Kircher adduces a letter from one of his correspondents in Madrid who writes about Borri. This correspondent communicated with Borri, who at that time was in Portugal, on the subject of longitude and magnetic declinations. Borri, according to this letter, considered himself as the inventor of the device to find longitude at sea, which was very important for navigation at that time.[167] According to Martino Martini (1614-1661), a Jesuit missionary, the technique seemed to involve the construction of a chart mapping points of equal magnetic declination, an azimuthal compass, and a technique for measuring the declination at any time of day.[168] According to Kircher's correspondent, Borri "had the nerve" to claim this prize in spite of the

---

[164] De Carvalho, "Galileu e a cultura porgutuesa," pp. 465-466.

[165] For a detailed overview of the work see: A. A. de Andrade, "Antes de Vernei nascer ... o P. Cristovão Borri lança, nas escolas a primeira grande reforma científica (Before Vernei was born ... Father Cristoforo Borri Launches the First Major Scientific Reform in the Schools)," *Brotéria* XL, 4 (1945): 369-379. Also Lynn Thorndike, *A History of Magic and Experimental Science* (New York, NY: Columbia University Press, 1958) VII:55-58; and de Carvalho, "Galileu e a cultura porgutuesa," pp. 464-465.

[166] Thorndike, *A History of Magic and Experimental Science*, p. 465.

[167] Kircher, *Magnes*, p. 502.

[168] Gorman, "The Angel and the Compass," p. 244.

correspondent's effort to dissuade him, pointing out dubious aspects of Borri's theory due to the unreliability of the magnetic device. Moreover, Borri accused this correspondent of not being willing to help him gain access to the king. When he did get the king's attention, however, his invention, according to the correspondent, was rejected.[169] Valentin Estancel, a Jesuit astronomer who taught in Portugal, also referred to Borri's presentation at the court as a fiasco, saying that instead of gaining the 50,000 cruzados promised by the Spanish crown, Borri earned the reputation of being "presumptuous and bizarre."[170] Similar epithets, according to Ribeiro dos Santos, writing in 1812, were applied to Borri's method, which was said to have "little reliability and solidity."[171] The best result that Borri achieved there was that the king ordered his invention to be used by his fleet departing for India, and this outcome is what unites these various accounts of events with Borri's.

But even if Borri had not gotten the desired recognition of the Spanish crown, his work undoubtedly provoked discussion and even won approval among the scientists. One of the famous mathematicians of that time, Francesco Stelluti (1577-1652), on December 2, 1628, at the end of the year when Borri completed his *Arte de navegare*, wrote to Galileo, whose close friend he was, about his meeting with Pietro della Valle. The latter told him about a Portuguese Jesuit who found an instrument to define longitude. Despite the erroneous identification of the Jesuit as Portuguese, there is little doubt that della Valle was referring to Borri and the instrument is identified as *horivolo con polvere* (watch with sand, that is, hourglass) to observe longitude. Stelluti, too, expresses uncertainty about the invention but he is also very interested in and enthusiastic about it as, according to him, it being "easier and more precise than all the other inventions before, that it will be embraced by everybody and of great use to navigation and cartography."[172]

It is possible that he was not successful in some other matters that he also tried to pursue in Portugal and Spain. Borri did not report on these to Pietro della Valle or if he did those letters have not survived. In one of the sessions of the Royal Council, he discussed inadvertent discoveries by a Dutch boat. Originally, to get from Europe to Asia, the Dutch followed the course of their predecessors, the Portuguese, that is, after doubling the Cape of Good Hope, they would proceed along the east coast of Africa to Madagascar, and from there cross the Indian Ocean to the East Indies (modern Indonesia). Later they found that turning eastward from the Cape of Good Hope and then to the north could bring them faster and more safely to their destination. In 1616, Dirk Hartog, captain of the ship *Eendracht*, deviated from this course and found himself off the West coast of Australia. Borri advocated sending an expedition there. The Council did not reach any decision about this, except to refer it to the king, who did nothing about it. Borri did not give up on this idea and, two years later, in 1629 or 1630, he found in Madrid a certain captain of the navy and persuaded him to apply for a license from the Royal Council to make this exploration. The Council, however, was

---

[169] Kircher, *Magnes*, p. 502.

[170] De Carvalho, "Galileu e a cultura porgutuesa," p. 448.

[171] Ribeiro dos Santos, "Memórias históricas sobre alguns matemáticos portugueses e estrangeiros domicilidrios em Portugal ou nas Conquistas," *Memórias de literatura portuguesa publicadas pela Academia Real das Ciências de Lisboa* (Lisbon, 1812), vol. VIII, part I, p. 188, cited in de Carvalho, "Galileu e a cultura porgutuesa," pp. 436-437.

[172] Galileo Galilei, *Opere*, vol. XIII (Florence: Tip. di G. Barbèra, 1906), pp. 459-60.

uninterested and responded that the monarch "already had more land than he could maintain; it is not worthwhile to search for more."[173] And Borri went back to Rome.

The Return of the Prodigal Son

Whether he went to Rome from his own volition, as he wrote to della Valle, or was called by the Congregation for the Propagation of the Faith, as della Valle affirms,[174] we do not know. While in Rome, according to Pietro della Valle, Borri received news from Spain on the success of the voyage of that armada, which navigated from Lisbon to India with his invention. The pilot of the armada used the old methods. But there was also on board "a Jesuit Father ultramontane, person skilled in Mathematics and well-instructed in Father Borri's invention, [whose observations] corresponded with Father Borri's map and with his invention." One day, the Pilot announced that, according to his calculations, they were at the distance of half a day from Goa. The Jesuit Father, however, decided that they were at the distance of half a day from the Maldives Islands, a place that was considered dangerous for navigation. At dawn of the following day, land appeared, considered by the Pilot and all other Portuguese to certainly be India. Thus, they prepared to disembark. But when they approached, it turned out to be the easternmost island in the Maldives chain. This recognition helped them to find one of the larger channels among the islands, which, according to the official report, "permitted them with God's help to be saved from the dangers in which they would otherwise find themselves, in more narrow channels. From this it is possible to comprehend how beneficial is this invention." The account of this was given to Father Borri in Rome from Spain, authenticated by the hand of the Notary with witnesses and with all legal solemnity.[175] But if all this indeed happened, it was one of the last bright moments of Borri's life.

Borri's return to Italy after fifteen years of absence brought him neither happiness nor peace. Having failed to persuade the Portuguese and the Spaniards to venture into new territories, Borri decided to try his hand in Rome. In 1630, he entered into correspondence with the Pope and the Sacred Congregation for the Propagation of the Faith, trying to persuade them to organize a mission to the *terra incognita australe* inadvertently discovered by the Dutch, "adding that he had failed to persuade Portuguese authorities to send an expedition to the new land."[176] Simultaneously, Borri tried to persuade the Pope and the Congregation to establish ecclesiastical missions in Madagascar and from there to initiate missions in the "southern island world." Borri wrote the already mentioned *Informatione del P. Christoforo Borro giesuita a S. S. [Sua Santità] d'una nuova India per portar in quella con sua autorità apostolica mandar a piantare, e propagare la santa fede à petitione della Santa Congregatione de Cardinali de propaganda fide* (Information of Father Christoforo Borro, Jesuit, to His Holiness on a new India in order to bring, plant, and propagate there with his apostolic power the Holy Faith, with a petition of the

---

[173] Ms. 677, Biblioteca da Universidade de Coimbra, fol. 253r, cited in dos Santos, pp. 132-133.

[174] Della Valle, "Lettera mia alla S. M. de Re di Portogallo," in Mercati, "Notizie," p. 42.

[175] Della Valle, ""Ricordi miei," in Mercati, "Notizie," pp. 38-39.

[176] Joe Morley, "Feature: First Priest to the Great South Lands," *The Catholic Weekly*, Sydney, Australia (April 14, 2002).

Sacred Congregation of Cardinals for the Propagation of the Faith). In this petition, Borri asks the Pope to be concerned about the souls perishing in Madagascar, especially with Prince André, a son of a Madagascar ruler who received Christian training in Goa, waiting "like Daniel in the lion's den" until the Pope would send missionaries to help him.[177] In 1613, Jesuits had persuaded a local king in one of the territories of Madagascar to let them proselytize in his kingdom and to take his son to Goa, where he was baptized and assumed the name André. The young prince returned to Madagascar in 1616 with Jesuits. Not long after that, his father decided to bring the evangelization of his kingdom to a halt and expelled the missionaries.[178] This was what brought to Borri's mind a comparison with Daniel and the lion's den. If Borri did not visit Madagascar, he could have met the prince in Goa in 1616 or, at least, heard his story there.

According to della Valle, Pope Urban VIII also saw the *Informatione* and considered it good.[179] While we undoubtedly should credit Borri for this success, Pietro della Valle was probably instrumental in Borri's writing of this work and in establishing Borri's contact with the Pope and the Congregation. In one of his letters, della Valle mentions that he "communicated" the work numerous times with Borri and also that he could testify to its correctness as one who saw it.[180]

Writing about places one had never visited was not unheard of. For example, Borri's famous contemporary, Athnasius Kircher, wrote on China and Egypt while never leaving Europe and relying on the letters and works of missionaries and travelers.[181] Another famous seventeenth-century traveler, the Frenchman Jean-Baptiste Tavernier (1605-1689), whose account will be discussed in this volume in connection with Samuel Baron's work, described the kingdom of Tonkin without ever going there, basing his description on what he reportedly heard from his brother.[182] Della Valle's observations of these places would undoubtedly add a welcoming touch to Borri's epistle. In addition to his knowledge of the places, by that time della Valle had had a good experience with similar requests. He returned to Rome in March 1626, not long before Borri, and, as a Roman patrician and intellectual, he had the Pope's ear. Already on April 11, 1626, he presented to the Pope the *Information of Georgia*, describing the homeland of his second wife, which was already a Christian (if not Catholic) country. Della Valle wrote his *Informatione* "to the end to persuade him [the Pope] to send a Mission of Priests thither in order to reduce those people to the union of the Roman Church." Already on May 4, 1626, the Pope spoke of this with the Congregation and they agreed.[183] It seemed that the Pope treated Borri graciously, and Borri even demonstrated to him his invention for defining longitude, the "Instrument, neither yet used nor named by

---

[177] Dos Santos, "Vicissitudes da obra," p. 139.

[178] Albert Kammerer, *La découverte de Madagascar par les portugais et la cartographie de l'île* (Lisbon: 1950), pp. 82-90.

[179] Mercati, "Notizie," p. 31.

[180] Ibid.

[181] Athanasius Kircher, *China monumentis* (Amsterdam: Apud Joannem Janssonium à Waesberge & E"Relation nouvelle et singulier du royaume de Tunquin," in J. B. Tavernier, *Recueil de plusieurs relations et traitez singuliers & curieux* (Paris: 1679).lizeum Weyerstraet, 1667).

[182] "Relation nouvelle et singulier du royaume de Tunquin," in J. B. Tavernier, *Recueil de plusieurs relations et traitez singuliers & curieux* (Paris: 1679).

[183] Pietro della Valle, *The Travels*, pp. 317-318.

others, he [Urban VIII] thus named it, and called it, very appropriately, by a Greek word Naugnomon,"[184] that is, "nautical gnomon," or "nautical sundial." Urban VIII (1568-1644), né Maffeo Barberini, was an offspring of one of the most famous Florentine families. Pope from 1623, Urban VIII patronized arts, architecture, and science, including bringing to Rome such renowned figures as Athanasius Kircher. Thus, della Valle's statement on the Pope's interest in Borri's invention is not ungrounded.

In a Crossfire

But instead of an all-round success, the result of these contacts for Borri was apparently an all-out war. According to della Valle:

> In Rome, Father Borri had a lot of troubles with his superiors; who did not like his direct contacts with the Pope; and with that Congregation, in relation to the propagation of the faith; but Father Borri innocently, as a newcomer to Rome and misinformed, undertook these tasks, believing that his Order with the Congregation, being of the same will, aimed towards the same goal to serve God.[185]

Borri's troubles in Rome were not limited to dealings with the authorities of his order as he also had "great troubles from the Spaniards" who were dissatisfied with Borri's return to Rome and his contacts with the Pope concerning missionary activities in India.[186] Della Valle describes Borri as being in conflict with the world, or at least with his own order and with Spain, which he had only recently left and which had seemed to be hospitable to him. This is not smoke without fire, and there was apparently a reason for Spanish dissatisfaction with Borri.

In his petition to the Pope, Borri writes about how providential it is that the need for missionaries he described coincides with a period when the Congregation for the Propagation of the Faith is ready to take the opportunity to open up a new mission field. Borri writes that he would offer to do it himself if he were not "hindered by the East Asian missions and by difficulties in his own order." Borri points out three ways to propagate the faith in the "new south Indies": 1) with the help of Spain and Portugal, 2) by means of the Pope, 3) by some other ruler.[187]

As a scientist, Borri is methodical. He had tried the first way and failed. So he moved to the second one. While della Valle mentions only the troubles caused to Borri by Spaniards, we should not exclude that it is possible that the Spaniards were joined by the Portuguese, whom della Valle perhaps leaves out of his accusation for the reason that his addressee was the King of Portugal. Borri had lost his faith in the Iberians. We also hear his request for changes in organizing mission activity in his *Account of Cochinchina*, in which he refers to the support given to missions by King Philip of Spain "and his council of the Indies," yet notes that "it is impossible" that Spain, "which supports other mighty weights" and bears "almost all the world" on its "shoulders," can sufficiently support all the

---

[184] Della Valle, "Ricordi miei," in Mercati, "Notizie," p. 41.

[185] Della Valle, "Lettera mia alla S. M. de Re di Portogallo," in Mercati, "Notizie," p. 42.

[186] Ibid.

[187] As cited in Schmidlin, "Die ersten Madagascarmissionen," pp. 197-198. I thank Arthur Gross of Cornell University for helping with this passage.

needs of overseas missions.[188] He desires that the Pope would commission the Congregation to supply what Spain cannot, but in doing so he was interjecting himself into the strained relationship between the Pope and Spain. Spain was suspicious of the Pope, who, according to a historian of the papacy, "was anxious for a balance of power since by reason of the exclusive preponderance of Spain in Italy, he had cause to fear not only for the autonomy of the Papal States but for that also of the Holy See itself."[189] Borri seems not to have been heedful of these subtleties.

It is evident that upon Borri's return to Rome, the relationship between the Jesuit Society and himself was irreparably damaged. General Vitelleschi does not allow Borri to publish his doctrine on the three heavens. Borri's letter to him, cited above, was intended to obtain Vitelleschi's permission for publication. However, the tone of the letter and the presentation of arguments suggest either the absence of any negotiating skills on Borri's side or his intention to sever his relation with the Society. He does sign the letter "the most humble son and servant," but essentially the letter consists of the description of injustices Borri endured from his superiors in the Society: General Acquaviva, who ordered him to leave his post at the Collegio di Brera, and General Vitelleschi himself who, according to Borri, initially promised him permission to publish his book but later revoked it, despite all the acclamations he had received in Portugal and Spain from the local scientists as well as from the French, Germans, Flemish, and Scotts, and even in Rome, where the "reviewers who by the order of Your Paternity saw my work and in general agreed with my doctrine."[190]

In addition to this, the traces of Borri's conflict with the Order flash in his correspondence with the Pope and the Congregation. As Dr. Schmidlin informs us in his article on the three hundredth anniversary of the Congregation for the Propagation of the Faith, Borri wrote that he was willing to be the one to establish the mission in Madagascar if he were not "hindered by the East Asian missions and by difficulties in his own order."[191] In addition to Borri's incompatibility with his Order, the relationship between the Congregation and the Jesuits did not thrive either. There were reasons for the Jesuits to be suspicious, if not apprehensive, of the Congregation for the Propagation of the Faith. The Congregation was receiving discouraging and critical reports from the missions in the West and East Indies. The Secretary of the Congregation, Francesco Ingoli, was an adversary of the Jesuits and put much of the blame for trouble in the missions on them for being too autonomous.[192] Already in 1625, three years after the creation of the Congregation, he presented to its cardinals a memo in which he listed obstacles to the propagation of Christianity in the Indies: discord between Jesuits and other orders, and the guilt of many missionaries "who only looked for amassing riches and to import them to Europe."[193] According to Dr. Schmidlin, the Jesuits were "so disinclined toward the Congregation that if the [Jesuit] fathers thought that Borri

---

[188] Borri in this volume, Part II, "Conclusion."

[189] Ludwig Freiher von Pastor, *The History of the Popes From the Close of the Middle Ages*, trans. Dom Ernest Graf, O. S. B., 2nd ed. (London: Routledge & Kegan Paul Ltd., 1955), XVIII:274.

[190] Borri, "Al molto Rev. Pre. Generale," in dos Santos, "Vicissitudes da obra," p. 146-148.

[191] Schmidlin, "Die ersten Madagascarmissionen," p. 198.

[192] Von Pastor, *The History of the Popes*, XXIX:263.

[193] Chappoulie, *Aux origines*, p. 76.

was dispensing such information and ideas to it [about plans for sending missions to new lands] they would find a way to expel him from Rome."[194]

On December 23, 1630, Borri's suggestion was indeed discussed at a meeting of the Congregation for the Propagation of the Faith, but no result was achieved.[195] This new failure did not deter Borri. The following year, 1631, he published *Relatione della nuova missione delli PP. della Compagnia di Giesù, al Regno della Cocincina,* the *Account of Cochin-China* presented in this volume. The *Account* was apparently written after Borri's arrival in Rome to support his attempts to persuade the Pope and the Congregation to expand mission activities into new territories. The book is dedicated to Urban VIII, not only because his work discusses conversion to Christianity but mostly, as Borri writes, "because Your Holiness showed to me an inclination to see it, that's why humbly prostrating to his feet I present it to him, and implore Your Holiness' Benediction."[196] Borri's statement confirmed his contacts with the Pope and even implied the Pope's encouragement of his work.

The context of adversarial relations between the Congregation and the Society of Jesus undoubtedly made it difficult for Borri to find his own voice in this account. He needed the approval of the Society for the publication and thus he had to gloss over all the contradictions and difficulties among the missionaries in Cochinchina. This explains the difference between his *Account* and Father de Pina's letter, the gloominess of which beclouds the rainbows of Borri's *Account.* While we do not know whether that letter was de Pina's momentary *cri de l'âme* or a habitual mode of internal correspondence, unlike Borri's *Account,* it was not intended for public eyes. Jesuit closeness about their internal affairs perhaps accounts for the high praise employed by the non-Jesuits Argelati and de Visch for Borri's

---

[194] Schmidlin, "Die ersten Madagascarmissionen," p. 198.

[195] Ibid. We do not know whether Borri had or he would have approached another ruler after his failures to persuade Rome, Spain, and Portugal to expand the missions, as was suggested by Schmidlin above. Joaquim de Caravalho included in his article a document demonstrating, in his opinion, Borri's contact with a Dutch scientist in order to inform the Dutch government of his method based on the map of magnetic declination. If true, this would give a whole new twist to Borri's personality, with his scientific ambitions dominating over both his religious affiliation and his political loyalties, as the Protestant Dutch were at that time bitter enemies of Portugal and Spain. However, the document that Caravalho presents (pp. 437-438) does not allow us to come to this conclusion. He reprints a letter written from Amsterdam by Gerhard Johann Vossius to Borri in response to Borri's request to promote an issue that they discussed while never identifying the matter. The letter is published in his Vossius' *Opera* (Amsterdam: P. & J. Blaev, 1699), p. 344. Vossius or Voss (1577-1649) was a German classical scholar and Calvinist theologian, without any evident connection to science. Moreover, the letter is dated in 1643 (eleven years after Borri's death); it implies that Borri and Vossius are relatives (as Vossius addresses Borri as his *Cognate optime,* "Dear relative"; the letter further indicates that Borri is married and has a father-in-law, Georgio Ratalliero Dubletio, apparently a high-ranking church official. It also implies that Borri lived in France, at least at the time of the letter, as Vossius asks Borri to convey his wishes for the health of Borri's wife and father-in-law, "unless they live in a different part of France" (*nisi alterum illorum Galliae adhuc tenent*). It is appealing to imagine Borri playing a trick on everybody and, instead of dying, leaving Italy, marrying, and then, through his father-in-law, attempting to get in touch with the Dutch. But if we resist this temptation and wait until a better corroboration surfaces, Borri's connection to the Dutch, if it existed, remains unproved.

[196] Borri, *Relatione della nuova missione* (Rome: F. Catanio, 1631), p. A2.

missionary activity as, not privy to the Society's affairs, they most probably received their information about this from Borri's own *Account*.

The flesh of Borri's *Account* was arranged upon the skeleton of a Cochinchina "which wants nothing to make it a part of heaven."[197] His Cochinchinese are predominantly friendly, kind, and childish. They, for example, "being soon taken with the curiosities of other countries, it comes to pass, that they put a great value upon, and buy at great rates, many things, which to others are of very small worth."[198] Moreover, "as ready as the Cochin-Chinese are to give, so are they as apt, if not more, to ask any thing they see, so that as soon as ever they cast their eye on any thing that is new to them, and curious, they say, *Schin Mocaii* [please give it to me]."[199] Presenting the Cochinchinese as children, Borri undoubtedly insists on the need of parenting, but the conditions of the parenting in his depiction are almost ideal.

Whether all the details of the *Account* corresponded to reality was beside the point. They did not. Sometimes we can see Borri's insufficient knowledge of the country, which perhaps unintentionally distorts the presentation of Vietnamese history or religion. Sometimes a discrepancy is more deliberate, as we see in Borri's compromising description of the easiness of learning the language. Even his reflection on living conditions can be contested. De Pina describes troubles caused by drinking water when he, with another missionary, went out to a mission. The water, he writes, "made us gravely ill. I was in bed for fifty days, then convalesced and relapsed for [a total of] three full months."[200] What a dissonance with Borri's mesmerizing, almost sumptuous, account of the exquisite fruits and foods of the country, its healthy climate, and skillful physicians!

But Borri's goal was to persuade the Congregation about the viability of the missions and the usefulness of science for missionary purposes. He enriched the usual reasons cited for European penetration into Asia, summarized as the "three Gs": God, Gold, and Glory; to these he added Science.

His *Account* became the last signifier of Borri's affiliation with the Society of Jesus. In January 1631, General Vitelleschi wrote a foreword to the *Account*, identifying its author as a member of his Order and one of the first missionaries to Cochinchina and, as it was the custom, conditioning the publication "if the Reverend Monsignor Vicegerent [of Rome] and the Reverend Father Master of the Sacred Palace approve."[201] These two officials, in charge of all the materials published by the members of religious orders, indeed approved. The same year, Borri's *De tribus coelis* was also published in Lisbon and then translated by della Valle in Rome.

---

[197] Borri in this volume, Part II, Section titled "Conclusion."

[198] Borri in this volume, Part I, Chapter VIII, Section titled "Trade of Cochin-China."

[199] Borri, Book I, Chapter V, "Liberality."

[200] De Pina's letter, cited in Jacques, *Portuguese Pioneers*, p. 42.

[201] Page A2 of the original *Relatione*. The Viceregent of Rome was Antonio Ricciulli (?-1643), Bishop Emeritus of Belcastro; see Patritius Gauchat, O. M., *Hierarchia catholica medii aevi* (Catholic Hierarchy through Times) (Monasterii: sumptibus et typis librariae Regensbergianae, 1935), vol. 4, p. 112. Master of the Sacred Palace was Nicolaus Riccardus. No further information is available.

A Layman of Two Religious Orders?

Either because of Borri's contacts with the Congregation or the publication of the *De tribus coelis,* the tension between Borri and the Jesuit order not only continued but became aggravated to the extent that "it became necessary [for] the Pope to issue a dispensation, which in a special edict allowed [Borri] to leave the Jesuit Order and to pass to the Cistercian Order."[202] Persecutions against Father Borri from all sides were so numerous that, according to della Valle, the "poor thing" (*poverello*) one day found himself in the house of Monsignor Vicegerent, either to talk about his problems or for some other reason, "when he suddenly was overcome with some grave pain, and after less then sixteen hours of the malady he passed away."[203] We do not know whether this is the same Vicegerent as the Vicegerent of Rome (at that time Antonio Ricciulli), who had recently approved his *Account*, or some other person.

Borri's fellow Jesuit, Julius Cordara, presented the case differently. According to him, Borri did not leave the Order through the Pope's dispensation but, on the contrary, was expelled from the Society by order of General Vitelleschi after he did not mend his ways upon his return to Rome from Spain.[204] As noted by Pietro della Valle, Borri subsequently joined the Cistercian Order. Carlos Sommervogel, the nineteenth-century Jesuit historian, is more particular on this period of Borri's life. Citing a letter from Father Venot to Father Ayrault, written on July 15, 1632, from Rome, Sommervogel states that Borri

> ... left the Jesuit Order to enter the Order of Bernadins of the St. Cross of Jerusalem[205] in Rome with the dispensation from the Pope to have his profession after three months of novitiate. But when the three months had elapsed, the abbey refused to admit him. He then went to another house of the Order of Cîteaux,[206] from which he was also dismissed after several weeks. He brought this order to court and won the process. On his way to announce his victory in court to the prelate, an accident happened, which put him into bed, where he died the following day, being May 24, 1632, at this prelate's house.[207]

Bartoli, who has also been cited in this essay, identified "the accident" as apoplexy.[208]

Even the date of Borri's death is not unambiguous and signifies a watershed in Borri's regard between the Jesuits and non-Jesuits. The aforementioned Father Ayrault's date is supported by the *Bibliotheca scriptorum societatis Iesu* published in

---

[202] Della Valle, "Lettera mia alla S. M. del Re di Portogallo," in Mercati, "Notizie," p. 42.

[203] Ibid., p. 42.

[204] Julio Cordara, *Historiae societatis Jesu*, p. 331.

[205] One of the houses of the Cistercian Order. The Order is otherwise known as the Order of Cîteaux or the Order of White Monks because of the color of the habit over which is worn a black scapular or apron.

[206] Petech, "Borri, Cristoforo," in Ghisalberti, *Dizionario*, p. 4, suggests that it was perhaps the House of S. Bernardo alle Terme.

[207] Sommervogel, *Bibliothèque*, vol. 1, col. 1821, under "Borri, Burrus, Christophe."

[208] Bartoli, *Dell'historia della Compagnie di Giesu*, III:707.

1676, which indicates that Borri died on May 24, 1632.[209] However, Pietro della Valle provides us with the date of May 14, 1632. Angelo Mercati, who discovered and published della Valle's letters, is puzzled because this date, according to him, differed from the commonly accepted day found in all other sources for Borri's death: May 24, 1632.[210] I found the matter even more puzzling since della Valle's correspondence with the religious authorities immediately upon Borri's passing is dated earlier than May 24.[211] It may be tempting to blame the ten-day difference in the dates to the switch from the Julian to the Gregorian calendar. The latter was introduced in 1582 by Pope Gregory XIII and was implemented rather swiftly in the Catholic countries in Europe. While some Protestants, especially in England and its colonies, were still using the Julian calendar at the time of Borri's death, it is hard to explain why della Valle, an Italian writing to Italian religious authorities, would chose to use the Julian calendar. It turns out that della Valle was not alone in his dating of Borri's death. De Visch, the seventeenth-century historian of the Cistercian order, who like della Valle was chronologically close to Borri's time, publishing his work in 1649, also dates Borri's death on May 14, 1632.[212]

Moreover, according to Father Venot, as cited by Sommervogel, Borri died "not being a Jesuit, nor Bernardine, nor even of a religious order."[213] In contrast to this portrayal is that of the eighteenth-century historian, Argelati, not affiliated with any religious order, who wrote on eminent Milanese. He, perhaps too generously, identified Borri as "of Two Religious Orders" (*Geminos Reliogiosos Ordines*).[214] The seventeenth-century Cistercian historian de Visch, more rigorous in his approach, wrote that Borri was recalled to Rome and expelled from the Society

> because he seemed to deviate from the Society. He joined his mind to our Order and because of the outstanding gifts of his mind, the subtlety of his intellect, his eminence in all sorts of teaching, he was accepted by our fathers, among whom, under the name Onufriy, after some time he became distinguished.[215]

De Visch's description indicates that Borri did find a new home among the Cistercians some time before his death.

Coda

After his death, the Congregation for the Propagation of the Faith was interested to collect Borri's works "for public service," as is evident from a note written by Francesco Ingoli, the aforementioned Secretary of the Congregation and the Jesuits' adversary, conveying to della Valle a request from Cardinal

---

[209] Pietro Ribadeneira, Philippo Alegambe, and Nathanaele Sotvello, *Bibliotheca scriptorum societatis Iesu* (London: Gregg International Publishers, 1969; 1st edition Rome, 1676), p. 138.

[210] Mercati, "Notizie," p. 39, fn. 32.

[211] Ibid., pp. 23-30.

[212] De Visch, *Bibliotheca scriptorum sacri ordinis cisterciens*, p. 71, under "Christophorus Borrus."

[213] Sommervogel, *Bibliothèque*, vol. 1, col. 1821, under "Borri, Burrus, Christophe."

[214] Argelati, *Bibliotheca scriptorum mediolanensium*, p. 238, under "Burrus, Christophorus."

[215] De Visch, *Bibliotheca scriptorum sacri ordinis cisterciens*, p. 71, under "Christophorus Borrus."

Barberini.[216] The note was written on May 19, 1632, a year after Borri left the Jesuit order and only five days after Borri's death, if it is true that he died on May 14. On May 21, 1632, della Valle responded that one of Borri's books, titled *Hidrografia, overo Exame de Pilotos* (Hydrography, or Examination of Pilots), written in Portuguese, was "ordinary in Portugal, but here [in Italy], where Spanish books are rare, is not located, and even though I looked for it with great effort, I could not find it."[217] He sees its value in the description of Borri's invention, of which della Valle knew in Persia before he met Borri, when a Portuguese gave it to him to read. "Later in India, Father Borri communicated to me this invention, of which I had already heard, if only in theory at that time and not yet tested, as was done later in the voyage to Portugal."[218]

Two of Borri's works were found: the *De tribus coelis* and the *Informatione* on the Indies. There were two copies of the latter: one, written by Borri's hand, "lacked precision," as he was editing it; the other one, made by the hand of a copyist, was easier to read and more precise, "but the Father," recalls Pietro della Valle, "told me that the copyist made errors in this, because of not having a good intention in his character." However, Pietro della Valle, having the original, could correct it easily as he had read and discussed the original with Borri many times.[219]

But three things that Pietro della Valle considered very important were missing: a book manuscript on navigation, a navigational map, and a mathematical instrument to determine longitude, that is the aforementioned *naugnomon*. Mercanti identified the missing manuscript as *Tratade de navegar* but, since the letter does not provide any details except for the general reference to its usefulness, it is uncertain whether della Valle indeed referred to *Tratade* (which discusses the hourglass theory) or to some other writing that discusses the *naugnomon*. I am actually inclined to assume the latter, as della Valle later paired the manuscript with the instrument, made of brass or some other metal, whose description is closer to the *naugnomon* than to the hourglass. But whatever the case, the manuscript was not found in 1632 after Borri's death. Della Valle believed that

---

[216] Francesco Ingoli, "Per gli libri del Padre Borro in nome del Sig. Card. Barberino," in Mercati, "Notizie," p. 28. There Barberini is alternatively spelled as Barberino or Barbarino. At that time, there were three Cardinals Barberini in Rome, namely, Antonio Barberini,, Senior (1569-1646), a brother of Urban VIII; Cardinal Antonio Barberini, Junior (1607-1671), Urban VIII's nephew; and Cardinal Francesco Barberini (1597-1679), another nephew of Urban VIII. I assume that the Barberini on whose behalf Ingoli wrote to della Valle was Cardinal Francesco Barberini, who between 1626 and 1633 was Librarian of the Holy Roman Chuch, a *mecenate*, or patron, of arts and sciences, who founded the famous Barberini Library, which became a part of the Vatican Library in 1902.

[217] Della Valle, "Al Sig. Ingoli, 21 Magio 1632," in Mercati, "Notizie," p. 28. It is unclear to what book he refers as this title appears on no lists of Borri's works. However, judging from his description, this can be either the aforementioned *Arte de navegar* (hourglass) or *Regimento* (naugnomon). Della Valle thinks that the book was published (he says *fra i libri stampati,* "among published books") and that it was very popular in Portugal. We do not have evidence that either of these two works had been published by 1632. As for the popularity of the book in Portugal, this information could have reached della Valle from Borri himself, as Borri's accounts to della Valle appear to contain some exaggeration. After a first mention, della Valle does not refer to *Hidrographia* any more. Later, della Valle is occupied with the search for the manuscript (instead of *libro stampato* he uses the expression *un libro manoscritto*; p. 32) dealing with magnetic declinations, apparently the *Regimento*. We do not know if he found the *Hidrografia* or the *Arte de navegar*.

[218] Ibid., p. 29.

[219] Ibid., pp. 31-32.

Father Christopher Scheiner (1573-1650), a German Jesuit and Borri's friend, had a copy of it.[220] But "as for the original," Pietro della Valle complains, "Father Scheiner said that he did not have it," and that it remained in the hands of a copyist, a certain Laertio Alberti da Orte, who had departed from Rome by that time. Father Borri, while still alive, was very unhappy about da Orte's behavior, and, according to della Valle, not being able to recover his original, took this fellow, da Orte, to court. However, due to da Orte's absence from Rome and Borri's premature death, the process did not yield any results. Thus, Pietro della Valle suggested that the situation was not critical since even without the original, producing a copy of Schreiner's copy would be a solution.[221]

While Father Schreiner was keen on having a copy of the navigational map, Borri kept taking it back from him, perhaps, as della Valle suspects, because he had not finished working on it yet. However, Father Mascarenhas, Assistant of Portugal in the Society of Jesus, had another copy of this map, done by one of the most famous carthographers, Matteo Greuter (1556-1638), with the assistance of Borri. Pietro della Valle saw it many times attached to the wall in Mascarenhas's cell, but Mascarenhas refused to surrender it.[222] Not possessing the map, Father Scheiner, according to della Valle, nevertheless had the *naugnomon* with which the map was produced and of which Borri was so proud. Pietro della Valle warned Father Ingoli that Father Scheiner was soon to return to his native Germany, so prompt measures should be undertaken.[223] Such was the situation on May 21, 1632, a week after Borri's death.

Soon afterwards, the Inquisition launched severe sanctions against new theories. In Florence, in 1632, Galileo published his *Dialogo dei due massimi sistemi del mondo* (Dialogue Concerning the Two Chief World System), which unequivocally supported the Copernican system. In 1633, he was summoned to Rome and put on trial on suspicion of heresy. He recanted. His and Copernicus's works were put into the *Index Librorum Prohibitorum*, where they remained until 1758.

Perhaps after the *Dialogo*'s publication, the Congregation for the Propagation of the Faith and the Vatican itself had lost interest in Borri's work, being overwhelmed by the burden of fast unfolding events. There appears to be no further information about the fate of Borri's works until della Valle updates the status of these items in his letter to the King of Portugal dated October 23, 1650. Father Macarenhas had by then departed Rome, and the map simply remained in the hands of Jesuits in the cell of Mascarenhas's successor, Father Nuno da Cunha, where, after many tireless efforts and difficult negotiations, della Valle found and recovered it, together with the "Instructions or the Regiment for the Pilots."[224]

---

[220] At the same time, Scheiner was Galileo's bitter rival because of the existing controversy about the discovery of sunspots, which both of them claimed. See William R. Shea, "Galileo, Sunspots, and Inconstant Heavens," *Galileo's Intellectual Revolution: Middle Period, 1610-1632* (New York, NY: Science History Publications, 1972), pp. 49-74. Perhaps the friendship between Borri and Scheiner emerged, among other factors, from their shared opposition to Galileo.

[221] Della Valle, "Al Sig. Ingoli, 21 Magio 1632," in Mercati, "Notizie," pp. 33-34.

[222] Ibid., p. 34.

[223] Ibid., pp. 34-35.

[224] Della Valle, "Lettera mia alla S. M. del Re di Portogallo," in Mercati, "Notizie," p. 44.

The *naugnomon* was a different matter. Despite della Valle's warnings, nothing was apparently done to prevent Father Schreiner from taking Borri's work to Germany, to where he indeed departed in 1633 and where he presented them to the Emperor; and "there, without being more seen, nor used, they became kept, solely for vanity, amidst mathematical curiosities."[225] In his letter to the Portuguese king, Pietro della Valle does not forget to take credit for all the difficult investigations he had undertaken:

> It is of the utmost importance for the navigation of India and of Brazil, and it is a pleasure for me to give this small service of diligence that I committed to find them; it is certain that if not for me they would never be found and would stay simply buried here in Rome in the cell of the Fathers Assistants for Portugal, without being used, neither perhaps known, as they should be.[226]

The Swedish scientist, Johan Fredrik Nyström, apparently saw Borri's map, either in Germany or in Portugal, and wrote that Borri had obtained compass readings of isogones in the Atlantic and Indian oceans and produced what he called "no doubt the first real isogone map." Nyström considered Borri a predecessor of Edmund Halley (1656-1742), a famous English astronomer and mathematician who in 1701 published a *General Chart of the Variation of the Compass*.[227]

In Memoriam: Chacun À Son Goût

Pietro della Valle is whole-hearted in his support of Borri, presenting him as a genius highly esteemed abroad though little understood in his homeland. But other people remembered Borri differently. Borri's story, according to the seventeenth-century Jesuit Bartoli was, "an example and a warning, especially for those who for the divine ministry must have virtues similar to the Apostle."[228] Not all the Jesuits had only critical words for Borri. Cordara, the eighteenth-century Jesuit historian, wrote that Borri "soon after he had put aside the tunic of the Society, while he was enjoying the first fruit of his recovered liberty, has perished overcome by the sudden force of the disease."[229] Cordara seemed to understand that Borri's problem arose from conflict between an individual and the organization to which he belonged. Saying that Borri died "while he was enjoying the first fruit of his recovered liberty," Cordara implies that the Jesuit Society was Borri's cage. He perceived him as a suffering soul who actually had to pay for a choice he had made in his youth, that is, to join the Society of Jesus. He considered Borri as "a man of very lamentable memory, who fell disgracefully because of his own pristine zeal, [who while] eager to heal the misfortunes of others had created

---

[225] Ibid.

[226] Ibid., p. 45.

[227] Johan Fredrik Nyström, *Geografiens och de geografiska upptäckternas historia* (The History of the Geography and Its Discoverers) (Stockholm: C. E. Fritzes Kongl. Hofbokhandel, 1899), p. 399. Thanks to Professor Fredrik Logevall of Cornell University, who translated this passage for me.

[228] Daniello Bartoli, *Dell'historia della Compagnie di Giesu*, III:707.

[229] Julio Cordara, *Historiae societatis Jesu*, p. 331.

the most grave misfortune for himself."[230] Cordara's reference to the misfortunes of others might well imply Borri's zeal to arrange missions into the new lands, in one of which, Madagascar, Prince Andre was alone "in the Lion's den."

These accounts create three different versions: Borri as a scientific success and treasure (della Valle), Borri as a villain (Bartoli), and Borri as a tragic figure (Cordara).

In the nineteenth century, Carlos Sommervogel (1834-1902), a French Jesuit scholar, who has often been cited in this essay, took another approach, as is evident in his entry on Borri in the *Bibliothèque de la Compagnie de Jésu*. His edition of the *Bibliothèque* was not the first one, and he definitely was not a newcomer to it. He was one of the assistants of Augustin de Backer (1809-1873), the editor of the two previous editions of the *Bibliothèque*. Noting "occasional errors and omissions" in the first edition, Sommervogel "made a systematic examination of the whole work,"[231] and consequently, in the revised edition of the *Bibliothèque* (1869-1876), Augustin de Backer credited Sommervogel as his co-author. In the second edition, Borri's life is described briefly and nonchalantly: place of origin, entrance to the Society of Jesus, missionary activity in Cochinchina, teaching in Coimbre and Lisbon, and invitation to the Spanish court. De Backer ended his entry on Borri as follows: "He left the Society [of Jesus] to enter the Order of Cîteaux, where he took the name of Don Onofrio; he died in 1632."[232] When in 1890 Sommervogel, as de Backer's successor, published the new edition of the *Bibliothèque*, he kept the first lines of the entry on Borri but changed and expanded the rest based on several letters. The first is a letter from Father Charles Venot (1574-?) to a certain Father Ayrault. Venot's description of Father Borri's misfortunes and ramblings in Rome create a picture of a hapless chap spending the last months of his life in a miserable commute among religious houses and dying as a member of none of them, while, as we have seen, there is plenty of evidence to the contrary. This information is quite unique, contradicting not only materials previously published by others (as for example, the Cistercians) but also the previous edition of the *Bibliothèque*. One wonders about Sommervogel's reasons for including it. What was Father Venot, a French-based Jesuit, as is clear from Sommervogel's own entry on him, doing in Rome? What was his relation to Borri? Why did his information supersede that of the other sources? Sommervogel provides no answers to these questions. Nor can we find any indirect corroboration in Venot's other works, as the only other written sources by Father Venot, discovered by Sommervogel, are three more letters, two of which are to the same Father Ayrault.[233]

Sommervogel skillfully elaborated on Father Venot's image of Borri by including other examples of potentially controversial, if not derogatory, comments made by two other people. Curiously enough, one of these two was Pietro della Valle, whose observation on the necessity for Borri to change his name is repeated by Sommervogel, "as it was unpleasant to the Portuguese ears." Taken by itself,

---

[230] Ibid.

[231] J. H. Pollen, "Society of Jesus," *The Catholic Encyclopedia* vol. XIV (New York, NY: Robert Appleton Company, 1912), p. 110.

[232] Augustin de Backer, in collaboration with Alois de Backer and Carlos Sommervogel, *Bibliothèque des écrivains de la Compagnie de Jésus* (Liége: A. de Backer; Paris: C. Sommervogel, 1869), vol. I, p. 777, under "Borri, Borrus, Christophe.

[233] Carlos Sommervogel, S. J., *Bibliothèque de la Compagnie de Jésus* (Paris: Alphonae Picard; Bruxelles: Oscar Schepens, 1898), vol. 8, col. 564-565, under "Venot, Charles."

this comment might not create an image of a hexed or jinxed person, but it enhances Venot's description. There is no doubt that Sommervogel did this consciously as he chose to use only part of della Valle's statement about Borri. He ignores that della Valle immediately goes on to describe Borri as a "great mathematician."[234]

In addition to the citations from Father Venot and Pietro della Valle's letter, Sommervogel employs comments made by Father Dominique Le Jeunehomme (1590-?), about whom Sommervogel had very scant information, limited to the fact that he was a French Jesuit who in 1627 went to Lisbon and wrote *Relation d'un voyage de la Flèche à Lisbonne en 1627*.[235] Based on the citations from this work used by Sommervogel, Le Jeunehomme was allegedly commissioned to translate Borri's *Tratade de navegar* from Portuguese into Latin, and this seems to be their only connection. The reason that Father Le Jeunehomme gives for Borri's writing in Portuguese is remarkable: Borri wrote in Portuguese "since the gentleman while traversing the seas and the lands, everywhere in the Orient and Africa, forgot his native Italian, and did not remember his Latin."[236] Surely Borri did not forget his native Italian, nor did he forget his Latin. Portuguese was the language which he used in his teaching, along with Latin, as is evident from his lecture notes preserved in the institution where he taught in Portugal.[237] In Jesuit schools, use of Latin was mandatory in public lectures of rhetoric, philosophy, and theology, though not in lectures on practical subjects such as navigation, astrology, and mathematics.[238] Consequently, it is peculiar to note that the only manuscript in Latin at the Colégio de Santo Antão is by Borri, which, after a general introduction, contains his lecture on cosmic spheres.[239]

Father Le Jeunehomme's statement is very significant, as to a certain extent it reflects the complex relationship between Borri and his superiors in Rome and many of his contemporaries among the Jesuits and, as it turned out, those in the next generation. They could not afford not to notice Borri and his theories because others were noting his views, but neither could they forgive him any deviation from their standards, so they punished him by mockery if no other means were at hand.

Sommervogel does not explain why, considering all the various sources for Borri undoubtedly available to him, he chose to give particular emphasis to Fathers Venot and Le Jeunehomme, both French and neither closely associated with Borri or with any significant legacy in the religious or intellectual history of their Order, as is evident from Sommervogel's own entries on them in his *Bibliothèque*. Disregarding all the sources giving a positive spin on Borri, he created a new, almost farcical, image of him, evincing an unabated disdain for this black sheep of the Society of Jesus.

Unfortunately, perhaps due to Sommervogel's authority, his entry on Borri has become a standard reference in the twentieth century for scholars dealing with

---

[234] Della Valle, *The Travels*, part 3, p. 81.

[235] Sommervogel, *Bibliothèque*, vol. 4, col. 799, under "Jeunehomme, Dominique."

[236] Ibid., vol. 1, col. 1822, under "Borri, Burrus, Christophe."

[237] Dos Santos, "Vicissitudes da obra," p. 133.

[238] Ugo Baldini, *Saggi sulla cultura*, p. 151.

[239] Ms. 2378, as indicated in Ugo Baldini, *Saggi sulla cultura*, pp. 151-152, fn. 73.

Borri, including Petech's entry on Borri in *Dizionario biographico degli italiani*,[240] Caravalho's "Galileu e a cultura portuguesa,"[241] dos Santos's "Vicissitudes da obra do P. Christóvão Borri,"[242] and Vu Khanh Tuong's dissertation, "Les missions jesuites avant les missions étrangères au Vietnam."[243] Even the celebrated scholar and professor of the École Française d'Exrême-Orient, Charles Maybon (1872-1926), used Sommervogel's entry as the main source for his biographical essay on Borri introducing the French translation of his *Account*.[244] From Maybon, Borri's biography found its way into the Vietnamese edition of Borri's account.[245]

Borri was different from Sommervogel's caricature. He had a proud and inflexible character, which got him into trouble with his superiors in Rome and in Cochinchina. At a time when few suffered for their scientific views, he nevertheless did. He, like many of us, did not like to admit his failures, and he glossed them over, as for example in his letters to della Valle about his dealings at the Spanish court. Sometimes he chose to exaggerate his successes, as with his reported nomination as Bishop of Macao and the fight between the Spanish and Portuguese crowns over him in the same letters.

But he possessed an extraordinary stubbornness in achieving his goals, be this in conducting his research, introducing his inventions to the Portuguese and Spanish courts, publishing his works, or attempting to expand missions into new territories. Any means would work: litigation,[246] insubordination, trespassing, and outright disregard for the rules of his Order. But all this was connected to his great passion for science, which he pursued tirelessly and self-righteously. The lack of his insistence in matters pertaining to missionary activity suggests the secondary role it played in his life. He volunteered to go to Asia in order to check his theories; while in Cochinchina, he apparently failed to prove that the mission's work took precedence over his scientific research; when recalled to Macao, and then in Goa, he did not seek another missionary position but instead proceeded to Portugal to develop his theories and demonstrate his inventions. Near the end of his life, he ardently advocated the expansion of missions into Madagascar, Australia, and other places in the South Seas, but, after his apparent failure at the Spanish court, it would be hard to claim that he did this to bring Christianity into those territories

---

[240] Petech, "Borri, Cristoforo," in Ghisalberti, *Dizionario*, p. 4.

[241] De Carvalho, "Galileu e a cultura porgutuesa," pp. 423, 427.

[242] Dos Santos, "Vicissitudes da obra," pp. 140-141.

[243] Vu Khanh Tuong, "Les missions jésuites," pp. 254, 256.

[244] Charles Maybon, "Notice sur Cristoforo Borri et sur les editions de sa relation," *Revue Indochinoise*, 1909, pp. 343-348. Republished in *Bulletin des Amis du Vieux Hué* 3-4 (1931), pp. 269-276 together with an excellent translation of Borri's work as *Relation de la nouvelle mission des pères de la Compagnie de Jésus au royaume de la Cochinchine*, by Lt.-Col. Bonifacy, who taught Vietnamese history at the University of Hanoi, and with Leopold Cadière's Preface in the volume "Les européens qui ont vu le vieux Hué" (pp. 261-405).

[245] Hồng Nhuệ, Nguyễn Khắc Xuyên, Nguyễn Nghị, "Lời Giới Thiệu"(Introduction) in Cristophoro Borri, *Xứ Đàng Trong Năm 1621* (Cochinchina in 1621), translated and annotated by Hồng Nhuệ, Nguyễn Khắc Xuyên, Nguyễn Nghị (Hochiminh City: Nhà Xuất Bản Thành Phố Hồ Chí Minh, 1997), pp. 5-10.

[246] I have mentioned in this essay two instances of Borri resorting to litigation. While either or even both of them can be questioned, the fact that two independent sources describe two different occasions of Borri initiating a judicial process suggests his propensity in this direction.

more than to expand scientific exploration to areas that were important for his research on determining longitude.

Onward, Britannia!

Taking into account the means of communication in the seventeenth century, Borri's *Account* proved to be quite a hit, with its popularity in Europe comparable to that of *Harry Potter* or *The Da Vinci Code*. Within two years, the *Account* was translated into five languages. In 1631, the same year of its original publication in Italian, Father Ant. de la Croix, S. J., translated it into French.[247] The following year, 1632, a Latin translation by another Jesuit, Father J. Bucelleni, appeared in Vienna.[248] The same year F. Jacobus Susius, S. J., translated and published Borri's *Account* in Dutch.[249]

Apparently, by that time the breakup between Borri and the Society of Jesus had became widely known and no other Jesuit ever again translated Borri's work. But the *Account* proved to be viable even without the patronage of the Society. In 1633, again in Vienna, a German translation appeared.[250] And the same year, the *Account* crossed the Channel to flourish in English editions, of which we now have six. But these six editions are reprints of only two translations. Robert Ashley published the first translation in 1633.[251] The second, by an anonymous translator, appeared in Churchill's *Collection of Voyages and Travels* in 1704.[252]

Robert Ashley (1565-1641) entitled his edition *Cochinchina: Containing many admirable Rarities and Singularities of that Countrey. Extracted out of an Italian Relation, lately presented to the Pope, by Christophoro Borri, that lived certaine yeeres there.*[253] The difference in Borri's and Ashley's goals announces itself already in the title page of their editions. The place allotted to the dedication to Pope Urban VIII in Borri's book is occupied by a famous maxim from Seneca: *Cum hac persuasione vivendum est: Non sum uni angulo natus; Patria mea totus hic mundus est* (Live in this belief: "I was not born for any one corner of the universe; this whole world is my

---

[247] *Relation de la nouvelle mission au royaume de la Cochinchine* (Lille: Pierre de Rache, 1631). According to C. Maybon, A. De Bellecombe published a new translation of the *Relatione* in 1852 titled *Mission en Cochinchine* (Maybon, "Notice," p. 275). In this case, Lieutenant-Colonel Bonifacy's excellent, and apparently the first annotated, translation of Borri's work, *Relation de la nouvelle mission des pères de la Compagnie de Jésus au royaume de la Cochinchine,* is the third French translation.

[248] *Relatio de Cocincina R. P. Christophori Borri e Societate Jesu* (Vienna: Domo Professa Societatis Jesu, 1632).

[249] *Historie van eene nieuvve seyndinghe door de paters der Societeyt Iesv in't ryck van Cocincina* (Louvain: By de weduwe van H. Haestens, 1632).

[250] *Relation vod dem newen Königreich Cochin China* (Gedruckt zu Wien in Oesterreich bey Michael Riekhes). Another German edition was published in M. C. Sprengel and G. Forster, *Neue Beiträge zur Volker- und Länderkunde* (Leipzig: P. G. Kummer, 1793), vol. 2, pp. 27-110.

[251] Ashley's edition was reprinted in 1970 by Walter J. Johnson.

[252] Awnsham Churchill and John Churchill, eds., *A Collection of Voyages and Travels, some now first printed from original manuscripts, others now first published in English* (London, 1704), vol. 2, pp. 787-838, reprinted in the 1732 edition of the same Collection (vol. 2, pp. 721-765), as well as in a new edition in 1744 (vol. 2, pp. 699-743). Borri's *Account* was also reprinted in John Pinkerton's *A General Collection of the best and most interesting Voyages and Travels* (London: 1811), vol. 9, p. 772-828. In 2002, the 1732 edition was reprinted (New Delhi, Madras: Asian Educational Services, 2002).

[253] London: Printed by Robert Raworth, 1633.

country").[254] This allusion to worldly affairs is fully supported in Ashley's choice of his dedication "To the Right worthy Knight Sir Maurice Abbot, Governor of the Honourable Company of Merchants, trading to the East Indies, and the rest of that renowned Society." In his "Epistle Dedicatory" to Sir Abbot, Ashley explained his desire to publish Borri's work by the great effect it had on him and expressed his hope that the book "might also happily be usefull to our Countrymen that trade and traffique in those Easterne parts," and he continued, "the remotest traffique is always most beneficial to the publick Stocke, and the Trade to the East Indies doth farre excell all others."[255] In his Foreword, addressed to his fellow countrymen, Ashley pointed out that their potential lack of interest in Cochinchina should be overcome due to two reasons: the first is curiosity, since the book would expand their horizons, and the other is its usefulness, because as time passes England might find itself more involved in the trade of that area. And why would it be otherwise, since, citing Borri, Ashley affirms that Cochinchina was a welcoming country willing and eager to accept any foreigners for trade.[256]

Unlike Borri's scientific or ecclesiastical mission, Ashley's goal was either to promote his book or to promote trade between England and Cochinchina and adjacent areas, or both. Apparently assuming that the entire second part of Borri's *Account* on local religious life and Catholic missionary activity in Cochinchina would hardly be of interest to his readers among the merchants in Protestant Britain, Ashley excluded it from his work, indicating in the title that the work contains "extractions" from Borri's *Account*. He pretty loyally kept to the original in his translation of the first part of the book with one notable exception: the touchy issue of the relationship between the Portuguese and the Dutch in Cochinchina commanded his special attention.

Ironically, the passage in question from Borri opens with the same statement Ashley used in his Preface: "the King of Cochin-China gave free admittance to all nations whatsoever," a circumstance the Dutch decided to put to the test. The Portuguese, however, held a monopoly on European trade in Cochinchina at that time and managed to elicit from the ruler of Cochinchina a promise to deny the Dutch, their enemies, the right to trade in Cochinchina. Nevertheless, while the Portuguese envoy who obtained this promise, Ferdinando da Costa, was still at the Cochinchinese court, a Dutch ship arrived there in an attempt to gain a foothold. The ship brought rich gifts to the ruler, who, having accepted the gifts, granted the Dutch request to trade. Infuriated, the Portuguese demanded that the ruler expel the Dutch, which was then done. The ruler moreover ordered the destruction of the Dutch vessel and the seizure of its goods. In addition, he gave the Portuguese further concessions, including land on which to build a city, an invaluable offer in Borri's eyes, as a fleet prepared to counter the Dutch could be kept there.[257]

The first unpleasant encounter between the Dutch and the Cochinchinese occurred in 1601 when the Dutch sent two ships to China, the *Harlem* and the *Leyde*. The ships stopped somewhere on the coast of either Champa or Cochinchina, and, according to the records of the Dutch East India Company: "It is

---

[254] On the front cover of Ashley's translation of Borri's work. Seneca, *Epistularium moralium ad Lucilium*, translated by Richard Gummere, Book III, Epistula XXVIII: 4 (Cambridge, MA: Harvard University Press; London: William Heinemann LTD, 1917), 1:200-201.

[255] Ashley, "The Epistle Dedicatory," in Borri, *Cochinchina*, Ashley trans., p. A2.

[256] Ashley, "The Preface Apologetical," in Borri, *Cochinchina*, Ashley trans., p. A4.

[257] Borri, Part I, Chapter VIII, Section "Dutch banish'd."

difficult to imagine a worse reception than the one that here awaited the navigators: twenty-three people were massacred, and van Groesbergen [Gapsar Gorensbergen, commander of the small fleet] himself was a prisoner for some time." After being freed, they continued their way along the shores of Cochinchina. Groensbergen dispatched two merchants, Jeronime Wonderaar and Albert Cornelisz, who

> passed also Touron [Đà Nẵng] and Faifo [Hội An], who attracted a big number of merchants, Portuguese and Japanese. Further southward there was a sea city Sinoa, where the son of the king resided. In Tachem [Cachiam], the reception given by the king was more welcoming, but this visit did not produce anticipated results.[258]

The Dutch never succeeded in establishing good relations with Cochinchina. They mainly traded with Tonkin, while Cochinchina kept an alliance with the Portuguese.

The description of the strength of the Portuguese at the court, and of a fickle Cochinchinese ruler's conduct towards the Dutch, who at that time still were British allies,[259] could easily turn the English from a Cochinchinese enterprise even before it started, especially taking into account that the English, like the Dutch, had already had an unpleasant encounter in this country. In fact, it may be that Borri's sad tale about the Dutch attempt to trade in Cochinchina confuses Dutch with English traders, for a very similar event did take place involving an English merchant ship. According to English records, in 1613, an English ship arrived at Faifo and the king cordially received one of the merchants aboard, Walter Carwarden, from whom he received gifts. But when Carwarden unloaded his cargo, he and his companions were massacred.[260] The Dutch explained the incident in the following way: "The English merchant learnt at his own expense what it cost to speak of the king of Annam [Chúa Nguyễn, ruler of Cochinchina] in insulting terms. He was put to death and his cargo ended up at the king's [possession]."[261]

Even if Borri's Dutch story is a garbling of this episode, it is unclear whether Ashley knew about the English merchant's experience in Cochinchina. As it is, Ashley condensed and rewrote three pages of Borri's *Account*, eliminating the Portuguese victory and the Dutch defeat, which together with the omission of Borri's second part of the book, turned the *Account* into an alluring, if deluding, vignette for English traders and travelers into the land of Cochinchina.[262]

Only seventy years later, a full translation of Borri's *Account* was introduced to English-speaking readers. It appeared in Awnsham and John Churchill's *A Collection of Voyages and Travels* and is quite accurate, which explains our choice to use it for this book.

---

[258] W. J. M. Buch, "La Companie des Indes Néerlandaises et l'Indochine," *Bulletin de l'Ecole Française d'Extrême-Orient* 36 (1936): 115.

[259] Twenty years later, the First Anglo-Dutch war over sea trade broke the alliance.

[260] Borri, *Relation de la nouvelle mission*, Bonifacy, trans., p. 335 n. 82 and Charles B. Maybon, *Histoire moderne du pays d'Annam* (Paris: Librairie Plon, 1920), p. 65.

[261] Buch, "La Companie," p. 117.

[262] A footnote with Ashley's interpretation of this subject can be found in the body of the *Account* (Part I, Chapter VIII, at the beginning of the Section "Dutch banished."

Long Live Vietnam!

In 1997, Borri's *Account* was published in Vietnam for the first time in Vietnamese translation.[263] The Vietnamese translators, Hồng Nhuệ, Nguyễn Khắc Xuyên, and Nguyễn Nghị, worked from Bonifacy's French translation. Despite some mistakes,[264] most of the translation is faithful to the French. However, in addition to translating, the translators edited the *Account*, introducing new ideas and completely changing the goals and focus of Borri's work.[265] Borri wrote to urge the expansion of missionary activities in Cochinchina, combining geographical, historical, cultural, religious, and ethnographic information with a narrative about the difficulties, successes, and importance of proselytizing there. The Vietnamese translators pursued different goals.

First, the translators eliminated almost all mention of the missionary activity conducted by Borri and his fellow Jesuits and their predecessors. Thus, six chapters of the second part of the *Account* discussing ways of conversion, construction of churches, and persecutions, are completely omitted.[266] Some other chapters were selectively translated so as not to spoil an idyllic picture of the country.[267] Sometimes, the translators keep a significant portion of a chapter but supplant its

---

[263] Cristophoro Borri, *Xứ Đàng Trong Năm 1621* (Cochinchina in 1621), trans. and annot. Hồng Nhuệ, Nguyễn Khắc Xuyên, & Nguyễn Nghị (Hochiminh City: Nhà Xuất Bản Thành Phố Hồ Chí Minh, 1997).

[264] For example, Borri's statement that "The Cochin-Chinese not being so fond of their own customs, as to despise those of strangers, as the Chinese do, ... " (translated even more transparently into French by Bonifacy) in the Vietnamese translation reads differently: *Dân Đàng Trong rất trọng những tục lệ của họ. Họ khinh những tục lệ của người ngoại quốc như người Tàu* (Cochinchinese very much respect their [Cochinchinese] customs. They despise the customs of strangers, as the Chinese [do]). See Borri in this volume, Part I, Chapter V, Section titled "The scholars"; Borri, *Relation de la nouvelle mission*, Bonifacy, trans., p. 313; Borri, *Xứ Đàng Trong*, p. 58.

[265] I cannot say to what extent the translators initiated changes introduced into the Vietnamese version and to what extent changes may have been initiated by state authorities. Thus, my usage of the word "translators" here encompasses the people who literally worked on Borri's account and also those who may have directed them.

[266] These are the following chapters in Part II: Chapter I "Of the First entering of the Fathers of the Society of Jesus into that Kingdom: And of the two Churches built at Turon and Caccian"; Chapter II "Of the Persecution the New Church of Cochin-China endur'd, at its first institution: and how I was Sent Thither to be Assisting to It, by my Superiors"; Chapter V, "How God Made Way for the Conversion of the Province of Pulucambi, by Means of the Noblest Persons in It"; Chapter VII, "How God Open'd Another Way to Christianity, by Means of the Omsaiis, or Heathen Priests"; Chapter IX, "How God Opened Another Way to the Conversion of the Meaner Sort by Miraculous Means"; Chapter X, "Of the Churches and Christians of Faifo, Turon, and Cacchiam."

[267] Compare, for example, Borri's Chapter IV (Part II), especially the section titled "Fathers in distress," in which he describes the fathers' distress upon the death of their main protector, with Chapter 10 in the translation. Borri wrote: "Three years pass'd after this manner, and yet we were not so much troubled at our own wants, which God knows were very great, as to see every day less hopes of promoting the service of God among those pagans, having during those three years converted but very few, and what with unspeakable labour and toil. Things being in this posture, in some measure desperate, we being inclinable to believe the time was not yet come, when it would please God to enlighten the darkness of those people, either because our sins obstructed it, or for some other hidden judgments of God." The translators condensed this to a description of the fathers' loneliness and avoided Borri's portrayal of further troubles. Borri, *Xứ Đàng Trong*, p. 106.

meaning with their own interpretation. For example, Chapter VI, "How God Open'd Another Way to Christianity, Through the Means of the Learned People among the Heathens," in the Vietnamese translation becomes a chapter titled "Astronomy" (*Thiên Văn*).[268] The new title reflects the changes undertaken in this chapter to eliminate Borri's description of his use of astronomy to convert Cochinchinese. For example, the concluding part of Borri's section titled "The fathers foretell the eclipse truer than the Cochin-Chinese astrologers" is omitted. This section tells of a hapless Cochinchinese astrologer unable either to correctly predict an eclipse without Borri's help or to admit his inability to do this. Borri wrote that the *omgne*, or Cochinchinese astrologer,

> repaired immediately to the Father to know the precise time of the eclipse; who having shewed him that it was to be exactly at eleven the following night, he still continued doubtful of the truth of the matter, and therefore would not wake the prince till he saw the beginning of the eclipse. Then he ran to rouze him, and he coming out with some of his courtiers, performed the usual ceremonies and adorations to the moon. Yet he would not make the matter publickly known, for fear of utterly discrediting their books and mathematicians, **though all men conceived a great opinion of our doctrine, and particularly the *omgne*, who from that time forwards for a whole month came to hear the catechizing, diligently learning all that belongs to our holy faith. However, he was not baptized, wanting resolution to overcome the difficulty of the multiplicity of women, as the ambassador Ignatius had done before. He forbore not nevertheless publickly with much fervour to declare our doctrine and law were true, and all others false, and said he would certainly die a Christian, which mov'd many others to desire to be baptized."[269]**

The translators dispensed with the part in bold,[270] seemingly in order to avoid the topic of astronomy as a means of conversion. But then why not to throw the chapter out completely, as was done with some other chapters? Probably because Vietnamese historians consider science to be something their ancestors could learn from foreigners. Retaining this chapter might also serve to explain the reason Borri was in Cochinchina, since removing most discussion of proselytizing would leave the reader curious about what those fathers were doing in Cochinchina. Borri the astronomer is more palatable to Vietnamese historians than Borri the Christian missionary. The Vietnamese translators also omit Borri's own explanation of his sojourn in Cochinchina in Chapter XI, where he wrote: "When the superiors of Macao sent me into Cochn-China, they told me, they did not absolutely design I should continue in that mission, but only to learn the language, that I might afterward discover the kingdom of Tunchin."[271]

---

[268] Borri, *Xứ Đàng Trong*, pp. 107-117.

[269] Borri in this volume, Part II, Chapter 6, Section titled "The fathers foretell the eclipse truer than the Cochin-Chinese astrology."

[270] Borri, *Xứ Đàng Trong*, p. 114.

[271] Borri in this volume, Part II, Chapter XI, Introductory paragraph, and Borri, *Xứ Đàng Trong*, p. 122.

The omitted passage cited above also suggests the translators' desire to avoid any portrayal of backwardness in their country. This *omgne* was prevented from conversion (in itself a topic to be avoided) by his unwillingness to part with the custom of polygamy. For the same reason, the authors omitted the end of this chapter altogether, which describes the respect gained by the missionaries through calculating the time of eclipse and the punishment inflicted by the ruler on the *omgne*.[272] Elsewhere, Borri, and the Vietnamese translators, discuss punishments commonly imposed on *omgne* who commit errors, such as being made to forfeit land previously awarded to them, which the translators apparently considered unobjectionable,[273] but the punishment of "making them kneel a whole day in the court of the palace, bare headed, exposed to the heat of the sun, and to the scorn of all the courtiers"[274] was seemingly viewed as rather barbaric by the translators, who replaced it with a vague comment that the "mathematicians" were punished by the ruler.[275]

The translators also mitigate Borri's description of Cochinchinese "superstition" when he wrote: "The reason why they make such account of foretelling the eclipse, is because of the many superstitions at that time used towards the sun and moon."[276] The Vietnamese version reads: *Trong thời gian đó, họ giữ những tập tục xung quanh mặt trời và mặt trăng*[277] (At that time, they held habits and customs with regard to the sun and the moon), thus replacing the condescending word "superstition" by the neutral and more respectful compound "habits and customs."

The translators also avoided the word "heathens," either completely omitting it (along with the sentence, paragraph, or even chapter where it was used) or replacing it by a different expression, for example by the compound *lương dân*,[278] which comes from a Chinese compound 良 民 meaning "loyal subjects or law-abiding people" and in modern Vietnamese means "ordinary people, or good people." Eliminating or replacing words such as "superstition" and "heathens" reflects an effort to shift the discussion of Vietnamese religions and rites. Two chapters give us the best perspective on this: Chapter IV and Chapter VIII of Part II. Chapter IV, titled by Borri, "Of the Governor of Pulucambi's Death," is reduced by the translators to roughly one-eighth its original length. They omit Borri's description of posthumous rites performed for the governor in sections titled "Heathen ceremonies at the governor's death," "Sorcery to discover the state of the soul departed," "Heathen canonization," "The governor's funeral," and "The fathers questioned concerning the governor's soul." They replace all these sections with one sentence: *Về các nghi lễ ma chay phúng điếu chúng tôi không thể tường*

---

[272] Borri in this volume, Part II, Chapter 6, Section titled "Astrology in great esteem."

[273] Borri, *Xứ Đàng Trong*, p. 108

[274] Borri in this volume, Part II, Chapter 6 , Section titled "An eclipse of the sun mistaken."

[275] Borri, *Xứ Đàng Trong*, p. 117, which corresponds to Borri's "… his astrologers, who escap'd not unpunish'd." Borri in this volume, Part II, Chapter 6, section titled "An eclipse of the sun mistaken."

[276] Borri in this volume, Part II, Chapter 6, Section titled "Superstitions concerning eclipses."

[277] Borri, *Xứ Đàng Trong*, p. 108.

[278] Borri in this volume, Part I, Chapter 6, Section titled "Matrimony"; Borri, *Xứ Đàng Trong*, p. 80.

thuật hết các chi tiết vì sẽ không bao giờ cùng (As for the funeral, offerings [to the deceased person], and condolences, we are not able to completely relate all the details because we would never finish)."[279] This is an interpretation of Borri's sentence, "It would be endless to relate them all."[280] However, this sentence opens Borri's description of the rites, while in the Vietnamese version it mutes all descriptions.

The translation of Borri's Chapter VIII, "A Short Account of the Sects in Cochin-China," is converted into *Đời Sống Tinh Thần Ở Đàng Trong* (Spiritual Life in Cochinchina). The substitution of "Spiritual Life" for "Sects" avoids an image of fragmented groups designated by a word that for missionaries was derogatory and commonly applied to "heathens." Instead, "spiritual life" implies something valued by every civilized society. But the changes introduced by the translators into the chapter itself go far beyond replacing the title. They actually start the chapter with the last paragraph of Borri's previous chapter, Chapter VII, which they omit. The paragraph describes the vast and beautiful temples in Cochinchina, and the translators use it to draw a parallel between Catholicism and Buddhism that was never intended by Borri. According to Borri, the Cochinchinese

> make so many processions that they outdo the Christians in praying to their false gods. There are also among them some persons resembling abbots, bishops, and arch-bishops, and they use gilt staves, not unlike our crosiers, insomuch that if any man come newly into that county, he might easily be persuaded there had been Christians there in former times; so near had the devil endeavoured to imitate us.[281]

The translators change "false gods" to Buddha and instead of a reference to "outdoing," we see an equalizing description: "They organize solemn processions and festive occasions and offerings to worship Buddha as we find among our most zealous Catholics."[282] Imitation and the devil completely disappear from the text. Borri's unquestionably muddled description of Cochinchinese religious doctrines also disappears, but his positive comparison of Buddha with Aristotle is retained.

Another matter pursued in the translation is political correctness and international relations. For example, in Chapter VII, Borri, describing Zen Buddhism, wrote "the second doctrine being made publick, the Chinese received it, **and above others the *bonzis*, who are generally the meanest and most inconsiderable people in *Japan*, who being zealous for their spiritual advantage admitted this doctrine,** and preserved it in twelve several sorts of sects all differing from one another . . ." The text in bold did not find its way into the Vietnamese translation. Vietnamese readers are spared the disparaging references to the bonzes, as well as to the errors in Cochinchinese religious practice and doctrine that are described in the rest of the chapter and which the translators omit. The omission also removes any offense to the Japanese, even at the expense of denying their origination of the twelve sects, which Borri attributes to them, and

---

[279] Borri, *Xứ Đàng Trong*, p. 106.

[280] Borri in this volume, Part II, Chapter IV, Section titled "Heathen ceremonies at the governor's death."

[281] Borri in this volume, Part II, Chapter VII, Section titled "Temples."

[282] Borri, *Xứ Đàng Trong*, pp. 118-119.

gives this honor instead to China.[283] China is very important to Vietnam, and we find corroboration of this in the following passage in Chapter XI, "Of the Kingdom of Tunchim":

> On the north of it [Tonkin] is China, without the defense of a wall, the trade and commerce between the Chineses and Tunchineses being so mutual and constant, that it will not allow of wall and gates shut, as they are against other foreigners. **This is the reason that induces the fathers of our society to attempt the entrance into China that way, knowing they shall not on this side meet with all those impediments that strangers meet with throughout all the rest of the kingdom, and more especially about Canton.**[284]

The omission of the part in bold removes from Vietnam any potential accusation of facilitating the penetration of Christianity into China and creates a picture of good neighborliness and equality regardless of the fact that Vietnam was a tributary state of China.

Similarly, the translators omit Borri's mention of Laos as a tributary state of Tonkin in the context of political relations among the Vietnamese states:

> Yet he [the king] is always own'd as superior to the Chiuua of Tunchim, by the king of Cochin-China, and by that other Chiuua, we observ'd in the first book to be fled into the province bordering upon China, tho' these are continually at war against one another; **and the king of Lais bordering upon Tunchim, pays him a certain tribute.**

The Vietnamese version reads: *Các chúa Đàng Ngoài và cả Đàng Trong đều công nhận ông là kẻ bề trên và cả một chúa khác chúng tôi đã nói ở phần một, ông này đã trốn lánh trong tỉnh giáp giới Trung Quốc, mặc dầu ông vẫn luôn làm ngụy* (The warlords of both Tonkin and Cochinchina recognized him [the Lê king] as superior and there is another warlord of whom we talked in the first part, who fled into the province bordering with China, although he is still a puppet).[285] The omission of Laos in the translation concerns international politics and is one of two points worthy of our attention in this passage. The other point is the treatment of the situation in Tonkin and Cochinchina and relations between them. Borri calls the ruler of Cochinchina a "king," but the translators consistently translate his position as *chúa* or (war)lord. For Borri, Cochinchina and Tonkin are two kingdoms with "the language being the same, as formerly it was but one kingdom."[286] However, the omission of the word "formerly" in the Vietnamese version *ngôn ngữ là ngôn ngữ chung vì cả hai xứ đều thuộc về một quốc gia* (the language is the same because both lands belong to the same state)[287] leaves no

[283] Ibid., p. 119.

[284] Borri in this volume, Part II, Chapter XI, Section titled "A description of Tunchim"; Borri, *Xứ Đàng Trong*, p. 122.

[285] Borri in this volume, Part II, Chapter XI, Section titled "The Government"; Borri, *Xứ Đàng Trong*, pp. 125-126.

[286] Borri in this volume, Part II, Chapter XI, Introductory paragraph.

[287] Borri, *Xứ Đàng Trong*, p. 123.

72 Views of Seventeenth-Century Vietnam

doubt for Vietnamese readers that Borri is talking about one kingdom, something Vietnamese authorities today insist to have always been the case. Perhaps this is one reason to omit the last part of this chapter where Borri describes conversions (which is the other reason for omission) and expresses hope that "these kingdoms of Tunchim and Cochin-China, will soon be united to the flock of the church, acknowledging and giving the due obedience to the universal pastor and vicar of Christ our Lord on Earth." For the Vietnamese translators, there is no need to unite something that already constitutes one country and certainly not on the basis of Christianity.

The reference to "another warlord of whom we talked in Part I, who fled into the province bordering with China although he is still a puppet" is to Mạc Kính Cung, a descendant of Mạc Đăng Dung, who in 1527 overthrew the Lê dynasty. Up until recently, the Mạc have been vilified in Vietnamese historiography, and this is apparently what prompted the translators to refer to the Mạc leader as a "puppet," a term absent in Borri's work.[288] The Vietnamese translators also omit Borri's mention of the warlords being "continually at war against one another" to avoid acknowledging that Vietnamese rulers engaged in war with each other. Indeed, Borri wrote about the Mạc and warfare in Chapter VII of Part I, which the translators chose to ignore. Thus, Borri's title for this chapter, "Of the Power of the King of Cochin-China, and of the Wars he has in his Kingdom," turned into *Lực Lượng của Chúa Đàng Trong* (Of the Power of the Warlord of Cochinchina). In order to avoid a warmonger image, the translation eliminates from this chapter all descriptions of internal conflicts not only between the Mạc and the Lê and the Trịnh families in Tonkin,[289] but also of all the conflicts the Cochinchinese *chúa* had to deal with, namely: "defense against the king of Tonkin"; second, civil war in Cochinchina itself; and third, a "continual war" against Champa, described in Borri's section titled "Wars in Cochinchina." Two sentences survive in the Vietnamese translation. One affirms that warfare is conducted in the same way in both Cochinchina and Europe, and the other mentions Cochinchinese assistance to the Cambodian ruler in his war against Siam,[290] this being an indirect involvement to support a neighbor.

The Conclusion, reduced to about one-third the length of the original, epitomizes the revisionist project of the Vietnamese translators. In Borri's work, the entire Conclusion is devoted to the need for expanding the work of proselytizing in the world generally and in Cochinchina particularly. To this end, he describes how perfect this place is for the propagation of Christianity, reiterating his praise of its people, its natural riches, and its climate. The translators entirely eliminate Borri's goal, but keep his argument, albeit slightly modified. If Borri describes Cochinchinese as "admitting of all strangers in their kingdom, and being well pleas'd that every one should live in his own religion," the Vietnamese version keeps this, but replaces "religion" by "laws and practices." In addition to the people's wonderful disposition, another factor that Borri considers important is the

---

[288] In recent years, some works have appeared that consider the Mạc in a more positive light. For example: Nguyễn Đức Diệu et al., *Vương Triều Mạc* (Kings of the Mac Dynasty) (Hanoi: Nhà Xuất Bản Khoa Học Xã Hội, 1996); Nguyễn Đức Diệu et al., *Văn Bia Thời Mạc* (Inscriptions of the Mac Period) (Hanoi: Nhà Xuất Bản Khoa Học Xã Hội, 1996).

[289] Borri in this volume, Part I, Chapter VII, Section titled "King's power."

[290] Borri, *Xứ Đàng Trong*, p. 84.

relative ease of learning the language: "Nor is it necessary before preaching to spend many years in studying their letters and hierogliphicks, as the fathers in China, for here it is enough to learn the language, which as has been said is so easie, that a man may preach in a year."[291] In the Vietnamese translation, this statement reads: *cũng không cần nghiên cứu tường tận về học thuật và chữ viết của họ trước khi giảng dạy họ, như các cha dòng ở Trung Quốc phải làm và tiêu phí những năm đầu tiên là những năm tốt nhất, bởi vì chỉ cần học tiếng nói của họ, thứ tiếng rất dễ, như chúng tôi đã viết, đến nỗi chỉ trong một năm là đã có thể nói được dễ dàng*[292] (Nor is it necessary to exhaust yourselves studying their learning and letters before you teach them, as the fathers in China have to do and waste the first years, which are the best, because [they] have only to study their spoken language, a kind of easy language, as we have written, to the extent that already in a year one can speak with ease). The substitution of "teaching" or "speaking" for "preaching" is a transformation from a work of intervention by a proselytizer to a work of appreciation by a tourist. Borri's *Account* is an encouragement by a foreigner for other foreigners to come with their ideas to change a country that is not theirs.

The Vietnamese translation is an invitation for the Vietnamese to enjoy the history and culture of their country, which was so much admired (and admired only!) by this Westerner. It is also an invitation for foreigners to come and enjoy this wonderful land. This invitation is a *bonbonnière*, full of sweet and peaceful images of the country, where, as the translation of the *Account* suggests, it is so pleasant to live and easy to get by. One would ask: "But how many foreigners can read this translation?" Relatively few, but perhaps the message can reach them through other channels. The Vietnamese have already developed a tourist itinerary that includes "Borri Country."[293] In short, this translation gives a new twist to Borri's work and legacy, enabling him to participate in recreating a "Phantasmatic Cochinchina," this time by Vietnamese and this time for both internal and external consumption.

---

[291] Borri in this volume, Part II, Chapter VI, Section titled "Conversion of a great lady," mentions that he had only "some knowledge of the Cochin-Chinese language" in the context of events occurring after he had already been three years in Cochinchina. The omission of this entire chapter in the Vietnamese translation eliminated a potential contradiction in Borri's statements.

[292] Borri in this volume, Part II, "Conclusion"; Borri, *Xứ Đàng Trong*, pp. 128-129.

[293] See the following sites: http://www.discoveryvietnam.com/packagetour3.htm. http://www.infohub.com/TRAVEL/SIT/sit_pages/12908.html. On day nine of these tours, "You will head out towards Lam Dong Province through 'Borri Country,' once the home of Jesuit missionaries."

THE REAL TONKIN

Very little is known about the life of Samuel Baron. Aside from a few mentions in the records of the Dutch and English East India Companies and in the diary of the London scientist Robert Hooke, not to mention a bit of graffiti on a rock reported by the French in the nineteenth century, nothing remains from him except his account of Tonkin. This account is remarkable for its informed detail about Tonkinese life, government, society, culture, and religion. Baron was apparently born and raised in Hanoi among the Dutch merchants and their Vietnamese women who from 1637 labored to turn a profit in local and regional markets. His father died in 1664, five years after sending him to Europe.

When Baron returned to Asia in the early 1670s he had gone over to the English, and the Dutch and the English were at war. His activities with the English East India Company during this time are obscure. Aside from some allusions to adventures in Taiwan, all that can be known for sure is that he established a good relationship with William Gyfford, who sailed to Tonkin in 1672 and remained there as chief of the English Company until 1674. These were difficult and unprofitable years for the English in Tonkin, and blame for this threatened to come upon Gyfford personally. There is no evidence that Baron was with Gyfford in Tonkin during this time, but his account, dedicated to Gyfford, bears the mark of being an explanation for the lack of English success in the Tonkin market, attributing failures to intractable local conditions. His basic argument is that European expectations of profitable trade in Tonkin were unrealistic, that merchant dreams were sure to break upon the rock of the real Tonkin.

In 1677, Baron appears briefly in the company of Robert Hooke in London. Hooke, a prominent scientist, was interested in learning about foreign lands and Baron was apparently able to satisfy some of his curiosity about Asia, particularly Tonkin. Shortly thereafter, Baron was off again to Asia, and in the late 1670s and early 1680s he spent quite a lot of time in Tonkin. In 1679, Jean-Baptiste Tavernier published an account of Tonkin in Paris. An English translation of this was published in London in 1680, and Hooke immediately sent a copy to Baron asking for his opinion. Tavernier had never been to Tonkin and had based his work on hearsay, supposition, and the account of a Jesuit missionary published some years before. Baron wrote his account to point out all the errors in the fantasy concocted by Tavernier and to provide a truthful description of the real Tonkin.

Baron wrote at least parts of his account while in Vietnam, but he finished it and sent it off to London at the English Fort St. George (Madras, India) in 1685. In his prefatory note to John Hoskins and Robert Hooke, he indicates that he is about to depart for China. There is no further information about him. His account of Tonkin is clearly based on extensive local knowledge and first-hand experience. But the account itself and the form of its development was elicited by a desire to disabuse readers of two discernible illusions about Tonkin, one about prospects for trade and the other about falsities and misinformation purveyed by Tavernier who never was there. Baron's voice is pitched at the confident angle of one who knows the real Tonkin.

A Dutch Father

Samuel Baron's father, Hendrik Baron, was an employee of the Dutch East India Company in Tonkin during the middle decades of the seventeenth century. In company records, he is identified as the person temporarily in charge of Dutch affairs at Hanoi in 1650, when the head of operations was absent, having departed on a voyage to Japan.[294] In the following year, when a company inspector found irregularities at Hanoi and the head was dismissed, it was recorded that Hendrik Baron was not culpable.[295] In that year, 1651, he was described as "a long-time resident of Tonkin and fluent in the language" as explanation for choosing him to be put in charge of a Dutch house at Faifo (Hội An), the chief port of Cochinchina.[296] This was an ill-fated experiment, for the Dutch had but recently allied with the Tonkinese in their wars against the Cochinchinese, and there was much mutual suspicion between the Dutch and the southern rulers. It is not surprising that, in a matter of months, Baron and four other Hollanders in Faifo were confined to a prison and shortly thereafter expelled from Cochinchina.[297] At the beginning of 1652, Baron was in Batavia, apparently on his way back to Tonkin.[298]

In 1659, Baron saw off his son on a ship sailing from Batavia to the Netherlands[299] and then returned to Tonkin.[300] During the next four years, Baron continued to be occupied with the Tonkin trade, traveling regularly between Batavia and Hanoi.[301] In May 1663 he was put in charge of operations in Tonkin, where he remained until his death on March 21, 1664.

Hendrik Baron's son's name appears in Dutch East India Company records of 1659 as Salomon.[302] This was either an error—entered mistakenly in place of "Samuel"—or else the young man changed his name when he arrived in Europe. We can only conjecture the age of Samuel Baron when his father sent him to Europe in 1659. Given the rigors of travel, it is most likely that he was at least in his teens. The Dutch had maintained a headquarters in Hanoi since the late 1630s, making it possible that Hendrik Baron had taken up residence there at that time.

Samuel Baron was described in a 1678 record of the Dutch East India Company as a "Tonkinese half-breed."[303] The chief of the English Company at Bantam in 1674 wrote vaguely that he had been born "on the coast of China."[304] When he first appears in the diary of the London scientist Robert Hooke, on May 29, 1677, he is

---

[294] W. J. M. Buch, "La Compagnie des Indes Néerlandaises et l'Indochine," *Bulletin de l'Ecole Française d'Extrême-Orient* 37 (1937): 132.

[295] Ibid., pp. 133-4.

[296] W. J. M. Buch, "La Companie des Indes Néerlandaises et l'Indochine," *Bulletin de l'Ecole Française d'Extrême-Orient* 36 (1936): 194-5.

[297] Buch, "La Compagnie des Indes Néerlandaises et l'Indochine," *(BEFEO 37)*, p. 145.

[298] Ibid., p. 146.

[299] Charles B. Maybon, "Une factorerie anglaise au Tonkin au XVIIe siècle (1672-1697)," *Bulletin de l'Ecole Française d'Extrême-Orient* 10 (1910): 169, note.

[300] Buch, "La Compagnie des Indes Neerlandaises et l'Indochine," *(BEFEO 37)*, p. 142.

[301] Ibid., pp. 143, 144, 160.

[302] Maybon, "Une factorerie anglaise au Tonkin."

[303] Ibid.

[304] Ibid.

identified as "of Funquin [*sic*]."[305] When his "description of Tonqueen" was published, he was denoted as "a native thereof." In his dedication, Baron claims to have been born in Tonkin. From all of these indications, it is reasonable to assume that his mother was Vietnamese.

A context for Baron's birth may be found in William Dampier's account of his visit to Tonkin in 1688. Dampier remarks upon the custom of Vietnamese women hiring themselves out as temporary wives to foreign sailors and merchants, and writes:

> For 'tis said, that even while they are with Strangers, they are very faithful to them; especially to such as remain long in the Country, or make annual Returns hither, as the Dutch generally do. Many of these [i.e., the Dutch] have gotten good Estates by their Tonquin Ladies, and that chiefly by trusting them with Money and Goods. For in this poor Country 'tis a great Advantage to watch the Market; and these Female Merchants having Stocks will mightily improve them, taking their Opportunities of buying raw Silk in the dead Time of the Year.[306]

Perhaps this passage gives us a glimpse into one aspect of Hendrik Baron's long residence and apparent success as a merchant in Tonkin.

Baron Goes Over to the English

We have no information about Samuel Baron in the 1660s. At some point, he changed his allegiance from the Netherlands to England, perhaps after the death of his father in 1664. In 1672, Dutch company records noted that he had gone over to the English,[307] this at a time when war had again broken out between the English and the Dutch. In 1674, the chief of the English company at Bantam wrote that Baron was a naturalized Englishman and had been in company service for three years.[308]

According to a letter from the London office of the English East India Company to its headquarters in Bantam, Java, dated September 21, 1671, Samuel Baron informed the officers of the company at the time they hired him that he was born in Tonkin, that his paternal grandfather had been "a Scotchman," his father was "a Dutch man," and his mother was "of the race of the Portugal."[309] Baron, seeking employment with the English East India Company, was apparently trying to ingratiate himself with the English by emphasizing his connection with Scotland through a grandfather and by denying his Eurasian heritage by claiming a Portuguese mother. This can be surmised from further mention in the letter that

---

[305] Henry W. Robinson and Walter Adams, eds., *The Diary of Robert Hooke (1672-1680)* (London: Taylor & Francis, 1935), p. 293.

[306] William Dampier, "Mr. Dampier's Voyages, Vol. II, Part I: His Voyage from Achin in Sumatra, to Tunquin, and Other Places in the East-Indies," in *A Collection of Voyages, in Four Volumes* (London: James and John Knapton, 1729), II:51.

[307] Maybon, "Une factorerie anglaise au Tonkin."

[308] Ibid.

[309] Oriental and Indian Office Collection, The British Library, London: No. E-3-87 London General to Bantam 21 September 1671. I am indebted to Hoang Anh Tuan for this information.

Baron "gave us some reasons why he left the Dutch service and offered himself to ours" and the observation that "though he be not of our nation, yet by the grandfather he is very near it." The English found him, according to the letter, to be "an active, intelligent person with competent abilities for his years," implying that, despite his experience in "the Dutch service" and being "well acquainted with" Tonkin, Taiwan, Japan, and China, he was still rather young. The letter instructs the agent in Bantam to establish a trading base in Tonkin and notes that Baron would be useful in that endeavor. Nevertheless, the London office warned that in case of the death or absence of the Company's chief in Tonkin, Baron was not to replace him, "for though we have respect for this person for so little acquaintance we have with him, yet we do not think it would be so convenient to have a stranger to be chief in our factories."

Samuel Baron was involved in discussions at Bantam in 1672 about setting up an English headquarters in Tonkin. Because of some unspecified delay involving the availability of shipping and Baron's prior assignment to go to Taiwan and Japan, he did not sail to Tonkin with the first English ship in 1672.[310] In that year, William Gyfford, with whom Baron was closely associated, established the English company's presence in Tonkin, where he remained in charge for the next four years. Baron later dedicated his "Description" to Gyfford in language that indicates his personal acquaintance with Gyfford's activities in Tonkin, indicating either that Baron was also there or that he had heard about the vicissitudes of the English in Tonkin during that time from others.

While Gyfford was in Tonkin setting up a base for company operations, Baron was off to Taiwan. A letter from him arrived in Bantam in June 1672, perhaps sent from Taiwan.[311] In April 1673, news reached Bantam that Baron had been imprisoned in Taiwan, and a documentary fragment that appears to pertain to this event records that "the ship and all others belonging to him were disposed of into other hands."[312] This was a volatile period for the region. The Dutch had been driven out of their fortress on the island a decade earlier by Chinese coastal forces resisting the rise of the Qing dynasty. The Dutch had allied with the Qing against the local forces in hopes of recovering their position there, but nothing came of this alliance until 1683, when the Qing finally gained control of the island. It appears that in 1672-3 Baron ran afoul either of the anti-Qing forces on Taiwan or of the Dutch who were then at war with the English.

In 1676, after four years in Tonkin, Gyfford was dismissed from his post and summoned to London to answer charges that he had engaged in private business and mismanaged the Company's affairs there.[313] This did not greatly damage Gyfford's career with the Company, for in 1684-85 he was the Company's governor at Madras, which became the Company's base of operations in Asia when Bantam was abandoned to the Dutch in 1682. During Gyfford's residence in Tonkin, the English there languished from Company neglect, Dutch hostility, and what they perceived as the cupidity of corrupt officials, the anti-trade policies of the government, scarcities of items to purchase, lack of a market for their merchandise,

---

[310] Maybon, "Une factorerie anglaise au Tonkin," pp. 170, 193-4.

[311] Ibid., p. 197.

[312] Ibid., p. 171.

[313] According to Hoang Anh Tuan, "From Japan to Manila and Back to Europe: The Abortive English Trade with Tonkin in the 1670s," *Itinerario* 29, 3 (2005): 84. In his dedication, Baron hyperbolically says that Gyfford was in Tonkin "the space of well nigh six years."

and the Vietnamese themselves, who were "unreasonable and truthless."[314] Gyfford's efforts to trade under such conditions were unorthodox and easily perceived by distant Company officials as seeking private profit at Company expense.[315]

When he wrote his account of Tonkin in the early 1680s, Baron echoed all the English complaints about the difficulties of doing business there in a way suggesting that he may indeed have given testimony on Gyfford's behalf when Gyfford was summoned to London. In his dedication to Gyfford, Baron refers to Gyfford "having suffer'ed strange rudeness and harsh usages from the natives, their usual welcome to new-comers," and he itemizes the obstacles to English trade in Tonkin: "the Dutch war, want of shipping [and] supplies . . . incapacity to trade." He also dilates upon Gyfford's excellent qualities that enabled him to obtain some measure of success: "prudence and dexterity . . . generosity . . . liberal spirit . . . affable, courteous and complaisant." He notes that Gyfford was selfless in his pursuit of the Company's good, that he eventually "gained the good-will of [the local] courtiers and merchants," and that he upheld himself with "honour." The presence of Baron in London shortly after the time of Gyfford's summons suggests that these comments may paraphrase testimony on Gyfford's behalf.

Adventures

In 1677, Baron appears in London as an acquaintance of Robert Hooke and Thomas Hoskins, who were active in the Royal Society and in scientific activities of that time.[316] Hooke and Hoskins took an interest in people who had traveled in foreign lands. Baron appears in Hooke's diary from May to October as one of his regular companions.[317] In the October entries, Hooke tells of preparing a letter for Baron to deliver to an acquaintance of his who was apparently then traveling in Asia. Baron is not mentioned again in the diary until March 1679, when Charles Chamberlain, an agent of the English East India Company and apparently Hooke's intermediary for news of Baron, informs Hooke that Baron is "going to Tunkin."[318]

In the meantime, the Dutch company in Batavia had noted Baron's arrival in Bantam aboard an English ship in June 1678.[319] He must have then proceeded to Tonkin, for a letter received in Bantam from Tonkin by the English East India Company dated in December 1678 mentions "errors committed by Baron."[320] What this was about remains a mystery. It appears that Baron was in Tonkin in 1680 because as late as the nineteenth century, a rock could be seen from the Đáy River with the inscription "Baron 1680."[321] According to Chapter VI, he was doing business in Tonkin during the years 1678-1682 and to facilitate his activities had

---

[314] Ibid., pp. 76, 85.

[315] Ibid., pp. 83-84.

[316] Lisa Jardine, *The Curious Life of Robert Hooke: The Man Who Measured London* (New York, NY: Harper Collins, 2004), pp. 8-9, 272, 283.

[317] Robinson and Adams, eds., *The Diary of Robert Hooke*, May 29 (1677); June 23 (1677); August 2, 24 (1677); September 6, 22, 28 (1677); October 4, 8, 25, 26, 28 (1677).

[318] Ibid., March 18 and 21, 1679.

[319] Maybon, "Une factorerie anglaise au Tonkin."

[320] Ibid., p. 181.

[321] M. A. C. J. Geerts, "Voyage du yacht hollandais *Grol* du Japan au Tonquin," *Excursions et Reconnaissances* 13 (Saigon, 1882): 8, n. 1.

established a relationship of "adoption" or patronage with one of the local princes. We learn from Chapter XIII that in 1682 he arrived in Tonkin from Siam. Baron was apparently in Tonkin when Trịnh Tạc died in 1682, for he includes a detailed description of the funeral ceremonies in Chapter XVII. In Chapter XI, Baron writes that it is 1683, and he is in Tonkin.

During this time, Baron appears to have had many adventures. In Chapters VI and XII, he writes that his trading activities in Tonkin were protected by a Trịnh prince, the only surviving son and heir apparent of Trịnh Căn, who was the son and heir of Trịnh Tạc, the ruling lord (*chúa*). Baron writes that he had in his possession the seal of this prince and that this protected him from difficulties with local and court officials. In return, Baron writes that he "always gave [the prince] presents at my arrival from a voyage" (Chapter VI). Baron appears to have entered into competition with Chinese merchants, for twice he reports that he found himself in troubles because of Chinese hostility toward him. In Chapter V, he writes that on one occasion he took passage on a Chinese junk, but the Chinese stranded him and three others on an island in the western part of the "Bay of Tonqueen." He eventually found passage on a small boat that was "sewed together with rattans," on which he sailed all the way to Siam in twenty-three days. When he eventually returned to Tonkin, his story aroused widespread interest, and Vietnamese officials questioned him about what he had seen along the Cochinchinese coast and in Siam and even asked if he would lead two or three hundred soldiers to raid the Cochinchinese coast using such sort of small boats. He says that he refused this suggestion by saying that he was a merchant, not a soldier, but that his refusal was later held against him when he was "accused by the Chinese" (Chapter XII). This may have been related to his "troubles" in 1682 upon the death of Trịnh Tạc, when he refers to his patron as follows (Chapter VI):

> This prince, tho' he be of a generous, noble mind, and had an extraordinary kindness for me, yet I was not the better for him in my troubles; for on the decease of his grandfather, it pleased God to visit him, in the height of his prosperity with madness, which was the overthrow of my business, by incapacitating him to protect me in my greatest trouble and necessity; but lately I understand he is recover'd again.

This prince, not mentioned in Vietnamese sources, never lived to become the ruler; his father Trịnh Căn was, upon his death in 1709, succeeded by a great-grandson.

Baron dated and apparently sent off his "Description" in 1685-6 from Fort St. George (Madras), the headquarters of the English East India Company, where his patron, William Gyfford, was then serving as governor. In his dedication to Hooke and Hoskins, he says that he is conveying his "Description" to these two men via Charles Chamberlain, and he asks that they send the money "the said description will yield" by Chamberlain to Gyfford "whose liberality has chiefly supported my expences." Judging from this, it appears that Baron hoped to repay a debt to Gyfford with whatever he could gain from his writing. Baron's reference, in his dedication to Gyfford, to "the troubles I was in" while writing his account probably relate to the situation described at the end of the previous paragraph and may have included financial difficulties that involved Gyfford and the English East India Company. In his dedication to Hooke and Hoskins, Baron names four men, one being Charles Chamberlain, apparently all associated with the English East India Company, whom he calls his "benefactors," and who may indeed have been his creditors. Chamberlain and two of the other three men mentioned here appear on a list of men qualified for employment by the English East Company for the year 1675.[322]

Against Tavernier

Aside from discharging a debt, there was another motivation for Baron to write his account. In 1680, an English translation of Jean-Baptiste Tavernier's account of Tonkin, published the previous year in French, appeared in London.[323] Although a rather famous world traveler whose writings received wide acclaim during his lifetime, Tavernier did not actually visit Tonkin. He claimed to have based his account upon the testimony of his brother, who supposedly did go to Tonkin, and upon information available to him during his residence in Batavia and Bantam on the island of Java (June-October 1648). According to his dedication to Gyfford and to his "Advertisement," Baron was requested by Hooke and Hoskins to note the errors in Tavernier. He organized his account following the topics in Tavernier, frequently pausing to dispute with Tavernier on various points. At some point Baron decided to expand his critique of Tavernier into a full account of his own, in his words, "finding it much more easy for me to compose a new description of Tonqueen (the country of my nativity, and where I have been conversant with persons of all qualities and degrees) than to correct the mistakes of others."

---

[322] English East India Company, "A List of Their Names Who by their Adventures and Capable of being Chosen Committees for the Year 1675." Aside from Chamberlain, James Houblon and John Paige are listed here; I conjecture that these last two are the men whose names Baron spells James Hobland and John Page. I have found no trace of the fourth man, William Moyor.

[323] Jean-Baptiste Tavernier (1605-1689) was a French traveler who gained fame for making six journeys to Asia between 1631 and 1668; he spent most of his time in Persia and India, but during his third voyage spent around four months in Java (June-October 1648), during which time his brother, whom he encountered there, died. In 1669, he was ennobled for his contributions to geography and commerce, whereupon he purchased the Barony of Aubonne in the canton of Vaud on the north shore of Lake Geneva, which joined the Swiss Federation in 1803. In 1685, he was forced to sell the barony due to financial difficulties, and he shortly after died in Moscow while en route once more to Asia. In 1676, he published *Six Voyages* in Paris, which did not mention Tonkin. This was quickly translated into English by J. Phillips and published in London in 1677 and again in 1678. In 1679, Tavernier published in Paris his second large work, *Recueil de plusiers relations et traitez singulier et curieux de J. B. Tavernier qui n'ont point esté mis dans ses six premiers voyages, divise en cinq parties* (Collection of several unique and interesting accounts and essays of J. B. Tavernier that were not among his six first voyages, divided into five parts), of which part four is "Relation nouvelle et singulier du Royaume de Tunquin" (New and unique account of the Kingdom of Tonkin). The following year, an English translation of this book appeared in London: Jean-Baptiste Tavernier, *A Collection of Several Relations and Treatises Singular and Curious* (London: A. Godbid & J. Playford, for Moses Pitt at the Angel in St. Paul's Churchyard, 1680), which included "A New and Singular Relation of the Kingdom of Tunquin." In the early twentieth century, Tavernier's account of Tonkin was published in *Revue Indochinoise* X:504-517, 610-160, 744-750, 806-811, 894-900 (October-December 1908) and XI:43-51 (January 1909). For more on Tavernier, see the Introduction of William Crooke, ed., *Travels in India by Jean-Baptiste Tavernier, Baron of Aubonne, Translated from the original French Edition of 1676 with a biographical sketch of the Author, Notes, Appendices, etc.*, 2 vols. (London: Oxford University Press, 1925).

Baron's account was compared favorably with Tavernier's account a century later in Abbe Richard's *Histoire Naturelle, Civil, et Politique du Tonquin*, which was based upon the account of a French missionary who lived for twelve years in Tonkin. Abbe Richard wrote:

> The Jesuit missionary Father Alexandre de Rhodes and the traveler Tavernier were the first to give some idea of this country. The Jesuit, solely occupied by his religious interests, did not speak of the condition of the peoples of this kingdom and of the government except to the extent that it was related to his purpose. Tavernier recounted nothing about this topic that one should believe; and the best that one can think to his credit is that he had been deceived by his brother, whom he said had been in Tonkin and had observed all that which he ascribed to it: but his account is so little in conformity with the truth that it is doubtful that he ever set foot in the place. On the contrary, Baron, an Englishman, born in Tonkin where he was raised and where he passed a long succession of years, had no goal in composing his account of this country but to undeceive the public of the widely accepted errors in Tavernier's work.
>
> So one can generally agree with the authenticity of Baron's account of Tonkin and can consider it as a reliable guide, at least for what happened up to 1685, when he departed the country ... [324]

Abbe Richard, in a note to the above passage, suggests that Tavernier, "being very ignorant and barely able to write," had dictated his accounts of various countries to copyists who added their own ideas, and that he easily confused items about one kingdom with those of another, and that he poorly remembered information he received from a French missionary whom he met during the course of his travels. But amidst the errors and confusions in Tavernier's account of Tonkin there are some verifiable items that may not be explained by Abbe Richard's supposition. Prior to the publication of Tavernier's account in 1679, less well-known accounts of Tonkin were published by two French Jesuits who had served as missionaries there: Alexandre de Rhodes,[325] who is mentioned by Abbe Richard, and Joseph Tissanier.[326] While Tavernier alludes to the account of de Rhodes, he makes no mention of Tissanier. Nevertheless, Louis Malleret, in an article published in 1932, has shown that Tavernier lifted whole passages out of Tissanier.[327] Seven years earlier, William Crooke had commented: "In a certain

---

[324] Richard (Abbe), *Histoire naturelle, civile, et politique du Tonquin* (Paris: Chez Moutard, 1778), pp. vi-viii.

[325] Alexandre de Rhodes, *Histoire du royaume de Tunquin et des grands progrez que la predication de l'evangile y a faits en la conversion des infidèlles, depuis l'année 1627 jusques à l'année 1646*, trans. from Latin by R. P. Henry Albi (Lyons: Chez Jean Baptiste Devenet, 1651).

[326] Joseph Tissanier, *Relation du voyage du P. Joseph Tissanier de la Compagnie de Jésus, depuis la France jusqu'au royaume de Tonkin, avec ce qui s'est passé de plus memorable dans cette mission durant les années 1658, 1659, et 1660* (Paris: Edm. Martin, 1663). A third Jesuit, an Italian, had also produced an account of Tonkin at that time: Gio. Filippo de Marini, *Relation nouvelle et curieuse des royaumes de Tunquin et de Lao*, translated from Italian by L.P.L.C.C. (Paris: Gervais Clouzier, 1666).

[327] Louis Malleret, "Une source de la relation du voyageur Tavernier sur le Tonkin," *Bulletin de la Société des Etudes Indo-Chinoises de Saigon*, nouvelle serie 7,1 (Janvier-Mars 1932): 115-125.

sense, to a limited degree, Tavernier may have been a plagiarist, but he openly avowed his endeavours to obtain information wherever he could."[328] Despite cribbing from the writings of authors more knowledgeable about Tonkin than himself, Tavernier failed to avoid Baron's indignant debunking, apparently because the English translation of his account attracted the interest of Hooke and Hoskins, who, having undoubtedly heard much about Tonkin directly from Baron, immediately requested from him an itemization of errors.

Epilogue

Baron's dedication to Hooke and Hoskins implies that he expected his account to be published without delay. However, it was not published until the 1732 edition of Awnsham and John Churchill's multi-volume *Collection of Voyages and Travels*.[329] No explanation was provided for the gap of nearly half a century between Baron's dispatch of his manuscript to London and it's eventual publication. We might surmise that, if the manuscript indeed arrived in the hands of Hooke and Hoskins sometime in 1686 or shortly thereafter, it was lost in the shuffle of accounts from foreign lands that Hooke had solicited from many travelers. Hooke indeed did bring to publication some of these accounts, but it is likely that Baron's manuscript languished, perhaps in the papers of the Royal Society if not in the personal papers of Hooke or Hoskins, as Hooke became increasingly distracted from this time with personal feuds and failing health.[330]

After Hooke's death in 1703, his papers were scattered, though many of the more purely "scientific" materials eventually appeared in the Repository of the Royal Society that was completed in 1712.[331] How Churchill's editors discovered Baron's manuscript is not known. At least one anonymous editor was conversant with Biblical studies and incorporated into Chapter XIV of Baron's work an entire entry from Dom Augustin Calmet's *Dictionary of the Holy Bible*, of which the first English translation, by D'Ogley and Colson, was published in the same year, 1732.[332]

Baron had an interesting life. In 1673 he had been imprisoned on Taiwan and lost his ship and crew. In 1678, records of the English Company noted unspecified "errors" that he committed in Tonkin. In the early 1680s, he was abandoned by a Chinese shipmaster on an island and later "accused by Chinese" in Tonkin; he refers to "the trouble I was in" at that time and mentions that the prince who was

---

[328] William Crooke, ed., *Travels in India by Jean-Baptiste Tavernier*, ch. I, p. xxvi.

[329] Awnsham and John Churchill, *A Collection of Voyages and Travels*, 2nd ed. (London: John Walthoe et al., 1732), vol. 6. Baron's account also appears in volume 6 of the third edition published in 1744-46.

[330] L. Jardine, *The Curious Life of Robert Hooke*, pp. 272 ff.

[331] Ibid., pp. 305 ff.

[332] Twenty years after Baron's account first appeared in Churchill, Abbe Antoine Francois Prevost included a partial French translation of Baron's account in his *Histoire Generale des Voyages* (Paris: Didot, 1751) IX:91-123, entitled: Baron, "Description du Tonquin." He ignores half of Baron's chapters, rearranges the rest, and summarizes rather than translates. In 1914-15, H. Deseille published a more faithful French translation with annotations: S. Baron, "Description du royaume de Tonkin," trans. H. Deseille, *Revue Indochinoise* XXII, no. 7 (July 1914): 59-75; no. 8 (August 1914): 197-208; no. 9-10 (September-October 1914): 331-343; no. 11-12 (November-December 1914): 429-454; *Revue Indochinoise* XXIII, no. 3-4 (March April 1915): 291-301; No. 5-6 (May-June 1915): 443-454.

his patron and protector pleaded temporary insanity to avoid assisting him in a time of need. He was apparently inclined to find himself in tight spots, but he did not lose confidence that with the written word he could strike blows for truth. Perhaps he kept himself busy amidst his troubles by writing, possibly while in prison.

Baron's discussions of several topics reveal his depth of knowledge. He gained his knowledge from his years of residence in Hanoi and from information gained from educated Vietnamese. He shows himself relatively well informed about the history of the country; about education, examinations, and academic degrees; about Trịnh family politics; about the organization of provincial governments and of the central government; about the court and legal system; about public ceremonies conducted by the king (*vua*) and the lord (*chúa*); about the mutiny of soldiers in the capital in 1674; about the funeral of Trịnh Tạc in 1682; about Confucianism, Buddhism, and Daoism; about clairvoyants, sorcerers, and geomancers; about fruits; and about daily life among the Vietnamese.

The interest that Baron's "Description of the Kingdom of Tonqueen" holds for us today is in what it tells us about the northern Vietnamese in the mid-seventeenth century and also about the Englishmen who sailed to distant lands at that time. Baron's strong, confident, expressive idiom is very close to that of John Bunyan, who wrote from prison around the same time. While Bunyan voiced the excitement of spiritual pilgrimage, Baron voiced that of the merchant adventurer. In both voices there is a sense of conviction and momentum, of engagement with error in defense of truth, of getting somewhere interesting. In his dedication to Hooke and Hoskins, Baron informs his London friends of his future plans: "I am now on a voyage to China, where if I can pick up any curiosity, or discover any thing worthy your sight or information, you are sure to hear from me." This is the last we hear of Samuel Baron. What curiosities, if any, Baron may have encountered in China after he sent off his manuscript to London are lost to us today. But his sense of anticipation remains.

A

COLLECTION

OF

Voyages and Travels,

SOME

Now first Printed from *Original Manuscripts*,

OTHERS

Now first Published in ENGLISH.

In Six VOLUMES.

With a General PREFACE, giving an Account of the
Progress of NAVIGATION, from its first Beginning.

Illustrated with a great Number of useful Maps and Cuts,
Curiously Engraven.

Vol. II

L O N D O N:
Printed by Assignment from Messrs. CHURCHILL,

For JOHN WALTHOE, over-against the *Royal-Exchange, in Cornhill;* THO.
WOTTON, at the *Queen's-Head* and *Three Daggers* over-against St. *Dunstan's* Church
in *Fleetstreet;* SAMUEL BIRT, in *Ave-Mary-Lane, Ludgate Street;* DANIEL
BROWNE, at the *Black-Swan,* without *Temple-Bar;* THOMAS OSBORN, in
Gray's-Inn; JOHN SHUCKBURGH, at the *Sun,* next the *Inner-Temple-Gate,* in
Fleetstreet; and HENRY LINTOT, at the *Cross-Keys,* against St. *Dunstan's* Church, in
Fleetstreet. M DCC XXXII.

THE
CONTENTS
OF THE
SECOND VOLUME

MR. John Nieuhoff's *remarkable voyages and travels in-*
to Brazil, *and the best parts of the* East-Indies. *Tran-*
slated out of Dutch.   Page 1
The true travels and adventures of captin John Smith, *into*
Europe, Asia, Africa, *and* America, *from the year* 1592
to 1629.   329
Two journals: The first kept by seven sailors, in the isle of
S. Maurice *in* Greenland, *in the years* 1633, *and* 1634,
who pass'd the winter, and all died in the said island. The
second, kept by seven other sailors, who in the years 1633,
and 1634, *winter'd at* Spitzbergen. *Done out of* Low
Dutch.   369
A true and short account of forty two persons, who perish'd
by shipwreck near Spitzbergen, *in the year* 1646. *Out of*
Low Dutch.   381
An account of Ireland, *sent to monsieur* de la Mothe de Vayer,
by la Peyrere. *Done out of* French.   383
An account of Greenland, *to monsieur* de la Mothe de Vayer,
by la Peyrere. *Done out of* French.   399
Captain Thomas James's *strange and dangerous voyage in his*
intended discovery of the north-west passage into the South-
Sea, *in the years* 1631, *and* 1632, *with many curious Ob-*
servations.   429
An account of two voyages: The first of Feodor Iskowitz
Backhoff, *the* Muscovite *envoy, into* China: *The second, of*
Mr. Zachary Wagener, *through a great part of the world*
into China. *Translated from the* High Dutch.   489
The life of Christopher Columbus, *and the history of his dis-*
covery of the West-Indies; *written by his own son,* D. Fer-
dinand Columbus. *Translated from the* Italian.   501
Pyrami-

Pyramidographia: *Or, A description of the* Pyramids *in* Egypt:
  By John Greaves, *professor of* Astronomy *at* Oxford; *with*
  additions of his own.   Page 625
A discourse of the Roman Foot *and* Denarius, *from whence,*
  as from two principles, the measures and weights used by the
  ancients, may be deduced. By the same John Greaves.   675
An account of Cochin-China; *in two parts: The first treats*
  of the temporal state *of that kingdom: The second, of what*
  concerns the spiritual. *By the* R. F. Christopher Borri, *of*
  the society of Jesus. *Translated from the* Italian.
                                                            721

VOYAGES

AN ACCOUNT OF COCHIN-CHINA.
IN TWO PARTS.

THE FIRST TREATS OF THE TEMPORAL STATE OF THAT KINGDOM.

THE SECOND, OF WHAT CONCERNS THE SPIRITUAL.

WRITTEN IN ITALIAN

BY THE R. F. CHRISTOPHER BORRI, A MILANEZE, OF THE SOCIETY OF JESUS, WHO WAS ONE OF THE FIRST MISSIONERS IN THAT KINGDOM.

This account is so short, it requires not much preface, or to say the truth, any at all; a little time sufficing the curious to inform himself of the value and contents of it. Who the author was appears by the title, and what the cause of his going into that kingdom, his profession and only business being to preach Christianity to the infidels: he lived five years among them, and learn'd their language to perfection; and therefore his relation is not like those of travellers, who just pass through a country; or merchants, that touch at ports upon the business of trade, and consequently deliver very fabulous accounts, either to make their travels the more surprizing, or for want of knowing better, taking things upon hear-say, and not understanding their language to get certain information. This father on the contrary frequently conversing with all sorts of people, and having a settled residence there for years, had the opportunity of knowing what he writ. He gives the description of the kingdom, a considerable part whereof he travell'd over: he speaks of its product, which he had the benefit of for sustenance and cloathing: he tells us the temper and seasons of the air, which he several times felt: he relates the inundations which he often saw: he gives an account of their sects, which he learn'd from their priests, or *omsays*,[1] whom he converted to Christianity: he sets down the power and

---

[1] The term "omsays" is an Anglicized plural used by the anonymous author of this introduction for Vietnamese *ông sãi*; see Chapter 2 of Part 2 in Borri where it is spelled "omsaii" by the translator; in Borri's Italian original, it is spelled "onsaij." The plural of the second syllable of this expression is given in Baron, Chapter 18, as "Sayes"; it might plausibly be argued that what is being transcribed is not *sãi* but rather *thầy*, a term of address meaning "master" and used for monks and teachers, but Baron, in Chapter 18, clearly distinguishes between *sãi* ("Sayes" in plural form) and *thầy* (which he spells "thay"). Alexandre de Rhodes, in his seventeenth-century dictionary, identifies *sãi* as "bonze" and describes such people as what we would consider to be "monks"; the same is true in the early nineteenth-century dictionary of Taberd. Alexandre de Rhodes, *Dictionarium Annnamiticum, Lusitanum, et Latinum* (Rome: Sacr. Congreg, 1651), col. 671. A. J. L. Tabert, *Dictionarium Anamitico-Latinum* (Serampore: J. Marshnam, 1838), p. 435.

government of the kingdom which he could be no stranger to, being familiar with several men in great authority: and to conclude, he particularizes how far the christian faith has been there propagated; which he well knows, as having been himself a labourer in the vineyard for the first five years; and after that, receiving it from those that succeeded him. In fine, the relation is curious, tho' short, and seems to carry all the air of truth imaginable, besides the general approbation it has always received in all parts, which is the greatest commendation that can be given it.

AN
ACCOUNT
of
COCHIN-CHINA.
The FIRST PART.

OF THE
Temporal State of the Kingdom of *Cochin-China*.

CHAPTER I.

OF THE NAME, SITUATION, AND EXTENT OF THIS KINGDOM.

{Name of *Cochin-China*.}[1]

Cochin-china, so call'd by the *Portugueses*,[2] is by the natives called *Anam*, signifying a western country, because it lies well west of *China*;[3] for which same reason the *Japoneses*, in their language, give it the name *Cochi*,[4] signifying the same as

---

[1] The original *Relatione* is not divided into sections. The section titles were added by the translator.

[2] See Introduction.

[3] Annam (Annan in Chinese) means "Pacified South." This title was originally applied to the territory of modern northern Vietnam when it became a frontier province of the Tang empire (618-907). Borri's suggestion to explain the term "Annam" by its being west of China is not as absurd as it might seem, for on early European maps northern Vietnam is indeed west of what was known as China, the region of Canton; for example, see the map opposite page one in Alexandre de Rhodes, *Histoire du royaume de Tunquin et des grands progrez que la predication de l'evangile y a faits en la conversion des infidèlles, depuis l'année 1627 jusques à l'année*, trans. from Latin by R. P. Henry Albi (Lyon: Jean Baptiste Devenet, 1651). Thus, Borri's apparent error simply reflects a common perception of his time. In the seventeenth century, the Jesuits commonly arrived in the Vietnamese territories after sailing west from Macau.

[4] Usually transcribed as *Koshi* in modern Japanese, from Chinese Jiaozhi (Vietnamese Giao-chi).

Anam, in the *Cochi-Chinese* [*sic*] language. But the *Portugueses*, having, by means of the *Japoneses*, been admitted to trade in Anam, of the *Japonese* word *Cochi*, and this other word *China*, compounded the name *Cochin-China*, applying it to this kingdom, as if they call'd it *Cochin* of *China*, the better to distinguish it from *Cochin*, the city in *India*, inhabited by the *Portugueses*: and the reason why, in the maps of the world, we generally find *Cochin-China* set down under the denomination *Cauchin-China*, or *Cauchina*[5] or the like, is no other but the corruption of the right name, or that the authors of those maps would signify, that this kingdom was the beginning of *China*.

{Its bounds.}

This kingdom, on the south, borders upon that of *Chiampá*,[6] in 11 degrees of north latitude, on the north somewhat inclining eastward toward *Tunchim* [Tonkin],[7] on the east is the *Chinese* Sea, and on the west-northwest the kingdom of *Lais*.[8]

{Extent.}

As to its extent, I shall here speak only of *Cochin-China*, which is part of the great kingdom of *Tunchim*, usurped by a king who was grandfather to him now reigning in *Cochin-China*, who rebelled against the great king of *Tunchim*:[9] for as yet the

---

[5] Variations in transliteration can be accounted for by a word passing through different languages and by the absence of an established system of transliteration. Speakers of the same language transcribed names they heard differently. We see in Borri's work that the same word now commonly transcribed as Tonkin is transliterated as Tunchim and Tonchin on adjacent pages. On Cauchin (or Cauchim), see: Pierre-Yves Manguin, *Les Portugais sur les côtes du Viêt-Nam et du Campa: Etude sur les routes maritimes et les relations commerciales, d'après les sources portugaises: XVI, XVII, XVIII siècles* (Paris: Ecole Française d'Extrême-Orient, 1972), p. 42, n. 2. For a full discussion of this term, see the Introduction.

[6] Champa was a kingdom that went through many transformations along what is now the central coast of Vietnam, beginning from the second century CE, when it first appeared in Chinese records. The Chams, of Malayo-Polynesian ethnicity and language, received their prevailing cultural influence from the Indian subcontinent rather than from China, which set them apart form the northward-looking Vietnamese. In the fifteenth century, the Chams were defeated by the Vietnamese, and much of their territory was annexed and opened to Vietnamese immigrants. Remaining Cham lands were annexed by the Vietnamese in the seventeenth century.

[7] Borri never went to Tonkin, but he knew it was between Macao and Cochinchina and that he had to go west from Macao to reach Cochinchina, which is apparently why he thinks Tonkin is east of Cochinchina.

[8] The reference is to Laos. In the Italian original, Borri writes Lai, a plural form of the Italian appellation Lao, referring to the people inhabiting this country. The English translation adds an "s."

[9] The ruler of Cochinchina during Borri's time was Nguyễn Phúc Nguyên, also called Sãi Vương (ruled 1613-35). The "great king of Tunchim" is apparently a reference to the Mạc kings who ruled from Hanoi during most of the sixteenth century (1527-92). The "grandfather" is Nguyễn Kim (d. 1545) who initiated a movement against the Mạc to restore the Lê dynasty; however he did not, as Borri indicates, "usurp" Cochinchina, for it was after his death that his son Nguyễn Hoàng (1525-1613) shifted the family into the southern frontier and there established what the Europeans called Cochinchina in an area that had been garrisoned by Vietnamese soldiers since the late fifteenth century. When the Nguyễn family eventually established its power there in the late sixteenth century, it was allied with the forces that in the north were fighting the Mạc on behalf of the Lê. For more on this, see K. W. Taylor, "Nguyen Hoang and the Beginning of Vietnam's Southward Expansion," in *Southeast Asia in*

Portugueses have traded only in this province; and here only the fathers of the society have been conversant, in order to introduce Christianity: yet, at the end of this account, I shall discourse concerning some particulars of *Tunchim*, where our fathers got footing since my return into *Europe*.[10]

Cochin-China extends above a hundred leagues along the sea, reckoning from the kingdom of *Chiampá*, in the aforesaid 11 degrees of north latitude, to the gulf of *Ainam*,[11] in the latitude of 17 degrees, or thereabouts, where the king of *Tunchim's* dominions begin.[12] The breadth is not much, being about twenty miles, all the country plain, shut up on the one side by the sea, and on the other by a ridge of mountains inhabited by the Kemois,[13] which signifies a savage people; for tho' they are *Cochin-Chineses*, yet they no way acknowledge or submit to the king, keeping the fastnesses of the uncouth mountains, bordering on the kingdom of *Lais*.

{Division.}

---

the *Early Modern Era*, ed. Anthony Reid (Ithaca, NY: Cornell University Press, 1993), pp. 42-65. Borri's statement reflects the following perceptions: first, that Tonkin and Cochinchina were previously one country; second, that rulers of the South were "usurpers"; and third, that the only lawful dynasty in the country was in Tonkin.

[10] The Catholic mission first developed among the Vietnamese in Cochinchina. It was not until March 1626 that Father Giuliano Baldinotti, an Italian Jesuit, with a Japanese lay-brother, Giulio del Piani, went to Tonkin, where they stayed for only about six months, during which they achieved no significant success and finally left for Macao. *Biên Niên Lịch Sử Cổ Trung Đại Việt Nam* (Annals of Ancient, Medieval, and Modern History of Vietnam) (Hanoi: Nhà Xuất Bản Khoa Học, 1987), p. 307; A. Bonifacy, *Les débuts du Christianisme en Annam des origines au commencement du 18e siècle* (Hanoi: Impremerie Tonkinoise, 192-?), pp. 18-9. The account of Baldinotti under the title *Relatione del viaggio di Tunquino nuovamente scoperto* was published in Rome in 1629. For its translation into French see *Bulletin d'Ecole Française d'Extrême-Orient* 3 (1903): 71-78. In 1627, Jesuit Fathers Alexandre de Rhodes and Pedro Marquez or Marques were dispatched to Tonkin to establish a basis for the propagation of Christianity there. They were expelled from Tonkin in 1630, but de Rhodes shortly returned and stayed there until 1633.

[11] The Gulf of Ainam is called after the large island (Hainan) that on early European maps is named Ainam or Hainam. The common English term today is the Gulf of Tonkin.

[12] The border between the Nguyễn and the Lê at Borri's time was along the Gianh river. Later, the Nguyễn built a wall some short distance south of this river to defend against northern invasions. See L. Cadière, "Le mur de Đồng Hới," *Bulletin de l'Ecole Française d'Extrême-Orient* 6 (1906): 87-254.

[13] The reference is to the mountain chain presently called Trường Sơn that composed the western frontier of Cochinchina. *Kẻ Mọi*, "uncivilized people," is a vernacular Vietnamese expression applied to the upland minorities in Central Vietnam. An apparent variant of this expression was applied to the mountains inhabited by these people on the map in Alexandre de Rhodes, *Histoire*, where this mountainous region is called *Ru Moi*. The phrase *Ru Moi* also appears at this place on some other early European maps. G. F. Marini, a Jesuit missionary in Tonkin in the mid-seventeenth century, also refers to the place as *Ru Moi*, "where savage people live, of whom a part obey to two kings of Fire and Water." Gio. Filippo de Marini, *Relation nouvelle et curieuse des royaumes de Tunquin et de Lao*, tr. L.P.L.C.C. (Paris: Gervais Clouzier, 1666), p. 35. The meaning of the word *ru* is unclear, and it later disappeared from European maps and accounts, being replaced by *Ke Moi*, for example, on de Rhodes's map edited by the Jesuits and found in the later edition (1666) of his work.

Cochin-China is divided into five provinces; the first bordering on *Tunchim*, where this king resides, is call'd *Sinuvá*;[14] the second *Cachiam*;[15] here the prince, the king's son, resides and governs;[16] the third, *Quamguya*;[17] the fourth *Quignin*, by the *Portugueses* call'd *Pullucambi*;[18] and the fifth, confining on *Chiampa*, is *Renran*.[19]

---

[14] De Rhodes's map lists this province as *Thoanoa*, the modern Vietnamese spelling of which is Thuận Hóa, the province where Huế, the Nguyễn capital, was located; the Portuguese called this place Sinoa (*Sinuvá* here is a misprint; Borri's original spells it *Sinuua* in Chapter 7 of Part I) after the Chinese pronunciation of Thuận Hóa, *shunhua* in Pinyin, transcribed in some early European texts as *Sun-Whua*.

[15] Modern Quảng Nam province. Cachiam, spelled Cacciam in Borri's original, apparently takes its roots from Kẻ Chàm, Kẻ Chiam, or Kẻ Chiêm, which, in turn, derives from Vietnamese for Champa, Chiêm Thành. For many centuries, Quảng Nam had been the center of a major Cham kingdom.

[16] Nguyễn Phước Lan (1601-48), known also as Công Thượng Vương (Duke Công Thượng), son of Sãi Vương, who succeeded him on his death in 1635.

[17] On the de Rhodes's map it is Quam ghia. In modern orthography it is Quảng Nghĩa or Quảng Ngãi.

[18] De Rhodes's map in *Histoire* indicates it as Quinhin or Pulocambi. The modern spelling for Quinhin is Qui Nhơn. According to Daniello Bartoli, *Dell'Historia Della Compagnia di Giesu, La Cina, Terza Parte, Dell'Asia* (Rome: Nella Stamperia del Varese, 1663), III:707, Pulocambi is Malay for "Goat Island," in reference to an island shaped like a goat. Today this is Bình Định province, the capital city of which is Qui Nhơn.

[19] Also called Ranran. The name probably derives from the main river Đà Ràn. Today this place is the province of Phủ Yên.

CHAPTER II.

OF THE CLIMATE, AND NATURE OF THE COUNTRY OF COCHIN-CHINA.

{Great heat of *India*.}

Tho' this kingdom, as has been said, lies between 11 and 17 degrees of north latitude; hence it follows of course, that the country is rather hot than cold, and yet it is not so hot as *India*, tho' it be in the same latitude, and within the torrid zone. The cause of the difference is, because in *India* there is no distinction of the four seasons of the year, so that the summer lasts there nine months without intermission, without seeing so much as a cloud either day or night, and therefore the air is continually, as it were, inflamed with the great reflection of the sun-beams. The other three months are call'd winter, not because there is any want of heat, but because at that time it generally rains day and night; and tho' to appearance, such continual rains should naturally cool the air, yet they falling in the three months of *May, June,* and *July,* when the sun is in its greatest elevation, and in the zenith of *India,* and no winds blowing but what are hot, the air continues so inflam'd, that sometimes the heat is more intense than in summer, when for the most part there are pleasant winds blowing from the sea, which cool the ground, wherewith, if Almighty God did not relieve those countries, they would be uninhabitable.

{Four seasons in *Cochin-China*.}

But *Cochin-China* enjoying the distinction of the four seasons, tho' not in so perfect a manner as *Europe,* is much more temperate; for tho' its summer, which comprehends the three months of *May, June,* and *July,* be violent hot, because it lies within the torrid zone, and because the sun is then in its zenith, yet in *September, October,* and *November,* the autumn season, the heat ceases, and the air becomes very temperate by reason of the continual rains, which at this time usually fall upon the mountains of the *Kemois,* whence the waters running down in abundance do so flood the kingdom, that meeting with the sea, they seem to be all of a piece. These inundations during these three months, for the most part happen once a fortnight, and last three days at a time. They serve not only to cool the air, but to fertilize the earth, making it fruitful and abounding in all things, but particularly in rice, which is the most common and universal food of all the kingdom. During the other three winter months, which are *December, January,* and *February,* there are cold northerly winds, bringing cool rains, and so sufficiently distinguishing the winter from other seasons. To conclude, in *March, April,* and *May,* the effects of spring appear, all things being green and blossoming.

{Notable Inundations.}

Now since we have spoke of these inundations, I will not conclude this chapter without first observing some curiosities that occur on occasion of them.

The first is, That all men in general wish for them, not only that they may cool the air, but much more for the fertilizing of the earth; for which reason as soon as they appear, all the people are so pleas'd and joyful, that they express it by visiting, feasting, and presenting one another, all of them crying, and often repeating *Daden Lut, Daden Lut* [Đã đến lụt, đã đến lụt]; that is, the inundation is come, it is here; and this is done by persons of all degrees, even to the king himself.

And in regard the inundations often come so unexpectedly, that very often when they do not think of it at night, they find themselves the next morning surrounded with water; so that they cannot go out of their houses, throughout the whole kingdom, as has been said; hence it is that abundance of cattle are drowned, for want of time to retire to the mountains, or higher grounds.

{A pleasant law.}

For this reason there is a pleasant sort of law throughout the kingdom; which is, that if any oxen, goats, swine, or other beasts, are drowned, the owner loses them, and they belong to him that first takes them, which causes much sport and jollity; because when the *Lut* happens, they all go out in boats to seek the drowned cattle; upon which they afterwards feast and treat one another.

{Beneficial sport.}

Nor are the younger sort without their pastime; for there being in those fields of rice, an infinite number of rats, their nests filling with water, they are forced to swim out, and get upon the trees to save themselves; and it is pleasant to see the boughs loaded with rats, like fruit hanging on them. Then do the boys run out in their boats, striving to out-do one another, in shaking the trees, that the rats may fall and be drowned; which childish pastime is wonderful beneficial to the country, delivering it from those mischievous creatures, that otherwise, by degrees, would devour all the harvest.

{Markets and fairs on the water.}

In short, the *Lut* causes another considerable advantage; which is, that it affords every body the opportunity of furnishing his house with all necessaries, because the country being all navigable, during three days, commodities are very easily convey'd from one city to another, and therefore then are held the greatest fairs and markets, and with greater concourse of people than at any other time in the year. Then also it is, that they lay in provision of wood to burn and build, bringing it from the mountains in boats; which to this purpose come into the streets, and into the very houses, built for this purpose upon high pillars, that water may have free passage, the people living during that time in the upper floors; to which it were a wonder if the *Lut* should ever rise, they being built according to the situation of the place, to such a height as they know by long experience, is sufficiently above the waters.

CHAPTER III.

OF THE FRUITFULNESS OF THE COUNTRY.

{Rice.}

It is an easy matter to conceive the fertility of *Cochin-China*, by the advantages accruing from the *Lut*; yet we will mention some other particulars relating to it. The *Lut* leaves the land so fruitful, that rice is gathered three times a year,[1] in such great plenty and abundance, that there is no body will work for gain, all persons having enough to live on plentifully.

{Oranges.}

There are great quantities of fruit of several sorts, all the year about; and they are the same with those in *India*, *Cochin-China* being within the same climate. But to come to particulars; the oranges there are bigger than ours in *Europe*, and very full; the rind of them is thin, tender, and so well tasted, that it is eaten with the juice, which has a pleasant relish like lemons in *Italy*.

{Banana's.}

There is a sort of fruit which the *Portugueses* call *Banana's*, and others *Indian* figs; though, in my judgment, the name of a fig is neither proper to those in *India*, nor in *Cochin-China*, because neither the tree[2] nor the fruit has any resemblance with our figs; the tree being like that we call *Indian* wheat,[3] but higher, and the leaves so long and broad, that two of them would serve to wrap a man in quite round, and from head to feet. Hence some have taken occasion to say, that this was the tree in paradise, with the leaves whereof *Adam* covered himself. This tree at the top produces a cluster of twenty, thirty, or forty of these *Banana's* together; and each of them is in shape, length, and thickness, of an indifferent citron in *Italy*. Before the fruit is ripe, the rind is green; but afterwards yellow, as the citrons are. There is no need of a knife to pare this fruit, for the rind comes off as we shell beans. This fruit has a most fragrant smell; the pith or flesh of it is yellow, and firm, like that of a

---

[1] First, *lúa mùa* (seasonal rice); second, rice, that develops within three months, hence the name *lúa ba giăng* (rice of three moons) or *lúa chiêm* (fifth-month rice); and third, *lúa thông* (belated rice). See Ch. Crevost and Ch. Lemarie, *Catalogue des produits de l'Indochine* (Hanoi: Imprimerie d'Extreme-Orient, 1917), 1:24-5.

[2] Indeed, strictly speaking, bananas are herbaceous plants and not trees, as they do not have a wooden trunk but a stem.

[3] The original calls it Turkish wheat; Christoforo Borri, *Relatione della nuova missione delli PP. della Compagnia de Giesu, al Regno della Cocincina* (Rome: F. Catanio, 1631), p. 14.

bergamot pear,[4] when full ripe, that melts in the mouth. By this it appears to be no way like our fig, except in the taste and sweetness.[5] There is another sort of them, which is only eaten roasted, and with wine: the stem dies every year, when it has produced the fruit, and leaves a young sprout at the foot, which grows up against the next year.[6] That which in *Italy* they call an *Indian* fig, is nothing like the plant, or fruit of this *Banana* we now speak of; nor is this which we have in *Italy* called an *Indian* fig, in those parts.[7] This fruit is common throughout all *India*. There is another sort in *Cochin-China*, that is not found in *China*, nor *India*: It is as big as the largest citrons we have in *Italy*; so that one of them is enough to satisfy a man. These are nourishing, very white within, and full of black round seeds, which chew'd together with the white substance, are of a delicious taste, and a good medicine against the flux.[8]

{Can.}

There is another fruit in *Cochin-China*, which I have not seen in any other country of *India*; and this they call *Can*; the outward form and nature is like our pomegranate; but within it contains a substance almost liquid, which is taken out, and eaten with a spoon; the taste is aromatic, and the colour like that of a ripe medlar.[9]

---

[4] It seems that Borri refers here to bergamot orange, or *Citrus bergamia*, which originated in South Italy, because bergamot pear, a winter pear, was cultivated mainly in England and could hardly be familiar to Borri. Bergamot orange, however, is also a pear-shaped fruit. It has been used also for extraction of oil, which, because of its fragrant smell, has been widely used in perfume production.

[5] The description fits that of *chuối mật* (Musa nana) or *chuối tiêu* (Musa paradisiaca).

[6] *Chuối sứ*.

[7] As it is, this sentence seems obscure. In Italian, it reads: "Questo, che quì in Italia si chiama Fico d'India non ha che fare, nè con la pianta, nè con frutto con queste banane, delle quali noi hora parliamo, anzi che ne anche questo, che si trouva in Italia in quelle parti è chiamanoto fico d'India." Borri, *Relatione della nuova missione delli PP. della Compagnia de Giesu*, pp. 15-16. "This, which is called an Indian fig in Italy has nothing in common with either a plant or a fruit of this banana, of which we are speaking now; moreover, what is found in Italy is not called an Indian fig in this region [Cochinchina]."

[8] Borri, apparently, refers to *chuối hột*, the biggest among the species of bananas in Cochinchina. It has red-greenish skin and retains its seeds. Crevost and Lemarié, *Catalogues*, 1: 275.

[9] The word *Can* used by Borri is not associated with any known fruit at the present time and is not used in other accounts. We can try to infer what he meant only by comparing his information with other possible fruits: their form and nature (pomegranate), substance (liquid), and color (medlar). Medlar, while unripe and even when picked from the tree, retains a yellow-greenish color, but as it becomes ripe through the months-long process of fermentation in a cool place, its pulp becomes extremely soft and its color changes to golden-brownish. Bonifacy suggested to see in this *can* a "passion fruit," which according to him the Vietnamese call *dưa gan tây*, which Borri corrupted into *can*. Bonifacy identifies it as *Passiflora guadrangularis*, which in English means "giant granadilla." A. Bonifacy, *Les débuts du Christianisme en Annam des origines au commencement au 18e siècle* (Hanoi: Impremerie Tonkinoise, 192-?), p. 20. This fruit might reach one foot in diameter, thus exceeding the "outward nature" of pomegranate, to which Borri compared it. It has a yellow color. Passion fruit, or *qủa lạc tiên*, indeed has glutinous juicy fragrant pulp with numerous seeds. The Vietnamese translators of Borri, puzzled by this *can*, are more inclined to consider the option that this may be a reference to dragon fruit (*thanh long*); see Cristoforo Borri, *Xứ Đàng Trong Nam 1621* (Cochinchina. Year 1621), trans. Hồng Nhuệ, Nguyễn Khắc Xuyên, Nguyễn Nghị

{Gnoo.}

They have another peculiar to the country, that grows, and is like our cherries, but tastes like raisins, and is call'd *gnoo*.[10]

{Melons.}

There are also melons, but not so good as ours in *Europe*; nor are they eaten without sugar or honey. The water-melons are large and delicate.

{Giacca.}

There is a large fruit they call *giacca*,[11] which is common in other parts of *India*, but much larger in *Cochin-China*: It grows on a tree as high as the walnut, or chestnut,

---

(Hochiminh: Nhà Xuất Bản Thành Phố Hồ Chí Minh, 1998), p. 22, fn. 1. This is not very plausible, because dragon fruit, although comparable to pomegranate in its shape, is of red color, and its "substance" is not as liquid as that of the passion fruit. Furthermore, I was informed that *thanh long* appeared in South Vietnam only recently. Thus, I am inclined to agree with Bonifacy's opinion. It is possible, however, that Borri refers not to *Passiflora guadrangularis* but to some other kind of the 120 species comprising the Passifloraceae family, several of which existed in Cochinchina. The passion fruit got its name from its flower, which is not related, as commonly assumed, to "amorous" qualities of the fruit, but rather reflects Christ's passion and passion for Christ. The first European missionaries who discovered the plant in Latin America saw in the structure of the plant the iconography of Christ's crucifixion (nails, crown of thorns, etc.).

[10] *Nho* in modern Vietnamese orthography. It has come to signify "vine" or "grapes." Borri definitely does not recognize Cochinchinese grapes as grapes with which he was acquainted in Europe, as is seen from his statement. Moreover, further in the text he directly says that there were no grapes in Vietnam. On the other hand, Crevost and Lemarié at the beginning of the twentieth century list grapes among the fruits of Cochinchina and apply the same word, *nho*, to them. Crevost and Lemarié, *Catalogues*, 1:219-20. Thus, there are two possibilities. First, the berries that Borri saw were indeed grapes but they looked different from what he knew as grapes. Or, they were not grapes, and real grapes appeared in Cochinchina only later, brought there by Europeans. If that were the case, what then might this *gnoo* refer to? We might plausibly assume that it refers to one of the species from the Sapindaceae family, among which we find mangosteen, genips, longans, and lychees. All of them have some of the features described by Borri. Probably, even though mangosteen, also known as "queen of fruits," has a purple color, grape-like taste, and is native to Southeast Asia, we should exclude it from the list of possibilities due to its tennis-ball size and segmented, tangerine-like structure, which does not exactly correspond to Borri's comparison to cherries. Genips, while having a grape-like taste and a consistency similar to cherries, is green and is not "peculiar" to Vietnam but rather to other parts of the world. Lychee, although grown in northern Vietnam, was not found in central or southern Vietnam, according to Crevost and Lemarié, *Catalogues*, 1: 221. Thus, only longan (*long nhãn* in Vietnamese, meaning "dragon's eye" or also called simply *nhãn*) is left to fit Borri's description. Longans do resemble the shape of cherries, they have a pit similar to cherries, and they grow on a tree, not on a vine like grapes do. It should be noted that by the time Alexandre de Rhodes published his dictionary in 1651, only two decades after Borri's work, *nho* had become identical to the meaning we employ now, as we find in his dictionary: "nho: vitis sylvestris" (wild vine, wild grape). See Alexandre de Rhodes, *Từ Điển Annam-Lusitan-Latinh* (Annamite-Portuguese-Latin Dictionary), ed. and trans. Thanh Lãng et al. (Hochiminh City: Nhà Xuất Bản Khoa Học Xã Hội, 1991), col. 553.

[11] The jackfruit is native to India, from where it traveled to other parts of Asia, including Cochinchina. The appellation takes its roots from the Malayalam word *cakka*, later apparently

and has much longer prickles than the *jubeb*.[12] It is as big as a very large pompion [pumpkin] in *Italy*, so that one of them is a man's load. The out-rind is like that of a pine-apple, but soft and tender within. This fruit is full of certain yellow round kernels, like a small piece of coin, that is round and flat; and in the middle of every one of them, is a stone that is thrown away. There are two sorts of this fruit; one in *Portuguese* is call'd a *giacca barca*: The stone of this is thrown away, and the pulp is stiff; they do not take out the stone of the other; nor is the pulp hard, but soft as glue;[13] both these in taste somewhat resemble that delicious fruit called the *durion*, whereof we shall speak next.

{Durion.}

This *durion* is one of the most delicious fruits in the world, and found only in *Malaca*, *Borneo*, and the adjacent islands. The tree differs little from the *giacca* last mentioned, and the fruit itself is like it without, and that resembles the pine-apple, even in the hardness of the rind. The meat within is very white about the bone, to which it sticks like glue, and tastes very much like our *mangiare bianco* (a dainty among the *Italians*).[14] This meat and liquor is divided into ten or twelve little apartments, in each of which the flesh and moisture is about its stone, which is as big as a large chestnut. And it is to be observ'd, that when they break open the shell of this fruit, there comes from it an ill scent, like that of a rotten onion, all the substance within remaining of a most sweet and inexpressible flavor; whereupon I will relate what happened in my presence: a prelate arrived at *Malaca*, and one there opened a *durion* before him to give him a taste; the prelate was so offended at that nauseous smell that came from it when broke, that he would not taste it by any means. Being afterwards set down to dinner, they gave the rest of the company *mangiare bianco*; but on this prelate's plate they laid the white substance of this fruit, which is so like the *mangiare bianco*, that he could not distinguish the difference by the sight. The prelate tasted it, and thought it so much more delicious than usual, that he ask'd, what cook dress'd it so rarely? Then he that had invited him to dinner, smiling, told him, It was no other cook but God himself, who had produc'd that fruit, which was the very *durion* he would not taste. The prelate was so astonished, that he thought he could never eat enough; and they so dear, that even at *Malaca*, where they grow, they sometimes cost a crown apiece.

---

corrupted by the Portuguese into *jaka*. Its weight can be as much as ninety pounds, its rind is covered with numerous spines. The fruit is considered a great delicacy.

[12] Borri refers here to jujube, a Chinese date, which spread all over the world and is a delicious sweet fruit. While the fruit has a very thin and edible skin, the tree, on which the fruits grow, is often very thorny.

[13] *Qủa mít mật* and *qủa mít giai* respectively.

[14] Or "Bianco Mangiare" (literally "to eat white"), which is a delicious old Italian dessert prepared of all white ingredients: sugar, milk, ground almonds, and egg whites.

{Ananas.}[15]

Cochin-China abounds in another sort of fruit, by the *Portugueses* call'd *ananas;* which tho' it be common in all *India,* and *Brazile,* yet because I have not found it well describ'd by those that have writ of it, I would not pass it by. The fruit does not grow on a tree, nor from a seed, but on a stalk, like our artichokes, and the stem and leaves are much like those of the thistle or artichoke. The fruit is like a cylinder, a span long, and so thick that it requires both hands to grasp it. The pulp within is close, and like a radish, the rind somewhat hard, scaly like a fish. When ripe, it is yellow both within and without, is par'd with a knife, and eaten raw, the taste of it an eager sweet, and as soft as a full ripe *bergamot* pear.

{Areca.}

There is besides, in *Cochin-China,* a fruit peculiar to that country, which the *Portugueses* call *areca*. The trunk of it is as strait [straight] as a palm-tree, hollow within, and produces leaves like those of the palm, only at the top among these leaves, there grow some small boughs, which bear the fruit in shape and bigness like a walnut, green without, just as the nut is; within it is white and hard like a chestnut, and has no taste at all. This fruit is not eaten alone, but is wrapp'd up in leaves of *betle* [betel], well known in *India,* which are like our ivy-leaves in *Europe,* and the plant itself clings to trees like the ivy. These leaves are cut in pieces, and in them they wrap a bit of *areca,* each of them making four or five morsels; and with the *areca* they put some lime, which is not there made of stone, as in *Europe,* but of oyster-shells; and as among us there are cooks and caterers, & c. so in *Cochin-China* there is one in every family, whose business is to wrap up these morsels of *areca* in *betle,* and these persons being commonly women, are call'd *Betleres*. They fill their boxes with these morsels, and chew them all day, not only when they are at home, but when they are walking or talking, at all times, and in all places, never swallowing, but spitting them out when they are well chew'd, retaining nothing but the relish and virtue of it, which wonderfully comforts the stomach. These morsels are so much in use, that when one of them goes to make a visit, he carries a box full of them, and presently presents some to the party visited, who claps it into his mouth; and before the visitor departs, he that is visited sends to his *Betler* woman for a box of the same, and presents it to the visitor, to return his kindness; and these morsels must be still making. And there is so much of this *areca* us'd, that the greatest revenues of that country come from the fields of it, as among us of olive-gardens, and the like.

{Other growth.}

Tobacco is also us'd there, but not so much as *betle*. The country also abounds in all sorts of pumpions[16] and sugar canes. The *European* fruits are not yet come thither;

[15] Pineapple. The Europeans first discovered it on the coast of Brazil, where it was called "anana," which in the indigenous language meant an "excellent" or "fragrant" fruit. The name subsequently entered Portuguese, French, and Italian. The Spaniards, however, created a new appellation based on the shape of the fruit—"pina," from "pinecone"—and the English language elaborated on the Spanish name, adding the word "apple" to it.

[16] Another variant spelling of the aforementioned word *pompion,* that is, pumpkin.

but I believe grapes and figs would take very well. Our herbs, as lettice [lettuce], endive, colworts, and the like, come up well in *Cochin-China*, as they do throughout all *India*: But they all grow into leaf, without producing any seed, so that it must still be supplied out of *Europe*.

{Cattle and fowl.}

There is also plenty of flesh, by reason of the great multitude not only of tame cattle, as cows, goats, swine, buffaloes, and the like; but of wild, such as deer, much bigger than those of *Europe*, wild boars, *& c.* and of hens both tame and wild, of which sort the fields are full, turtles, pigeons, ducks, geese, and cranes, which are savory enough; and in short, other sorts, which we have not in *Europe*.

{Fish.}

Their fishery is very great, and fish so delicious, that tho' I have travell'd so many countries, I do not think I have met with any to compare to that of *Cochin-China*. And the country, as was said before, lying all along upon the sea, there are so many boats to go out a fishing, and they bring in so much fish to all parts of the kingdom, that it is really very remarkable to see the long rows of people continually carrying fish from the shore to the mountains; which is duly done every day, for four hours before sun-rising.[17]

{Balachiam.}

And tho' generally among the *Cochin-Chineses*, fish is more valu'd than flesh, yet the main reason why they apply themselves so much to fishing, is to furnish themselves with a kind of sauce, which they call *balachiam*,[18] which is made of salt

---

[17] The part of the sentence—"which is duly done every day, for four hours before sun-rising"—is not an exact translation of the original, which reads: "il che infallibilmente si sà ogni giorno dalle vent' hore, fino alle vent-quattro" (Borri, *Relatione*, pp. 23-24) and should be literally translated as "which is done without fail each day from the twentieth hour to the twenty-fourth hour." While it is possible that the translation simplifies the phrase and just refers to the night time as "four hours before sun-rising," Bonifacy states that the time was counted in Italy starting from the evening at 6 pm and all Catholic offices used to follow it. In which case "from the twentieth to the twenty-fourth hour" will coincide with the time range of 2 pm to 6 pm. (Bonifacy, *Les debuts*, p. 295, n. 26). However, it is not clear who is right here. Bonifacy obviously refers to the "Divine Office" or "Catholic hours," prayers required to be recited by clergy during certain hours of the day. The day was divided into a night watch ("Vigil," between 6 pm and 6 am) and a day watch ("Matins," from 6 am to 6 pm), but the first hour, Prime or *prima hora*, is considered to be at 6 am, apparently because night prayers were gradually co-joined with the day prayers. If we count from 6 am, the time indicated by Borri will be between 2 am and 6 am. But we really do not know what count he used, and I could not locate any supporting evidence from other sources.

[18] The reference is definitely to the famous Vietnamese condiment *nước mắm*. While Borri calls *nước mắm* "balachiam," William Dampier, who visited Tonkin in 1688, distinguishes between "balachaun" and *nước mắm*: "*Balachaun* is a Composition of a strong Savour; yet a very delightsome Dish to the Natives of this Country. To make it, they throw the Mixture of Shrimps and small Fish into a Sort of weak Pickle made with Salt and Water, and put it into a tight earthen Vessel or Jar. The Pickle being thus weak, it keeps not the Fish firm and hard, neither is it probably so designed, for the Fish are never gutted. Therefore in a short Time they turn all to a Mash in the Vessel; and when they have lain thus a good while, so that the Fish is

fish macerated and steep'd in water. This is a sharp liquor, not unlike mustard, whereof every body lays in such store, that they fill barrels and tubs of it, as many in *Europe* lay in their stocks of wine. This of itself is no food, but serves to sharpen the appetite to the rice, which they cannot eat without it. For this reason, tho' rice be the general and most common sustenance in *Cochin-China*, there must be vast quantities of *balachiam*, without which it is not eaten, and consequently there is continual fishing. There is no less plenty of shellfish, oysters, and other product of the sea, especially of one sort, which they call *cameron*.[19]

Besides all this, providence has furnish'd them with a sort of food so rare and delicate, that in my opinion it may be compar'd to the *manna*, wherewith the chosen people of God were fed in the desert. This is so peculiar to *Cochin-China*, that it is nowhere else to be found: and I will give an account of what I know of it by experience, and not by hear-say, having seen and eaten of it several times.

{Wonderful nests.}

In this country there is found a small bird like a swallow, which fastens its nest to the rocks, the sea-waves break against. This little creature with its beak, takes up some foam of the sea, and mixing it with a certain moisture it draws from its own stomach, makes a sort of slime, or bituminous substance, which serves to build its nest, which when dry and hardened, remains transparent, and of a colour between green and yellow. The country people gather these nests, and being soften'd in water, they serve to season meat, whether fish, flesh, herbs, or any sort whatsoever; and give every thing so different a relish, and so proper to it, as if they had been season'd with pepper, cinnamon, cloves, and the richest spice; this nest alone being enough to season all sorts of provisions, without salt, oil, bacon, or any other addition; and therefore I said I thought it like manna, which had in it the taste of all the most delicious meats; saving that this is the work of a small bird, and that was made by God's angels. And such great store of them is found, that I myself saw ten small boats loaden with nests, taken among the rocks, in not above a mile's distance. But they being so precious a commodity, only the king deals in them, they being all kept for him; and his greatest vent[20] is to the king of *China*, who values them at a great rate.

They eat no sort of white meats,[21] looking upon it as a sin to milk the cows, or other creatures: and the reason they give for this nicety is, that milk was by nature

---

reduced to a Pap, they then draw off the Liquor into fresh Jars, and preserve it for use. The masht Fish that remains behind is called *Balachaun*, and the Liquor pour'd off is called *Nuke-mum*. The poor People eat the *Balachaun* with their Rice. 'Tis rank-scented, yet the Taste is not altogether unpleasant; but rather savory, after one is a little used to it. The *Nuke-mum* is of a pale brown Colour, inclining to grey; and pretty clear. It is also very savory and used as a good Sauce for Fowls, not only by the Natives, but also by many *Europeans*, who esteem it equal with *Soy*." William Dampier, "Mr. Dampier's Voyages, Vol. II, Part I: His voyage from Achin in Sumatra, to Tunquin, and other Places in the East-Indies," in *A Collection of Voyages, in Four Volumes* (London: James and John Knapton, 1729), II:28. Bonifacy, *Les debuts*, p. 296, n. 27, suggests to look for the roots of the appellation *balachiam* in the Cham name for it, *baraval* or *barahauk*.

[19] I suppose this to be the *Portuguese* word *camerano*, signifying shrimps or prawns.

[20] In the original it says "spaccia" (p. 26) from the verb "spacciare" (to sell), thus, the meaning is "sale."

[21] Butter or cheese.

appointed for sustenance of the young ones: as if the owner of the young ones could not dispose of their sustenance.

{Camelions eaten.}

They eat some things which we loath, and count venomous, as camelions, which are here somewhat bigger than those that are sometimes brought dry'd up into *Italy*, out of the other countries. I saw a friend buy some ty'd together in a cluster, and lay them upon the live coals, which having burn'd the string, they walk'd about gently, as they used to do till they felt the heat of the fire; which being a violent cold nature, they resisted a-while, but were at last broil'd: my friend took them up, and scraping off the burn'd skin with a knife, the flesh remain'd extraordinary white; then he bruis'd and boil'd them in a certain sort of sauce like butter, and then eat them as a great dainty, inviting me to bear him company: but I had enough with the sight of it.

{All wear silk.}

Cochin-China abounds in all other things necessary for the support of human life; and in the first place for cloathing: there is such plenty of silk, that the peasants and mechanicks[22] generally wear it; so that I was often pleas'd to see men and women at their labour, carrying stone, earth, lime, or the like, without the least fear of spoiling or tearing the rich cloathes they had on. Nor will they wonder at it, who shall know, that the mulberry-trees, whose leaves feed the silk-worms, grow in vast plains, as hemp does among us, and run up as fast; so that in a few months the said worms appear upon them, and feed in the open air, spinning their thread at the proper time, and winding their bottoms in such plenty, that the *Cochin-Chineses* have not only enough for their own uses, but they furnish *Japan*, and send it to the kingdom of *Lais*, whence it afterwards spreads as far as *Tibet*; this silk being not so fine and soft, but stronger and more substantial than that of *China*.

{Buildings.}

The structures the *Cochin-Chineses* use of wood, are nothing inferior to those of any other part of the world; for without falsifying this country has the best timber in the universe, in the opinion of all that have been there to this time.

{Incorruptible trees called *Tin*.}[23]

Among the variety and multitude of their trees, there are two that most usually serve for building, and are so incorruptible, that they do not decay in the least, either under ground, or under water; and they are so solid and heavy, that they do not swim upon the water, and a log of them serves instead of an anchor to a ship. One of them is black, but not so as ebony; the other is red, and both of them, when the bark is taken off are so smooth and slick, that they scarce need any plaining. These trees are call'd *Tin*; and they would not deviate much from the truth, who should say, they were that incorruptible wood, which *Solomon* made use of for building the temple:

[22] The original reads "zappatori e manoali." Borri, *Relatione*, p. 27.
[23] Ironwood.

for we know the scripture gives them a name much like this, calling them *ligna thyina*.[24] The mountains of *Cochin-China* are all full of these trees, all strait, of such a prodigious height, that they seem to touch the clouds, and so thick that two men cannot fathom them. Of this timber the *Cochin-Chineses* build their houses, every man being free to cut down as many as he pleases.

{The houses.}

The whole fabric of their houses rests upon high, solid and well settled pillars, between which they place boards to remove at pleasure; either to exchange them for cane-lattices, which they weave neatly, to let in the air in hot weather; or to leave free a passage for the water and boats, at the time of the inundation, as we observ'd above. They also have a thousand curious inventions, and ingenious contrivances to set off their houses, with carving, and other works on wood, which are a very great ornament.

{Aquila, and Calamba, odoriferous wood.}

Since we have begun to talk of the trees, before we proceed upon any other matter, I will here mention something of a sort of wood, accounted the richest commodity that can be carried out of *Cochin-China* to other parts; which is the most famous wood called *Aquila*, or Eagle-wood,[25] and *Calamba*;[26] which are the same thing as to the tree, but differ in their value and vertue.[27] Of these trees, which are thick and high enough, the *Kemois* mountains are very full; if the wood be cut off a young tree, it proves *Aquila*, or Eagle-wood, and this there is most plenty of, every one cutting as much as he can: but when the wood is of an old tree, that proves *Calamba*; which were very hard to be found, had not nature itself provided for it, causing these same trees to grow on the tops of inaccessible mountains, where growing old without being exposed to destruction, some boughs of them now and then drop down, breaking off, either for want of moisture, or through age, and are therefore found rotten and worm-eaten, infinitely exceeding the common *Aquila* or Eagle-wood, in vertue and sweet scent; and this is the so highly valued and famous *Calamba*. The *Aquila* is sold by any body, but the *Calamba* belongs only to the king, because of the high value of its perfume and vertue. And to say the truth, it is so sweet where they gather it, that some pieces being presented me, for a trial, I buried them above a yard and a half under ground, and yet they discovered themselves by their fragrancy. The *Calamba*, where taken, is worth five ducats a pound; but in the port of *Cochin-China*, where the trade is, it bears a much greater price, and is not sold under sixteen ducats a pound. In *Japan* it is worth two hundred ducats a pound; but if there be a piece big enough for a man to lay his head on like a pillow, the *Japoneses*

---

[24] Ligna Tinea in the original (Borri, *Relatione*, p. 29). Vulgate 2 Chronicles, 9:11 reads: "de quibus fecit rex de lignis scilicet thyinis gradus in domo Domini et in domo regia…" "The king made of the algum trees terraces for the house of Yahweh, and for the king's house…" Algum, or sometimes almug, probably refers to the sandalwood tree. The Vietnamese translation for this term in the Chronicles is *đàn hương*. Borri possibly refers here to *Pterocarpus santalinus* or to *Adenanthera Pavonina*, which is taller than the former. Both can be used for construction.

[25] Lignum aquile, one of the less famous species of the *Thymelaeaceae* (aloe) family.

[26] *Aquilaria agalocha* or *Aquillaria malaccensis*, or aloes wood, a very rare and expensive tree.

[27] i.e. "virtue," meaning qualities.

will give after the rate of three or four hundred ducats a pound: the reason of it is, because they instead of a soft down-pillow, when they sleep, lay their head on some hard thing, and generally it is a piece of wood, which everyone, according to his ability, endeavours to have of as great value as he can; and a piece of *Calamba* is looked upon as a pillow fit for none but a king, or some great lord. Yet the *Aquila*, though of less price and esteem than the *Calamba*, is so considerable, that one ship's load of it enriches any merchant for ever: and the best advantage the king can allow the governor of *Malacca*, is to grant him one voyage of *Aquila*; because the *Brachmans* [Brahmans] and *Banians*[28] of *India* using to burn their dead with this sweet wood, the consumption of it is continually very great.

{Great wealth of *Cochin-China*.}

To conclude, *Cochin-China* abounds in rich mines of the most precious metals, especially of gold: and to reduce to a few words, what might be said more at large on the plenty of this country, I will conclude with that which the European merchants trading thither commonly say of it; which is, that in some measure the wealth of *Cochin-China* is greater than that of *China* itself; and we all know how rich that country is in all respects.

I ought in this place to say something of the beasts, whereof we before observed there was great variety and numbers in *Cochin-China*; but that I might not dilate too much, I will only treat of the elephants and abadas,[29] or rhinocero's, chiefly found here; of which many curious things may be said, which perhaps very many have not heard of.

---

[28] Also spelled *bania* or *baniya*, the word refers to one the Indian castes, a majority of whose members are occupied with trade or moneylending. They usually follow Vishnaism or Jainism, observing a strict vegetarian diet and believing in the transmigration of souls. The *banians* were a wonder for the Europeans when they discovered them. One of the Europeans working in India in the eighteenth century, in a lengthy tractate on the *banians*, whom he mistakingly calls a "sect" instead of a "caste," mentioned also their burial rituals. "First, they beare the dead body to a river's side appropriate to such purpose, where, setting the corps downe on the ground, ... After this, putting combustible matter to the body, accended and lighted by the help of sweete oyle, and aromatical odours shrewed thereon." See Henry Lord, "A Discussion of Two Foreign Company Sects in the East-Indies; viz. The Sect of the Banians, the Antient [*sic*] Natives of India and the Sect of the Persees, the Ancient Inhabitants of Persia," in *A Collection of voyages and Travels*, ed. Awnsham Churchill (London: John Walthoe et al., 1732), vol. 6, p. 319. Given the importance ascribed in this description to aroma during the funeral, we can see that aquila was a valuable commodity for them.

[29] Portuguese for "rhinoceros."

CHAPTER IV.

OF THE ELEPHANTS AND ABADAS, OR RHINOCERO'S.

{Elephants, their age.}

There are abundance of elephants in the woods of *Cochin-China*, which they make no use of, because they know not how to take, or tame them: therefore they bring them tame and well taught from *Cambogia*, a neighboring kingdom. These are twice as big as those of *India*, the round print of their feet they leave behind them, is not less than half a yard diameter; the two teeth striking out of the mouth, whereof ivory is made, are very often four yards and a half long; that is, those of the males, for those of the females are much shorter; by which it is easy to compute, how much those elephants of *Cochin-China* are bigger than those shewn about in *Europe*, whose teeth are not above three quarters of a yard long. The elephants live many years; and I asking, How old one might be? the driver of it told me, It was sixty years old before it came from *Cambogia*, and had lived forty [years] in *Cochin-China*: and having myself several times travelled upon elephants in that kingdom, I can relate many things that will seem strange, but yet are very true.

{They carry by land and water.}

An elephant generally carries thirteen or fourteen persons, who are thus disposed of: as we lay a saddle on a horse, so they clap a certain machine upon the elephant, which is like a coach, wherein there are four seats; it is fastened with chains under the elephant's belly, as a horse's saddle is girt. The coach has two doors on the sides, where six persons sit, three on a side; and another behind, where there are two more; and lastly, the *nayre*,[1] who supplies the place of a coachman, sits over the elephant's head, and guides him. Nor have I travelled in this manner by land only, but very often by sea too, crossing arms of it above a mile over: and it was wonderful to any body that knew it not before, to see such a vast great lump of flesh swimming under such a weight, so that it look'd like a boat rowing. True it is, the beast groan'd under the toil, occasioned by the unreasonable bulk of its own body, and the difficulty of breathing; and therefore to ease itself in that pain, it sucked in water with the trunk, and spouted it out so high, that it look'd like some great whale gliding across the ocean.

---

[1] *Nayre*, variously *Nayar* or *Nair*, refers to a caste of rulers and warriors, in what is now the state of Kerala on the Malabar coast of southwest India, that was encountered by Europeans beginning in the sixteenth century. Here, Borri uses this term for "mahout."

{They help up passengers.}

For the same reason of its mighty corpulency, it finds much difficulty in stooping down; and this being absolutely necessary for the conveniency of passengers to get up to, or down from the coach, he does it not but when commanded by the *nayre*; and if when he is kneeling, any one stops but never so little, upon ceremony, or any other account, he rises up, not having patience to continue in that posture, it is so painful.

Nor is it less wonderful to behold, how at the *nayre's* command he makes, as it were, a ladder of his limbs, for the greater conveniency of those that are to get up into the coach: the first step is his foot, which is high enough; for the second, he turns out the first joint above the same foot, distant enough from the other; for the third he bends his knee; for the fourth, his hip-bone, sticking out to that purpose; and from whence, he that gets up, lays hold of a chain fastened to the coach itself, where he seats himself.

{How they sleep.}

By this it plainly appears, how much they are mistaken, who say and write, that the elephant can neither kneel nor bow down; and that the only way to take him, is to cut the tree he leans against to sleep: for that falling together with the false support, and not being able to rise, he becomes a certain prey to him that lies in wait: which is all a fable, though it be true that he lies not down to sleep, that being an uneasy posture to him, as has been said, but sleeps always standing, with a continual agitation of his head.

{Their vast strength.}

Upon occasion of war or battle, they take off the roof of the coach, whence, as it were from a tower, the soldiers fight with muskets, arrows, and sometimes a small piece of cannon, the elephant being strong enough to carry it, his strength being answerable to all the rest: and I have been on one myself, that would carry vast weights upon his trunk; and another that lifted up a great piece of cannon with it; and another, who by himself launch'd ten galliots one after another, taking hold of them very dexterously with his teeth, and shoving them into the sea. I have seen others pull up large trees with as much ease as we do a cabbage or a lettice: with the same ease they throw down houses, leveling whole streets when they are commanded, either to do harm to an enemy in war, or to stop the fury of the flames upon occasion of any fire.

{The trunk.}

The trunk's length is proportionable to the height of the rest of his body, so that he can take up any thing off the ground with it without stooping. It is made of abundance of small sinews knit together, which makes it so pliable, that he can take up the least thing, and yet so strong and firm as we have shewn.

All the body is covered with a rough ash-colour skin. An elephant's usual day's journey is twelve leagues, and his motion has the same effect upon those that are not used to it, as that of a ship has at sea.

{Great sense of the elephant.}

I shall say nothing more wonderful concerning the elephant's docility, or aptness to learn, than what is generally reported; by which it will appear, there was reason to say, *No beast was more sensible*[2] *than the elephant;*[3] for it does such things as seem to be the acts of prudence and understanding. In the first place, though the *nayre* makes use of a certain instrument of iron a yard long, which has a hook at one end, wherewith he strikes and punches him, that he may be watchful, and mind what he bids him do, yet for the most part, he governs him only by words; by which it appears he understands the language very well; and some of them understand three or four that are very different according to the several countries they have lived in. Thus he that I travelled on, seemed to understand the language of *Cambogia*, whence he came, and that of *Cochin-China*, where he was. And who would not admire to hear the *nayre* discourse with his elephant, tell him the way and road he is to take, what place he is to pass by, what inn they are to lie at, what they shall there find to eat; and in short, give him an exact account of all that is to be done during the journey? and to see the elephant perform what he expects from him, as regularly as any man of good sense could do; insomuch, that when the elephant seems to have understood what place he was to go to, he takes the shortest cut to it, without minding the beaten road, rivers, woods, or mountains, but goes on, not doubting to overcome all difficulties, as in effect he does; for if any rivers be in the way, he either fords or swims them; if woods, he breaks the boughs of the trees, pulls them up whole, or cuts them with a sharp iron like a scythe, which to this purpose is fastened to the fore-part of the top of the coach, wherewith upon occasion having first laid hold of the boughs, he cuts them with his trunk, and makes himself way, cutting through the thickest forest, where it is easily known to have been an elephant that made the way; and all this he does with great ease and expedition, in obedience to the *nayre*.

{The elephant understands what is said.}

One only thing disturbs this creature, and puts it to great pain; which is, when a thorn, or such like thing, runs into the bottom of his foot, which is extraordinary soft and tender, and therefore he treads very cautiously, when he goes thro' places where there may be danger of such an accident. I went a journey once with seven or eight elephants in a company, and heard the *nayres*, every one warn his own beast, to look out carefully where he set his feet; for they were to pass over a sandy place about a mile in length, where thorns grew up among the sand; upon this intimation all the elephants held down their heads, and looking out, as it were, for some small thing that is lost, they walk'd that mile very cautiously, step by step; till being told there was no more to fear, they lifted up their heads, going on as they had done at first. Being come at night to the inn, the *nayres* sent the elephants to the wood to feed, without taking the coach off their backs; and I asking, why they did not take it down, they answerd, That the elephants fed on the boughs of trees, and therefore they left the coach on their backs, that they might cut them with that iron we said was before it. The next day being come, where there was no wood, every *nayre* carried a large

---

[2] i.e. "clever."

[3] In the original this phrase is in Latin: "Elephanto belluarum nulla prudentior." Christoforo Borri, *Relatione*, p. 38.

bundle of green boughs for his elephant. I took particular satisfaction to observe one, who more nimbly than the rest, laying hold of those boughs with his trunk, barked them with his teeth, and then eat them up as quick, and with as good a gust, as we would a fig, or any other sort of fruit. Discoursing the next day with my fellow-travelers, who were about twenty, I told them, how much I was pleased to see that elephant eat the boughs so cleverly. Then the *nayre*, by order of the elephant's master, called him by his name, which was *Gnin*, he being at some distance, but presently lifted up his head to give ear to what was said to him. *Remember,* said the *nayre, that father, the passenger that looked upon you yesterday, when you was eating; take such a bough as one of them was, and come before him, as you did yesterday.* No sooner had the *nayre* spoke the words, but the elephant came before me with a bough in his trunk, singling me out among all the company, shew'd it me, bark'd, and eat it; then inclining himself very low, he went away, as it were, laughing, making signs of joy and satisfaction; leaving me full of astonishment, to see that a beast should be so apt to understand, and do what it was commanded. Yet the elephant is obedient to none but the *nayre*, or his master: and he will only endure to see them get upon him; for if he should see any other person mount, there were danger that he would throw down the coach with his trunk, and kill him; and therefore when any body is to get up, the *nayre* generally covers his eyes with his ears, which are very large and ill shap'd.

{How they are corrected.}

If at any time the elephant does not obey so readily as he should, the *nayre* beats him cruelly on the middle of his forehead, standing himself all the while upright on his head: One time when I was upon him, with several others, the *nayre* beat him, as has been said, and every stroke he gave him, it looked as if we should have been all thrown down headlong. Generally they give him six or seven strokes on the middle of the forehead; but with such force, that the elephant quakes, and yet bears all patiently. There is only one time when he obeys neither the *nayre*, nor any other body; which is, when on a sudden he is inflamed with lust; for then, being quite besides himself, he bears with no body, but lays hold of the coach with all that are in it, killing, destroying, and beating every thing to pieces. But the *nayre* by certain signs discovers it a little before it comes, and getting down speedily with all the passengers, unloads, him, taking down the coach, and leaves him alone in some by-place, till that fury be over; after which, being sensible of his error, and as it were ashamed of himself, he goes with his head low to receive the blows that are to be given him, thinking he has deserved them.

{Now useless in war.}

Formerly the elephants were of great use in war, and those armies were formidable that carried great troops of them into the field; but since the *Portugueses* found out the way of using artificial fireworks to them, they are rather hurtful than otherwise; for not being able to endure those sparks of fire which get into their eyes, they betake themselves to flight, breaking their own armies, killing and confounding all that stands in their way.[4]

---

[4] Despite what Borri says here, elephants were trained to endure explosions and fireworks and remained important in Cochinchinese armies throughout the seventeenth century and later. Li Tana, *Nguyễn Cochinchina* (Ithaca: Cornell Southeast Asia Program Publications, 1998), pp. 41-

{The rhinocerous.}

The tame elephant fights with only two creatures, which are the wild elephant, and the abada, or rhinoceros; the latter it overcomes, by the first is generally conquered. The rhinoceros is a beast of shape between a horse and an ox, but as big as one of the smallest elephants, cover'd all over with scales, as it were so many plates of armour. He has but one horn in the middle of the forehead, which is straight and pyramidal, and his feet and hoofs are like those of an ox. When I was at *Nuocmon*,[5] a city in the province of *Pulucambi*, the governor went out to hunt a rhinoceros, that was in a wood near our dwelling place. He had with him above a hundred men, some a foot, and some a horseback, and eight or ten elephants. The rhinoceros came out of the wood, and seeing so many enemies, was so far from giving any tokens of fear, that it furiously encountered them all; who opened and making a lane, let the rhinoceros run through: It came to the rear, where the governor was a-top of his elephant, waiting to kill it; the elephant endeavors to lay hold with his trunk, but could not by reason of the rhinoceros's swiftness and leaping, that striving to wound the elephant with its horn. The governor knowing it could receive no hurt, by reason of the scales, unless they struck it on the side, waited till leaping it laid open the naked place, and casting a dart, dexterously struck it through from side to side, with great applause and satisfaction of all the multitude of spectators; who without any more to do, laid it upon a great pile of wood, and setting fire to it, leap'd and danc'd about, whilst the scales were burning, and flesh roasting, cutting pieces as it roasted, and eating them. Of the entrails, that is the heart, liver, and brain, they made a more dainty dish, and gave it to the governor, who was upon a rising ground, diverting himself with their merriment. I being present, obtained the hoofs of the governor[6]; which are looked upon to have the same quality and virtue, as the claws of the great beast (or the hoof of the elk) and so the horn is good against poison, as is the unicorn's.

---

43. See "Les Européens qui ont vu le vieux Hue: Cristoforo Borri," *Bulletin des Amis du Vieux Hué* 18, 3-4 (July-December 1931): 306, n. 36.

[5] Nước Mặn (Salt Water) was a port and the residence of the governor, the modern city of Qui Nhơn in Bình Định province.

[6] i.e., "obtained the hoofs" *from* the governor.

CHAPTER V.

OF THE QUALITIES, CUSTOMS, AND MANNERS OF THE COCHIN-CHINESES; OF THEIR WAY OF LIVING, THEIR HABIT AND CURES.

{Colour and disposition of body of the *Cochin-Chineses*.}

The *Cochin-Chineses* are in colour like the *Chineses*; that is, inclining to an olive-color: I mean those that are nearest the sea; for those up the inland, as far as *Tonchin*, are as white as the *Europeans*. The shape of their faces is exactly like the *Chineses*, with flat noses, little eyes, but of an indifferent stature, not so small as the *Japoneses*, nor so tall as the *Chineses*. Yet they are stronger and more active than either of them, and braver than the *Chineses*, but are out-done by the *Japoneses* in one thing, which is the contempt of life in dangers and battles; The *Japoneses* seeming to make no account of life, nor to apprehend the least fear of death.

{Their civility.}

The *Cochin-Chineses* are naturally the most courteous and affable of all the *Eastern* nations; and tho' on the one side they value themselves much upon their valour, yet on the other they look upon it as a great shame, to suffer themselves to be transported with passion. And whereas all the other *Eastern* nations, looking upon the *Europeans* as a profane people, do naturally abhor them, and therefore fly from us when first we come among them: in *Cochin-China* it falls out just contrary; for they strive who shall be nearest us, ask a thousand questions, invite us to eat with them, and in short use all manner of courtesy with much familiarity and respect. So it happened to me and my companions when we first came there, being as it were, among friends of an old standing. This is a very good disposition to facilitate the preaching of the gospel
.

{Liberality.}

This loving and easy disposition is the cause of much concord among them, they all treating one another as familiarly as if they were brothers or of the same family, tho' they have never known or seen one another before; and it would be look'd upon as a most vile action, if one man eating any thing, tho' never so little, should not share with all about him, giving every one a bit. They are also naturally kind and free-hearted to the poor, to whom it is customary among them never to deny an alms, when asked; and it would be reputed a great fault to deny it, as if it were due to them. Thus it happened, that some strangers escaping from a shipwreck in a port in *Cochin-China*, and not knowing the language to make known their want, but learning only this word *doii*[1] [Đói], which signifies *I am hungry*: when the natives saw strangers at their doors, crying out *doii*, as if the greatest misfortune in the world had befallen them, every one strove to be before another in giving them to eat; so that in a short time they gathered so much provision, that a ship being afterwards given them by the king to return to their country, they took such an affection to that country, where they found all things for their sustenance at such an easy rate, that not a man of them would go away; so that the captain of the ship was forced to drive them aboard with many blows and cuts, which he effectually did, loading the ship with the rice they had gathered only by going about, crying, *I am hungry*.

But as ready as the *Cochin-Chineses* are to give, so are they as apt, if not more, to ask any thing they see, so that as soon as ever they cast their eye on any thing that is new to them, and curious, they say, *Schin Mocaii*;[2] that is, *Give me one of these things*: and it is such a rudeness to refuse them, tho' the thing be rare and precious, that whosoever should do it, would be ever after looked upon as a vile person; so that a man must either hide, or be ready to give what he shews. A *Portuguese* merchant disliking this uncommon custom, as not used to it, resolved, since every one asked of him whatsoever he saw, to do the same with them: accordingly he came to a poor fisherman's boat, and laying hold of a pannier full of fish, in the country language said to him, *Schin Mocaii*; the honest man made no answer, but gave him all the pannier as it was, for him to carry home, as he did, admiring the liberality of the *Cochin-Chineses*; but taking compassion on the poor fisherman, he afterwards paid him the full value of it.

{Their breeding.}

The manner of breeding and civility the *Cochin-Chineses* use, is more or less the same with that of the *Chineses*, always punctually observing all niceties; we know these latter observe between superiors and inferiors, equals, and the respect due to ancient persons, ever preferring the eldest, of what degree soever, and giving them preference before the younger. Wherefore some of those gentlemen coming often a visiting to our house, tho' the interpreter told them, that a father we had there somewhat elder than the rest, was not our superior: yet they could never be brought to pay their respect to the young superior, before the old man. In every house, tho' never so poor, the *Cochin-Chineses* have three sorts of seats: the first and meanest, is a mat upon the bare floor, on which persons of equal quality sit, as those that are of the same family. The next is, a low stool, covered with a very fine mat; which is for persons of better account. The third is a couch about three quarters of a yard high, on which only the lords and governors of places sit, or persons dedicated to the divine service, and on this they always make our fathers sit.

This good nature and civility of the *Cochin-Chineses*, makes them so courteous to strangers, whom they allow to live according to their own laws, and to wear what clothes they please; and so they praise their customs, and admire their doctrine,

---

[1] In the original, it is written *doij*. In the modern orthography, it is spelled *đói*. Christoforo Borri, *Relatione*, p. 49.

[2] In the original, it is written *Scin mocaij*. See ibid., pp. 49-50. In the modern orthography it is *Xin một cái*.

frankly preferring them before their own; quite contrary to the *Chineses,* who despise all but their own customs and doctrine.

{Fashion of clothes.}

As for their habit, we have before observed, that it is the general custom in *Cochin-China* to wear silk; It only remains to speak of the fashion of their clothes. To begin with the women; I think the modestest garb of all *India*; for even in the hottest weather, they suffer no part of the body to be uncovered: they wear five or six petticoats one over another, all of several colours, the first reaches to the ground, which they trail along the ground with such gravity and state, that the tips of their toes are not seen; the second is half a span shorter than the first: the third shorter than that; and so one over another; so that all the several colors appear: and this is the women's habit from the waste [waist] downwards, for on their bodies they wear doublets checkered of several colours; over all they have a veil; but so thin, that tho' it covers them, yet it is transparent, and shews all their gaiety with modesty, and makes a beauteous majestic appearance. Their hair is loose, spreading over their shoulders, so long that it reaches to the ground, and the longer the greater beauty it is reckon'd. On their head they wear such a broad cap, that it covers all their face, so that they cannot see above four or five paces before them; and these caps are interwoven with silk and gold, according to the quality of the person. The women when met, are not obliged to any other return of civility, but to lift up the brims of their caps, so much, as their face may be seen. The man, instead of breeches, swathe themselves with a whole piece of stuff, putting on over them five or six long and large gowns all of fine silk, and of several colors, with wide sleeves, like those of the monks of the order of St. *Benedict*;[3] and these gowns, from the waste downwards, are all flashed curiously so that as a man moves he makes a shew of all those several colours together, and if any wind blows to lift them up, they look like peacocks with their fine feathers spread abroad.

{Hair and nails never cut.}

They let their hair grow as the women do, down to their heels, and wear the same sort of hats, or broad caps. Those who have any beard, and they are but few, never cut it; being in this like the *Chineses,* as they are in suffering the nails of their hands to grow, which the people of note never pare; this being a mark of distinction between them and the commonalty, who always keep them short, for the conveniency of their trades; whereas the gentry have them so long, that they cannot grasp any small thing in their hands. Nor can they approve of our fashion of cutting our hair and nails[4] being of opinion, that they were given by nature, as an ornament

---

[3] The order, also known as "black monks," was founded in the sixth century by St. Benedict (480?-547?).

[4] Jean Koffler, who spent several years in Cochinchina in the mid-eighteenth century, in his work *Historica Cochinchinae descriptio,* published in 1803, observed that "short hair was the sign of a commoner"; Jean Koffler, "Description historique de la Cochinchine," *Revue Indochinoise* XVI,12 (December 1911): 582. Marini, a missionary in Tonkin in the mid-seventeenth century, wrote: "Men as well as women wear their hair rolled up because they lived under the Chinese domination…, but being liberated from their captivity to mark their liberty, as they say,

to man: so that some discourse arising once concerning hair, they started an objection, which was not so easy to answer at sight, saying: *If the Saviour of the world, whom in your actions you profess your selves to imitate, wore his hair long, after the manner of the* Nazarites, *as you your selves do affirm, and shew by your pictures, why do not you do so too?* Adding, *That our Saviour's wearing long hair, demonstrated it to be the better fashion.* But at last they were satisfy'd with the answer we made, that this imitation did not consist in the outward dress.[5]

{The scholars.}

The scholars and doctors are somewhat more gravely clad, without so many colours and flashes, and therefore cover all their gowns with one of black damask. They also wear a thing like a stole about their necks and a blew [blue] silk maniple on their arms, covering their heads with caps made after the manner of mitres.

Both men and women carry fans in their hands, rather for ornament than use, and they are not unlike to those the women in *Europe* use. For mourning, as we *Europeans* use black, they wear white. They never uncover their heads in saluting, that being looked upon as an uncivil action. Wherein they agree with the *Chineses*, among whom that custom is reputed so unmannerly, that to comply with them in this particular, the fathers of the society were forced to obtain leave of pope *Paul* the fifth,[6] to celebrate the holy sacrifice of the mass covered. In short, the *Cochin-Chineses* wear neither shoes nor stockings, only saving their feet with leather soles fastened across the toes with silk, like sandals; nor do they think it indecent to go quite barefoot; and though going shod or unshod, they are apt to dirty their feet, they value it not, there being in every house at the door of the chief room, a large pan of clean water, in which they wash their feet, leaving those soles or sandals they use there, to take them again when they go away, because they cannot then dirt their feet, all the floors being covered with mats.

The *Cochin-Chineses* not being so fond of their own customs, as to despise those of strangers, as the *Chineses* do, our fathers in those parts have no occasion to change their habit, wherein they differ but little from the generality of all *India*. They wear a thin cotton cassock, which they call *Ehingon*, and is generally blue, without any cloak, or other upper-garment. They have no shoes,[7] neither after the *European*, nor country [local] fashion; the first they cannot get, because there is no body knows how to make them; and the latter they cannot endure, because of the pain it is to any body that is not used to it, to have his toes spread at a distance from one another, by

---

against the Chinese sentiments, they leave their hair hang lose neglectfully." Gio. Filippo de Marini, *Relation nouvelle et curieuse des royaumes de Tunquin et de Lao*, pp. 70-1.

[5] A similar problem existed in China with the advent of Buddhism, when Buddhism was considered an alien religion. One of the objections that the Chinese had against the Buddhists was that they shaved their heads, thus altering their appearance given to them by God and their parents. Marini describes the situation between the Buddhist monks and lay people in Tonkin as follows: "Bonzes are shaved-head by some vanity and presumption. Seculars, they say, whose actions are mortal and of no consideration, who do not have any merits, should, in fact, have their hair long so that the Idol could pull them easily to Heaven; but not them [bonzes], whose proper merits will serve them as wings to rise [there]." Marini, *Relation nouvelle*, p. 71.

[6] 1550-1621, elected to be Pope in 1605.

[7] The original reads *non usano però scarpe* (p. 57): "but they do not use shoes."

reasons of the buttons that fasten them on, and therefore they choose as the less evil, to go quite barefoot, though it exposes them to continual pains in the bowels, especially at first, by reason of the dampness of the country, and their not being used to it. True it is, that in time nature complies, and the skin grows so hard, that it is no pain to walk upon stones or briars. When I returned to *Macao*, I could not endure shoes, thinking them a weight and encumbrance to my feet.

{Their diet.}

The chief sustenance of the *Cochin-Chineses* is rice; and it is wonderful, that tho' the country abounds in flesh, fowl, fish, and fruit, of so many several sorts, yet when they eat, they first fill their belly with rice, and then taste of other things, as it were for fashion-sake. They make more account of rice than we do of bread, and that it may not clog them, they eat it alone without any seasoning of salt, sugar, oil, or butter, but boiled in so much water as will keep it from burning to, so that the grain remains whole, only soften'd and moisten'd. For this very reason that the rice is not seasoned, it is the easier of digestion, and therefore they that live upon rice, as they do in the east, commonly eat it at least four times a day, and a great quantity of it to support nature. The *Cochin-Chineses* eat sitting cross-legg'd on the ground, with a round table before them breast-high, with mouldings, or adorned with silver or gold, according to the people's quality or wealth. It is not very large; because the custom is for every man to have one to himself; so that at a feast, as many guests as there are, so many tables are provided, and the same is done when they dine privately; only, sometimes man and wife, or father and son, will make a shift with the same table. They neither use knives nor forks; of the first they have no need, because every thing is brought up from the kitchen cut into small bits; the place of the last is supplied by two little sticks, wherewith they neatly and very readily take up any thing; nor have they any need of napkins, for they never foul their hands, nor touch any thing with them.

{Their treats.}

There are frequent invitations among neighbours, and at these entertainments they provide other sorts of dishes than what we have hitherto spoke of; for they make no account of rice, supposing every man has enough of that at home; and tho' he that treats be never so poor, he does not come off with credit, unless every guest's table be served with at least an hundred dishes; and it being the custom to invite all their friends, kindred, and neighbours, there is no feast where there is less than thirty, forty, fifty, sometimes a hundred, and even two hundred guests: I was once myself at a solemn entertainment, at which no less than two thousand were feasted, and therefore these banquets must be made in the country, that there may be room for so many tables. Nor must any body admire that the tables being small, they be furnished with a hundred dishes at least; for upon these occasions they very curiously make frames of sugar canes on the table, on which they dispose of the said dishes; and there must be in them all the varieties of meat the country produces, as well flesh as fish, and butcher's meat, as fowl, wild and tame creatures, with all sorts of fruit the season affords; for if but one were wanting, it would be a great fault in the entertainer, and they would not count it a feast. The men of quality that are invited eat first, being waited on by their chief servants. When the masters have tasted of all they like best, these same principal servants take their places, and eat, being waited on by the inferior sort; then these succeed in their places; and because all of them are not able to consume such plenty, and according to custom all the dishes must be emptied; when these are satisfied, then the very meanest servants of every great man come in, and do not only eat their belly full, but put up all the fragments in bags they carry for that purpose, and carry them home, where they merrily divide it among the boys, and other mean fry, and so the feast ends.

{Their drink.}

Cochin-China produces no grapes, and therefore instead of wine they drink a liquor distilled from rice, which tastes like brandy, and resembles it in colour and harshness, spirit and briskness, and they have such plenty of it, that all people in general drink as much as they will of it, and are as drunk as people are among us with wine. Graver persons mix that liquor with some other water distilled from *calamba*, which gives it a delicious smell, and is a delicate composition.

Between meals they drink hot water, wherein they boil the root of an herb they call *chià*,[8] from which the liquor takes name. It is cordial, and helps to dispel humours from the stomach, and advance digestion. The *Japoneses* and *Chineses* use such a sort of drink, only that in *China*, instead of the root, they boil the leaves of the herb; and in *Japan*, a powder made of the same leaves; but the effect is the same, and they call it *chià*.

Amidst this great plenty of meat, and abundance of provisions, it is incredible how much hunger and thirst we *Europeans* endure; not so much for want of food, as because we are not used to that diet, nature finding a very great miss of bread and wine; and I believe the *Cochin-Chineses* would be in the same condition, should they come into *Europe*, where they would be deprived of their usual sustenance of rice, tho' they had plenty of other delicate provisions. To this purpose I will not omit to relate what happened to us with a governor of *Cochin-China*; he being a friend of ours, was invited by us to eat at our house; and the more to shew our affection, we endeavoured to have several dishes dressed for him after the *European* manner. He sat down to table, and when we expected he should acknowledge our kindness, commend the cookery, and thank us for the rarity, because we had been at much trouble about it; when he had tasted them all, he could not eat of any one, though out of civility he strove against his stomach; and we were forced to dress more meat after the country fashion, the best we could, whereof he afterwards eat very favourily, to his own and our satisfaction. Yet providence does not neglect a thousand ways to support those that undergo these hardships for the preaching of the gospel, finding means, even in this world, to requite what they suffer for the sake of God, as happens in this particular of food, as was before-said of going bare-foot; for by degrees nature grows familiar with it, and comes to be so habituated to the custom of

---

[8] *Trà*, tea. Tea did not become known in Europe until rather late, in the late sixteenth and early seventeenth centuries. It was the Dutch who introduced it to Europe. Tea was an exotic product for the first Europeans. Alexandre de Rhodes commented on it: "In my opinion one of the things that contributes most to the health of these people who so often reach a ripe old age is tea, used very widely throughout the Orient, and which is beginning to be known in France through the medium of the Dutch, who bring it from China and sell it in Paris for thirty francs a pound, which they bought in that country for eight to ten cents." Alexandre de Rhodes, *Rhodes of Vietnam*, trans. Solange Hertz (Westminster, MD: The Newman Press, 1966), p. 31.

the country, that it looks strange when to return to its first ways. This happen'd to me, who, when I returned from thence, coveted nothing but the rice of *Cochin-China*, which I thought satisfied me more than any other thing.

{Physicians.}

As for physicians, and their way of practice, there are abundance of doctors, not only *Portugueses*, but natives; and it often is experimentally known, that the country physicians easily cure several diseases, which the *European* physicians know not what to do with; so it sometimes happens, that after our physicians have given over a patient, they call one of the country, and he cures him.

{Way of practice.}

The physicians of the country use this sort of practice; being come to the patient's bedside, they stay a little to settle themselves after the motion of coming; then they feel the pulse for a long while together, very attentively, and with much consideration; after which they usually say, You have such a distemper; and if incurable, they honestly say, I have no cure for this disease; which is a sign the patient will die. If they find the disease curable, they say, I have a medicine that will cure him; and I will do it in so many days. Then they agree what they are to have if they cure the sick man, bargaining the best they can, and sometimes they draw up writings to bind the contract. After this the physician himself prepares the medicine, without the help of an apothecary; for which reason there are none in the country; and this they do, that they may not discover the secret of the art they work; and because they will not trust another to put together the ingredients they prescribe. If the patient recovers within the time appointed, as generally happens, he pays the price agreed on; if he miscarries, the physician loses his labor and medicines.

{Medicines.}

The medicines they give are not like ours, which cause a loathing, and are laxative; but theirs are palatable as their broths, and nourishing without any other sustenance, which makes them give the patient several doses in a day, as we give broth at so many hours interval; and these do not alter the course of nature, but only help the usual operations of nature, dispersing the peccant humours, without wracking the patient.

{A notable story.}

I remember a passage worth the relating in this place: A *Portuguese* falling sick, sent for the *European* physicians; who having used their endeavors, gave him over. When they were gone, a physician of the country was called; who undertook to cure him in so many days, strictly injoining him, whilst he was under his hands, to have a care of having to do with women, upon pain of certain death, from which the virtue of his medicine could not deliver him. They agreed upon the price, and the physician undertook to cure him in thirty days. The patient took the medicines prescribed him, and in a few days found himself so well recovered, that he was not afraid to transgress the physician's injunction; who coming to visit him, by the alteration of his pulse discovered the sick man's incontinency, and bid him prepare to die, because there was no cure for him; but that he should pay him his money, since it was none of his fault that he must die. The case was try'd; the sick man was adjudged to pay; and so he died.

{Bleeding.}

Bleeding is also used, but not so much as in *Europe*, nor is it done with a steel lancet; but they have abundance of goose-quills, in which they fix some bits of fine porcelane, made sharp, and shaped like the teeth of a saw, some bigger, some less, of several sizes. When they are to let blood, they apply one of these quills to the vein, proportionable to the bigness of it, and giving it a fillip with the finger, open the vein, only so much of the porcelane entering as is requisite; and what is most wonderful, when they have drawn the blood, they use no fillet or binding to stop it; but wetting their thumb with spittle they press the orifice, so that the flesh returning to the place whence it was parted, the blood is stopt, and runs out no more; which I suppose to proceed from the manner of opening the vein, as it were sawing it with that porcelane full of teeth, and therefore it closes again the easier.

{Surgeons.}

There are also surgeons, who have some wonderful secrets, whereof I will give but two instances, one practiced upon my self, the other upon one of our brothers, my companion: I happened to fall from a very high place, with my breast against the corner of a stone, whereupon I presently began to spit blood, and had a wound in my breast outwardly.

{Great cures.}

We applied some medicines after our *European* manner, but to no purpose. A surgeon of the country came and took a quantity of a certain herb like that we call mercury, and making it into a plaister, laid it on my breast, then he caused some of that herb to be boiled for me to drink, and made me eat the same herb raw; and thus in a few days perfectly cured me. I, to make another experiment, caused the leg of a hen to be broke in several places, and making a plaister as he had done for the same herb, bound it upon the broken leg, and in a few days it was whole and sound.

A scorpion bit a brother of ours, my companion, in the neck; and in that kingdom the bite of a scorpion is mortal. All his throat swelled immediately, and we were about giving him extreme unction. A surgeon was sent for, who immediately set a pot of rice a boiling in nothing but fair water, then clapping the pot to the brother's feet, covered him and it close with cloths, that the steam might not go out, and as soon as the said steam and hot smoke of the rice came up to the place where the bite was, the brother felt the pain assuage, the swelling in his throat fell, and he remained as sound as if nothing had ailed him.

Many other instances might be added, but I shall only say, that the medicines in those parts have a greater virtue than when they come to us; and particularly I can affirm, that I brought with me a small cask of *rhubarb,* which was extraordinary good there, and when I came into *Europe,* having spent two years by the way, I found it so changed, that I scarce knew it myself, so that those medicines lose much of their virtue in bringing from those countries to our parts.

CHAPTER VI.

OF THE CIVIL AND POLITICAL GOVERNMENT OF THE COCHIN-CHINESES.

I will give a brief account of as much as may suffice for the reader's information; for it would be too tedious, and from the purpose of this my short relation, to discourse of every thing in particular. The government of *Cochin-China*, in general, is a medium betwixt those of *China* and *Japan*: for whereas the *Japoneses* make less account of learning than military knowledge: and on the contrary, the *Chineses* attribute all to learning, taking little notice of warlike affairs.[1] The *Cochin-Chineses* following the example of neither, equally incourage learning, and skill in war, according as occasion offers; sometimes preferring the soldier, and sometimes the scholar, and so repulsing them as appears most convenient.

{Learning.}

In *Cochin-China* there are several[2] universities, in which there are professors, scholars, and degrees conferred by way of examination, in the same manner as is practiced in *China*; the same sciences being taught, and the same books and authors read;[3] that is, *Zinfu*, or *Confucius*, as the *Portugueses* call them;[4] which are authors of such profound learning, and in such esteem and reputation amongst them, as *Aristotle*[5] is among us, being much ancienter than he. These books of theirs are full of erudition, of stories, of grave sentences, or proverbs, and such like things, for the directing a civil life, as are *Seneca*,[6] *Cato*,[7] and *Cicero*,[8] among us; and they spend

---

[1] This is a very interesting observation as it reflects Borri's knowledge of the governments in both China and Japan.

[2] In the original Italian, *molto*, "many." Borri, *Relatione*, p. 70.

[3] While the government in the North was mostly built on the civil service, the Nguyễn government relied heavily on the military, especially during the first period of its existence, since they were at war with the Trịnh lords. The civil service exams were held there on a less frequent and less regular basis than in the North, but they were still based on the same Confucian Classics and commentaries to them, as in the North.

[4] This sentence is obscure as it is not clear whether *Zinfu* is the same person as Confucius or these are two different people. On the one hand, "or" implies that they are the same person; on the other hand, Borri uses the plural for "authors" and uses the pronoun "them." The name *Zinfu* is a mystery.

[5] 384-322 BCE. Greek philosopher and mathematician.

[6] Lucius Annaeus Seneca (3-4 BCE-65 CE). A Spanish-born Roman philosopher, a tutor and later advisor to Emperor Nero (r. 54-68), one of the most famous Stoic philosophers.

many years in learning the true sense of the phrases, words, characters, and hieroglyphics, they are writ in; but that they most value is moral philosophy, or ethicks, economy, and policy. It is comical to see and hear them, when they are studying, read and repeat their lessons in such a tone as if they were singing, which they do to use themselves to it, and give every word its proper accents, which are many, every one expressing a several thing: and therefore one would think, that to converse with them, a man must understand the grounds of music.

The language they generally speak, is different from that they read and teach at the schools, and which their books are writ in: as among us the vulgar language differs from the *Latin* used in the schools. Wherein they differ from the *Chineses*, who, if they are learned, or noble, always use the same language, which they call of *mandarines*; that is, of doctors, judges, and governors, and the characters they use in writing and printing their books, are above eight thousand, all differing from one another. And for this reason the fathers of the society spend eight, and even ten years, in studying the *Chinese* books, before they can be masters, and go abroad to converse with them. But the *Cochin-Chineses* have reduced the characters to three thousand, which they generally make use of: and these are enough to express themselves in their harangues, letters, petitions, memorials, and such things which do not belong to printed books; [9] for those of necessity must be in *Chinese* characters. The *Japoneses* have been more ingenious, who, tho' in all that belongs to books, whether written or printed, they agree with the *Chineses*, yet for common uses have found out forty-eight letters, wherewith they express whatsoever they please, as well as we do with our alphabet: and yet the *Chinese* characters are in such esteem even among the *Japoneses*, that these forty-eight letters, notwithstanding the use they are of above the others, are contemned in comparison of them; insomuch, that in scorn they call them women's letters.[10]

The ingenious invention of printing was found out in *China*,[11] and *Cochin-China*, long before it was in *Europe*: but not in such perfection: for they do not compose joining letters and characters, but with a graver, penknife, or such instrument, cut and carve the characters upon a stone as they will have them in their books: on this board so carved they lay their paper, and print it off, as we in *Europe* do copper-plates, or the like.

Besides these books of morals, they have others, which contain things they account sacred; as for instance, the creation and beginning of the world: of the rational souls of demons: of idols, and of their several sects. These books are called

---

[7] Marcus Porcius Priscus (234-149 BCE). A Roman orator, statesman, and writer, called Cato for his skillfulness (from Latin *catus*—sharp intellect). He advocated a return to conservative values of Roman morality.

[8] Marcus Tullius Cicero (106-43 BCE). A Roman orator and statesman.

[9] Borri is here referring to the demotic Vietnamese writing called *nôm*.

[10] The reference is to the *hiragana* system of writing composed of forty-eight characters. "*Hira* means 'commonly used,' 'easy,' 'rounded.'" Campbell et al., eds., *The Japan Encyclopedia* (Tokyo: Kodansha, 1993), p. 731. *Hiragana* was developed from simplified Chinese characters. "In its early [ninth century] forms, *hiragana* was used by women [who were not permitted to learn the Chinese script], while the unsimplified *kanji* were used by men; for this reason, the earliest *hiragana* was also called *onnade*, 'women's hand.' By the end of the ninth century, *onnade* ceased to be a system limited to women … ." Ibid.

[11] Ninth century.

Sayc Kim, to distinguish them from the profane, which they call *Sayc Chiu*.[12] Of the doctrine of their sacred books, we shall treat in the second part of this account, where the subject will be more suitable.

{The language.}

Though the language of the *Cochin-Chineses* be in one respect like that of the *Chineses*, both of them using all monosyllables, delivered in several tones and accents; yet they utterly differ in the word itself, the *Cochin-Chineses* being more full of vowels, and consequently softer and sweeter, more copious in tones and accents, and therefore more harmonious. The language of *Cochin-China* is, in my opinion, the easiest of any, for those that have a musical ear, to take the tones and accents; for it has no variety by way of conjugation of verbs, or declination of nouns, but one and the same word, with the addition of an adverb, or pronoun, signifies the present, the preterit, and future tenses, the singular number, and the plural; and in fine, serves for all moods, tenses, and persons, and the diversity of numbers and cases. For instance, this word, *To have*, which in the [Cochin] *Chinese* language[13] is *Co* [*Có*], by only adding a pronoun, serves all occasions, saying, *I have, Thou have, He have*; the name of the person making that diversity, which we express by altering the termination, thus, *I have, Thou Hast, He has*. In the same manner they make the several tenses; saying, for the present, *I now have*; for the preterit, *I heretofore have*; and for the future, *I hereafter have*: And so without ever altering the word *Co*; by which it appears how easily this language may be learned: as it happened to me, who in six months understood so much, that I could discourse, and even hear their confessions, tho' not so perfectly, for it requires at least four years to be a master [*This variety of moods and tenses, appears better by the* Latin, *or other languages, than in* English, *where we use much the same method, as he represents in* Cochin-China; *our variations the same, being but few, as to instance in the same word,* I have, You have, We have, They have, I shall have, May we have: *and so in this, and many others.*][14]

{Rewards for military men.}

But to return to our relation: I was saying, that the *Cochin-Chineses* reward not only the learned with dignities, employments, and revenues; but that they make great account of good soldiers, in which particular they act differently from us; for instead of assigning brave commanders, some land, earldom, or marquisate, as a reward of their valour, they allot him such a number of people, and vassals, belonging to the king himself, who, whatsoever part of the kingdom they live in, are obliged to own him as their lord, to whom they have been assigned by the king,

[12] Sayc Kim is Sách Kinh in modern spelling, denoting "sutras" or classic Confucian books. As for *Sayc Chiu*, its original is more uncertain. It is possible that *Sayc Chiu* stands for Sách Chữ, meaning "book in letters or in characters" to distinguish between the sacredness of the *kinh* and the mundaneness of the *chữ*, while also highlighting the difference between classical Chinese in the first case (as *kinh* is a Chinese word) and the demotic Vietnamese (*nôm*) in the second case, as *chữ* is vernacular. It should be noted that *chữ* can signify any script, including Chinese, as for example in the compound *chữ Hán*, "classical Chinese."

[13] In the original it is "in Cochin-Chinese language." See Christoforo Borri, *Relatione*, p. 75. The English translation dropped "Cochin."

[14] This bracketed comment is from the translator.

being bound upon all occasions to serve him with their weapons, and to pay him all those duties they before paid to the king himself; and therefore, as we say, such a one is lord, earl, or marquess of such a place; they say, such a one is a man of fifty, such a one of a thousand men, to such a one the king has added three thousand, to such a one two thousand; their dignity, wealth, and grandeur increasing by the addition of many vassals. We shall speak of the wars of this kingdom in the next chapter.

{Trials at law.}

It remains that we say somewhat worth being known of the civil government. In the first they govern rather after a military manner, than by judges, counsellors, and lawyers, and their formalities; the vice-roys and governors of provinces performing that function: for every day they give publick audience for four hours daily, in a large court within their own palace, two hours in the morning, and two after dinner. Hither all suits and complaints are brought, and the vice-roy, or governor, sitting on a tribunal raised like a balcony, hears every man in his turn; and these governors being generally men of sound judgment, capacity, and experience, they easily discover the truth of the matter by the questions they put, and much more by the common consent of the stander-by, which is gathered by the applause they give the plaintiff, or defendant, and accordingly they immediately, without delay, give judgment with a loud voice, which is immediately executed without any demur, or appeal, whether the sentence be death, banishment, whipping, or fine, every crime being punish'd as the law appoints.

{False witnesses, how punished.}

The crimes generally try'd and severely punished are many, but they are particularly rigid against false witnesses, thieves, and adulterers. The first of these being convicted of having given false evidence, are themselves indispensably condemned, as if they themselves had committed the crime they accuse others of. And if the crime they alleged deserved death, they are sentenced to die: and experience teaches, that this way of trial is very proper to find out the truth.

{Thieves.}

Thieves, if the theft be considerable, are beheaded; if small, as for example, a hen, for the first offense they have a finger cut off, for the second another finger, for the third an ear, and for the fourth the head.

{Adulterers.}

Adulterers, both men and women, indifferently are cast to the elephants to be killed, which is done thus: They lead the criminal out into the field, where in the presence of an infinite number of people flocking together, he is set in the middle, with his hands and feet bound, near an elephant, to whom the condemned person's sentence is read, that he may execute every part of it orderly; first, that he lay hold of, grasp, and hold him fast with his trunk, and so hold him in the air, shewing him to all the company; then, that he toss him up, and catch him upon the points of his teeth, that his own weight may strike them through him; that then, he dash him against the ground; and lastly, that he bruise and crush him to pieces with his feet: All which is exactly performed by the elephant, to the great terror and amazement of the spectators, who are taught by this punishment, at another man's cost, what fidelity is due between married persons.

{Matrimony.}

Since we are upon this point of matrimony, it will not be from the purpose to deliver some farther particulars concerning it, before we conclude this chapter. The *Cochin-Chineses*, though heathens, never use to contract matrimony within those degrees forbid by the laws of God and nature, nor within the first degree of the collateral line of brothers and sisters. In other degrees, matrimony is lawful to every man with only one woman; though rich men use to have many concubines, under pretense of grandeur and generosity, looking upon it as covetousness, not to have as many as every man's income will conveniently maintain; and these are called second, third, fourth, and fifth wives, and so on, according to every one's rank, all which wait upon the first, which is accounted, and really is the true wife, whose business it is to choose the others for her husband. But these marriages of theirs are not indissoluble, the laws of *Cochin-China* allowing of divorces, but not at the will of either party, it being first requisite, that the person suing for it, convict the other of many offenses; which being made out, it is lawful to dissolve the first marriage, and marry again. The husbands bring the portion, and leave their own houses to go to the wife's; upon whose fortunes they live, the women managing all the household affairs, and governing the family, whilst the husband lives idle at home, hardly knowing what there is in the house, satisfied that they have meat and clothes.

CHAPTER VII.

OF THE POWER OF THE KING OF COCHIN-CHINA, AND OF THE WARS HE HAS IN HIS KINGDOM.

{Their skill in cannon and small arms.}

I took notice at the beginning of this account, that *Cochin-China* was a province of the great kingdom of *Tonchin*, usurp'd by the grandfather of the king now reigning; who being made governor of it, rebelled against the said king of *Tonchin*; to which he was not a little encouraged, by having in a short time got together a great many pieces of cannon, of the wrecks of several *Portuguese* and *Dutch* ships, cast away upon those rocks, which being taken up by the country people, there are above sixty of the biggest, at this time, to be seen in the king's palace. The *Cochin-Chineses* are now become so expert in managing artillery, that they perform it better than the *Europeans*, practicing continually to shoot at a mark, with such success, that being proud of their skill, as soon as any *European* ship arrives in their ports, the king's gunners challenge ours, who being sensible that they cannot stand in competition with them, as near as they can, avoid this trial of skill, being convinced by experience, that they will hit any thing as exactly with a cannon, as another shall do with a firelock; which they are also very expert at, often drawing out into the field to exercise.

{Gallies, scymitars, and horses.}

Another great encouragement to rebellion, was, his having above a hundred gallies, which rendering him formidable at sea, and the artillery by land, he easily compass'd his designs against the king of *Tonchin*. Besides, by reason of the constant trade in *Japan*, there were in *Cochin-China* abundance of *Catana's*,[1] which are scymitars made in *Japan*, and excellently tempered. And all the country abounding in horses, which tho' small, are handsome and mettlesome, on which they fight, casting darts, and daily exercise themselves.

{King's power.}

The power of this king is so great, that whensoever he pleases, he can bring 80,000 fighting men into the field, and yet is always in fear of the king of *Tonchin*, whose power is four times as great; to whom, for quietness sake, he, by agreement, pays a tribute, of all such things as his kingdom affords, and are useful for that of *Tonchin*, particularly of gold, silver, and rice; furnishing, besides all this, plank and

---

[1] *Catana* is a Japanese word for scimitar, a curved sword.

timber for building of gallies. And for the same reason he was about entering into a league with the fugitive son [Mạc Kinh Cung] of the late king [Mạc Mậu Hợp],[2] who lorded it in the utmost province of *Tonchin*, which borders upon *China* [Cao Bằng],[3] that in case he succeeded, and became master of *Tonchin, Cochin-China* might remain free from all tribute and acknowledgment.[4]

For the better understanding hereof, it is to be observed, that when I was in *Cochin-China*, that kingdom [Tonkin] was in the possession not of the precedent king [Mạc Mậu Hợp], but[5] the tutor or governor [Trịnh Tùng][6] of that son [Mạc Kinh Cung], who made his escape from the said governor to save his life. The said prince [Mạc Kinh Cung] lived like a fugitive, in the farthest province adjoining to *China* [Cao Bằng]; where being known to be what he was, that is, the late king's son, he was received by that people as their sovereign lord, and by his good government he had so strengthened himself, that his tutor [Trịnh Tùng], already declared king of *Tonchin*,[7] was much afraid, seeing him [Mạc Kinh Cung] grow so great, lest he should agree with the king of *Cochin-China*, who is on the opposite side, to catch him [Trịnh Tùng] between them, and expel him his unjust possession.[8] He therefore every year form'd a considerable army to destroy the aforesaid prince [Mạc Kinh Cung], but always to no purpose, because the army being of necessity to march five or six days, through a country where there is no other water to drink, but that of some

---

[2] Ruled from 1562 to 1592; the last king of the Mạc dynasty to rule from Hanoi.

[3] In 1592 the Mạc were driven from the capital city into the northern provinces of Tonkin and concentrated in the northernmost provinces of Cao Bằng and Lạng Sơn. King Mạc Mậu Hợp was captured. His son Mạc Kinh Cung (r. 1593-1625) was proclaimed king to succeed him. With the help of the Ming dynasty in China, Cao Bằng was secured for the Mạc. They remained there until 1667. Trần Trọng Kim, *Việt Nam Sử Lược* (Short History of Vietnam) (Nhà Xuất Bản Văn Hóa Thông Tin, 1999), pp. 302-6.

[4] Borri refers to contacts between the Nguyễn and the Mạc families. While we do not have historical evidence corroborating this statement, it is only logical to assume that after 1600, when the Nguyễn began to be estranged from the Trịnh, who were based in Hanoi, they would approach the Mạc in search of an ally against the Trịnh.

[5] This is an imprecise translation of the original, which reads . . . *stava in possesso de Regno del Tonchin, non il figlio del Re passato, ma* . . . (". . . already in possession of the Kingdom of Tonkin, not the son of the preceding king, but . . ."). Borri, *Relatione*, p. 83. The English translation gives two variations for the Italian *Rè passato*: in the previous paragraph it was translated as "late king" and here it is "precedent king." But Borri definitely implies one and the same king, Mạc Mậu Hợp, and uses the same words in reference to him.

[6] In the original, Borri uses the Italian word *aio*, which means "tutor." See Borri, *Relatione*, p. 83. Borri mistakenly refers here to the warlord Trịnh Tùng (r. 1570-1623)—who was a leading figure in defeating the Mạc in 1592—as the tutor of the "son who made his escape," conflating Mạc Kinh Cung with King Lê Thế Tong (r. 1573-1599). Lê Thế Tong ascended the throne at the age of seven, and Trịnh Tùng was the one who really governed the country as if he were the young king's "tutor." The Trịnh family used the Lê kings as figureheads until the end of the dynasty in 1788.

[7] Borri conflates the Mạc with the Lê and thinks that the Trịnh occupy the throne in Hanoi.

[8] As it has been said above, the Trịnh lords were the real rulers, or in Borri's terms "kings," of Tonkin. The Nguyễn lords accused the Trịnh of usurping the Lê king's royal authority. The Mạc had been expelled into the northern mountains from their possession of the capital in the 1590s by an alliance of the Trịnh and Nguyễn; however, the Nguyễn subsequently established themselves on the southern coast in defiance of the Trịnh. Continuing warfare between the Trịnh and Mạc, combined with the increasingly hostile relations between the Trịnh and Nguyễn, which broke into open warfare shortly after Borri departed Vietnam, served to make natural allies of the Nguyễn and the Mạc against the Trịnh.

rivers coming from the enemies country, the army always found it poison'd by the prince's party, with a sort of herb, the effect whereof was such, that it destroyed both men and horses; which obliged him always to retire after much trouble and expence cast away.[9]

{Wars in Cochin-China.}

The military discipline, and art of war, in *Cochin-China*, is almost the same as in *Europe*, the same form being observed in drawing up, fighting, and retiring. This king has generally war in three parts of his kingdom: First, he is always upon his defense against the king of *Tonchin*, who, as has been said, continually threatens and assaults his frontiers, and therefore the king of *Cochin-China* has his residence in *Sinuua*, the extreme part of his dominions, the better to oppose him, and march his forces towards the confines of *Tonchin*, which is a powerful province, and generally under experienced and martial governors.[10]

The next is a sort of civil war, raised by two of his own brothers, who aiming to be equal in command and power, not satisfied with what has been allotted them, have rebelled against him, and craving succours from *Tonchin*, gave him perpetual trouble. Whilst I lived in those parts, they having got some pieces of cannon, which they carried upon elephants, fortified themselves so well upon the frontiers, that the king's army marching against them, was in the first engagement routed, with the loss of 3,000 men; but coming to a second battle, the king's brothers lost all they had gained before, being both made prisoners; and they had both immediately lost their lives, had not his majesty's natural clemency and brotherly affection prevailed, and taken place of his anger, so far as to spare their lives, yet so as to keep them prisoners.[11]

---

[9] It should be noted that this passage, starting from the previous paragraph with the words "And for the same reason he was about entering into a league with the fugitive son of the late king," has been completely omitted from the Vietnamese translation of Borri's work; see Cristoforo Borri, *Xứ Đàng Trong Nam 1621* (Cochinchina. Year 1621), trans. Hồng Nhuệ, Nguyễn Khắc Xuyên, Nguyễn Nghị (Hochiminh: Nhà Xuất Bản Thành Phố Hồ Chí Minh, 1998), p. 84. We can hardly attribute it to a random omission, but it rather shows that this digression into early-seventeenth-century Vietnamese history depicting possible connections between the Nguyễn and the Mạc rulers and the reference to the Mạc being "received by that people as their sovereign lord, and by his good government" is still a highly censored issue in Vietnamese historiography.

[10] See the next footnote. Shortly after Borri's departure from Cochinchina, the Trịnh indeed launched the war against the Nguyễn in 1627, after Nguyễn Phúc Nguyên (or Chúa Sãi) refused to pay tribute for three years (Trần Trọng Kim, *Việt Nam Sử Lược*, pp. 318-9). The war lasted for fifty years.

[11] Two of Nguyễn Phúc Nguyên's brothers, Phúc Hạp and Phúc Trạch, established relations with the Trịnh, who were to attack from the north, and rebelled against Nguyễn Phúc Nguyên in 1620. The brothers were defeated and captured, while the northerners, seeing this event and that the Nguyễn astutely agreed to pay tribute, decided not to attack at that time. Phúc Hạp's and Phúc Trạch's fate afterwards, however, is not completely clear. *Đại Việt Sử Ký Toàn Thư* (Complete History of Great Viet) simply states that they were apprehended and murdered (*bị bắt giết*); see *Đại Việt Sử Ký Toàn Thư* (Hanoi: Nhà Xuất Bản Khoa Học Xã Hội, 1993), bản ký, 21:2a (3:324), under the year 1620. Southern annals, however, report the brothers being put in prison, where they soon died of some illness. But they are not in complete agreement. Some, like *Việt Nam Khai Quốc Chí Truyện* (Story of the Foundation of the Vietnamese State), say Nguyễn Phúc Nguyên was furious and wanted to execute his disloyal brothers, but the majority of the mandarins interceded, and the brothers were imprisoned instead; other sources

The third place where he has continual war, is on the west side, and utmost bound of his kingdom called *Renran*, against the king of *Chiampá*; whose efforts being weaker, are sufficiently repulsed by the troops of that same province, and the governor.

He is also in continual motion, and making warlike preparations to assist the king of *Cambogia*, who has married his bastard daughter, sending him succours of gallies, and men, against the king of *Siam*; and therefore the arms of *Cochin-China*, and their valour, is famous and renowned, as well by sea as by land.[12]

{The gallies.}

At sea they fight in gallies, as has been said, each of which carries cannon, and is manned with musketeers: Nor will it seem strange, that the king of *Cochin-China* has an hundred, or more gallies in a readiness, when the method of furnishing them is known. It is therefore to be observed, that the *Cochin-Chineses* do not use to have a crew of criminals, or other slaves, to row in their gallies; but when they are to go out to fight, or for any other purpose, the way to man them immediately is this: A great number of officers, and commissaries, go out privately and scouring on a sudden all together throughout the whole kingdom, with the king's authority, press all they find fit for the oar, conducting them all together to the gallies, unless they be exempted by birth, or any other privilege. Nor is this method so troublesome as it appears at first sight; for in the first place they are well used and paid aboard the gallies; and besides, their wives and children are fed and provided with all things necessary, according to their condition, all the while they are from their houses. Nor do they only serve at the oar, but upon occasion lay hold of their weapons, and behave themselves bravely; for which purpose every one has his musket, darts, and scymitar allotted him; and the *Cochin-Chineses* being of an undaunted spirit, and brave, they give good tokens of their valour, either rowing to join their enemies, or with their arms when joined. Their gallies are somewhat less, but particularly narrower than ours, but so neat, and so well adorned with gold and silver, that they afford a glorious sight. Chiefly the stern,[13] which they account the most honourable post, is all over gold, there the captain and persons of chief note have their station;

---

present Nguyễn Phúc Nguyên as the one who wanted to pardon his brothers and who stood against the mandarins who insisted on their death. See Nguyễn Khoa Chiêm, *Viêt Nam Khai Quốc Chi Truyện* (Story of the Foundation of the Vietnamese State), trans. and annot. by Ngô Đức Thọ and Nguyễn Thúy Nga (Hanoi: Nhà xuất bản Hội Nhà Văn, 1994). L. Cadière sees in the latter case an attempt to present Nguyễn Phúc Nguyên in a more favorable light; see L. Cadière, "Le mur de Đồng Hới," *Bulletin de l'Ecole Française d'Extrême-Orient* 6 (1906): 119 and n. 1; also *Đại Nam Thực Lục Tiền Biên* (Chronicle of the Nguyễn Dynasty, Premier Period), 2:5b, and *Đại Nam Liệt Truyện Tiền Biên* (Collection of Biographies of the Nguyễn Dynasty, Premier Period), 6:30. Both of these documents can be found in *Đại Nam Thực Lục* (Chronicle of the Nguyễn Dynasty), vol. I (Tokyo: Keio Institute of Linguistic Studies, 1961), pp. 32, 287.

[12] In 1620, Nguyễn Phúc Nguyên gave a daughter in marriage to the king of Cambodia, who was seeking to counter pressure from Siam with an alliance with the Vietnamese. As a result of this, in 1623 the Vietnamese were allowed to establish an outpost at the future site of Saigon. G. Coedes, *The Making of South East Asia* (Berkeley, CA: University of California Press, 1967), p. 198.

[13] This word is mistranslated. In the original, it is *prora*, "prow," which also fits the description of the captain's post provided by Borri. See Borri, *Relatione*, p. 88.

and the reason they give for it is, that it being the captain's duty to be the first upon any danger, it is fit he should be in the properest part of the gally for that purpose.

Among other sorts of defensive arms they use in war, they have certain oval, hollow targets,[14] so long that they cover a man quite, and so light, that they can manage them without any trouble. The cities of this kingdom have a great advantage in the manner of their houses, which being all of wood upon pillars of timber, as has been said before, when the enemy comes so strong, that they perceive they cannot oppose him, every man flies to the mountain with what he has, firing the houses, so that the enemy finds nothing but the ruins left by the flames, and having no place to fortify himself, nor any thing to subsist on, is forced to retire back to his own country, and the inhabitants returning to the same place in a short time, with great ease rebuild their houses.

---

[14] Borri uses the word *rotella* in the original (p. 88), which means a small wheel or a round shield. Ibid.

CHAPTER VIII.

OF THE TRADE AND PORTS OF COCHIN-CHINA.

{Trade of *Cochin-China*.}

The great plenty *Cochin-China* affords of all things necessary for the support of human life, as has been said before, is the cause that the people have no curiosity, or inclination to go into other kingdoms to trade; and therefore they never go so far to sea, as to lose sight of their beloved shore; yet they are very ready to admit of strangers, and are very well pleased they should come not only from the neighbouring countries, but from the remotest parts to trade with them. Nor do they need to use any art for this purpose; strangers being sufficiently allured by the fruitfulness of the country, and the great wealth which abounds there; and therefore they resort thither not only from *Tonchin, Cambogia, Chincheos,*[1] and other neighbouring places, but from the remotest, as *China, Macao, Japan, Manila,* and *Malacca,* all of them carrying silver to *Cochin-China,* to carry away the commodities of the country, which are not bought, but exchanged for plate, which is here put off as a commodity, being sometimes worth more, and sometimes less, according as there is more or less plenty of it, as is usual with silk and other goods.

All the coin they use is of brass, and of the same value, like a *quatrine,*[2] 500 of which make a crown. These pieces are quite round, with the king's arms and ensign stamped on them, and every one of them has a hole through the middle, which serves to string them by thousands, and every thousand is worth two crowns.[3]

{Rich trade of the *Chineses* and *Japoneses*.}

The *Chineses* and *Japoneses,* drive the chief trade of *Cochin-China;*[4] which is managed at a fair held yearly at one of the ports of this kingdom, and lasting about four months. The *Chineses,* in their vessels they call *junks,* bring the value of four or five millions in plate; and the *Japoneses,* in their ships called *sommes,*[5] an infinite

---

[1] In the original it is said *Cicnceas* (p. 90). Antony de Herrera's map of 1622 places Chincheo on the coast of China farther south from Canton. See Antonij de Herrera, "Indiae Occidentalis descriptio," *Descriptio Indiae Occidentalis* (Amsterdam: Apud Michaelem Colinium bibliopolam, 1622).

[2] *Quattrino* is Italian money.

[3] On trade, see Li Tana, *Nguyễn Cochinchina* (Ithaca: Cornell Southeast Asia Program Publications, 1998), pp. 78-98.

[4] While China historically was a primary and major trade partner, Japan entered the scene relatively late in the sixteenth century, but indeed became a major trade partner in the seventeenth century.

[5] This term is unidentified.

quantity of very fine silk, and other commodities of their country. The king has a vast revenue from this fair by customs and imposts, and all the whole country receives great profit. The *Cochin-Chineses* applying themselves very little to arts, because plenty makes them lazy; and being soon taken with the curiosities of other countries, it comes to pass, that they put a great value upon, and buy at great rates, many things, which to others are of very small worth; as for instance, combs, needles, bracelets, and pendants of glass, and such like women's tackling. I remember a *Portuguese,* who bringing into *Cochin-China* from *Macao,* a box full of needles, which could not be worth above thirty ducats, made about a thousand of it, selling that for sixpence in *Cochin-China,* which had not cost him above a farthing at *Macao.* In short, they out-bid one another, in buying any thing that is very new and strange without sparing for price. They are very fond of our hats, of caps, of girdles, shirts, and all other sorts of garments we wear, because they are quite different from theirs; but above all, they put a great value upon coral.

{Sea ports.}

As for their ports, it is wonderful that in a coast little more than an hundred leagues in length, there should be above sixty most convenient landing-places; which is so, because there are many large arms of the sea. But the principal port, to which all strangers resort, and where the aforementioned fair is kept, is that of the province of *Cacchian;*[6] which has two mouths, or inlets from the sea, the one called *Pulluchiampello,*[7] and the other of *Turon,*[8] being at first three or four leagues distant from one another, but running in seven or eight leagues like two great rivers, at last join in one, where the vessels that come in both ways meet. Here the king of *Cochin-China* assigned the *Chineses* and *Japoneses* a convenient spot of ground, to build a city for the benefit of the fair. This city is called *Faifó,* and is so large, that we may say they are two, one of *Chineses,* the other of *Japoneses;* for they are divided from one another, each having their distinct governor, and the *Chineses* living according to the laws of *China,* as the *Japoneses* do according to those of *Japan.*[9]

---

[6] Previously mentioned as Cachiam.

[7] This is an island in the South China Sea, close to the city of Hội An (Faifo). On Alexandre de Rhodes's map it is listed as Polociampello. According to Bonifacy, "pulo-" or "polo-" is an "island" in Malay; see "Les Européens qui ont vu le vieux Hue: Cristoforo Borri," *Bulletin des Amis du Vieux Hué* 18,3-4 (July-December 1931): 333, n. 81.

[8] Also Touron or Tourane. Modern Đà Nãng, a city in what is now Central Vietnam, located southward from Hue on the Han river. The territory where the city was located became a part of Quảng Nam province after the Vietnamese advanced to this region in the sixteenth century. Because this site featured a safe harbor, a port appeared here. In the late eighteenth century, Faifo (Hội An) lost its significance. Thereafter Turon experienced its heyday as one of the most important ports in the country. As for its appellation, it was initially called Cửa Hàn, "a closed port" (on de Rhodes's map it is called Che An), or also, as Chapuis states, Thủ Hàn— "closed customs," which the Portuguese corrupted into Touron. See A. Chapuis, "Les noms annamites," *Bulletin des Amis du Vieux Hué* XXIX/1 (January-March 1942): 95.

[9] The reference is to the city of Hội An. It is unclear how the name Hội An was transformed into Faifo. Some sources say that initially the name of the city was Hải Phố, "Sea Streets," and the Europeans corrupted this name into Faifo or, as it is on de Rhodes's map, Haifo. But we do not have any Vietnamese documents from that time supporting the name Hải Phố. It is possible that, on the contrary, the Europeans somehow corrupted the name Hội An to Faifo and from this the Vietnamese later conjectured Hải Phố as an alternative name of the city. This city-port appeared not long before Borri arrived in Cochinchina, at the beginning of the

{All nations admitted to trade.}

And because, as we said before, the king of *Cochin-China* gave free admittance to all nations whatsoever, the *Dutch* resorted thither with all sorts of commodities. Hereupon the *Portugueses* of *Macao* resolved to send an embassador to the king, to demand in their name, that the *Dutch*, as mortal enemies to their nation, should be excluded all *Cochin-China*.[10] One captain *Ferdinand de Costa*, a man well known for his valour, was appointed to go upon this embassy; which he delivered and was favorably heard, with assurances of obtaining his demands.

{*Dutch* banish'd.}

Nevertheless, whilst he was yet at that court, there arrived a *Dutch* ship, and coming to an anchor in the port, some of them landed with much mirth and jollity, and presently went with rich presents to the king: He accepted of them very graciously, and granted them the usual liberty of trading freely in his kingdom. *Costa*

---

seventeenth century. It became the most lively port on the Vietnamese coast and attracted merchants from China, Japan, Portugal, and Malaya. Separate quarters for Chinese and Japanese were established there. While this was interpreted by some as a sign of benevolence from the Cochinchinese government, we can assume that it was also a precaution and a measure of convenience: to have foreigners concentrated would facilitate collecting taxes, observing administrative formalities, and also surveillance.

[10] Ashley's interpretation of Borri's Italian original removes all expressions of hostility or inhospitableness on the part of the Cochinchinese. He replaces Borri's text, starting from here and going to the end of the penultimate paragraph in the chapter, with: "Wherein they imployed a brave Captaine, called *Ferdinand de Costar*, who effected it with good successe, yet not without much difficulty; prevailing so farre, that the King by his Edict or Proclamation, forbad the *Hollanders* to approach the Countreyes under his obedience, or paine of their lives. But those of *Macao* apprehending afterwards, that the said Edict was not well observed, thought good to send a new Embassage into *Cochin-China*, to obtaine a Confirmation thereof; and charged their Deputies to make the King understand, that the affaire concerned his owne Interest, and that if hee did not prevent it, he might have cause to feare that the Hollanders in time (being so crafty and cunning as they are) would assay to invade some part of his Kingdome of *Cochin-China*, as they had already some other places of the *Indies*. But certaine Persons of good understanding in that Countrey, advised them not to speake in that sort to the King; because that would be the very way to make the *Hollanders* have permission to come to Traffique in that Countrey, and to invite all *Holland* thither; The Maxime of the *Cochin-China* being, not to acknowledge ever any the least apprehension of any Nation in the World. Cleane contrary to the King of *China*, who fearing all, shutteth the Gate against Strangers, permitting not traffique in his Kingdome." See Christoforo Borri, *Cochinchina: Containing Many Admirable Rarities and Singularities of that Countrey. Extracted out of an Italian Relation, lately presented to the Pope, by Christophor Borri, that lived certaine yeeres there*, translated by Robert Ashley (London: Robert Raworth, 1633), the last page (unnumbered). The points of difference are evident: 1) Borri does not mention any difficulties in da Costa's mission; 2) Ashley omits the appearance of the Dutch ship in Cochinchina after the ruler's order and instead brings a Portuguese ship there to insist on the banishment of the Dutch, as though the first attempt did not work; 3) Dispensing with the arrival of the Dutch ship, Ashley easily finds a way to leave in silence the entire incident of the assault on the Dutch crew and their goods, as well as the sneaky and treacherous attitude of the Cochinchinese ruler; 4) Ashley avoids any positive mention of the Portuguese, be that Borri's description of the Portuguese as "good and sincere friends of Cochinchina," or the whole first paragraph of the section titled "Portuguese favour'd in Cochin-China," which describes all the favors the Cochinchinese ruler granted to the Portuguese.

hearing of it, went presently to the king, and complaining, That his majesty did not keep his word with him, in a *Portuguese* bravado gave a stamp on the ground to shew his resentment. The king and all the courtiers were pleased at his passion, and bidding him have patience, and expect the event, for he should find he had no cause to complain, dismissed him. In the mean while he ordered all the *Dutch* to go ashore, and land all their goods against the fair at *Turon,* as the *Portugueses* did, which they perform'd: But as they were going upon the river in boats, they were on a sudden assaulted by the gallies, which destroyed most of them. The king remained master of their goods; and to justify this action, alleged, that he very well knew the *Dutch,* as notorious pirates, who infested all the seas, were worthy of severer punishment; and therefore, by proclamation, forbid any of them ever resorting to his country; and it was actually found, that those very men had robbed some vessels of *Cochin-China,* and therefore he took this just revenge; admitting the *Portugueses* as good and sincere friends: Who not long after sent another embassador from *Macao,* to obtain of the king a confirmation of the aforesaid edict, at the instance of *Acosta,*[11] alledging as a motive, the danger that the *Dutch,* in time, might cunningly possess themselves of some part of *Cochin-China,* as they had done in other parts of *India.* But the new embassador was advised by knowing men of that country, not to mention any such thing to the king, because that very thing would be a motive to him to grant the *Dutch* a free trade, and invite all *Holland* to come over; he pretended to be afraid of no nation in the world; quite contrary to the king of *China,* who being afraid of every body, forbids all strangers trading in his kingdom; and therefore the embassador must urge other motives to obtain his desire.

{*Portugueses* favour'd in *Cochin-China.*}

The king of *Cochin-China* has always shewn himself a great friend to the *Portugueses* that trade in that kingdom, and has several times offered them three or four leagues of the fruitfulest country about the port of *Turon,* that they may build a city there with all sorts of conveniencies, as the *Chineses* and *Japoneses* have done. And were it allowed me to give his Catholick majesty my opinion in this point, I should say, he ought, by all means, to command the *Portugueses* to accept of the kind offer made them, and to build a good city there as soon as possible; which would be a refuge, and brave defense, for all the ships that pass by towards *China:* For here a fleet might be kept in readiness against the *Dutch,* that sail to *China* and *Japan,* who of necessity must pass through the middle of the bay, that lies between the coast of this kingdom, in the provinces of *Ranran* and *Pulucambi,* and the rocks of *Pulusisi.*[12]

This is what small matter I thought I could with truth give an account of, concerning the temporal state of *Cochin-China,* according to the knowledge I could

---

[11] Misspelling of the aforementioned Ferdinand de Costa.

[12] Pulo Cecir is an island about forty miles off the coast, mostly east and a bit south of Phan Thiết, called "Puolo Cecir de Mer" on colonial maps to distinguish it from "Puolo Cecir de Terre," an island of the same name adjacent to the coast near Cà Ná. Today it appears on Vietnamese maps as Phú Qúy. Many sixteenth–seventeenth century European maps of the South China Sea show a large zone of reefs and rocks dangerous to ships beginning in the area of this island and extending north and east, which we can understand as an indication of what have been called the Spratly and Paracel Islands (Trường Sa and Hoàng Sa on Vietnamese maps today), what Borri here calls the rocks of *Pulusisi.*

gain in some years I resided there; as will further appear in the second part of this relation.

The End of the First Part.

An *Account of* Cochin-China.

The Second PART.
TREATING
Of the SPIRITUAL STATE of *Cochin-China*.

CHAPTER I

OF THE FIRST ENTRING OF THE FATHERS OF THE SOCIETY OF JESUS INTO THAT KINGDOM: AND OF THE TWO CHURCHES BUILT AT TURON *AND* CACCHIAN.[1]

{The Jesuits the first that taught Christianity in *Cochin-China*.}

Before the fathers of the society of Jesus went into *Cochin-China*, it was the custom of the *Portugueses* trading thither, to carry thither with them from *Malacca*, and *Macao*, and the *Spaniards* from *Manila*, some chaplains, to say mass and administer the sacraments to them, during their stay there, which generally was three or four months in a year.[2] These chaplains having no other obligation but only to serve the *Portugueses*, never thought of promoting the spiritual welfare of the natives of that country, not applying themselves to learn their language, nor using any other means to communicate the light of the gospel to them. And yet there was one of these who had the face to publish in *Spain*, in a book call'd, *The Voyage of the World*, that he had catechis'd and baptis'd the infanta or princess of *Cochin-China*,

---

[1] Spelled "Cachiam" in Chapter I of Part I.

[2] The winds on the central coast of Vietnam generally blow from the north during winter and from the south during summer. Ships would stay in port until the winds changed to enable a return journey, meanwhile allowing merchants to complete their business.

and a great many of her ladies:[3] whereas never infanta, nor any other person of all that royal family, till this time, had shewn any inclination to become Christian, notwithstanding we fathers go every year to visit the king, and discourse with all the great men of the court; and yet the infanta has not given any token of being a Christian, or so much as knowing what a Christian is. And it may well be discern'd, how falsely he talks in this point, by the other fables he adds in the same book, concerning that infanta; as that she would have marry'd the said chaplain, and the like. We know of none but some fathers of the order of St. *Francis*,[4] that went from *Manila*,[5] and one of St. *Augustine*,[6] from *Macao*[7] to *Cochin-China*, merely for the conversion of those souls. But they meeting with no success, by reason of the many several difficulties that occur'd, they return'd to their countries: Providence so

---

[3] Pedro Ordonez y Cevallos was a Spanish traveler, born in Andalusia in the second half of the sixteenth century and who died in Spain about 1620-5. A soldier in his youth, he set out for America and Europe in search of adventures. Later he renounced his army career and became a priest; see Romanet du Caillaud, *Essais sur les origines du Christianisme au Tonking and dans les autres pays annamites* (Paris: Augustin Challamel, 1915), pp. 83-4. Upon his return to Spain, he published an account of his travels. It was published under the title "Viage del Mundo" (Madrid, 1614, 1616, and 1691). His work is one of the most controversial existing accounts of Vietnam. And it is one of the controversial passages of this work that Borri mentions here: describing the baptism of Princess Mai Hoa, the sister of King Lê Thế Tông (r. 1573-1599), who, according to Cevallos, wished to marry him. According to his account, he baptized not only the princess but her entire entourage. Some, like Caillaud, a French Canadian interested in Christian missions in Tonkin at the beginning of the twentieth century, and C. Poncet, Provicar Apostolic of the Foreign Mission in 1941, are supporters of Cevallos's account. See Caillaud, cited above, and C. Poncet, "La princess Marie d'Ordonez de Cevallos," *Bulletin des Amis du vieux Hué* 4 (1941): 351-9. But Cevallos's supporters are few. Others, as, for example, Borri and Bonifacy, are indignant about it and dismiss Cevallos's account as pure fiction; see Auguste Bonifacy, *Les débuts du Christianisme en Annam des origines au commencement du 18e siècle* (Hanoi: Impremerie Tonkinoise, 192-?), p. 5. Furthermore, Alexandre de Rhodes's and other missionaries' accounts do not mention Cevallos at all. It is hard to resolve the issue: we do not have any evidence of Cevallos's trip to Vietnamese lands, not to mention his numerous conversions. They have not been reflected in either Vietnamese nor Western historiography. Cevallos's account is still awaiting its researcher.

[4] The Franciscan Order consists of followers of St. Francis of Assisi (1182-1226).

[5] Diego de San Jose o de Oropesa, a Spanish Franciscan missionary (?-1590), native of Oropesa, in the Toledo area, was sent as head of a mission from the Philippines to Vietnam and China in 1583. He was accompanied by FF. Bartolome Ruiz, Francisco de Montilla, Ortiz Cabezas, and four lay brothers: Cristobal Gomez, Diego Jimenez, Francisco de Vllarino, and Manuel de Santiago. They were greeted by King Mạc Mậu Hợp (r. 1562-92). Diego de San Jose was imprisoned on Hainan island after his ship was swept there during a storm. Due to the intervention of Father Matheo Ricci, a Jesuit missionary to China, he was liberated, went to Macao, and then arrived back in Manila in 1585. He died near Acapulco while returning to Spain in 1590. J. Ignacio Tellechea Idigoras, "Expedition franciscana a Cochincina y China" and Diego de San Jose, "Relacion inedita de Fray Diego de San Jose sobre la mision franciscana a Cochinchina y su paso por China (1583)," Archivo Ibero-Americano 209-12 (1993): 449-87, especially pp. 452-6, 460-2.

[6] The order of St. Augustine is a mendicant order established as a result of the unification of several religious communities in the thirteenth century. Its members follow the teaching of St. Augustine of Hippo (354-430). I could not identify the Augustinian Borri refers to.

[7] Macao is a small territory on China's southern coast. In the sixteenth century, it became an important Portuguese outpost, and missionaries arriving on Portuguese ships transformed Macao into an East Asian center of Christianity.

ordering it, which had design'd that land to be cultivated by the sons of the holy patriarch *Ignatius*:[8] which was done as follows.

{Manner of their going thither.}

Certain *Portuguese* merchants acquainted the superiors of the society of Jesus at *Macao*, with the great advantages that might be gain'd, to advance the glory of God in *Cochin-China*, if there were undaunted and zealous labourers sent thither; and particularly one captain earnestly pressed the father provincial, not to abandon a kingdom so capable of being instructed in the holy faith. The proposal seem'd to the father very agreeable to the spirit of our vocation, and therefore without demurring upon the execution of it, he made choice for this enterprise of F. *Francis Buzome*, who had been professor of divinity at *Macao*, by birth a *Genoese*, but educated in the kingdom of *Naples*, where he was admitted into the society, and whence he set out for *India*, together with F. *James Caravalho*, a *Portugueze*, who from *Cochin-China* was to attempt to go over to *Japan*, as he did. This was he, who being put into a pool of cold water in the dead of winter, and exposed to the wind and snow, gave up his life for the sake of his Redeemer, freezing leisurely to death. F. *Caravalho*, being gone, F. *Buzome* was left alone in *Cochin-China*, with only a lay-brother to attend him: being zealously inflam'd with the desire of saving souls, he us'd all possible means for their conversion, and to this purpose began his mission at *Turon*.
{Mistaken conversions.}

But as yet he knew not the language, nor could he find any interpreter that knew any more *Portuguese* than what was requisite for buying and selling, and some words or phrases, which the interpreters of the chaplains of ships, who were there before the fathers of the society, made use of to ask the *Cochin-Chineses*, Whether they would be Christians? After this manner they had made some, but such as might rather be accounted so by name than by profession; for they did not so much as understand what the name of a Christian meant: and this by reason of the phrase the interpreters us'd to ask them, Whether they would be Christians: for the words they made use of, signify'd nothing more, than that they would become *Portuguezes*: which F. *Francis Buzome* found out by this following accident: A play was acted in the public market-place, at which the father saw one in the habit of a *Portuguese*, brought in by way of ridicule, with a great belly so artificially made, that a boy was hid in it; the player, before the audience, turn'd him out of his belly, and ask'd him, Whether he would go into the belly of the *Portuguese*? Using these words, *Con gnoo muon bau tlom laom Hoalaom chiam*? [*Còn nhỏ muốn vào trong lòng Hoa Long chăng?*] That is, *Little boy, will you go into the belly of the* Portuguese, *or not*? The boy answer'd, *He would*: and then he put him in again, often repeating the same thing to divert the spectators. The father observing, that the phrase the player so often repeated, *Muon bau tlom laom Hoalaom chiam*, was the same the interpreters us'd, when they ask'd any one, Whether he would be a Christian? presently conceiv'd the mistake the *Cochin-Chineses* were under; who thought, that to become a Christian was only to cease being *Cochin-Chinese*, and become a *Portuguese*; which to make sport was express'd in the play, by making the boy go into the belly of him that acted the *Portuguese*. The

---

[8] St. Ignatius Loyola (1491-1556), together with his followers, among whom was St. Francis Xavier, the first missionary to Japan, founded the Society of Jesus (also known as the Company of Jesus, or Jesuits) in the 1530s.

father took care, that so pernicious an error should spread no farther, teaching those already baptis'd their duty, and instructing those that were newly converted, what it was to be baptis'd and become a Christian, taking particular care that the interpreters should be well inform'd in this particular, that they might afterwards serve faithfully in teaching of others; changing the abovemention'd phrase into this, *Muon bau dau Christiam chiam?* [*Muốn vào đạo Christian chăng?*] That is, *Will you enter into the Christian law, or no?* His great diligence and charity was so successful, that within a few days he began to reap the fruit of his labours, as well by the reformation of those who before were Christians only in name, as the conversion of many more.

{Churches erected.}

Nor was the fame of his charity and zeal for the gaining of souls confin'd to *Turon,* his usual place of residence, but spread abroad into other places; he labouring in all places to instruct, convert, and dispose the people to receive baptism with such fervour, and so great a concourse about him, that in a short time those new Christians built a very large church at *Turon,* in which the most holy sacrifice of the mass was publicly celebrated, and the Christian doctrine preach'd and taught, by means of the interpreters, then well instructed; all persons being very much taken with F. *Francis Buzome;* who besides his being a person of great knowledge and virtue, entirely gain'd the affections of those heathens, by his great meekness and affability, insomuch that they all flock'd after him. This particularly happened at *Cacchiam,* the city where the king resides,[9] six or seven leagues from *Turon,* up the river.

Here F. *Buzome* made so great an impression, that a place was presently allotted him for a church, which was built in a very short time, every body contributing to the expence, and to the work, according to their power. Besides, he had a good house assign'd him, fit for to make a residence of fathers, who were to go thither in time to instruct that people in matters of faith: all which was done with the assistance of a most noble lady, who was converted, and in baptism took the name of *Joanna.* She not only undertook the foundation of the house and church, but erected several altars and places of prayer in her own house, never ceasing to bless and praise God for the mercy shewn her, in enlightening and drawing her to the faith. All this his divine majesty brought to pass in the space of a year, through the means of his servant, F. *Francis Buzome;* whose fame being spread as far as *Macao,* the following year our father provincial thought fit to send him another father, that was younger, with a *Japonese* brother, that learning the language, he might afterwards preach without standing in need of an interpreter. This was F. *Francis de Pina,* a *Portuguese,* who had learn'd divinity under F. *Francis Buzome.* And tho' this second year the increase was not answerable to that of the first, as to the conversion of souls, yet the

---

[9] As noted above, Cacchiam (variously Cachiam), Kẻ Chiêm, or Kẻ Chàm refers to the modern province of Quảng Nam; here it refers to the place from which this region was ruled at that time, near modern Điện Bàn at the confluence of the Thu Bồn and Vĩnh Điện rivers; the former flows to the sea via Hội An (Faifo) and the latter flows to the sea via the modern city of Đà Nẵng (Turon, variously Touron or Tourane). The Nguyễn lord ruled not from here but further north; the "king" here refers to the son and designated heir of the lord who customarily resided in this place because of its importance for controlling foreign trade. On Kẻ Chàm, Faifo, and Tourane, see Roland Jacques, *Portuguese Pioneers of Vietnamese Linguistics prior to 1650* (Bangkok: Orchid Press, 2002), p. 25.

advantage was much greater in the sufferings of a cruel persecution, rais'd by the enemy that sow'd the tares, who could not endure to see the divine seed grow up so prosperously in those parts, and endeavour'd to choke it; as shall be shewn in the next chapter.

OF THE PERSECUTION THE NEW CHURCH OF COCHIN-CHINA ENDUR'D, AT ITS FIRST INSTITUTION: AND HOW I WAS SENT THITHER TO BE ASSISTING TO IT, BY MY SUPERIORS.

{Cause of the persecution.}

The persecution against the fathers took its beginning from an accident at first sight ridiculous, and of no moment, which afterwards gave them much cause to lament. That year there happened an universal barrenness throughout the whole kingdom, for want of the usual inundation in autumn; which, as was said in the first part, is so necessary for bringing up the rice, the chief support of life in that country. Hereupon their priests, whom they call *omsaiis*,[1] held a great council, to find out the case why their idols were so angry with all their kingdom, that seeing the people starve to death about the fields, yet they were not the least mov'd to compassion for so great a calamity. It was there unanimously agreed, that there was nothing new in the kingdom, so opposite to the worship of the idols, as the admitting of strangers freely to preach up a law there, that utterly contradicted the honour given to those idols; and that they being justly provok'd at it, reveng'd themselves by denying them their desired rain.

{The fathers banish'd.}

This being agreed on as a most undoubted truth, according to their ignorance, they presently went in a tumultuous manner to the king, and press that the preachers

---

[1] In the original it is written *onsaij*, i.e. *ông sãi*, "temple warden." Usually, this term relates to laypersons who live in temples and carry out auxiliary functions but do not rigidly adhere to the tenets of Buddhism. The word used for "priests," as Borri called them, is a Sino-Vietnamese word *tăng* or *thầy tu* (bonzes), designating members of the Buddhist clergy, who devote their lives to observing the doctrine. Adriano di St. Thecla, an Italian missionary in eighteenth-century Tonkin, describes *ông sãi* as "mostly uneducated, [who] do not rigidly observe the rules of their sect, and are assigned to their temples by the elders of the villages." Adriano di St. Thecla, *Opusculum de Sectis apud Sinenses et Tunkinenses: A Small Treatise on the Sects among the Chinese and Tonkinese: A Study of Religion in China and North Vietnam in the Eighteenth Century*, ed. and trans. Olga Dror (Ithaca, NY: Cornell Southeast Asian Program Publications, 2002), pp. 206-7. However, sometimes the meaning of the compound *ông sãi* overlaps with that of *tăng* or *thầy tu*. I think this was especially the case for the Europeans, who mostly saw and had to deal with people working in village pagodas and extrapolated the appellation *ông sãi* to refer to higher representatives of the Buddhist hierarchy.

of the new law may be banish'd all the kingdom, that being the only means to appease the wrath of their gods. The wise king laugh'd at their project, knowing it to be a foolish notion of those priests, and made little account of it, having a great esteem for the fathers, and a kindness for the *Portugueses*. Yet this favor of the king avail'd them but little to oppose the fury of the ministers of Satan; for they so stirr'd up the people to press that the preachers of the gospel might be expell'd the kingdom, that the king, not able to resist without danger of a mutiny, sent for the fathers, and with much concern told them, He was sensible of the folly of the people, and ignorance of the priests; but that it was not prudence to withstand a multitude, so eagerly bent upon such an affair as that was, which was design'd for the removing so general a calamity; and therefore they must depart this kingdom as soon as possible. The fathers having heard these words with tears in their eyes, seeing themselves oblig'd to forsake those new and tender plants of Christianity, yet ever submitting to the will of God, went away to embark; but being got aboard, in obedience to the king's command, they could never get out of the harbour, because at that time a sort of contrary winds, which usually hold three or four months, had begun to blow, which by the *Portugueses* are call'd *Moncao*,[2] or general winds. The *Cochin-Chineses* observing it, would not allow them to return into the city, but oblig'd them to remain upon the shore depriv'd of all human comfort, and expos'd to the burning heat of the sun, which in those parts is very violent. It was a great satisfaction to them in the midst of their sufferings, to see the constancy of some of those new Christians, who never forsook their masters, following, accompanying, and relieving them the best they could, becoming voluntary companions in their sufferings. F. *Buzome* had here a new trial of his virtue; for the uneasiness of this uncomfortable life, in a few days, caus'd an imposthume[3] to break out in his breast, from which abundance of corruption ran, and was a mighty weakening to him.

{An hypocrite priest of the idols detected and punish'd.}

The infernal fiend, not satisfied to have brought the preachers of the gospel to this miserable condition, made yet farther efforts to discredit their doctrine, and catholick religion, making use to this purpose of one of those *omsaiis*, who living a solitary life, was therefore in great reputation of sanctity. This man coming one day from his hermitage, publicly boasted, That by his prayers he would cause the idols immediately to send rain; and without more to do, went away follow'd by an innumerable multitude to the top of a mountain, where he began to call upon his devils, and striking the earth three times with his foot, the sky was presently clouded, and there fell a shower of rain; which tho' not sufficient to supply the want, yet was enough to give a reputation to that minister of hell, and to discredit our holy faith; every one saying, They had not yet seen the foreign priests obtain so much by their prayers of the great God, whose servants they profess'd themselves. This accident troubled the fathers more than the misery they liv'd in: but Providence

---

[2] *Monção* in Portuguese means monsoon. This word derives from the Arabic word *mawsim,* "time or season." Monsoon is a wind blowing in opposite directions according to two main seasons: during spring and summer it blows from the southwest, and during fall-winter from the northeast. Not only do these winds determine the climate of the countries in their area, but they were responsible for establishing a scheduled maritime trade system, connecting Asian countries with each other and with other parts of the world.

[3] An abscess.

comforted them by the means of the lady *Joanna* abovementioned. She, as it were, with a prophetick spirit, bid them not be concern'd at any thing that had happened; for in a little time God would make the hypocrisy of the *omsaii*, and the vanity of his idols, known to all men, by destroying the reputation he had gain'd till then; all which was verified to a tittle soon after. For the fame of his sanctity being spread abroad upon account of the rain, and coming to the king's ear, he presently sent for him, and gave him an apartment in the palace. There he fell in love with one of the king's concubines, and found no difficulty to compass his design; but the matter being known, tho' in *Cochin-China* this be accounted a most heinous crime, and it be death to have to do with a woman the king had once touch'd; yet they could not proceed to execution against him, as being a person sacred among them, but according to the form appointed by their laws. The king therefore gave the sentence, That the *omsaii* should vanish; but that he should neither go east, west, north, nor south, nor through any part whatsoever of his kingdom. This decree being publish'd, was immediately executed in such a manner, that the *omsaii* vanish'd with great shame, and was never more seen in the kingdom, nor out of it.

{The church burnt.}

But the devil being enraged, vented his fury against God's servants, stirring up the people to fire the church in *Turon*, to the great grief of the fathers, who beheld all from the shore without hopes of redress.

{The author in *Cochin-China*.}

In the mean while the news of the fathers' misfortune was spread all about the neighbouring countries, and even as far as *Macao*, which was a great trouble to the fathers of that college, who pitying their brethren, resolv'd to send them some relief by a *Portuguese* vessel that was ready to sail to *Cochin-China*; and the fathers judg'd the business might succeed the better, if two fathers going in it, one had the name of a chaplain of the ship, to return in it; and that the *Cochin-Chineses* might have no cause to complain, or be incens'd, he that remain'd was to go disguis'd: F. *Peter Marques*, a *Portuguese*, was appointed chaplain; and I had the good fortune to be his companion, obedience so ordering it: for tho' I had been destin'd for *China* by our father general, I freely and affectionately embraced the opportunity of dedicating myself to God in the mission of *Cochin-China*, and for the comfort of those afflicted fathers, seeing myself quite shut out of *China*, by reason of the persecution rais'd there. I set out from *Macao* in the habit of a slave, and soon arrived in *Cochin-China* upon my birth day, which was very near opening the way for me to a blessed life; but it pleas'd Providence to order matters otherwise, either because my sins made me unworthy of such a mercy, or for other causes only known to God: as the vessel was entering the harbour, upon which there were abundance of the country people, there happened, I know not how, a quarrel between two *Portugueses*, and one of them falling down for dead, the other leap'd into the sea to escape the wounded man's friends and companions, who would have kill'd him. He swam a-while, but being tir'd, drew towards the ship again, to save himself from sinking, and endeavouring to catch hold could not, because they were ready above with half-pikes, javelins, and swords, to wound him. I seeing him in that distress, endeavour'd to relieve him; and tho' I was in a servile habit, ran among them, and calling out to one, and pulling another, took such pains that I appeas'd them. The *Cochin-Chineses* who were aboard the ship, seeing the *Portugueses* pacified at the sight of a slave, began presently to suspect the matter; and knowing by experience, that the *Portugueses*, when in a passion, are not so easily quell'd, unless religious men interpose, said to one another, This man is certainly no slave, as his habit seems to suggest; and being no merchant, as the rest are, he is certainly one of their religious men, that endeavours, contrary to the king's command, to be conceal'd in our country, but we will discover him to the king himself, that he may be punish'd as he deserves. Immediately they flock'd about me, and tho' I did not understand their language, yet I plainly perceived they had all a jealousy of me; and notwithstanding all my endeavours not to discover myself, I could not prevent their sending advice to court. When I had satisfy'd myself as to this point, believing I was certainly a dead man, I resolv'd to die as what I was: accordingly I put on my habit of the society, a surplice over it, and a stole about my neck; and in that habit I began publickly to preach the faith of Christ by means of the interpreter; then erecting an altar on the shore, I said mass, and gave the communion to the *Portugueses* that were present, standing ready for whatsoever it should please God to appoint: But it pleas'd him not that I should then shed my blood for him. Whilst my cause was in hand, it rain'd so abundantly day and night, without ever ceasing, that every man apply'd himself to tilling of the ground, and sowing of rice; and perhaps reflecting that they had obtain'd that at my arrival, which they had so long wish'd for, looking upon it as a good omen; and concluding it was not the fault of the fathers that they had wanted rain, they repented them of all they had done against us, and never gave us any farther trouble, but suffer'd us to live freely throughout the kingdom.

{Charity of *Japonese* Christians.}

Matters being thus pacified, I resolved to go look out for F. *Buzome*, and his companion, since I was gone thither to that end; and whilst I was endeavouring to hear some news of him, the report of my arrival being spread about the city, that lady *Joanna* above-mentioned found me out. By her I understood that F. *Francis de Pina*, with the *Japonese* brother, had been privately conveyed by *Japonese* Christians to the city *Faifó*, all people certainly concluding that the fathers were then got out of the kingdom. Upon this information, F. *Peter Marques*, who knew the language of Japan very well, would have us go to *Faifó*, where we found F. *Francis de Pina*, who was there hid, but very well used by those good *Japonese* Christians, to whom he privately administered the sacraments. We received incredible joy in meeting: for besides the general charity of religion, we had been companions, and great friends, in the college of *Macao*; and the kindness of the *Japonese* was extraordinary, for they treated us during a fortnight very splendidly, with great demonstrations of affection and joy.

Here I also understood how, through God's special providence, F. *Buzome* was also safe in the kingdom, as if God had particularly defended him for the good of that mission, where whilst he was upon the strand amidst so many afflictions, and with that imposthume in his breast, the governor of *Pulucambi* came to *Turon*; who seeing that man so ill used, that he looked like a walking ghost, being moved to compassion asked who he was, and what misfortune had brought him to that miserable condition. He was told all that had happened; and that the want of rain being laid to his and his companion's charge, he had been banished by the king's order. The governor was not a little amazed, and laughed to think that this should be attributed to a poor religious man, which could no way depend on him; therefore he ordered him to be taken from that open shore, and carry'd into one of his gallies, in which he carry'd him to his province, entertained him in his own house, had him looked after by the most skilful physicians in that city, and made his own children attend him during a whole year; for so long his sickness lasted: all men admiring that a heathen should behave himself so charitably towards a stranger utterly unknown to him, only out of mere natural compassion.

Thus we were four priests of the society in *Cochin-China*: F. *Buzome*, at *Pulucambi*, one hundred fifty miles from the port of *Turon*; F. *Peter Marques* remained at *Faifó*, as superior, and to serve the *Japoneses*; keeping F. *Francis de Pina* for his companion: and I returned to *Turon*, there to serve the *Portugueses*, to say mass, preach to them, and hear their confessions, and learning at the same time the language of *Cochin-China*, endeavoured, with the assistance of the interpreters, to persuade some of those heathens to be baptized; and above all, to encourage and confirm those that were already baptized. Soon after my first coming, there happened a mean accident worthy to be known: I was called to make a dying infant a Christian; I did so, and it soon after gave up the ghost. I was concerned, not knowing where to bury it, which made me think of fixing a burying-place for all the Christians that should die for the future. To this purpose I ordered a mast of a ship that was cast by, to be taken, and a stately cross to be made of it; which done, I invited all the *Portugueses*, and sailors, to help to carry it to the appointed place, I attending with my surplice and stole. Whilst the hole was digging to erect the holy cross, a company of armed men came out from the neighbourhood, who with their muskets threatened to kill me; which I perceiving, caus'd the interpreter to endeavour to know of them, what it was they would be at? And was told, they would not have that cross erected there, because they feared the devils would infest their houses. I answer'd, It would be quite contrary: because the cross had such a virtue, that it put the devil to flight. With this they were so well pleased, that laying down their arms, they all ran to help: and thus the cross was set up to the general satisfaction of all parties, and the burial-place fixed. Soon after the governor of *Pulucambi* came thither, and brought F. *Buzome* with him; and we met all four fathers of the society, to our unspeakable joy at *Faifó*, together with two lay-brothers, one a *Portuguese*, and the other a *Japonese*. After a charitable reception, we consulted together about the most proper means of promoting that mission. It was unanimously agreed, that F. *Peter Marques* should stay at *Faifó* with the *Japonese* brother, because he was a good preacher; and the other three, with the *Portuguese* brother, should follow the governor of *Pulucambi*, who earnestly desired it; which was accordingly done, as shall be here related.

CHAPTER III.

THE GOVERNOR OF PULUCAMBI INTRODUCES THE FATHERS OF THE SOCIETY INTO HIS PROVINCE, BUILDING THEM A HOUSE AND CHURCH.

F. *Francis Buzome*, F. *Francis de Pina*, and I, set out from *Faifó* for *Pulucambi*, with the governor of that province; who all the way treated us with inexpressible courtesy and kindness, always lodging us near himself, and behaving himself in such manner, that there being no human motives to incline him so to do, it plainly appeared to be the work of Providence.

{Great goodness of the governor of *Pulucambi*.}

He appointed a galley only to carry us and our interpreters, not suffering so much as our baggage to be put aboard it, but ordered another boat for it. In this easy manner we traveled twelve large days journey, putting into a port morning and evening, and all the ports being near great towns or cities of the province of *Quanghia* [*Quảng Ngãi*], in which province the governor had as much power as in his own at *Pulucambi*;[1] all people ran to pay their respects and acknowledgments, bringing him rich presents, the first of which always fell to our share, he himself so ordering it, every one admiring to see us so honoured; which gained us much esteem and reputation among those people, that being the design of the governor: and this was much forwarded by the great account he made of our intercession, when any criminal was to be punished: for we no sooner opened our mouths, but we obtained all we desired; by which means we not only gained the reputation of being great with the governor, but of having compassion and kindness for those people, who therefore loved and respected us. Besides, during the whole voyage, he treated us as if we had been some great lords, contriving sports and pastimes in all parts, causing the gallies sometimes to represent a sea-fight, sometimes to row for rewards. Nor did there a day pass but he came aboard our galley to visit us, seeming much pleased with our conversation, especially when we discoursed of religion and our holy faith. In this manner we came to the province of *Pulucambi*, thro' which we had still some days journey to make, before we arrived at the governor's palace, who for our greater diversion, would have us travel by land. To this purpose he ordered seven elephants to be provided; and the more to honour us, would have one for each, causing an hundred men, some on horseback, and some a foot, to attend us: and the

---

[1] The modern province of Bình Định.

journey being for recreation, we spent eight days in it, being royally entertained wheresoever we came; but particularly in the house of a sister of his, we had a most splendid entertainment, not only for the variety and number of dishes, but much more for the rarity of the dressing, all things being dressed after the *European* manner, though neither the governor, nor any of the family, were to taste of them.

{His grandeur, and affection for the fathers.}

Being at length come to the governor's palace, all the entertainment and dainties of the journey concluded in such a reception as he used to make for kings and great princes, treating us for eight days together in most splendid manner, making us sit in his royal throne, and eating with us himself in publick, with his wife and children; to the great astonishment of all that city, where it was unanimously affirmed, such a reception had never been seen, unless it were for some royal person: and this was the cause of the report generally spread throughout the kingdom, that we were a king's sons, and were come thither about matter of great concern; which being known by the governor, he was mightily pleased; and before the chiefest men of the court he publickly said, *It is very true, that the fathers were the sons of a king, for they were angels, come thither, not for any want or necessity of their own, being provided with all things in their own countries, but only out of pure zeal to save their souls*: And therefore he advised them, *to give ear to the fathers, and observe the law they would preach to them, learn the doctrine they taught, and receive the faith they delivered: for* (said he) *I have often discoursed and conversed with these men, and plainly perceive by the doctrine they teach, that there is no true law but theirs, nor no way but that they shew, which leads to eternal salvation. But take heed what you do; for unless you learn that true doctrine, which I, your chief, bring to you by means of these fathers, your neglect and infidelity will be punished eternally in hell.* Thus spoke that lord, becoming a preacher of the gospel, though himself a heathen: all men being the more amazed and astonished at it, because of the great conceit they had of his wisdom.

{The fathers settled.}

After the first eight days, we gave him to understand, that we would rather go live in the city, the better to promote the preaching of the gospel, which we could not so well attend in the palace, because it was three miles from the city, in an open field, according to the custom of the country. The governor would not have parted with us, because of the great affection he had for us, but preferring the publick good before his own satisfaction, he immediately ordered there should be a very convenient house provided in the city *Nuoecman*:[2] and moreover told us, we might see above a hundred houses that were about his palace, and take our choice of the convenientest of them, to make a church of it; and acquainting him with it, he would provide all that was necessary. We returned him thanks for so many favors bestowed on us during our journey, and those we still received. Having taking our leaves for the present, we mounted the elephants again, and with a great attendance went away to the city *Nuoecma*n, which extends itself five miles in length, and half a mile in breadth, where we were by the governor's order received with extraordinary

---

[2] A different spelling for the city mentioned in Chapter 4 of Part I as Nuocmon, referring to Nước Mặn, modern Qui Nhơn.

honour. He not being able to endure to be so far from us, came the next day to visit us, to know whether the house he had given us was convenient; and told us, he knew that we being strangers, could not have money and other necessaries, but that he took upon him to provide every thing; and immediately ordered a good sum to be paid us monthly, and every day flesh, fish, and rice to be sent in for us, our interpreters, and all the servants of the house: and not so satisfied, he frequently sent us so many presents, that they alone were sufficient to furnish us plentifully with all things. The more to honour and credit us among all men, he one day gave publick audience in the court of our house, in the manner as we said above was practiced in *Cochin-China*. Here several criminals were tried, every one receiving sentence according to his crime; among the rest, two were condemned to be shot to death with arrows, and whilst they were bound, we undertook to beg their pardon; which was immediately granted, and he ordered them to be discharged, publickly protesting, he would not have done it at the request of any other, but to these holy men, who teach the true way for the salvation of souls, (said he) I can deny nothing; and I am myself impatient to be rid of those impediments that obstruct my being baptized, and receiving their holy faith; which is what you all ought to do, if you desire to oblige me.

{A rare way of building a church.}

Then turning to us, he again desired we would appoint the place for the church, that he might give orders for its speedy fitting up. We shew'd him a place that seem'd convenient enough, and he approving of it, went away to his palace. Before three days were over, news was brought us, that the church was coming: we went out with great joy, and no less curiosity, to see how a church should come, which tho' we knew was to be made of timber, as had been agreed, yet it could not chuse [choose] but be a great pile, according to the space it must fill, standing upon great pillars. On a sudden, in the field, we spied above a thousand men, all loaded with materials for this fabrick. Every pillar was carried by thirty lusty men; others carried the beams, others the planks, others the capitals, others the bases; some one thing, some another, and so all of them went in order to our house, filling all the court, which was very large, to our unspeakable joy and satisfaction. One only thing displeased us, that we had not provisions enough in the house, to give so great a multitude a small entertainment; for tho' they were paid by the governor, yet it looked like ill-breeding to send them away without some refreshment: but we were soon eased of this trouble; seeing every one sit down upon the piece he brought, being obliged to keep and deliver it, and take out of his wallet, his pot with flesh, fish, and rice, and lighting a fire, fall to cooking very quietly, without asking any thing. When they had eaten, the architect came, and taking out a line, view'd the ground, mark'd out the distances, and calling those that carried the pillars, fixed them in their places; this done, he called for the other parts, one after another, that every man might give an account of what he brought, and go his way: and thus all things proceeding very regularly, and every man labouring his best, all that ·great pile was set up in one day; yet either through over-much haste, or the negligence of the architect, it proved somewhat awry, and leaning to one side; which being made known to the governor, he presently commanded the architect, upon pain of cutting off his legs, to call all the workmen he had need of, and mend it. The architect obey'd, and taking the church to pieces with a like number of workmen, rebuilt it in a very short time very compleately. And we blessed God, for that, at a time when Christians were so lukewarm, it had pleased him to stir up a heathen so zealously to build a church, in honour of his divine Majesty.

And to shew how affectionately the governor looked to our affairs, I will give one particular instance, and so end this chapter. In the months of *June, July,* and *August,* the south-west winds generally reign in *Cochin-China,* which causes such an extraordinary heat, that the houses are perfectly parch'd and dried up; and being all of wood, the least spark of fire, that through negligence, or other accident, falls upon them, immediately takes, as it would do in tinder; and therefore during those months there are generally great fires throughout the kingdom; for when it has taken hold of one house, the flame soon catches hold of those that lie the way the wind blows, and miserably consumes them. To deliver us from this danger, our house being in the middle of the city, and to make it farther appear what esteem the governor made of us, he put out an edict, commanding, that the tops of all the houses that lay south-west of us, should be taken off; and there were so many of them, that they extended at least two miles; which he did to the end, that if any of them took fire, it might be the easier to prevent its passing forward to ours: and this was readily performed by them all, by reason of the great respect they bore us.

CHAPTER IV.

OF THE GOVERNOR OF PULUCAMBI'S DEATH.

Our affairs advanced very prosperously in this city, and it was now the time, when the divine Providence was, according to its usual method, to give us a taste of sufferings, wherewith God frequently tries his servants; and so we ever see he gives such a mixture of prosperity and adversity, that they neither be depressed by the one, nor puffed up by the other: and as the primitive church was founded by the holy apostles upon these two pillars of prosperity and tribulation, even so it pleased the Almighty, that the new church of *Cochin-China* should be established by his apostolical ministers. The first beginnings of this mission were very successful, as has been seen in the first chapter of this second part; but very soon after ensued that terrible persecution for want of rain, which had like to have ruined all. Afterwards, with the favour of the governor of *Pulucambi*, the storms seemed to be blown off, and the budding vine seemed to promise abundance of fruit: but it pleased him that disposes of all things, that the governor of *Pulucambi*'s death, like a violent north wind, almost destroyed all in the bud.

{The governor's death.}

This misfortune happened as follows, the governor went out one day a hunting on his elephant, very well pleased, and the sport drawing him on, he made no reflection that he rode all day over a scorching plain, where the heat pierced his head in such a manner, that at night he fell into a burning fever; upon notice whereof, we hasted to the palace to visit, or rather to baptize him, if we found him in imminent danger. He kept us with him two days, we still pressing him to be baptized, as he had often said he would; to which he always answered, he was ordering his affairs for that purpose, but came to no conclusion. The third day he lost his senses, God so permitting, for causes only known to himself; and perhaps that vain honour he ever passionately coveted, was the reward of the good turns he did us: in fine, he began to rave, and so continued three days, till overcome by the violence of the distemper, he died without baptism.

Any man may guess how much we were concerned at this accident, seeing ourselves forsaken in a strange country, and destitute of all human help; but it chiefly grieved us, that a person so well disposed, and through whose means we had conceived hopes, that the faith might spread throughout the whole kingdom, should die so in our hands without baptism.

{Heathen ceremonies at the governor's death.}

Abundance of their rites and superstitious ceremonies were performed at this governor's death, at which we were present till the last. It would be endless to relate them all, and therefore I will set down two or three, by which the others used by those gentiles upon such occasions may be guessed at. First, whilst he lay in his agony, there was a multitude of armed men, who did not cease to cut and make thrusts in the air with the scymitars, cast darts, and fire muskets in the rooms of the palace; but particularly two, that stood on each side of the dying man, were continually striking the air about his mouth with their scymitars; and both these and the others being asked, Why they did so? told us, They frighted the devils, that they might not hurt the governor's soul, as it was departing his body. These superstitious ceremonies made us pity their ignorance, but not fear any harm to ourselves, as followed when the governor was dead: for we had much cause to fear being expelled that province of *Pulucambi*, and perhaps all the kingdom, with the loss of all we had acquired towards settling Christianity, and perhaps worse. It is the custom when any great person dies, for all the *omsaiis*, or priests of the country, to meet together, in order to find out, not the natural, but the superstitious cause of his death; and being agreed upon what it may be, immediately that thing to which it is attributed, is ordered to be burnt, whether it be a house, garment, man or beast. Accordingly all the *omsaiis* being assembled in a great hall, they began to argue this point: we, who were present, remembering the persecution for want of rain, there being at that time nothing extraordinary in the province, but the governor's kind reception to us, and his assigning a house, and building a church in the city, with such extraordinary tokens of affection for our holy law, did not at all question, but that these things being represented to them, they would lay the death of that lord to our charge, and consequently would order us all to be burnt alive, together with our house and church, and all our goods. Therefore we stood in a corner of the hall, recommending ourselves to God, and preparing ourselves for whatsoever his divine Majesty should suffer to be decreed against us; when one of the *omsaiis*, who was the eldest of them, and as it were their dean, standing up, said with a loud voice, that, in his opinion, the only cause of the governor's death, was the falling of a beam some days since in the new palace; and he was the more apt to believe it, because all the distemper was in his head, as appeared by his raving; an evident sign, as he said, of the stroke he had received in his head by the aforesaid beam: all which he meant metaphorically, and in a superstitious sense, and therefore it pleased the other *omsaiis*, who all unanimously agreed in the same sentiment: and so rising without more to do, they went and set fire to that palace, which was all reduced to ashes, whilst we gave thanks to God for having escaped so manifest a danger.

{Sorcery to discover the state of the soul departed.}

This done, some other *omsaiis* who profess necromancy, came to the governor's palace, to perform another superstitious ceremony, according to the custom of the country. The kindred of the party deceased looking upon it as a great blessing, that any body inspired by an evil spirit, should speak concerning the state of the soul departed; and to this purpose those wizard *omsaiis* were called, of whom they all earnestly beg that devilish favour, he that obtains it being much envied by the rest. These conjurers made their circles, and used several charms both in words and actions, that the devil might enter into some one of the governor's kindred, who were there in a suppliant posture, but all in vain. At last a sister of the governor's, for whom he had an extraordinary kindness, came in, and begging the same favour, immediately gave manifest signs that she was possessed: for being decrepit, by reason of her great age, and not able to go alone, she began, to the astonishment of the spectators, to skip as nimbly as if she had been a young girl, and the stick she threw from her hung in the air, all the while the devil was in her body during which time, talking in a raving manner, and doing many disorderly actions, she uttered several extravagancies about the state and place her brother's soul was in; and concluding her mad discourse, the devil leaving her, she fell down as if she had been dead, remaining so spent for the space of eight days, that she could not stir for meer [mere] weakness; all the kindred and friends flocking to visit her, and congratulate her happiness, in that she had been chosen among all the relations for an action (as they thought it) so glorious and honourable for the dead man.

{Heathen canonization.}

At length they began to order the funeral of this lord; and as in the catholick church it is the custom to honour the memory of men renowned for sanctity of life, by a solemn canonization; so in *Cochin-China*, the devil always mimicking holy things, the more to delude the people, it is customary to honour the death of those who have been universally reputed just men, and upright in their actions, and adorned with moral virtues, with great solemnity and magnificence, canonizing them, if we may so call it, after their manner, by eternizing their memory, and giving them immortal veneration. For this reason the governor of *Pulucambi*, who by all men, not only in his own province, but throughout all the kingdom, was, for his extraordinary natural parts, reputed a man of great wisdom, and incomparable prudence, his government being adorned with singular justice and integrity, together with an unusual inclination and affection for all needy persons, was judged not to require a doleful sad funeral pomp, as was due to others; but on the contrary, all demonstrations of joy and grandeur, which might declare him worthy of religious honours, and to be added to the number of their gods. This being decreed, they all endeavoured to lay aside their mourning and sorrow, and to express all pleasure and satisfaction; and to this purpose, all the governor's kindred, for the space of eight days, sumptuously treated all the people, during which time, they did nothing from morning till night, but eat and drink, sing, dance, and play upon musical and warlike instruments.

{The governor's funeral.}

After the eight days, the body was carried in a silver coffin gilt, under a canopy, to the city where he was born, called *Chifu*,[1] three days journey distant, attended by a multitude of all sorts of people, dancing and rejoicing, leaving the palace where he died utterly disinhabited, that it might run to ruin, and no sign of it remaining; so the memory of the governor's death might be lost in perpetual oblivion, he still remaining alive with perpetual praise and veneration in the hearts and mouths of all men. Being come to a spacious plain without *Chifu*, they all fell to work upon a palace, twice as magnificent and sumptuous as that the governor died in; and to make a great shew of the dead man's wealth, they built as many gallies as he used to keep, upon wheels, for them to run upon dry land. In the same manner they made wooden elephants and horses, and all other moveables used when the governor

---

[1] I could not identify the city. *Chifu* is transcribed *Kifu* in the original Italian.

went abroad when alive, without sparing any cost. In the midst of the palace they erected a stately temple, with a fine altar, on which they placed the coffin covered, and hid with such curious workmanship, that the hieroglyphicks, carving, and painting, greatly move those gentiles to respect. For three days continually they performed several sacrifices and ceremonies, by the ministry of five or six hundred *omsaiis*, all clad in white, who spent the time in singing and sacrificing, offering wine, oxen, and buffaloes, in great numbers; the publick entertainments continuing these three days, for above two thousand men of note, every one having his table to himself, according to custom, and each of them covered with above two hundred dishes. At the end of these three days they set fire to all that pile, burning the palace and temple, with all the perfumes and furniture, only saving the coffin with the body, which was afterwards buried, and privately removed to twelve several graves, that the people being always in doubt where it had been left, that uncertainty might increase the honor of the new idol, they adoring it in all those places where they thought the bones might be. Thus the solemnity ended for that time, till some months after, that is, in the seventh moon, according to their computation of time, it was repeated in the same manner as it had been performed at first; a few months after it was done a third time, and so from time to time for three years, all the revenues assigned the governor of that province by the king, being spent upon this solemnity for those three years; and therefore no other governor was appointed during that time, they being persuaded that the dead man's soul, which was placed among the gods, would continue in the government for those three years. However, his own son was appointed his deputy-governor, or lieutenant.

{The fathers questioned concerning the governor's soul.}

We three fathers of the society then in that province, were present at most of this solemnity; and tho' we did not attend at their superstitious ceremonies, yet to avoid being thought ungrateful and unmannerly, we were forced to accept of some invitations, in one of which we were forewarned we should be asked where the governor's soul was; assuring us, that if we said it was in hell, we should presently be cut to pieces. We were a little after publickly asked the question, and answered, That no man could be saved without baptism; but that through the mercy of God, and earnest desire to be baptized sufficing, where better cannot be; if the governor, at last, had such a desire, as it was likely he had, because of the affection he bore our faith, as was said above, and that he would have asked it, but that the violence of his distemper hindered, therefore it might be believed he was saved, and not damned.

This answer, tho' new, and unexpected, in some measure satisfy'd them, in token whereof they offer'd us some whole buffaloes, some boiled, some roasted, which had been sacrified to their new idol, the dead governor; but we refusing them, saying, "Our law forbid us to eat of that flesh so defiled by their sacrifice; instead of the dead sacrified buffaloes, they ordered others alive to be given us; the governor's kindred afterwards sending us elephants, that we might return on them to *Pulucambi*, with as much honor as when the governor was living.

{The fathers in distress.}

These were the last favours we received in virtue of the governor of *Pulucambi*'s favour; and therefore returning home, we were left like fatherless children, forsaken by all the world. Now no body minded us, the allowance of rice for our maintenance failed, and we having but twenty crowns, must in a few days have been reduced to great misery and want; and if any one fell sick, we durst not call any body to breath a vein,[2] because we had not wherewithal to pay for it; and tho' there were among them people very ready to supply the needy, especially with sustenance, as was said above, yet it was not convenient for us to ask any thing, lest we should lose all the advantage we made, as to the conversion of souls; because they would have said, we went not thither to preach the law of Jesus Christ, but to supply our wants under the protection of the governor. No body now came to our house that first shew of authority ceasing, and tho' we had learned the language of the country, yet they made no account of the words of three poor men, left in the midst of infinite idolaters, and despised our doctrines, as an invention of our own, carried thither to oppose their ancient sects and tenets.

Three years pass'd after this manner, and yet we were not so much troubled at our own wants, which God knows were very great, as to see every day less hopes of promoting the service of God among those pagans, having during those three years converted but very few, and that with unspeakable labour and toil. Things being in this posture, in some measure desperate, we being inclinable to believe the time was not yet come, when it would please God to enlighten the darkness of those people, either because our sins obstructed it, or for some other hidden judgments of God. But when our human frailty shewed itself most diffident of divine assistance, even then, the more to confound us, the God of mercy shewed the wonderful effects of his divine omnipotency, that the noble undertaking of converting souls might be wholly attributed to him, we then owning we had no power to proceed in it, and that we might know experimentally, that *neither he who waters, nor he who plants does any thing; but it is God that gives the increase,*[3] as will appear in the following chapter.

----

[2] Meaning to let blood.

[3] In the original this passage is in Latin: "neque qui plantat est aliquid, neque qui rigat; sed qui incrementum dat, Deus." This is from Vulgate, *Epistle of St. Paul to the Corinthians*, 3:7.

CHAPTER V.

HOW GOD MADE WAY FOR THE CONVERSION OF THE PROVINCE OF PULUCAMBI, BY MEANS OF THE NOBLEST PERSONS IN IT.

{The fathers disperse.}

We having nothing to maintain us at *Pulucambi*, and converting no body, dispersed ourselves into several parts: F. *Francis de Pina* went to live at *Faifó*, a *Japonese* city, as has been said, with a design to serve those Christians, whose pastor he had been before, and to live upon their alms. He being well skilled in the language of *Cochin-China*, and talking it naturally, never ceased there to preach our holy faith. F. *Francis Buzome* went away for *Turon*, carrying along with him the best interpreter we had, to endeavour to obtain some alms of the *Portugueses* there, that might at least maintain us two in *Pulucambi*, in our house at *Nuoecman*, till some supply came from *Macao*.

{Conversion of a great lady.}

Thus I was left in *Pulucambi*, solitary and disconsolate, without any hopes of the conversion of those gentiles. When one day being at home, far from any such thought, I saw a number of elephants before our door, with many ladies, and a large retinue of gentlemen, after whom followed a great lady, and principal matron, most richly clad, and adorned with abundance of rich jewels, according to the country fashion. I was much surprised at the unusual spectacle, and majesty of the lady, and in suspense, not imagining what might be the design of the new visit. Going out at last to receive her, I understood she was wife to the embassador the king of *Cochin-China* was sending to the king of *Cambogia*, which embassador was a native of *Nuoecman*, where we dwelt, and next the governor the chief man in that city, who was then at the court of *Sinuá*, treating with that king upon the subject of his embassy. After the usual ceremonies and compliments, according to the custom of the country, the lady being unwilling to lose time upon matters that were not to her purpose, *Let us come* (said she) *to the business I aim at; I have been fully informed, father, of your coming into this our country and province, and of the occasion of your coming; I see the holy and unblemish'd life you lead, I know you preach and teach the true God; and being satisfied that this is most agreeable to reason, am persuaded that there is no true law but yours, nor other God but yours, nor any way to life everlasting, but that you teach; and therefore my coming to your house, is for no other intent, but earnestly to beg of you, that bathing me in your holy water, you will add me to the number of Christians; this is the utmost of my wishes and desires.* In the first place I commended her good and holy resolution, exhorting her to return thanks to God for so signal a mercy bestowed on her, in calling her to the knowledge of his holy law, there being nothing in this world to be valued equal to the soul's salvation. Next I made my excuse for not complying out of hand with her pious and reasonable request; because, altho' I had some knowledge of the *Cochin-Chinese* language, yet it was not enough to instruct her in the lofty mysteries of our Christian religion; and therefore I advised her excellency to wait for F. *Buzome,* who in a few days was to return from *Turon,* having with him an excellent interpreter, by whose means she would be instructed as she ought to be to her own satisfaction, and obtain the end of her holy desires. *The great fire* (replied she) *that inflames my heart, will not allow of such a long delay; and the more, for that my husband is hourly expected from court, with whom I am soon to embark for the kingdom of* Cambogia, *where the dangers of the sea being frequent, a storm may happen to rise, where dying, I may perish for ever.* She added, that it was enough if I discoursed of matters divine, as I did of other things; for she should understand all I said. These visible tokens of her resolution obliging me to it, I began the best I could to inform her in several matters and principles of our holy faith. Soon after it pleased God, F. *Buzome* returned, and seeing this good success, gave infinite thanks to God. The lady was much pleased with the arrival of the interpreter, whom she had so earnestly expected, with whose assistance, and her continual application, study, and attention to catechizing, which was done for two hours before and two hours after dinner, in a fortnight's time she became perfect in the Christian Doctrine. Above all, what made the greatest impression on her heart, was the knowledge of Jesus Christ, true God, made man, and humbled for the sake of man; and therefore in some measure to imitate our Saviour's great humility, she for the future came to our house, which was a good mile from hers, not only without the state and elephants she used before, but bare-footed, in dirt, and upon stones, obliging her gentlemen and ladies, by her example, to imitate her devotion.

{Twenty-six baptized.}

In our spiritual discourses, and exposition upon the catechism, when we came to make mention of hell, describe its torments, represent the greatness, eternity, and variety of torments there suffered, the horrible company of devils, the darkness of those internal dungeons, and uninhabitable dens; and lastly, the torture of fire: both she and her ladies were so terrified, that having by themselves, all night, considered upon what they had heard, they came again the next day to tell us, they would all be Christians, to avoid that everlasting misery; But we telling them it was impossible, they being servants, and consequently concubines to the embassador, according to the custom of the country, as has been mentioned in the first treatise, the embassador's lady answered, *That impediment does not concern me. It is so,* said we, *for your excellency is your husband's only wife, and has not to do with other men, and therefore may freely be baptized.* At these words, lifting up her hands to heaven, she gave such tokens of joy, as if she had been besides herself, tho' she had never been truly so much herself, as when she shewed such signs of joy, for that which ought to be the only cause of all our satisfaction. Her women on the other side, seeing themselves excluded the way of salvation, cried out aloud, they would forbear being the embassador's concubines, since it obstructed their baptism, and was the way to damnation. The lady seconded their good purposes, taking upon her to deliver them from that sin, and get every one of them a husband. All lets and impediments being removed by these promises of the lady, and firm purposes of the women, one day, which was the joyfullest I ever saw in my life, the embassador's lady richly apparelled, and dressed with jewels, and nobly attended to our church by gentlemen, was baptized, with twenty-five of her women, and as chief of them called *Ursula*, to the glory of Jesus Christ, who by means of these few women, opened a way to the conversions made by our mission in *Cochin-China*.

{Zeal of the converts.}

After they were baptized, we went in procession to the palace of the embassador's lady *Ursula,* where there was an oratory in which she used before to perform her superstitious devotions to an idol. When we came in, we first sprinkled the house with holy water, and then the lady, and her women, couragiously laid hold of the idol, and throwing it violently against the ground, beat it to pieces, trampling on it; in whose place we set up a fine picture of our Saviour, which those new devout Christians falling down, devoutly worshipped, owning themselves his most humble and devout slaves. Then we put about their necks some *Agnus Dei's,* crosses, medals, and relicks, which they valued above the gold chains, and strings of pearls they were adorned with. Having obtained this victory over the devil, after saying the litany, and other prayers in the oratory, now blessed, F. *Buzome,* and I, returned home with that satisfaction and thanksgiving that every man may imagine. The embassador's lady, and her women, came after this, every day duly to mass, catechize, and other spiritual exercises, with great tokens of fervour, and Christian piety.

{The lady's carriage to her husband.}

At this time the embassador, husband to the lady *Ursula,* came from court, to depart in a short time upon his embassy to the king of *Cambogia.* It is the custom of that country, when the head of the family comes from afar off, for the wife, children, and rest of the family, to go out at least a mile upon the way to meet him. The lady *Ursula* failed to perform this ceremony being then retired in her oratory. The husband wondering at it, and suspecting she might be hindered by sickness, asked what was become of her; but understanding she was well, admired it the more, till coming to the gate of his palace, and missing the usual reception, he began to mistrust she was angry with him. At length he went up, and into the oratory, where he found his lady and her maids, with *Agnus Dei's,* and relicks about their necks, beads in their hands, and other Christian signs, praying before the image of our Saviour. The embassador was astonished at this sight, and his lady directing her discourse to him, bid him not admire that she had forbore the usual compliments to him, because she was raised to a higher pitch of honor than he was, both she and her women being children of the true God, and Saviour of the World, Jesus Christ, whose picture she shewed him, saying, he ought to adore him, if he would be equal to them in dignity. The embassador moved by his lady's words, and the beauty of the picture, with tears in his eyes fell down and adored, then standing up, he turned to his wife and women saying, *How is it possible you should be Christians? Have you a mind to leave me? Do not you know that the law the fathers preach forbid polygamy? Therefore you must either find another dwelling-place, or I leave this to you, and seek out another house.* His lady answered, *Neither need you depart, nor we leave you, for there will be a remedy for all things*: Wisely concealing for the present, the prohibition of plurality of wives, to avoid that difficulty which would have bred a disturbance. The embassador took heart at these words, and conceiving, as yet, that he need not be obliged to leave his women; thus piously imposed upon, he said, he would be a Christian too, and follow the good example set him by his wife and her women.

{The embassador instructed.}

The next morning betimes the embassador came to our house, to tell us, that since we had made his wife a Christian, he had a mind to embrace the same religion, if we thought it practicable. Very practicable, said we, full of joy and satisfaction at so grateful a question. For in case he were resolved, we would in a short time instruct him sufficiently to be baptized. He was pleased, and because the affairs of his embassy took up the day, so that he had not leisure to be instructed; upon his request we agreed to go to his house at night, where we began to catechize him, continuing it for twenty nights, four or five hours at a time, informing him in the mysteries of our holy faith, from the creation of the world, till the redemption of man, the glory of heaven, and pains of hell. It was no small matter for so great a person, and so full of business, to lose his sleep to hear the word of God; and he gave himself to them with great application, asking many very ingenious questions, which shewed his great wit. In all our discourses, our whole aim was to imprint the truth of our holy law in the heart of this nobleman, and make it agreeable to reason, that being made sensible of the great importance of salvation, and the terror of the pains of hell, and being well inclined to, and convinced of the certainty of our religion, he might afterwards make less difficulty in the main point concerning polygamy, which was the only thing he stuck at, and which we till then had designedly forbore to speak of. Having gone so far towards the embassador's conversion, we began to expound upon the commandments, where we informed him, that among Christians, it was unlawful to have many wives.

{Convinced about polygamy.}

This proposition was so unexpected, that like fire that has water thrown on it, the embassador presently cooled, and taking leave of us, said, this was a matter of great consequence, and therefore required time to come to a resolution. This answer was so displeasing and grievous to us, that returning home we spent that night in prayer and mortification, praying to God with all the fervour we could, that he would be pleased to put a happy conclusion to the work he had so well begun. Next morning one of the most learned *omsaiis* on the city came to us from the embassador, to examine the reasons for the prohibition of polygamy. Among other objections, this man made one, in his opinion, of the greatest force; which was, Why plurality of wives should be forbid, since generation and children were a work of perfection, and so agreeable to nature, chiefly when a man had a barren wife, as was the embassador's case, and might not have another to get heirs upon. We wanted not answers according to our divinity, but perceiving they were not satisfactory to them because they were not used to our theological notions, we at last added a reason out of scripture, whereof the embassador had before some knowledge from us, and it pleased God, this made an impression on his heart, and absolutely convinced him. This was putting of him in mind, that God being so just, and the law he had prescribed so agreeable to natural reason, as he himself had owned, he ought without doubt to obey in this point, since God himself commanded it; and this so much the more, in regard that God creating man, intimated the same to him, when there was most occasion for propagating [the] human race, and yet he gave *Adam* but one wife, whereas he could as easily have given him many more, that man might multiply the faster. This reason, I say, fully satisfied the embassador, yet finding it difficult to observe the precept, as being a thing he was much addicted to: *Is there no remedy,* said he, *or dispensation from the pope, or any other means, though never so difficult, to have this point remitted?* We told him, it was in vain to seek any redress whatsoever in this case; and therefore, if he desired to be saved, he must dismiss the other women, and stick to his wife. Then the embassador lifting up his eyes and hands to heaven, as it were struggling with himself, and pressed on by truth, with a generous resolution said, *If then multiplicity of wives be inconsistent with my salvation, let them all go in the name of God; for it is pity to lose an eternity of glory, for a transitory delight.* Then turning to his concubines, who were present with his wife, he discharged them all: but perceiving they laughed at his discharge, as a thing that would never stand good; to shew he was in earnest, he ordered his wife to pay them all off immediately, and let not one of them stay in his palace that night. After which turning again to the fathers, *Behold,* said he, *I have readily performed all you commanded me.* Having obtained our desires, we went home to give thanks to Almighty God.

{His conversion.}

But the devil found out a way still to make opposition, making use of the lady *Ursula*'s womanish temper; for she had not the heart to turn away those women she had bred up from their infancy in her house, and loved them as if they were her own children. Therefore some strife arising between the man and his wife, he pressing to have them gone, and she opposing, the embassador dissatisfied came to us to justify himself, and desire to be baptized, since the impediment was removed, he being willing the women should depart his house. We were about going to work, perceiving he spoke rationally, and particularly because he resolved they should not continue in his house as his concubines, but as his lady's servants. But the good man making a stand as if he were thinking, at last said he had a scruple to propose: *Since, according to what you fathers have taught me,* said he, *God sees into the heart of man, and cannot be deceived, tho' I desire to forsake and send away the women, yet whilst they continue in the house, I plainly see, either my ancient habit, or frailty of nature will easily cause me to fall again into sin; therefore methinks I do not proceed with due severity in this affair.* We perceiving by the embassador's discreet and Christian discourse, he foresaw the danger of being in the immediate occasion of sin, studied some proper means to remove so considerable an impediment; but nothing occurring for the present, he himself being very earnest upon the business, proposed a method, which we stuck to as the best of all others: *Fathers,* said he, *the fastest way I can think of is, that you as their directors powerfully persuade the Christian women that were my concubines, (for the heathens I will infallibly make my wife turn away) that in case through frailty I should be under any temptation they resist me resolutely; and forasmuch as I bear a great respect to, and stand in awe of our Saviour's picture placed in the oratory, if the women lie in that place, I will rather be torn to pieces than have any thing to do with them in the presence of that great Lord; and they being thus secured against me, till there be an opportunity of marrying them, it will be known abroad, that they are not kept in the house as my concubines, but only as servants to my only wife* Ursula, *and the people will be sensible I do not act contrary to the law of God.* This method was so well approved of, that the day after it was put in execution, the embassador was baptized in great state, attended by drums, fifes and other instruments, and he himself clad in rich apparel. With him were baptized twenty other gentlemen, his best friends, and he had the name of our holy patriarch *Ignatius* given him. After which, taking his wife *Ursula* by the hand, she renewed the old contract of matrimony as a sacrament of the church. The joy they all conceived at their baptism, and new marriage, was unspeakable.

It now remained that the embassador should depart on his embassy for *Cambogia*; and he ordered, that the ship which was to carry him, should have a cross in its colours, and the picture of the glorious father S. *Ignatius* his protector, causing all the jacks and pennants to express the religion he professed. Embarking with all his gentlemen and Christian women, he had a prosperous voyage from *Nuoecman* to *Cambogia*. When the squadron appeared, being well known to the people of *Cambogia* to be the embassador's, they were all astonished, seeing Christian colours set up; and therefore, they imagined that the king of *Cochin-China*, instead of the ordinary embassador, had sent some extraordinary *Portuguese* Christian; but their doubt was soon cleared, seeing the usual embassador land with a cross and medals on his breast, among the gold chains and jewels. This sight on the one hand, moved the *Portuguese* and *Japonese* Christians, who reside there on account of trade, to give shouts of joy, and bless God for this new off-spring *Cochin-China* had produced; and on the other, the heathens could not believe that the embassador, who before was observed to be excessively lascivious, should embrace the Christian religion, which forbids all immodesty. But the grace of the holy Ghost soon appeared to strengthen human frailty; for though the embassador at his palace in *Cambogia*, had double the number of concubines, as generally used to attend his wife, he ordered them to be all dismissed; nor did he ever lift up his eyes to look at them; which made his fame spread abroad, as of a man of singular sanctity and virtue; and being reputed a man of great knowledge, his example moved many of the most learned persons of *Pulucambi* to be baptized.

CHAPTER VI.

HOW GOD OPEN'D ANOTHER WAY TO CHRISTIANITY, THROUGH THE MEANS OF THE LEARNED PEOPLE AMONG THE HEATHENS.

{Means for the conversion of the Cochin-Chineses.}

God's infinite mercy, and his ardent desires for the salvation of mankind, finds out divers means suitable to the several conditions of persons, which are as it were so many ways to direct and lead them to that end for which they were created. Thus we see he himself in person called upon his people, and complying with the inclination of the persons, invited the wise men by means of the star; *Denis the Areopagite* the astronomer,[1] by the prodigy of the wonderful eclipse; S. *Augustine* by the knowledge of the true light and law, and the confusion and obscurity of former errors; and in fine, he calls the ignorant multitude, by the means of prodigies, wonders and miracles. So it fell out in the new church of *Cochin-China*; for when his divine majesty had by himself convinced some of the principal persons, as has been shewn, next he call'd not only the learned and wise philosophers and mathematicians, by means of some eclipses, as shall be shewn in this chapter, but also the *omsaiis* or priests, who were hardened in the errors of their heathen sects, to the knowledge of the true religion, as the following chapter will make appear. And lastly, in the next to that we shall set down, how he opened the way of salvation to the people by means of several prodigies and miracles.

{Astrology in great esteem.}

Now to come to the manner of converting the wise and learned *Cochin-Chinese*, reputed excellent mathematicians, by means of the eclipse. For the better understanding of what we are to say, it is requisite in the first place to be acquainted with a custom they have in this kingdom, relating to the science of astrology, but particularly of eclipses; for they make such a great account of it, that they have large halls where it is taught in their university; and there are special allowances assign'd the astrologers; as for instance, lands which pay them a tribute or stipend. The king has his peculiar astrologers, and so has the prince his son, who use all their art to set down eclipses exactly. But wanting the reformation of the calendar, and other

---

[1] Dionysius the Areopagite, who lived in the first century, was the Bishop of Athens. He was converted to Christianity through Paul's preaching. He studied astronomy in Egypt and is credited with some works on celestial subjects, which, however, were apparently written several centuries later. His teaching exerted a large influence on mystical philosophy.

matters, relating to the motion of the sun and moon which we have, they commit some mistakes in the calculation of the moons and eclipses, wherein they generally err two or three hours, and sometimes, tho' not so often, a whole day; tho' generally they are right as to the material part of the eclipse. Every time they hit right, the king rewards them with a certain quantity of land; and so when they mistake, that same quantity is taken from them.

{Superstitions concerning eclipses.}

The reason why they make such account of foretelling the eclipse, is because of the many superstitions at that time us'd towards the sun and moon, for which they prepare themselves in very solemn manner; for the king being told the day and hour a month before the eclipse happens, sends orders throughout all the provinces of the kingdom, for the learned and common sort to be in a readiness that day. When the time is come, all the lords in every province meet with their governors, commanders and gentry, and the people with their proper officers in every city and liberty. The greatest assembly is at court, where the principal men of the kingdom are, who all go out with colours and arms. First goes the king cloath'd in mourning, and after him all the court, who lifting up their eyes to the sun or moon, as the eclipse comes on them, make several obeisances and adorations, speaking some words of compassion for the pain those planets endure; for they look upon the eclipse to be no other, but that the dragon swallows up the sun or moon; and therefore, as we say, the moon is all or half eclips'd; so they say, *Da an nua, Da an het;*[2] that is, the dragon has eaten half, now he eats all.

{Their astrological terms and ours alike.}

Which way of expression, though it be nothing to the purpose, yet it shews that they assign the same ground for the eclipse originally that we do, which is cutting of the ecliptick, that is the sun's circle and the line of the course of the moon, in those two points which we call the dragon's head and tail, as astronomers well know: whence it follows, that the very same doctrine, and the same terms and names of the dragon, are common both to us and them, and so they give names like ours to the signs of the zodiac, such as *Aries, Taurus, Gemini,* &c. And thus in process of time the people have invented fabulous causes of the eclipse, instead of the true, saying that the sun and moon, when eclipsed are drown'd by the dragon; whereas, at that time they are really in the head or tail of the astronomical dragon.

Now to return to the compassion they have for those suffering planets; when the adoration is over, they begin first at the king's palace, and then throughout all the city to fire muskets and cannon, ring bells, sound trumpets, beat drums, and play upon other instruments, even to clattering of the kettles, and other utensils of the kitchen in all houses: and this is done, to the end the dragon may be frighted with the great noise, and not proceed to eat any more, but vomit up what he has already eaten of the sun or moon.

---

[2] *Đã ăn nửa, đã ăn hết.* Borri translates this phrase as "the dragon has eaten half, now he eats all," while it should be translated "has eaten half, has eaten all," as the word "dragon" is absent in the Vietnamese phrase.

{Conversions by means of an eclipse.}

When we were inform'd of this custom, the first eclipse that happened was one of the moon, in the year 1620, on the 9th of *December*, at eleven at night. I was then in the city of *Nuoecman* in the province of *Pulucambi*, where there was a commander of the ward[3] we liv'd in, whose son was become a Christian; tho' the father, as proud of his own learning, despis'd not only our religion, but our knowledge; and we earnestly desir'd his conversion, hoping that if he received the catholick faith, his example would induce those of his ward or quarter to do the same. This man came once to visit us before the eclipse of the moon happened, and in discourse we happened to talk of it, he positively affirming there would be no such eclipse: and tho' we demonstrated it to him, according to our calculation, and shew'd him the figure of it in our books, yet he would never believe it; alledging among other arguments for his obstinacy, that if any such eclipse were like to be, the king would doubtless have sent him notice a month before, according to the custom of the kingdom, whereas there wanted but eight days of the time by us appointed; wherefore he having no such advice, it was a certain sign that there would be no such eclipse. He persisting obstinately in his opinion, would needs lay a wager of a *Cabaia*,[4] which is a silk gown. We agreed to it upon condition, that if we lost we were to give him such a garment; but if we won, instead of paying the gown, he was to come to us for eight days together, to hear the catechize and mysteries of our faith expounded. He replied, he would not only do so, but the very moment he saw the eclipse would become a Christian: for he said, if our doctrine was so certain and infallible in such hidden and heavenly things as eclipses are, and theirs so erroneous, there was no doubt but our religion and knowledge of the true God was no less assured and safe, and theirs false. The day of the eclipse being come, the aforesaid gentleman, with a great many scholars, came to our house at night, bringing them as witnesses of the event. But because the eclipse was to be at eleven at night, I went to say my office, turning up the hour glass in the meanwhile. An hour before the time these men came several times, calling upon me by way of derision to see the eclipse, thinking I had not withdrawn to say my office, but had hid myself for shame that there would be no eclipse. Yet they could not but admire at my assurance in answering them, that the hour was not yet come, till the glass was run out, which they gaz'd at, as if it had been some wonderful thing. Then going out, I shew'd them that the circle of the moon on that side the eclipse began, was not so perfect as it should be, and soon after all the moon being darkened, they perceiv'd the truth of my prediction. The commander and all of them being astonished, presently sent to give notice of it to all the ward, and spread the news of the eclipse throughout the city, that every man might go out to make the usual noise in favour of the moon; giving out everywhere, that there were no such men as the fathers, whose doctrine and books could not choose but be true, since they had so exactly foretold the eclipse, which their learned men had taken no notice of; and therefore in performance of his promise, the commander, with all his family, became Christians, as did many more of his ward, with some of the most learned men in the city, and other men of note.

---

[3] Borri uses the word *rione*—"neighborhood, quarter."

[4] *Cabaya* means a robe in Portuguese.

{The fathers foretell the eclipse truer than the Cochin-Chinese astrologers.}

Such another accident happened at the same time, though among people of greater quality, and in a more eminent place. Tho' the king's astrologers had not foreseen this eclipse, yet those belonging to the prince at *Cacciam*, being more studious and intelligent, foretold it, but with a gross mistake as to time: for it was not of an hour or two, as is usual, but of a whole day, giving out that the full moon, and consequently the eclipse would be a day sooner than it was. F. *Francis de Pina*, who was then at court, had given notice of it to a courtier, who was very great with the prince, being his *omgne*;[5] that is, in the nature of master of the ceremonies. The father told him, That since the eclipse was not to fall out as their astrologers said, but as F. *Christopher Borri* affirmed, the following night, he should give the prince his master notice of it. But the *omgne* not giving entire credit to the father, would not do that duty of his office at that time. The hour appointed by the astrologers being come, and the prince having notice of it, he went out with his whole court, according to custom, to see and help the moon, that as they said was to be eclips'd; but finding he was deceiv'd, and growing angry with his mathematicians for their mistake, he ordered they should forfeit the revenue of a town, according to the custom before-mentioned. Hence the *omgne* took occasion to acquaint the prince that the *European* father had, before this happened, told him the eclipse would be the night following. The prince was mightily pleased that the fathers should hit right, when his mathematicians had miscarried.

The *omgne* repaired immediately to the father to know the precise time of the eclipse; who having shewed him that it was to be exactly at eleven the following night, he still continued doubtful of the truth of the matter, and therefore would not wake the prince till he saw the beginning of the eclipse. Then he ran to rouze him, and he coming out with some of his courtiers, performed the usual ceremonies and adorations to the moon. Yet he would not make the matter publickly known, for fear of utterly discrediting their books and mathematicians, though all men conceived a great opinion of our doctrine, and particularly the *omgne*, who from that time forwards for a whole month came to hear the catechizing, diligently learning all that belongs to our holy faith. However, he was not baptized, wanting resolution to overcome the difficulty of the multiplicity of women, as the ambassador *Ignatius* had done before. He forbore not nevertheless publickly with much fervour to declare our doctrine and law were true, and all others false, and said he would certainly die a Christian, which mov'd many others to desire to be baptized.

{An eclipse of the sun mistaken.}

Having talked of the eclipse of the moon, we will conclude with another of the sun, which happened on the 22nd of *May* 1621, which the king's astrologers foretold, as to last two hours; but having conceived a great opinion of us as to this particular, for their own greater security, they came to ask our opinions concerning it. I told

---

[5] *Ông nghè*. Alexandre de Rhodes gives a definition for *ông nghè* as a literati who holds an office; Alexandre de Rhodes, *Từ Điển Annam-Lusitan-Latin* (Annamite-Portuguese-Latin Dictionary), ed. and trans. Thanh Lãng et al. (Hochiminh City: Nhà Xuất Bản Khoa Học Xã Hội, 1991), col. 524. It denotes the person who succeeded in the highest (court) examinations. It also means "Hue court ministry clerk"; Đặng Chấn Liêu, et al., *Từ Điển Việt Anh* (Vietnamese-English Dictionary) (Hochiminh City: Nhà Xuất Bản Thành Phố Ho Chí Minh, 1999), p. 716.

them it was true there would be an eclipse of the sun, the figure whereof I shew'd in our *ephemerides*; but I purposely forbore to let them know, that it would not be seen in *Cochin-China*, by reason of the moon's parallax to the sun. Now they know not what the parallax is, which is the cause they are often deceiv'd, not finding the just time by their books and calculations. This I did, that their error being observ'd, our knowledge might appear the more: I therefore demanded time to find out the precise time; saying, in general terms, it was requisite to measure heaven by the earth, to discover whether that eclipse would be visible in their country; and I delay'd the answer so long, till the time of making known the eclipse being come, the astrologers satisfied that our book agreed with their opinion, without farther reflection, concluded the eclipse was most certain, and advis'd the king to publish it after the usual manner. When the astrologers has spread their false prediction throughout the kingdom, I gave it out that the eclipse would not be seen at all in *Cochin-China*. This assertion of ours was carried to the prince, who being doubtful in the matter, sent his mathematicians to me to ask my opinion, and argue the point. This dispute had no other effect on them, but only to increase their doubt, and hold the prince in suspense, whether he ought to send his orders throughout the kingdom, as the king his father had done, or publish the contrary; for on the one hand it wrought upon him to see that both their books and ours granted the eclipse, wherefore he thought it would be a dishonour to him, in case he happened not to have sent the usual advice; and on the other side, he had a great opinion of us on account of the antecedent eclipse of the moon. Hereupon sending to consult me again, I answered that having calculated the eclipse very exactly, I found it could not possibly be visible in his kingdom; and therefore he need not take any care to send advice about the country, for I would be answerable for his and his astrologers reputation, against the king and his mathematicians. He at last rely'd upon my words, and took no care to give notice in his liberty of the eclipse, the whole court and king's astrologers admiring at it, and they inquiring into the cause of the prince's neglect, were answer'd, that he had better mathematicians in his court than the king his father: by which they understood that some of our fathers being there, he forsook the opinion of the natives for theirs. However the publication they had made being irrevocable, the usual preparations were made against the day of the eclipse, till the hours being come, they experimentally perceived their error. The day was clear and not a cloud to be seen, and though it was the month of *May*, when the sun is there in the zenith, and the time of the day about three in the afternoon, when the heat is violent, yet the king did not omit to go out with his courtiers, enduring all the burning sun for a long time; but finding himself imposed upon, and being much incensed, as well by reason of the great heat he endured, as at the ignorance of his mathematicians, who had put him to that trouble, without any reason, he reprimanded them severely. They alleg'd for their excuse, that there would be an eclipse infallibly, but that they had made a day's mistake as to the conjunction of the moon, and therefore it would be seen the next day at that same hour. The king submitted to his astrologers, and coming out the next day at the same hour, suffered the same inconveniency of heat, to the great shame of his astrologers, who escap'd not unpunish'd; for he not only took away their revenues, but order'd they should kneel a whole day in the court of the palace, bare-headed expos'd to the heat of the sun, and to the scorn of all the courtiers. To return to the prince who had got the better in this point, he writ to his father in a jesting manner, That tho' he was his son, he had out-done him as to the eclipse, and had more learned men at his court.

It is not to be imagin'd how much reputation this accident gain'd us among the learned, insomuch that even the king's and prince's mathematicians came to us, earnestly begging we would receive them for our scholars[6]; and upon this account the fame of the fathers was everywhere so great, that not only our knowledge in astronomy, but our religion was extoll'd above their own; they arguing from the heavenly bodies to things above the heavens, as I said before.

---

[6] Here, "scholars" means "students."

CHAPTER VII.

How God Open'd Another Way to Christianity, by Means of the Omsaiis, or Heathen Priests.

{Conversion of a heathen priest.}

God in his infinite wisdom foreknowing of how great consequence it would be for the conversion of those heathens, that some of their priests or *omsaiis* should be converted, because of the great authority they have among all the people, it pleas'd his divine majesty to open even this way to his holy faith. An *omsaii* whose name was Ly, liv'd near to our house, and had the charge of an idol temple, and being a neighbour had frequent opportunities of conversing with us, and of coming to some knowledge of our rules, actions, and course of life. This pleas'd him so well, that proceeding still farther, he would needs be informed as to the law of God, whereof we gave him a full account; and coming to discourse of the resurrection of our Lord, shewing him how he rose again, that he and all men might rise again the last day, he was so pleas'd at it, that being inspir'd by God, he ask'd to be baptis'd, which was accordingly granted to him and all his family upon Christmas night, which he spent on his knees in prayer with floods of tears, uttering these words, *Tuii ciam biet* [*Tôi chẳng biết*]; that is, I knew not, as if he would have said, Forgive me my God, for till now I knew you not. Then continuing some time very still, as it were contemplating, he repeated the same words, making a sweet harmony to the new born infant. After baptism he took such an affection for us, that he resolved to come to us with all his family, that he might live under our rule; but being inform'd that could not be, because he was marry'd, he concluded to live nearer to our house, that he might regulate his actions by the sound of our bell, even to saying the long litany in his oratory; at the time, we used to say it every day, according to the custom of the society. And it is remarkable, that observing me at a certain hour us'd to say our beads walking, he would walk at the same time, to the amazement of his countrymen, who look upon walking as a strange and ridiculous action, because they never going a step but what is about business, or to some diversion, look'd upon our action of walking as idle, because we went to a place to no other end but to return; so that the people flock'd to see us walk, and admiring the strangeness of it said, *Omsaii di lay* [*Ông sãi đi lại*]; that is, the father goes and comes, goes and comes.

{A notable moral heathen.}

Yet their gazing did not make *omsaii* Ly leave his custom, which tended to nothing but to be like us in all points. He had but one wife, and had lived about thirty years, which was his age, so strictly up to the law of nature, that he had never, as he said, to that time, knowingly deviated in any matter of consequence from what was just and upright; and his adoring of idols was because he thought it contrary to reason not to adore them. This shews how true that doctrine of divines is, to wit, that God never fails to have baptism administered, either by the hands of men, as this was, or the ministry of angels, to a heathen who lives a good moral life, according to the dictates of reason, and law of nature. This *omsaii Ly* wholly devoted himself to the service of God, and after providing for the maintenance of his family, all he and they could earn was bestow'd upon our church, taking special care of its neatness and decency, and of adorning the altars.

{Other converts.}

Nor was this all God requir'd of this his beloved servant; for he so inflamed his heart, that he applied himself to preach the faith of Christ publickly, making the mystery of the resurrection the usual subject of his discourse, whereby he attracted and converted abundance, not only of the common sort, but several *omsaiis;* for tho' he was none of the most learned, yet his fervour so well supplied that defect, that among those who came to desire baptism, there was one of the most learned and famous men in the kingdom, whose authority, he himself proving the falsity of the heathen sects, immediately increased the harvest of the church. This man therefore took upon him to oppose the other gentiles, easily confuting them, as being well acquainted with the grounds they went upon; herein very much easing our fathers, who not being so well acquainted with their sects, could not so well oppose them.

{Several sorts of *omsaiis.*}

And in truth there was need of such a help; for there is such variety of *omsaiis* in that country, that it looks as if the devil had endeavoured among those gentiles, to represent the beauty and variety of religious orders instituted by holy men in the catholick church, their several habits answering their several professions; for some are clad in white, others in black, others in blue, and other colours; some living in community, some like curates, chaplains, canons, and prebends; others profess poverty, living upon alms; others exercise the works of mercy, ministering to the sick, either natural physick, or magick charms, without receiving any reward; others undertaking some pious work, as building of bridges, or other such things for the publick good, or erecting of temples, and going about the kingdom, begging alms to this purpose, even as far as the kingdom of *Tonchin;* others teach the doctrine of their religion, who being very rich, have publick schools, as universal masters. There are also some *omsaiis* who profess the farriers trade, and compassionately cure elephants, oxen, and horses, without asking any reward, being satisfied with anything that is freely given them. Lastly, Others look to the monasteries of women, who live in community, and admit of no man among them but the *omsaii* who looks to them, and they are all his wives.

{Temples.}

There are vast temples with beautiful towers and steeples, nor is there any town, tho' never so little, without a temple to worship its idols, which are generally very large statues, with abundance of gold and silver shut up in their breasts or bellies, where no body dares to touch it, till extreme necessity obliges some thief to gut the idol, without regard to so great a sacrilege as that is accounted among them; and what is very remarkable, they have chaplets and strings of beads about their necks, and make so many processions that they outdo the Christians in praying to their false gods. There are also among them some persons resembling abbots, bishops, and arch-bishops, and they use gilt staves, not unlike our crosiers, insomuch that if any man come newly into that country, he might easily be persuaded there had been Christians there in former times; so near has the devil endeavoured to imitate us. This will give us an opportunity of adding here a chapter of the sects in *Cochin-China*, to give some light how we may draw that people out of such darkness, and bring them into the light of the gospel.

CHAPTER VIII.

A SHORT ACCOUNT OF THE SECTS IN COCHIN-CHINA.

The end of all sects is either the god they adore, or the glory and happiness they expect, some believing the immortality of the soul, others concluding that all ends when the body dies.

{The philosopher Xaca.}

Upon these two principles the eastern nations build all their sects; all which took their origin from a great metaphysician of the kingdom of *Siam*, whose name was *Xaca*, much ancienter than *Aristotle*, and nothing inferior to him in capacity, and the knowledge of natural things.[1] The sharpness of this man's wit raising him to consider the nature and fabrick of the world, reflecting on the beginning and end of all things, and particularly of human nature, the chief lady of this worldly palace; he once went up to the top of a mountain, and there attentively observing the moon, which rising in the darkness of the night, gently raised itself above the horizon to be hid again the next day in the same darkness, and the sun getting up in the morning to set again at night, he concluded that as well moral as physical and natural things were nothing, came of nothing, and ended in nothing. Therefore returning home, he writ several books and large volumes upon this subject, calling them, *Of nothing*; wherein he taught that the things of this world, by reason of the duration and measure of time, are nothing; for tho' they had a being, said he, yet they would be nothing, nothing at present, and nothing in the time to come, for the present being but a moment, was the same as nothing.

{His opinion, that all this world is nothing.}

His second argument he grounded on the composition of things; let us instance, said he, in a rope, the which not being naturally distinguished from its parts,

---

[1] Thích Ca in Vietnamese. The reference is to Buddha. The term Xaca is used in many other European accounts. For example, de Rhodes says that "the Japanese call [Buddhism] *Xaca*, the Chinese *Xechia*, and the Tonkinese Thicca, by corruption of his [Buddha's] name." Alexandre de Rhodes, *Histoire du royaume de Tunquin et des grands progrez que la predication de l'evangile y a faits en la conversion des infidèlles, depuis l'année 1627 jusques a l'année 1646*, trans. from Latin by R. P. Henry Albi (Lyon: Jean Baptiste Devenet, 1651), p. 64. The name derives from Sanskrit "Sakya"—"one of the Sakya clan." Two points might be of interest here: first, that Borri, unlike de Rhodes, does not employ a Vietnamese appellation but only its Japanese or Thai pronunciation; second, F. Borri's reference to Buddha's origins in Siam possibly demonstrates that his informants presented him with a history of Theravada Buddhism (or the "Doctrine of the Elders"), predominant in South Asia and Thailand (Siam), Burma, Laos, and Cambodia, unlike the Mahayana (the Greater Vehicle), which spread to China, Japan, Korea, and North Vietnam.

inasmuch as they give its being and composition, so it appears that the rope as a rope is nothing; for as a rope it is no distinct thing from the threads it is compos'd of, and the threads themselves are no distinct thing from the hemp they are made of, and the hemp has no other being but the elements, whereof its substance consists; so that resolving all things after this manner into the elements, and those to a sort of *materia prima*, and mere *potentia*, which is therefore actually nothing, he at last proved, that as well the heavenly things, as those under heaven, were truly nothing.

{So of all moral things.}

In the same manner did he argue as to moral things; that the natural happiness of man did not consist in a positive concurrence of all that is good, which he looked upon as impossible, but rather in being free from all that is evil, and therefore said, it was no other thing but to have no disease, pain, trouble, or the like; and for a man to have such power over his passions, as not to be sensible of affection or aversion, to honour or disgrace, want or plenty, riches or poverty, life or death, and that herein consisted true beatitude: Whence he inferred, that all these things being nothing, they took their origin as it were from a cause not efficient but material, from a principle which in truth was nothing, but an eternal, infinite, immense, immutable, almighty, and to conclude, a God that was nothing, and the origin of this nothing.

{The world how made.}

As a prelude or introduction to his sect, this philosopher gave some account of the making of the world under two metaphors. The one was, that the world came out of an egg, which stretched out so vastly, that the heavens were made of the shell; the air, fire, and water, of the white; and of the yolk, the earth and all earthly things.[2] The other metaphor he took from the body of a vast great man, whom they call *Banco*, whom he would call *Microcosm*, saying; that the mass of the world came from him, his skull extending to form the heavens, his two eyes making the sun and moon, his flesh the earth, his bones the mountains, his hair plants and trees, and his belly the sea; and thus applying all the limbs and parts of man's body, to the fabrick and ornament of the world, he added, that the other men spread about all the world, were made of this great man's lice.[3]

---

[2] Egg is the foundation of world's creation in many cultures, the first or one of the first things that appeared from the emptiness.

[3] Ban Cổ in Vietnamese or Pangu in Chinese is the mythical progenitor of the Chinese. He is described in *Shiji* (Historical records), by Sima Qian, who lived approximately 145-90 BCE; see Chavannes, trans. and annot., *Les memoires historiques de Se-Ma Tsien* (Leiden: E. J. Brill, 1967). The general format of the Chinese creation myths begins with an egg, the first thing in the emptiness. Inside the egg was chaos and the first god was Pangu (male). When the egg broke, the universe was split into the heavens (*yang*) and the Earth (*yin*). After the breaking, Pangu had to hold up the heavens to keep them from crushing the earth. He lived ten thousand years, growing ten feet every day. He died after one day deciding to lie down to sleep. When he died, his body became the features of the earth and the animals. Then, Nunga (female), who is a human god with a human shape, except that she has a dragon tail instead of legs, appeared and admired the beauty of nature, but wanted more than simple animals. She made the people from the clay of the Yellow River. The world was broken by another god, Gong-Gong, only to be fixed again by Nunga.

{Another doctrine of the same philosopher.}

Having establish'd this doctrine of nothing, he gather'd some scholars, by whose means he spread it throughout all the east. But the *Chineses* who knew that a sect which reduced all things to nothing, was hurtful to the government, would not hearken to it, nor allow there was no punishment for wicked men, or that the happiness of the good should be reduced only to the being free from sufferings in this world; and the authority of the *Chinese* being so great, others following their example, rejected his doctrine. *Xaca* dissatisfied that he was disappointed of followers, changed his mind, and retiring writ several other great books, teaching that there was a real origin of all things, a Lord of heaven, hell, immortality, and transmigration of souls from one body to another, better or worse, according to the merits or demerits of the person; tho' they do not forget to assign a sort of heaven and hell for the souls departed, expressing the whole metaphorically under the names of things corporeal, and of the joys and sufferings of this world.

{The sect that believes all to be nothing.}

This second doctrine being made publick, the *Chineses* received it, and above others the *bonzis*, who are generally the meanest and most inconsiderable people in *Japan*, who being zealous for their spiritual advantage admitted this doctrine, and preserved it in twelve several sorts of sects all differing from one another, tho' that which is most followed and esteemed, is the opinion and sect that believes all to be nothing, which they call *gensiu*.[4] These sometimes go abroad into a field to hear a sermon, that is a discourse of bliss made by a *bonzo*, who treats of no other subject, but to persuade his congregation, that human bliss is nothing, and that he is happy who values not whether he has children or no children, whether he is rich or poor, sick or well, and the like; and the *bonzo* preaches this doctrine with such strength of argument, and vehemency, that the audience being fully bent upon the contempt of all things, which in themselves they look upon as nothing, suffering themselves to be in a manner transported, they express their satisfaction and happiness in this manner, that is, often crying out with a loud voice, *xin, xin, xin;* that is, nothing, nothing, nothing,[5] accompanying their voices with certain bits of boards they clap between the fingers of one hand striking them together with the other (as boys play on their snappers) and with this noise they are quite beside themselves as if they were drunk, and then they say they have done an act of bliss. The *Japoneses* and others making so great account of this opinion of nothing, was the cause that when *Xaca* the author of it was come to his last, calling together his disciples, he protested to them upon the word of a dying man, that in the many years he had lived and study'd, he had found nothing so true, nor any opinion so well grounded, as was the sect of nothing; and tho' his second doctrine seemed to differ from it, yet they must look upon it as no contradiction or recantation, but rather a proof and confirmation of the first, tho' not in plain terms, yet by way of metaphors and parables, which might all be applied to the opinion of nothing as would plainly appear by his books.

---

[4] A transcription of Japanese *Zen shu*, Vietnamese *Thiền tông* (Zen, *Dhyana*), brought to Japan from China in the seventh century; it was strongly established there by the twelfth century.

[5] *Xin* is apparently a transcription of Japanese *(mu) shin*, Vietnamese *vô tâm*, "no thought" or "thoughtlessness," an important idea in Zen Buddhism.

{Errors of the Cochin-Chineses.}

But it is time to return to our *Cochin-Chineses,* who not receiving this most foolish and vain doctrine,[6] which denying the substantial form, reduces all things to nothing, they generally throughout all the kingdom hold the immortality of the soul, and consequently the eternal rewards for the just, and punishments for the wicked, yet mixing a thousand errors with these truths. The first of which is, that they do not distinguish between the immortal soul and the demons, calling both by one and the same name *Maa,*[7] and attributing to them both the same practice of doing mischief to the living. The second is, that they assign one of the rewards of the soul to be transmigration from one body to another, more worthy, nobler, and in greater dignity; as from one of the common sort to a king, or great lord. The third, that the souls of the dead stand in need of sustenance and corporal food, and therefore at certain times in the year according to their custom, the children make plentiful entertainments for their dead parents, men for their wives, and friends for their acquaintance departed, expecting a long time for the dead guest to come and sit down at table to eat.[8] We one day confuted these errors with arguments which the philosophers call *à priori,* and therefore told them, that the soul was a spirit, and had no mouth or other material part to eat, and therefore they were deceived to think they could feed. And then *à posteriori,* for in case they did eat, then the dishes would not be as full after they had done as they were before. They laughed at these arguments, saying, these fathers know nothing; and to solve both difficulties, answered, that meat consisted of two parts, one the substance, the other the accidents of quantity, quality, smell, taste, and the like. The immaterial souls of the dead, said they, taking only the substance of the meat, which being immaterial, was proper sustenance for the incorporeal spirit, left only the accidents in the dishes, as they appear to our corporal eyes, to which purpose the dead had no need of corporeal parts as we said. Any wise man may by this false answer discover the acuteness of

---

[6] Let us notice the change of Borri's tone: at the beginning of this chapter he called Buddha "a great metaphysician," whose "sharpness" of "wit" prompted him to consider how the world was ordered. Here Borri refers to his alleged doctrine(s) as "most foolish and vain doctrine."

[7] *Ma,* meaning ghosts or evil spirits.

[8] Borri is describing ancestral worship. It definitely was not a part of Buddhist doctrine but a practice followed by nearly everyone, which proved to be the most formidable obstacle for Christian missionaries, as the Vietnamese, as well as the Chinese, could not bring themselves to forsake the rituals connected to ancestral worship. At the beginning, missionaries, especially Jesuits, having understood the importance of the veneration of the ancestors for indigenous people and striving to establish good relations with them, overlooked this practice. However, in the eighteenth century missionaries from other orders raised their voices to call for the elimination of the "pagan practice," which provoked the infamous Rites Controversy. While the Jesuits argued that these rites had social rather than religious character, Pope Clement XI decreed in 1715 that "[w]hether at home, in the cemetery, or during the time of a funeral, a Chinese Catholic is not allowed to perform the ritual of ancestor worship. He is not allowed to do so even if he is in company with non-Christians. Such a ritual is heathen in nature regardless of the circumstances." Dun J. Li, ed., *China in Transition, 1517-1911* (New York: Van Nostrand Reinhold, 1969), pp. 22-24. Indigenous people, hostile to the attempts to compel them to eliminate ancestral rites, turned against the missionaries and persecutions ensued. See more on the subject in D. E. Mungello, ed., *The Chinese Rites Controversy: Its History and Meaning* (San Francisco, CA: Institute Monumenta Serica, 1994).

the *Cochin-Chinese* philosophers, though they absolutely err as to the reality of the argument.

They also err in respect to the souls themselves, adoring those of men who were looked upon as holy in this world, adding them to the number of their idols, whereof their temples are full, placing them orderly according to their several degrees, in rows along the sides of the temples, the least first, and so bigger and bigger, till the last are extraordinary large. But the high altar being the most honourable place in the temple, is purposely kept empty, behind which is a vacant dark space, to express, that he whom they adore as God, and on whom the pagods [idols/images] call, who like us were visible and corporeal men, is invisible, wherein they think the greatest honour consists. Such a multitude of idols, by them accounted gods, giving us occasion to endeavor to demonstrate to them, that there can be but one only God: They answered, they agreed to it, supposing those that were placed along the sides of the temples, were not they that had created heaven and earth, but holy men whom they honoured, as we do the holy apostles, martyrs, and confessors, with the same distinction of greater and lesser sanctity, as we assign among our saints. And therefore to corroborate their assertion they added, that the vacant dark place about the high altar, was the proper place of the Creator of heaven and earth, who being invisible, and quite remote from our senses, could not be represented by visible images of idols, but that under that vacuity and darkness, the due adoration was to be given him as to a thing incomprehensible, using the intercession of the idols, that they may obtain favours and blessings of him. And altho' according to what has been hitherto said, they seem to have an efficient and intellectual cause for God, yet upon mature examination of the matter and their books, we find that they certainly adore a predominant element.

CHAPTER IX.

HOW GOD OPENED ANOTHER WAY TO THE CONVERSION OF THE MEANER SORT BY MIRACULOUS MEANS.

{Frequent apparitions of devils.}

It remains that we shew how God acting conformably to the mean vulgar people of *Cochin-China*, who were used to see phantoms, visions, and apparitions, the devil often appearing to them, was pleased to shew some miracles, to the end that declining in their opinion of diabolical prodigies, they might own the only Lord and singular worker of true wonders. The devils appear so frequently among those heathens, that not to speak of the oracles they deliver by the mouth of idols, which are in great esteem among the wretched gentiles, they walk about the cities so familiarly in human shapes, that they are not at all feared but admitted into company; and this is carried so far, that there are abundance of *Incubi* and *Succubi*.[1]

{Incubi and succubi.}

And among great people those husbands account themselves happy, who know their wives have such familiars; for generally they have to do with none but married women, publicly boasting that they are worthy to mix with a nature so much above their own as is the devils. It happened in my time, that a woman of great quality, mother to two sons who were Christians, envy'd by her neighbours, not so much for her beauty, as for her dishonest familiarity with the devil, positively refusing to become a Christian, came to die in labour, and by the assistance of the devil brought forth two eggs: Now it being held as most certain among them, that the devil her *Incubus* was god of the rivers, they did not bury the body in a cave, building a chapel over it as is the usual custom, but carrying it in solemn procession to a river cast it into the deep, together with the two eggs, saying, let her go to the lord of the river, since she was worthy to have to do with him when living. Among the common sort this filthiness is not esteemed an honour, but they rather account it a grievous distemper when their women are thus molested by the devil, as we should their being possesst [possessed]. These women therefore understanding that the religion of the fathers was altogether opposite to the devil, they imagined they might have

---

[1] Evil spirits or demons. *Incubus* is a male demon believed to have sexual intercourse with sleeping women. *Succubus* is a female demon believed to have sexual intercourse with sleeping men. In Vietnamese, *incubus* and *sucubbus* correspond to *con tinh*. See more on them in L. Cadière, "Le culte des arbres," *Bulletin de l'Ecole Française d'Extrême-Orient* 7,18 (1918): 34-39, and Bonifacy, in "Les Européens qui ont vu le vieux Hue: Cristoforo Borri," *Bulletin des Amis du Vieux Hué* 18,3-4 (July-December 1931): 392, n. 146.

some medicine against this distemper, calling holy things, as the water of baptism, *Agnus Dei*'s, and the like, medicines, and therefore came to our house to beg such medicines; and by the grace of God all those that carried away with them any bit of *Agnus Dei*, were never more molested by the devil, yet with this difference, that those who were not Christians saw the *Incubus* come to the bed's side, but had not power to lay hold on, or touch their persons, whereas the Christians perceive that he could not come near the chamber-door, which occasioned several to be baptized.

{Other monstrous visions.}

Tho' these *Incubus* devils appearing in human shapes, do no harm to the body, yet sometimes there are others that appear in horrid and frightful shapes, and the *Cochin-Chineses*, who have often seen, describe them after the same manner as we paint them, for example, with a cock's face, a long tail, a bat's wings, a hideous look, bloody flaming eyes; and when they appear in such shapes, they are much feared, being then generally hurtful to men, sometimes carrying them up to the tops of houses to cast them down headlong. We once heard a wonderful noise of people in our street, crying out very loud, *Maqui Maco*,[2] that is, the devil in a monstrous shape; whereupon some gentiles came running to desire us, that since we had weapons against those evil spirits, we would go relieve those distressed people who were infected by them. Having recommended ourselves to God, and arm'd ourselves with crosses, *Agnus Dei*'s, and relicks, we went two of us to the place where the devil was, and came so near, that we only wanted turning of a corner to be upon him, when he suddenly vanished, leaving three prints of feet upon the pavement, which I saw, and were above two spans long, with the marks of a cock's talons and spurs. Some attributed the devil's flying to the virtue of the holy cross and relicks we carried with us.

{Good visions.}

These frightful apparitions God has made use of to attract many to his holy faith, yet not denying them good visions, as will appear by the following accidents, which happened before me in that kingdom. The first was, that as we were one day in our own house, we saw a procession of a vast multitude of people in a field making towards us, whither when they came, being asked what they would have, they answered, that a most beautiful lady came from their land through the air, on a throne of bright clouds, who bid them go to that city, where they should find the fathers, who would shew them the sure way to bliss, and the knowledge of the true

---

[2] *Ma quỷ* means "demons and ghosts." It is not clear what is the original of *maco*. Bonifacy suggests that here is implied *ma cò*, a devil with long skinny legs like feathers *cò*. A. Bonifacy, *Les débuts du Christianisme en Annam des origines au commencement du 18e siècle* (Hanoi: Impremerie Tonkinoise, 192-?), p. 394, n. 150. However, the connection, between *cò* and long skinny legs, in my opinion, is not evident. I would suggest that *co* in the text stands for *cốt* from *cốt cách* "stature, figure." Thus, *ma cốt* would mean "a devil-like appearance," which will also bring us closer to Borri's translation "monstrous shape." The absence of the final *t* in the word *co* in the text can be accounted for by Borri's disregard of the *t* in final positions generally, as for example in the case *mocai* for *một cái* "one thing." Another possibility is that it comes from the compound *Bà cô*, "childless lady," one of the evil spirits. Cadière, "Le culte des arbres," pp. 31, 49. Or, this might simply indicate a female (*cô*) with an evil spirit (*ma*). In modern Vietnamese, *ma cò* means a pimp or a procurer/ess.

God of heaven. This made us give thanks to the blessed Virgin, whose this great benefit was owned to be, and having catechised and baptized the people sent them home well pleased.

The second was at another time, F. *Francis Buzome* and I returning homeward together, such a multitude of people came to another place, who having paid us very much respect, told F. *Francis Buzome*, they were come to him to teach them what he had promised them the night before when he was in their town. The father was astonished at their demand, having never been in the place they spoke of; but examining into the matter, I found that God of his infinite mercy had caused some angel in the father's shape, or in a dream had given those people some knowledge of our holy faith. The fame of these miracles being spread abroad, such numbers of people were converted, that the church given us by the governor was too little, and we were forced to build one larger; his wife, children, and kindred, with many other Christians contributing towards it.[3]

---

[3] F. Buzome died in 1639, long after Borri left the kingdom and after Borri's account was published, after spending twenty-four years in Cochinchina. According to de Rhodes, F. Buzome went to Macao "to transact some business for the king of Cochinchina, [and the news about the persecutions of Christians affected him so deeply] that he fell ill of a sickness that carried him off after a few days." Alexandre de Rhodes, *Rhodes of Viet Nam*, p. 79.

CHAPTER X.

OF THE CHURCHES AND CHRISTIANS OF FAIFO, TURON AND CACCHIAM.

{What the fathers did at *Faifó*.}

F. *Francis de Pina* being gone to *Faifó*, a city of the *Japoneses*, as was said before, he there joined F. *Peter Marques*, and they did great service in that city. The last of them, who was master of the *Japonese* tongue, in a short time reformed some of those Christians who were become libertines, and kept women, and converted many pagans. The other who understood the language of *Cochin-China* made many Christians, and having convinced some *bonzos* and *omsaiis*, by that means drew over many more to the holy faith; so that between *Japoneses* and *Cochin-Chinese*, that church for number and religious observance might compare with many in *Europe*; such was their piety, zeal, frequenting of the sacraments, and other godly works.[1]

{At Turon.}

The church of *Turon*, which we said in the second chapter of this book, the heathens burnt down during the first persecution, was by God's permission rebuilt by means of the fathers of the society, who gained many Christians in that city.

{At Cacchiam.}

Abundance of people were likewise converted to our faith at *Cacchiam*; which good work was much forwarded by the *Omgne*, who on account of the father's foretelling the eclipse so certainly as was before observed, publickly affirmed, there was no other true religion but that the fathers taught. This was the state of affairs there, when I came away out of that country for *Europe*, which was in the year 1622.

Afterwards by the annual letters sent me by those fathers, my companions left here cultivating that vineyard, I understood that there were still about a thousand converted and baptized in a year, and that Christianity flourished more than ever it had done at *Cacchiam* particularly. But now of late they write, that the king had forbid any more becoming Christians, and threatened to expel the fathers out of the kingdom, and this because the *Portuguese* trade failed. Yet it pleased God this persecution went no farther, the king being satisfied, provided one of the fathers

---

[1] Fr. Pina passed away in 1625, after Borri's departure from Cochinchina. "The good Father was asked to go visit the Portuguese, who had arrived within sight of the port of Cham where their ship lay at anchor. On concluding his visit he got into a boat to return to his flock, but a storm arose with such violence it upset the craft. The Father, finding himself hampered by his cassock, wasn't able to save himself by swimming like the others. He found burial in the waters and later in the tears of every last Christian in the whole country." Alexandre de Rhodes, *Rhodes of Viet Nam*, p. 52.

went away to *Macao*, to endeavour to persuade the *Portugueses* to continue the trade, as it seems was afterwards done; so that things are now quiet, and the fathers continue gaining new Christians as they did at first.[2]

---

[2] Apparently, Borri describes events that took place in 1625. As Alexandre de Rhodes relates: "Seeing the Portuguese hadn't come that year with their ships laden as usual, the king easily gave ear to the Christians' enemies." Ibid. But de Rhodes does not mention anyone sent to Macao to negotiate with the Portuguese; instead he reports that all the missionaries were ordered to be confined to Faifo, but they soon succeeded in lifting this restriction by petitioning the son of the Nguyễn lord. Ibid., p. 53.

CHAPTER XI.

OF THE KINGDOM OF TUNCHIM.

When the superiors of *Macao* sent me into *Cochin-China*, they told me, they did not absolutely design I should continue in that mission, but only to learn the language, that I might afterwards discover the kingdom of *Tunchim*. For this reason during those five years I dwelt there, I almost made it my business to inquire into, and get certain information of the affairs of that kingdom, the language being the same, as formerly it was but one kingdom. I will therefore say as much of it as any way concerns *Cochin-China*, which has some dependance upon *Tunchim*, and this according to the accounts given me by natives of *Tunchim*, who came to the province of *Pulucambi*, where I resided most part of my time; the rest I will leave to the news we shall receive from our fathers, who are there still making further discoveries.

{A description of Tunchim.}

This kingdom, besides *Cochin-China* which belongs to it, contains four other provinces, all extending equally in length and breadth. In the very center of them is the royal city of *Tunchim*, from which all the kingdom takes name, there the court is kept, and the king resides, being encompassed on all sides by those four provinces, composing a square four times as big as *Cochin-China*. On the east side of this kingdom is the gulf of *Ainam*, into which falls a great and navigable river that runs down eighteen leagues from the city *Tunchim*, and *Japonese* ships call'd *Jonks* go up it. The river generally overflows twice a year, in *June* and *November*, drowning almost half the city, but it lasts not long. On the south are the frontiers of *Sinuva*,[1] the court of *Cochin-China*, as has been observed already. On the north of it is *China*, without the defense of a wall, the trade and commerce between the *Chineses* and *Tunchineses* being so mutual and constant, that it will not allow of walls and gates shut, as they are against other foreigners. This is the reason that induces the fathers of our society to attempt the entrance into *China* that way, knowing they shall not on this side meet with all those impediments that strangers meet with throughout all the rest of the kingdom, and more especially about *Canton*. Lastly, on the west it borders on the kingdom of *Lai,* into which F. *Alexander Rhodes* of *Avignon* made his way through *Cochin-China;*[2] and this kingdom, I am of opinion, cannot but border upon that of

---

[1] See Borri, Part I, Chapter I, n. 12.

[2] Bonifacy argues that A. de Rhodes never visited Laos, but that the visit was carried out by one of the neophytes from Cochinchina, who assumed his name to visit Laos on his way to Tonkin; see "Les Européens qui ont vu le vieux Hue: Cristoforo Borri," p. 399, n. 154. And indeed I could not find a description of his own visit to Laos in de Rhodes's works. On the other hand, Giuliano Baldinotti, the first missionary to visit Tonkin (he arrived in 1626), summoned other missionaries from the south to explore this new domain, and Baldinotti's account, published in the same year, agrees with Borri's. According to Baldinotti, de Rhodes was on a mission there and reported the Laotians were "a people very much disposed towards

Tibet, newly discovered; which I am apt to believe, as well by reason of the extent and length of the land of *Tibet* and borders of *Lai*, because of the greatness and compass of these two kingdoms, it seems impossible that any other land should lie betwixt them;[3] as also much more on account of what the same fathers who were there relate of *Tibet*, who report that the farthest province of *Tibet* eastward borders upon, and trades with a people, who sell them raw silk and fine dishes, like those of *China*, and such like commodities, which we know *Tunchim* abounds in, and sell them to the *Laiis*.[4]

{The government.}

As to the government of this kingdom it is hereditary, and ruled as follows: The supreme regal dignity resides in one they call *Buna*;[5] but he of himself does nothing at all, all things being left to his favourite, whom they call *Chiuua*,[6] whose power is so absolute both in peace and war, that he is come by degrees to own no superior; the *Buna* remaining in his royal palace, quite cut off from all management of the publick affairs, satisfied with an exteriour respect due to him as a sort of sacred person, and with the authority of making laws, and confirming all edicts. When the *Chiuua* dies, he always endeavours to have his son succeed him in the government; but for the most part it falls out that the tutors of those sons aspiring themselves to that dignity, endeavour to murder them, and by that means possess themselves of the dignity of *Chiuua*.[7]

---

the acceptance of our law." See "La relation sur le Tonkin du P. Baldinotti," *Bulletin de l'Ecole Française d'Extrême-Orient* 1, 3 (1903): 78.

[3] The Chinese province of Yunnan lies between Laos and Tibet.

[4] Launay suggests that the first European missionary in Tibet was a Portuguese Jesuit, d' Andrada (?-1634), who arrived there in 1624, thus after Borri's departure from Cochinchina. He was joined by several other missionaries in the late 1620s. Adrien Launay, *Histoire de la Mission du Thibet* (Lille-Paris: Desclée de Brouwer, date unknown), 1: 23-30.

[5] As it has been said above, in the original this word is written *Bua*, spelled *vua* in modern Vietnamese orthography.

[6] *Chúa*, meaning prince or governor, a title similar to that of *shogun* in Japan, denotes a de facto ruler of the country, while a king or an emperor held only an honorific title and was a mere figurehead, with real control wielded by the *chúa*. Both the Nguyễn in Cochinchina and the Trịnh in Tonkin were called *chúa*.

[7] It seems that Borri may have mistakenly put the word *Chiuua* (*chúa*: prince, governor) instead of *Bua* (*vua*: king) in this sentence. It was hereditary succession among the *chúas*, but it was different with the kings. Between the mid-sixteenth century and Borri's time in Tonkin, the succession of the royal line was indeed disrupted or changed by the Trịnh lords. A quick glance will suffice to show the influence the Trịnh exerted on royal succession: King Lê Anh Tông (r. 1556-73), after he attempted to curb the Trịnh's power, was forced to abdicate in favor of his son. His successor was not his eldest son, but rather his fifth son (known as King Lê Thế Tông), who was put on the throne at the tender age of seven and ruled until 1599. He was not succeeded by his eldest son either, but by the second son (known as King Lê Kính Tông), when the latter was only twelve years old. Growing up, this king demonstrated some independent aspirations; as a result, he was forced to commit suicide or was killed in 1619. In this case, his eldest son, future king Lê Thần Tông, ascended the throne at the age of twelve. Furthermore, the Lê kings were forced to marry women from the Trịnh clan, whose leaders thus became close relatives of the kings and of their descendants. Borri's comment "that the tutors of those sons aspiring themselves to that dignity, endeavour to murder them, and by that means possess themselves of the dignity of *Chiuua*" may consequently be seen as a mistake, or it could also mean that, by controlling the royal family, the Trịnh were able to

{Power.}

The *Chiuua*'s power is so great, that suitable to the bigness of the kingdom, he is able to bring into the field three or four times the number of men as the king of *Cochin-China*, whose army, as was said above, amounts to 80,000 men. Nor is it any difficult matter for the *Chiuua*, as often as he pleases to raise 300,000 armed men or more, because the prime lords of his kingdom, such as among us, dukes, marquesses, and earls, are oblig'd in time of war to furnish them at their own expence. The *Buna*'s strength is not above 40,000 men for his guard. Yet he is always own'd as superior to the *Chiuua* of *Tunchim* [Trịnh], by the king of *Cochin-China* [Nguyễn], and by that other *Chiuua* [Mạc], we observ'd in the first book to be fled into the province bordering upon *China*, tho' these are continually at war against one another; and the king of *Lais* bordering upon *Tunchim*, pays him a certain tribute.

{Succession.}

Therefore when we say this crown is hereditary, it is to be understood only in reference to the *Buna* whose children always succeed, the royal race being continued in his family.[8] This is as much as I thought fit briefly to say of the kingdom of *Tunchim*, from what I could learn of it till my return into *Europe*.

Since then I have been inform'd, that F. *Julian Baldinotte*, an *Italian* born at *Pistoria* in *Tuscany*, was sent into that kingdom to make some way for the gospel, and arrived from *Macao* at the city *Tunchim*, after a month's sail.[9] As for what the said father found in that country, what pass'd between the king and him, the solemnity of his reception, and the first foundation he laid for Christianity, I refer the reader to the account given lately by that father himself; and we are still expecting fresh advices from the other fathers, as F. *Peter Marques* a *Portuguese*, and F. *Alexander Rhodes* of *Avignon*, who we said before had been in *Cochin-China* and are there still gaining Christians. We therefore hope both these kingdoms of *Tunchim* and *Cochin-China*, will soon be united to the flock of the church, acknowledging and giving the due obedience to the universal pastor and vicar of Christ our Lord on earth.

---

maintain their possession of real power as *chúa*. We have seen in Chapter 7 of Part I that Borri refers to the Trịnh as royal "tutors."

[8] The Trịnh had tried to preserve the royal blood in the succession. For example, when King Lê Trung Tông (r.1548-56) died without male descendants, they looked for some descendant of the royal house until they found Lê Duy Bang, a descendant of Lê Lợi, the founder of the Lê dynasty. Lê Duy Bang became King Lê Anh Tông (r. 1556-73). See *Đại Việt Sử Ký Toàn Thư* (Complete History of Great Viet) (Hanoi: Nhà Xuất Bản Khoa Học Xã Hội, 1993), bản kỷ 16:13a (3:129).

[9] Father Giuliano Baldinotte (Baldinotti in modern Italian orthography) (1591-1631) was the first Jesuit sent to Tonkin in 1626 from Macao with a Japanese, Giulio Piani, to find out about the situation there. "He was struck by the size and beauty of the kingdom and the natural goodness of the people no less than by their wonderful intelligence. It was then he regretted with all his heart not having learned the language so as to be able to implant the faith in ground that seemed so well prepared." Alexandre de Rhodes, *Rhodes of Viet Nam*, trans. Solange Hertz (Westminster, MD: The Newman Press, 1966), p. 54. He spent in Tonkin half a year, from March to August, and subsequently wrote an account, republished in Italian and translated into French in *Bulletin de l'Ecole Française d'Extrême-Orient* 3 (1903): 71-8. He and his work were mentioned above in connection with A. de Rhodes's trip to Laos.

THE CONCLUSION.

It is not possible but that such as have least inclination to the discovery of the world, and are most affected to their own countries and homes, must be excited by this short account to desire to see not only the variety but the truth of such strange things, which tho' they be not supernatural, may yet be term'd miracles of nature. Such are those I have said, I saw in *Cochin-China*, a land as to its climate and seasons of the year habitable, by reason of the fruitfulness of its soil abounding in provisions, fruit, birds, and beasts, and the sea, in choice and delicious fish; and most healthy, because of the excellent temper of the air, insomuch that those people do not yet know what the plague is. It is rich in gold, silver, silk, *Calambá*,[1] and other things of great value, fit for trade by reason of the ports and resort of all nations: peaceable, because of their loving, generous, and sweet disposition: and lastly secure, not only by the valour and bravery of the *Cochin-Chinese* accounted such by other countries, and their store of arms, and skill in managing them; but even by nature, which has shut it in on the one side by the sea, and on the other by the rocky *Alps*, and uncouth mountains of the *Kemois*.[2] This is that part of the earth call'd *Cochin-China*, which wants nothing to make it a part of heaven, but that God should send thither a great many of his angels; so S. *John Chrysostom*[3] calls apostolical men, and preachers of the gospel. How easily would the faith be spread abroad in this kingdom of *Cochin-China*, where there are not those difficulties which we fathers of the society dispers'd about the East, do meet with in other countries; for there is no need here of being disguis'd or conceal'd, these people admitting of all strangers in their kingdom, and being well pleased that every one should live in his own religion. Nor is it necessary before preaching to spend many years in studying their letters and hieroglyphicks, as the fathers in *China* do, for here it is enough to learn the language, which as has been said is so easie, that a man may preach in a year. The people are not shy, nor do they shun strangers, as is practic'd in other eastern nations, but make much of them, affect their persons, prize their commodities, and commend their doctrine.

They do not lie under that great impediment for the receiving the grace of the gospel, that is, the sin of sodomy, and others contrary to nature, which is frequent in all the other eastern countries, the very name whereof the *Cochin-Chinese* naturally abhor. In short, these people may very easily be taught the principal mysteries of our holy faith, they, as we have shewn, in a manner adoring but one only God, accounting the idols as inferior saints, allowing the immortality of the soul, eternal punishments for the wicked, and bliss for the just, using temples, sacrifices, processions; so that changing the objects, it would be easie to introduce the true worship. That there will be no difficulty in making out the mystery of the holy eucharist may appear by the distinction they make between the accidents and

---

[1] Calambac.
[2] See Chapter 1 of Part 1.
[3] 347-407, Archbishop of Constantinople.

substance of the meat they provide for the dead, as has been said above in this second book. All these things inflame the minds of the children of the society, who tho' recluse and shut up in the colleges and provinces of *Europe*, have an ardent desire to convert the world. And tho' many of them put it in practice with the assistance of the holy see apostolick, which with a fatherly care relieves the mission of *Japan*; as also by his catholick majesty king *Philip*, and his council of the *Indies*, who so frequently with incredible bounty, supply the *East* and *West Indies* with ministers of the gospel,[4] yet it is impossible that these two great pillars, which support other mighty weights, and bear almost all the world on their shoulders, can sufficiently supply all that daily occurs and is discover'd. I therefore trust in God, that his divine Providence will rouze up some generous soul, inflam'd with the zeal of God's honour, to send and maintain some evangelical ministers, who, satisfy'd with a religious and poor sustenance, may convey the food of the gospel not only throughout *Cochin-China*, but unto the great kingdom of *Tunchim*, founding a church and christian flock that may compare with the most renowned in the world.

FINIS

---

[4] The Council of the Indies, founded in 1524 by Charles I (1500-58), was to manage colonial possessions, politically, economically, and spiritually, thus being responsible for sending missionaries to the colonies to propagate Christianity. Its activity continued to approximately 1834. The Spanish kings, who between 1580 and 1640 were also kings of Portugal, were called Catholic kings. Borri apparently refers here to Philip IV (1605-65).

A

COLLECTION

OF

Voyages and Travels,

SOME

Now first Printed from *Original Manuscripts*,

OTHERS

Translated out of Foreign Languages, and now

First Published in ENGLISH.

To which are added,

Some Few that have formerly appeared in *English*,
but do now, for their Excellency and Scarceness,
deserve to be Reprinted.

In Six VOLUMES.

With a General PREFACE, giving an Account
of the Progress of NAVIGATION, from its first
Beginning to the Perfection it is now in, &c.

The Whole Illustrated with a great Number of useful MAPS and
CUTS, Mostly Engraven on Copper.

VOL. VI.

LONDON:

Printed by Assignment from Messrs CHURCHILL,
For JOHN WALTHOE over-against the *Royal-Exchange, in Cornhill;* THO. WOTTON at
the *Queen's-Head* and *Three Daggers* over-against St. *Dunstan's* Church in *Fleet-street;*
SAMUEL BIRT *Ave-Mary-Lane, Ludgate-street;* DANIEL BROWNE, at the *Black-Swan,*
without *Temple-Bar;* THOMAS OSBORN, in *Gray's-Inn;* JOHN SHUCKBURGH, at the
Sun, next the *Inner-Temple-Gate,* in *Fleet-street;* and HENRY LINTOT, at the *Cross-Keys,*
against St. *Dunstan's* Church, in *Fleet-street.* M.DCC.XXXII.

A
COLLECTION
OF
Voyages and Travels.
VOL. VI.

CONTAINING

I. A DESCRIPTION of the Kingdom of *T O N Q U E E N*. By SAM. BARON, a Native thereof.

II. T R A V E L S through *E U R O P E*. By Dr. JOHN GEMELLI CARERI. In several Letters to the Counselor AMATO DANIO, at *Naples*.

III. A VOYAGE to *V I R G I N I A*. By Col. Norwood.

IV. CAPTAIN PHILLIPS'S Journal of his Voyage from *England* to Cape *Mounseradoe* in *Africa*; and thence along the Coast of Guiney to *Whidaw*, the Island of St. *Thomas*, and so forward to *Barbadoes*. In which is contained an exact Account of the Longitudes, Latitudes &c. As also a Cursory Account of the Country, People, Forts, Trade, &c.

V. A V O Y A G E into the North-West. Passage. Written by JOHN GATONBE.

VI. A Relation of Three Years Sufferings of ROBERT EVERARD, upon the Coast if *Assada*, near *Madagascar*, in a Voyage to *India*; And of his wonderful Preservation and Deliverance.

VII. A familiar DESCRIPTION of the MOSQUETO Kingdom in *America*, with a Relation of the strange Customs, Religion, Wars, &c. of those Heathenish People.

VIII. A Discovery of Two Foreign Sects in the *East-Indies; viz.* The Sect of the BANIANS, the ancient Natives of *India*; and Sect of the PERSEES, the ancient Inhabitants of *Persia*. With the Religion and Manners of each Sect. By the Rev. Mr. HENRY LORD.

IX. An Account of the wonderful Preservation of the Ship T E R R A N O V A of *London*. By C . M A Y .

X. An Account of the King of MOCHA, and of his Country.

XI. Some Reasons for the Unhealthfulness of the Island of BOMBAY.

XII. A J O U R N E Y through Part of the *Low-Countries, Germany, Italy* and *France*. BY PHILLIP SKIPPON, Esq; (afterwards Knighted) in Company with the celebrated MR. RAY, MR. LISTER, MR. WILLUGHBY, MR. HENRY MASSINGBERD, &C.

A
DESCRIPTION

OF THE

Kingdom of *Tonqueen,*

BY

S. BARON, a Native thereof.

TO

SIR *JOHN HOSKINS*, KT.

AND

ROBERT HOOKE, ESQ.

Honoured Sirs,[1]

I send by this conveyance to Mr. *Charles Chamberlain*[2] the promised description of *Tonqueen*, wherein I think I have noted the most material passages of trade, government, and customs of the country, vice and virtue of the people, as least so far as will content and satisfy a moderate mind, and be sufficient for a new commissioner to conduct business by at his first entrance there. As to the imperfections and errors therein, you will be pleased to favour it with your exact survey and prudent correction, especially to remove or cancel what therein may be either against, or reflectingly spoken of Mons. *Tavernier*,[3] since the intention is to inform the reader of the truth, and not to carp and find fault with others; which when I did, was only for your particular perusal. The pictures are true and exact, tho' not according to art; the map, drawn and computed out of two others, is as near the truth as could be done in this place either by care or diligence. Of the whole the honourable president *Gyfford*[4] sends his judgment to you, whose liberality has chiefly supported my expences thereon; therefore I request you will be pleased to deliver to Mr. *Charles Chamberlain* the money the said description will yield, for the president's use. And if you should think convenient to dedicate it to the right honourable company, then to make honourable and particular mention of Mr. *John Page*, Mr.

---

[1] Robert Hooke (1635-1703), was an English physicist who conducted experiments in many fields of inquiry and was active in the Royal Society in London; for a biography, see Lisa Jardine, *The Curious Life of Robert Hooke, The Man Who Measured London* (New York: Harper Collins, 2004). Sir John Hoskins was a friend of Robert Hooke who was active in the Royal Society and served for a time as its president.

[2] Charles Chamberlain was an acquaintance of Robert Hooke who was active in the English East India Company.

[3] On Jean-Baptiste Tavernier, see the Introduction.

[4] William Gyfford, an agent of the English East India Company, established the English factory in Tonkin in 1672 and remained there in charge of it for four years. He was an agent in Madras from 1681 to 1684 and was then Governor of Fort St. George and President of Madras from 1684 to 1687.

James Hobland, Mr. *Charles Chamberlain,* and Mr. *William Moyor,*[5] my benefactors. I am now on a voyage to *China,* where if I can pick up any curiosity, or discover any thing worthy your sight or information, you are sure to hear from me; in the mean while I recommend myself to the continuation of your favour, as,

Fort St. *George* at
  Madras-patam,
  February, 2d.
  1685-6.

Honoured Sirs,
Your very humble devoted Servant,

Samuel Baron.

---

[5] Moyer aside, I have found evidence that these men were in the employ of the English East India Company; see the Introduction.

To the HONOURABLE
William Gyfford, *Esq;*
President of Coast Cormandell, Bengall, &c.

AND

Governor of Fort St. George

Honored Sir,

This is but a rough draught of what is in a more clear and lively manner impress'd in your honour's memory; I mean, the state and constitution of the kingdom of *Tonqueen*, since yourself was the first *English* man that, entring the country, open'd the trade, and settled there a factory for the honourable company; in effecting which your patience appear'd no less exemplary (having suffer'd strange rudeness and harsh usages from the natives, their usual welcome to new-comers) than your prudence and dexterity was eminent in that negotiation, wherein (I can say without incurring the imputation of flattery) your generosity respected the honour of your nation and common benefit much more than your particular interest, and with a liberal spirit bestow'd your wax and honey most freely on others, thinking, as that heroick *German* express'd himself to the emperor *Charles* V. *If my Labour is not for myself, 'tis for Posterity.*[6] Equal to this was your honour's deportment, affable, courteous, complaisant to the humours of those people, wherein your condescending temper was very conspicuous; which tho' it had been accustomed to live in other parts of *India* after another rate and splendor than the *Tonqueenese, Chinese* or *Japanese* willingly tolerate any stranger or foreigner to do in their country, did yet know readily how to please them, by your conformity and seasonable receding to their pride, whereby you presently so gain'd the good-will of courtiers and merchants (of which they are otherwise great niggards to new-comers, yet very loving to them that know their country and customs) as prov'd no small means to uphold afterwards the *English* name, your person, factory, and what else belong'd to your place, with honour, reputation and credit, notwithstanding the *Dutch* war,[7] want of shipping, supplies, and your incapacity to trade, which are moral distempers for a new-settled factory, all the time of your residence, until your departure thence, the space of well nigh six years, in which time you got much experience yourself, and gave so true and

---

[6] I have not located the source of this quotation, but Baron appears to attribute it to Martin Luther at the Diet of Worms in 1521.

[7] England and Holland were at war 1672-74.

exact a character of the country, whereof there had been before but a confus'd idea amongst the *English*, as was very advantageous to commerce.[8]

These, and the respects of your superintendency over the right honourable company's affairs in the South Seas, the honour of your many years acquaintance, have induc'd me to direct this description to your honour, who, as the most capable to judge and discern the truth thereof, so I hope will have the charity to construe with your innate candor my intention therein. I am sensible of the inconsiderateness of my labour herein, tho', to the best of my might, I did it as well as the troubles I was in would permit me; and that only the subject is to be taken notice of, which is such as Sir *John Hoskins* and Mr. *Robert Hooke,*[9] my most honour'd friends, assured me, by reiterated letters out of *England*, would be taking and acceptable, whose approved judgment, which I shall always reverence, did alone encourage me to undertake this task, were it but to satisfy their curiosity and noble desires, ever constant in assiduous application to advance learning, and enrich the publick by new discoveries, which otherwise I would not have ventur'd on; but since they were the promoters thereof, I submit it to their censure, according to the following advertisement, but leave the whole disposal to yourself, as from,

Fort St. *George* at *Madras-*
patam, on the Coast of
Cormandell, August 25,
Anno 1685.

Honoured SIR,

Your very humble obedient Servant,
Samuel Baron.

---

[8] On the difficulties of the English East India Company in Tonkin during the 1670s, when Gyfford was there, see Hoang Anh Tuan, "From Japan to Manila and Back to Europe: The English Abortive Trade with Tonkin in the 1670s," *Itinerario* XXIX,3 (2005): 73-92.

[9] Prominent figures in the London scientific community with whom Baron was acquainted; see the Introduction.

Advertisement.

MY design at first was not to undertake an historical narration of *Tonqueen*, but only to note the errors in Monsieur *Tavernier's* description of that country, as it was desired of me by Sir *John Hoskins* and Mr. *Robert Hooke* out of *England*; but having made some small progress therein, I was quickly tired with finding faults and noting mistakes, also thinking I should thereby give but small satisfaction to the curiosity of those worthy gentlemen, whose highly active genius's penetrate the very essence of the most occult things, and finding it much more easy for me to compose a new description of *Tonqueen* (the country of my nativity, and where I have been conversant with persons of all qualities and degrees) than to correct the mistakes of others; these considerations, together with ambition to do the publick acceptable service, and especially to demonstrate in some measure my thankfulness and profound respects to my much-honour'd friends Sir *John Hoskins* and Mr. *Robert Hooke*, induced me to undertake and finish this work, such as it is. I can freely declare that there is nothing inserted herein, but what I thought, to the best of my knowledge, to be exactly true and real. In dubious matters I had my informations from the most knowing and credible amongst the natives. As for the order and method, I follow'd Mons. *Tavernier*. The stile and diction thereof, since they are my first essays, must needs be very defective; therefore I intreat my friends to correct and alter what therein they may find amiss, and to dedicate it to whom they please; and in so doing they will infinitely oblige

Their most humble Servant,
Samuel Baron.

Note, *that the original Pictures, whereof those in this Book are but a Copy, were drawn on the Place by a* Tonqueeneer *of eminent Quality, and according to my Judgment are done as well as Things of that nature can be.*

CHAPTER I

THE DESCRIPTION OF TONQUEEN

TAVERNIERE'S ACCOUNT OF TONQUEEN *ANIMADVERTED ON.*[1]

The kingdom of *Tonqueen* has been discovered by the *Portuguese* above one hundred and twenty years since,[2] and the relations that *Padre Martin*[3] and *Alexander de Rodes*,[4] both Jesuites, give of it, is in general more true than this of *Taverniere*; for what contradictions we find in them, may be imputed to the alteration of things by mutation of time.

Taverniere talks of eleven or twelve voyages his brother made to *Tonqueen*, from *Acheen* [Acheh], *Batavia*,[5] and *Bantam*;[6] on the confidence of whose relation, together with what he inquired of the *bonzes*, or priests, that came while he was in *Bantam*, he has compiled his history,[7] as fabulous and full of gross absurdities as lines.

---

[1] This chapter is a response to Tavernier's first chapter: "A Discourse in general concerning the City of Tunquin, and of the Manner how the Author came to have knowledge thereof." See Jean-Baptiste Tavernier, "A New and Singular Relation of the Kingdom of Tunquin," in *A Collection of Several Relations and Treatises Singular and Curious* (London: A. Godbid & J. Playford, for Moses Pitt at the Angel in St. Paul's Churchyard, 1680). For more on Tavernier, see the Introduction.

[2] On the Portuguese arrival along the Vietnamese coasts, see Pierre-Yves Manguin, *Les Portugais sur les côtes du Viêt-Nam et du Campa: Etude sur les routes maritimes et les relations commerciales, d'après les sources portugaises: XVI, XVII, XVIII siècles* (Paris: Ecole Française d'Extrême-Orient, 1972).

[3] This refers to Gio. Filippo de Marini, *Relation nouvelle et curieuse des royaumes de Tunquin et de Lao*, trans. from Italian by L.P.L.C.C. (Paris: Gervais Clouzier, 1666).

[4] Alexandre de Rhodes, *Histoire du royaume de Tunquin et des grands progrez que la predication de l'evangile y a faits en la conversion des infidelles, depuis l'année 1627 jusques à l'année 1646*, trans. from Latin by R. P. Henry Albi (Lyon: Jean Baptiste Devenet, 1651).

[5] Modern Jakarta, headquarters of the Dutch East India Company in Asia.

[6] A major port and kingdom of that time on the western coast of Java. The Asian headquarters of the English East India Company was located there until 1682.

[7] Tavernier (p. 2) says his brother ". . . had made Eleven or Twelve Voyages from Batavia, Bantam, and Achem, to Tunquin. Other Observations I collected from the Tonquinesi themselves, with whom I have had several Discourses, during the time that I was at Batavia and Bantam, where they principally trade. And that which gave me more light was this, that those Merchants several times bring along with them some of their Bonzes or Priests, as also some of their Learned Men to teach their Children to Write and Read."

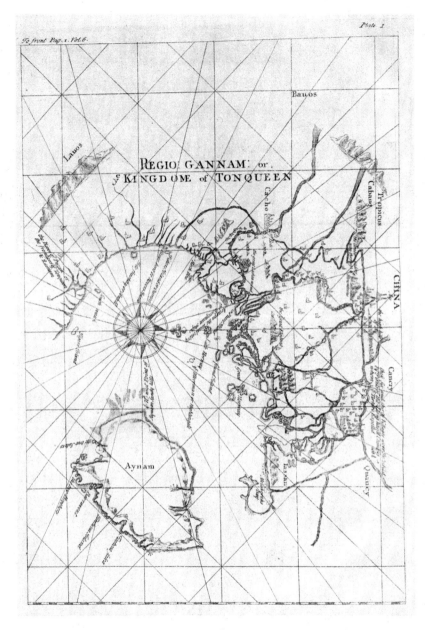

Plate 1: Regio Gannam or the Kingdome of Tonqueen

For first, the *Tonqueenese* have no *bonzes* or priests,[8] however they came to *Bantam* and *Batavia*; and then he saith, when the *Tonqueenese* make voyages, they take their wives and families with them; I suppose he means those voyages they make in the river of *Tonqueen*, from one village to another: but for foreign voyages they are altogether unacquainted with them, unless it be some few of the poorer sort that go to attend strangers, or are forced otherwise for a livelihood. He notes how the *Tonqueenese* were ravished with admiration, when he shewed them his Atlas, and some particular maps about the composure and structure of the whole world, and its several kingdoms and states,[9] which they heeded as much as a world in the moon. Neither can I hear of a *Taverniere* that has made eleven or twelve voyages to *Tonqueen* on his own account; only thus much I have heard, that there has been one *Taverniere*, a purser in the *Dutch* service, and once in Tonqueen.[10]

He commends his brother for a person of courage and cunning,[11] how justly I cannot tell; but this I am sure, he has used but little cordiality, and less sincerity, notwithstanding all his protestations, in his account of *Tonqueen*: He magnifies the great sums of money his brother carried always with him, when he went on that voyage; but it is too well known what a purser in the *Dutch* service can do, and what they are allowed to do; hindring so strictly the private trade.

He talks of a large present he gave the king and prince,[12] together with his favourable reception and familiar conversation with them; if this be true, I say the *Tonqueenese* are much degenerated, yet it cannot be denied, but that strangers at their first entrance into this country, had, in many respects, better usage than at present; but not so, as to permit themselves to play with a foreigner the good companion: at this time they keep their distance to all strangers, making but small account of them.

---

[8] In seeming to say that there are no bonzes, Baron appears to contradict what he says in Chapter 18: "... they have no priest ... to preach and propagate their doctrine; all they have, are their Sayes, or Bonzes, as M. Taverniere calls them (which, by mistake, he terms priests) which are a kind of friers or monks." "Sayes" is apparently a pluralized transcription of the Vietnamese word *sãi*, which today generally means temple warden or a layperson who administers temple affairs, but which in the seventeenth century meant a Buddhist monk or nun; see Alexandre de Rhodes, *Dictionarium Annnamiticum, Lusitanum, et Latinum* (Rome, Sacr. Congreg, 1651), col. 671. Baron objects to conflating *sãi* with priests, or bonzes. Bonzes, according to him, are "a kind of friers or monks," while he understands priests in a European Catholic sense as members of a global hierarchy. Here he reads Tavernier as saying that bonzes are the same as priests, and he objects by asserting that priests do not exist among the Tonkinese. While it appears that he is saying there are no bonzes, this is not what he intends.

[9] Tavernier, "A New and Singular Relation of the Kingdom of Tunquin," p. 2: "And as I was never without an Atlas and some other particular Maps, they ['these Bonzes and other Learned Men'] were ravish'd with admiration, when I shew'd them the Structure and Composure of the whole World, and the Situation of its several Kingdoms and Estates."

[10] Tavernier's brother ostensibly went to Tonkin before his death in 1648, at which time Baron's father would have been residing in Tonkin on behalf of the Dutch East India Company (see the Introduction), and when Baron himself was probably already a child or teenager, residing with his father.

[11] Tavernier, "A New and Singular Relation of the Kingdom of Tunquin," p. 2: "My Brother, who was a person both cunning and courageous ..."

[12] Ibid., p. 3: " ... a very noble Sword, of which the Handle and Hilt were all over enchac'd with Rubies and Emraulds, with a Backsword Blade. To this he added a pair of Pistols, adorn'd and inlaid with Silver, a Persian Saddle and Bridle, embroider'd with Gold and Silver, a Bow and Quiver full of Arrows, and six Pictures ... ."

To kiss the king's hand, is not the *Tonqueen* mode, much less permitted to strangers: and when he spoke the *Malayan* language so fluently, he might as well have spoken *French* to them, that understood not a word of either.[13] When he played amongst those lords, I wonder what game it was that he lost so many thousand crowns at, as he mentioned;[14] but it is most to be admired, that a calf and two jars of *Tonqueen* arrack, the usual largess and liberality of this king, (water distilled out of rice) should supply his great losses. He farther tells you, that by the great familiarity his brother had at court, and by the great discourses he had with a great many *Tonqueenese*, (who never stir out of country, however he met them at *Bantam* and *Batavia*) he laid the foundation of his work, which is both faithful and exact: Furthermore he saith, no other consideration, than speaking of truth has invited him to undertake this relation;[15] all which being notorious contradictions and false tales, shame, indeed, the author the more.

Our author, as all other *Europeans*, terms and intitles the general or *Choua*, king; because he disposes of the kingdom at his pleasure, receiving all foreign ambassadors, except that of *China*. However, this is a mistake; for they have their king or *Boua*, though he signifies no more than a cypher, as will be noted in several places of this relation.[16]

He not only vaunts of his cuts, which he says were drawn on the place, and will contribute much to the divertisement of the reader, but also praises, for it's exactness, the map which he gives of the country;[17] than which nothing can be more false, for

---

[13] Ibid., Tavernier, speaking of Tonkin (p. 2): "My Brother ... soon grew familiar with the Malaye, which is the Language of the Learned in those quarters of Asia, as Latin is among Us in Europe." Further (p. 3): "Thereupon having order to attend the Court, and coming to kiss the king's hands, the whole Assembly was surpris'd to hear a Stranger, born in a Country so far distant, speak the Malaye Language so fluently." Dampier, writing about his observations in Tonkin in 1688, is of Baron's opinion: "But for the Malayan Tongue, which Monsieur Tavernier's Brother in his History of Tonquin says is the Court Language, I never could hear by any Person that it is spoken there, tho' I have made particular Inquiry about it; neither can I be of his Opinion in that Matter." William Dampier, "Mr. Dampier's Voyages, Vol. II, Part I: His voyage from Achin in Sumatra, to Tunquin, and other Places in the East-Indies," in *A Collection of Voyages, in Four Volumes* (London: James and John Knapton, 1729), II:59.

[14] Tavernier, "A New and Singular Relation of the Kingdom of Tunquin," p. 3, where he is speaking of his brother at "the Court of Tunquin": "But that which fix'd him more in the good opinion and favour of the King and Lords of the Court, was his frolic and gentle behaviour in playing with them for several large Sums, insomuch that being one that ventur'd deep, he lost above 20000 Crowns in one Voyage. However the King, who was a generous Prince, would not suffer him to be a loser, but gave him those considerable Presents that supplied his losses."

[15] Ibid., p. 4: "Thus you see the Grounds and Foundations of this Relation, which is both fanciful and exact, and by which that noble Country, of which the Descriptions hitherto have been so obscure and uncertain, shall be truly discover'd and set forth, such as it is; declaring withal, that no other Consideration or Interest, then that of speaking truth, has incited me to undertake this Description."

[16] The distinction here is between the *vua*, vernacular Vietnamese for "king," which referred to the Lê emperor, who was a powerless prisoner of his palace, and the *chúa*, "lord," which referred to the leader of the Trịnh family, who was the actual ruler, commonly understood as "the king" by European visitors of that time. For example, see Chapter 15 of Gio. Filippo de Marini, *Relation nouvelle et curieuse des royaumes de Tunquin et de Lao*, pp. 301-327, wherein the funeral rites of the deceased *chúa* Trịnh Trắng in 1657 are narrated as the funeral of "the king."

[17] A reference to Tavernier, "A New and Singular Relation of the Kingdom of Tunquin," p. 4: "And I dare ingage, that the Map of the Country, and the Cuts which were drawn upon the place, will no less contribute to the divertissement of the Reader, then to the Explanation of the

compare it with our sea draughts, 'twill plainly appear what it is: But as fabulous stories and fictions, inventions at pleasure, are pleasuring only to the ignorant, so 'tis most certain, the ingenious reader will blame him for promising so much and using so little probity in his history.

Matter which they contain." By "cuts" is meant engravings for illustrations; "drawn upon the place" means that they were drawn in Tonkin, at the places they depict.

CHAPTER II.

OF THE SITUATION AND EXTENT OF TONQUEEN.[1]

We have no more reason to admire why our predecessors had no earlier knowledge of this kingdom than they had of that of *China*, because its discovery was something posterior to that; for the *Portuguese* had no sooner discovered the last, but they sent out ships to visit this also.

It is true, this kingdom was a province of *China* formerly, and pays tribute still to that emperor: But that was not the reason why we had no sooner knowledge thereof,[2] considering these people have been governed by their native princes for above these four hundred years without interruption, which was long before the *Portuguese* came to make their discoveries in *India*. The true reason seems to be, that the people did never stir abroad, nor do yet, for commerce or other association; and they somewhat affect in this the *Chinese* vanity, thinking all other people to be barbarous, imitating their government, learning, characters, &c. yet hate their persons.

I do not know why *Taverniere* saith most people should believe this country to be in a very hot climate, considering it is situated under the tropick, and some part of it more to the northward; nevertheless he affirms it to be very temperate, by reason of the great number of rivers (and altogether free from those sand-hills and barren mountains that cause such heat in *Commaroon*,[3] and other places in the gulf of *Persia*) that water it, together with the rain that falls in its season;[4] whereas the truth thereof is, that the rains, indeed, generally fall in the months of *May, June, July* and *August*, and sometimes sooner, which moistens the ground, but cause no fresh breezes at all; on the contrary, the said two months of *July* and *August*, make the weather here unsufferably hot. Doubtless the country would be plentiful in fruits, were there not so many inhabitants, who living by rice chiefly, find therefore the greater necessity to cultivate what ground they have with that grain, not neglecting the least spot.

---

[1] Jean-Baptiste Tavernier, "A New and Singular Relation of the Kingdom of Tunquin." Here Baron is referring to Tavernier, Chapter 2: "Of the Situation and Extent of the Kingdom of Tunquin." This chapter of Baron's is largely a running commentary upon Tavernier.

[2] Ibid., p. 5: "We shall have the less reason to admire wherefore our predecessors had so little knowledge of this Kingdom, when we consider that having formerly been a considerable part of China, the Inhabitants in the same manner as the Chinese did, kept themselves close within their own bounds, never minding to have any Commerce with other People, whom they contemn'd and lookt upon as Barbarians come from the other part of the World."

[3] This name remains unidentified.

[4] Tavernier, "A New and Singular Relation of the Kingdom of Tunquin," p. 5: "Most people believe this Country to lye in a very hot Climate; nevertheless it is now known to be very temperate, by reason of the great number of Rivers that water it; which together with the Rains that fall in their Seasons, cause a brisk freshness of the Air."

To the north-east of this kingdom lies the province of *Canton*; to the west it is bounded by the kingdoms of *Laos* and the *Bowes;*[5] to the north it borders on two other provinces of *China, Junam* [Yunnan] and *Quanci* [Guangxi], or *Ai;*[6] to the south and south-east on *Cochin-china.* The climate is temperate and wholesome, from *September* till *March*, sometimes very cold in *January* and *February;* though frost and snow are never seen here; for the months of *April, May* and *June* are not so healthful, both because of the rains and the fogginess of the air, and the sun's coming to the zenith; but *June, July* and *August* are excessive hot months. The winds here are divided between the north and south for six months and six months; the country is delightful from *May* till *August*, the trees being then in their verdure, and the fields all covered with paddy, very pleasant to the beholders.

The great winds that are called amongst our seamen the hurricanes, and known here by the name of *Touffoons,*[7] reign on this and the adjacent coasts, and the seas thereof are very terrible; but the time of their coming is very uncertain, sometimes once in five or six years, and sometimes in eight or nine; and though the wind is not known in other oriental seas by that name, and with that excessive violence, yet that which is called the *Elephant* in the bay of *Bengall* and the coast of *Cormandel,*[8] is not much inferior to this; and the sad effects thereof are but too often experienced by the seamen. I cannot find an astronomer in all *Tonqueen*, to ask from whence those winds should proceed, so I cannot affirm that they are caused by the exhalations of the mines of *Japan.*[9]

As for the extent of the country, which he makes equal to that of *France*, it is a gross mistake; for this kingdom is reckon'd by men experienced, to be not much bigger than *Portugal;* but may be thought to contain four times the number of inhabitants. *Taverniere* makes its limits to be unknown, forgetting that he had so lately described the borders and extent thereof.[10]

As for islands belonging to this kingdom, there are several in the bay of *Tonqueen*, the chief whereof is called by the natives *Twon Bene*,[11] and by the *Dutch, Rovers island.* It is situated in the latitude of 19 degrees 15 minutes north; is long one and a half, and broad half a league at most, the better part high land, and distant from the main one league, between which the main sea, ships may pass, as the *Dutch*

---

[5] This term, or variants of it (Bauos on Baron's map), appears in some early European accounts in reference to the mountains west of modern northern Vietnam. In Chapter XI, Baron says that part of Bowes was "maintain'd as conquer'd lands [by the Tonkinese], that people being of a different language and manner." This is plausibly a reference to the Tai rulers of the Sipsong Panna in the region of the modern border of Laos and China between the Mekong and Black (Sông Đà) Rivers.

[6] Ai or Ai-Lao was an ancient Sino-Vietnamese name for upland polities in the regions that are now along the borders of China, Laos, and Vietnam.

[7] Typhoon, in Vietnamese *đại phong*, "big wind."

[8] The Coromandel coast on the Bay of Bengal is in southeast India.

[9] Tavernier, "A New and Singular Relation of the Kingdom of Tunquin," p. 6: "The Astrologers of those parts believe that these terrible Tempests proceed from the Exhalations that rise out of the Mines of Japan."

[10] Ibid.: "In this fair extent of land, almost equal to that of Frence, are several Provinces, whose limits are not well known . . . ."

[11] This term is perhaps Vietnamese *Tuần Bến*, meaning "patrol station/harbor"; French colonial maps identified it as "Island of Biến Sơn" (Biến Mountain), and on modern maps it is identified as Nghi Sơn, at the border between Nghệ An and Thanh Hóa provinces.

did formerly; but the navigator must observe to keep the island side aboard, within a musket shot; where you will find six, seven, and seven and a half fathoms, ouzy ground. On the same side of the island, which is its west part, are two small bays, the northermost has a small pearl bank, but not rich, yet none dare to fish here without the king's special grant. In both the bays there is sweet water, which we found to be exceeding good, and esteemed the best we tasted there. At the south-west point of this island, is a ridge of rocks, extending from the said point 100 paces into the sea, and may be discovered at half ebb, by the breach thereon; for the rest, a clear coast.

Towards the north-west, is a fair bay, three fathom and a half and four fathom water, clay ground; here resort many fishing boats, besides what appertain to this village, whose inhabitants I compute between three or four hundred persons, most fishermen.

In this island is the watch-house general, which is a place of the greatest profit in the kingdom of *Tonqueen:* for all trading boats, either to the province of *Tingway* [Thanh Hóa] or *Guian* [Nghệ An], or from thence to the north, must stop here and pay custom, *viz.* for a large boat about half the value of a dollar and half, with some presents for the waiters, the rest proportionable; so that the customs of this place cannot yield less than a million of dollars *per annum.*

As for the ground, it is stony and mountainous, therefore not proper to manure; cattle we saw but few (tho' inhabitants told us of many antelopes that sheltered amongst the rocks and shrubs of the mountains) so that rice and other provisions for sustenance, are brought hither from the adjacent shore. Some good regulations would make this place plentiful, and with small expence this port might be a good one.

For cities and towns, excepting that of *Ca-cho*,[12] there are not above two or three in the whole kingdom of any note. As for *Aldeas* or villages, questionless the number is great, and more than I can exactly affirm, or any man else that hath not made it his business to inquire after them; neither is it an easy manner to find the truth thereof: the city of *Ca-cho* is the metropolis of *Tonqueen,* lieth in the latitude 21 degrees north, about 40 leagues from the sea, and may, for its capaciousness, be compared with many cities in *Asia,* and superior to most for populousness, especially on the first and fifteenth of their new moon; being their market days, or grand *Bazaar*; when the people from the adjacent villages flock thither with their trade, in such numbers, as is almost incredible; several of the streets, tho' broad and spacious, are then so crowded that one finds enough to do if he can sometimes advance through the multitude a hundred paces in half and hour. Every different commodity sold in this city is appointed to a particular street, and these streets again allotted to one, two, or more villages, the inhabitants whereof are only privileged to keep shops in them, much in the nature of the several companies or corporations in *European* cities. The courts of the king, general, princes, &c. *Grandesa,*[13] and high courts of justice are kept here, of which I can only say, they stand on large tracts of ground; the principal structure makes but a mean appearance, being built of wood, the rest of their houses of bamboos and clay, not well compacted; few of brick except the factories of strangers, which out-vie the rest. Stupendous, indeed, are the triple walls of the old

---

[12] Kẻ Chợ ("marketplace"), modern Hanoi.

[13] From Italian *grandezza* or Spanish *grandeza*, meaning "grand, magnificent," here used to indicate palatial architecture.

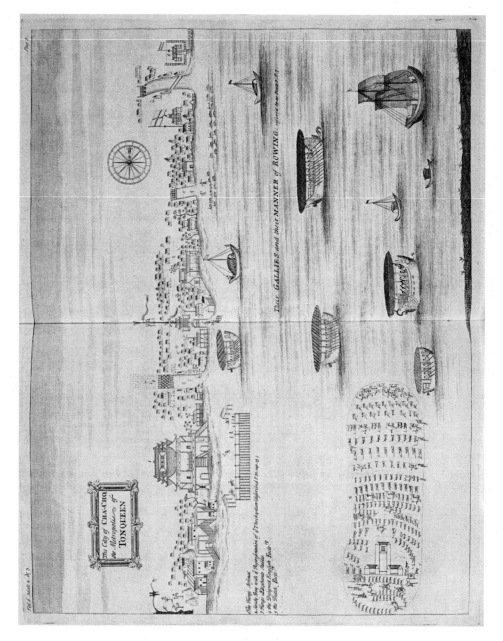

Plates 2/3: "The City of Cha-Cho, the Metropolis of Tonqueen." 1. The King's Arsenal.
2. Sandy Bay [Island] with the Representation of the Theckydaw. 3. King's Elephants' Stables.
4. The Designed English Factory. 5. The Dutch Factory.

city and palace; for by the ruins they appear to have been strong fabricks with noble large gates, paved with a kind of marble; the palace to have been about six or seven miles in circumference; its gates, courts, apartments, &c. testify amply its former pomp and glory. In this city is likewise quartered a formidable militia, to be ready on all occasions; and here also standeth the king's arsenal or magazine for war, seated on the bank of the river, near a sandy island, on which the *Thecadaw*[14] is kept, as hereafter will be mentioned. The river is called by the natives *Songkoy*,[15] or the head river: it rises in *China*, and after it has rolled many hundred leagues, it passes here and disgorgeth itself in the bay of *Aynam*,[16] by eight or nine mouths, most of them navigable for vessels of small draught. This river is exceeding commodious for the city, since all sorts of merchandise are brought hither as to the epitome of the kingdom, by an infinite number of boats trading up and down the country; yet they have their houses in their respective *Aldeas*, and do not live altogether in their boats as *Taverniere* reports, but when they are voyaging.[17]

---

[14] See Chapter XV, where this is spelled *Theckydaw*.

[15] Sông Cái, "the main river," (now called Sông Hồng, "Red River").

[16] *Hải-nam*, Vietnamese for the island of Hainan; the mid-seventeenth century Jesuit map of Vietnam identifies the Gulf of Tonkin as the Gulf of Hainam, Baron's "bay of Aynam."

[17] Tavernier, "A New and Singular Relation of the Kingdom of Tunquin," p. 6: " . . . many of the People choose rather to [live] upon the Water then upon the Land; so that you shall see the greatest part of their Rivers covered with Boates, which serve them instead of Houses; and which are very neat, though they also keep their Cattel in them."

CHAPTER III.

OF THE NATURE AND PRODUCTIONS OF THE KINGDOM OF TONQUEEN.[1]

This country is for the most part low and flat, not unlike the united provinces, especially for its moats and banks. The hills make the frontiers towards the north, west and south: it is watered by one special river, which disgorgeth itself into the sea, by many branches, most of them navigable for ships of mean burthen. These rivers swarm with boats and large barks, which make it very commodious for traders: indeed in this country grows neither corn nor wine, which is not occasioned by the want of rains, for both of them require rather dry than wet ground; but by reason the inhabitants do not much care for them, as being ignorant of their goodness, and therefore do not plant them. Rice, indeed, is the chief sustenance of these people; and the country produces sufficient quantities thereof; and if this grain would have grown only by the rains of the months of *June* and *July*,[2] we should not have experienced the sad effects of a most dreadful and calamitous famine, that swept away so many millions of souls, in these two preceding years.

From the rice they distil a liquor called arrack, but much inferior to aquavitæ. Their ploughs, and the manner of using them, are much after the *Chinese* fashion, described in the history of *China*: the paddy they tread out with their feet, wherein their practice has made them very expert.

The fruits are equally good in their kinds with those of other oriental countries, but their oranges, far exceed all that I have tasted: what *Taverniere* calls a palm-tree, is, indeed, a cocoa-nut,[3] the pulp within is white, and tastes something like an almond; this fruit is so plentiful in *Siam*, that they lade ships with the oil that is made of the said pulp, to supply their neighbours, which is used to burn in lamps.

The liquor thereof is very cold, and pleasant enough, but reckoned bad for the nerves: questionless it is the most useful tree that is found in *India*, serving for meat, drink, cloathing, firing, building, &c.

The *Guava* is a fruit much like his description; but he is mightily out in the effects thereof, for whether green or ripe, it is always binding, but not usually eaten green.[4]

The *Papay* [papaya] is a fruit indeed resembling a melon, and somewhat of the taste, not unpleasant.

---

[1] Jean-Baptiste Tavernier, "A New and Singular Relation of the Kingdom of Tunquin," Chapter III: "Of the Quality of the Kingdom of Tunquin."

[2] Ibid., p. 7: " . . . in all the country there grows neither corn nor wine, by reason of the want of rain, which never falls but in the Months of June and July."

[3] Coconut; ibid.

[4] Ibid: "[Guava] if they be eaten before they are ripe they bind the belly, whereas if they be eaten when they are come to full maturity they work a contrary effect."

The *Arreak* [Areca], called by the *Malays, Penang,* grows straight upright, bearing no branch, but at the top, like a crown; the fruit of which is in bigness like a large pigeon's egg, which most *Indians* use to eat with the leaf called Beetle [betel] by the *Portuguese, and Sera* by the *Malays:* it is good to sweeten the breath, fasten the teeth, and revive the spirits: in chewing, the juice thereof turns red; it is so much in use, that they think they do not make their friends welcome without presenting them with a dish of it. The *Tonqueenese, Siamese, Malays* and *Javas,* had rather lose a third of their diet than be without it. They have a fig called by them *Hungs,*[5] in taste something like a carrot, but much more pleasant; not at all like our *European* figs.

The other sort, called *Bonana,* or plantans, which he calls *Adam*'s figs, some are in length above a span, some less.[6]

The high-ways are here and there beset with trees and many sheds, where they sell tea and beetle, &c. very commodious for travellers: and for those exceeding great trees, that shade so many thousands of men, called the Banian-tree, I cannot contradict him;[7] but what I have seen at *Swallow Marreene,* at *Surrat,*[8] far exceed any of these in bigness.

In this country we have the fruit *Lechea* [lychee], call'd *Bejay*[9] by the natives, in great plenty; which indeed no where else comes to maturity but in latitude from 20 to 30 degrees north: It grows on high trees, the leaves resemble somewhat the laurel; the fruits in clusters on the branches, shew like so many hearts, of the bigness of a small hen egg; when ripe of a crimson colour; the shell thin and rough, yet easy to be pulled off; the kernel is full of a white juice. This fruit is of an excellent taste, and most pleasant to the sight, but it doth not last above forty days in season: the time of its maturity is *April,* about when the General will cause his *chiaop* [chop] or seal to be fixed on most trees of the best *Lachea*[10] in the country, belong to whom they will, which obliges the owner not only not to meddle with his own, but also to watch narrowly that others do not touch them, which would be to his peril, since it is ingrossed by the court, who allow him nothing for his fruit or pains.

The fruit called *Jean*[11] or *Lungung*[12] (that is, Dragons-eggs) by the *Chinese,* is very plentiful here: the tree much as the former, the kernel white, but exceeding luscious; the fruit round; and less than a small plumb, the skin not rough, of a pale olive colour, and near to a wither'd leaf. This fruit, though it pleases many of the *Tonqueenese,* yet it is reckon'd hot and unwholesome. The season is *May,* and lasts 'till *July.*

---

[5] Hồng: see Ch. Crevost and Ch. Lemarié, *Catalogue des produits de l'Indochine, Tome Ier: Produits alimentaires et plantes fourrageres* (Hanoi: Gouvernement Général de l'Indochine, 1917), pp. 257-160.

[6] Banana. See Tavernier, "A New and Singular Relation of the Kingdom of Tunquin," p. 8. A span, about nine inches, was measured from the end of the thumb to the end of the little finger on a hand with thumb and fingers spread.

[7] Ibid.: " . . . there are some of these Trees so big that two or three thousand men may stand under them . . ."

[8] Surat is a city in southeastern Gujarat state, west-central India, where the English established their first Indian factory in 1612. Swallow Marreene is unidentified.

[9] Apparently a transcription of Vietnamese *vải.*

[10] Spelled *Lechea* at the beginning of this paragraph.

[11] Unidentified.

[12] Longyan, commonly Anglicized as Longan, *long nhãn* in Vietnamese.

The *Na*,[13] or as the *Portuguese* call it, *Annona*,[14] *Pompelmoor*,[15] and two or three sorts of plums, with other kind of *Indian* fruits (except *Durrions* [durian], which will grow only in hot countries; that is, from *Siam* towards the South, as *Mallaya* [Malaya], *Mallacam* [Malacca], *Java*, &c.) are to be found here; but what exceeds all I have tasted in other parts of that kind, is the *Jaca*[16] or *Myte*[17] in *Tonqueen*. This is the largest fruit, I think, in the world, and because of its bigness provident nature has placed its growth on the stock or body of the tree, not on the branches, lest it should not be sufficient to bear the burthen: The skin when green, is very hard; but ripe, of a yellow colour, and easy to be cut with a knife. There are several sorts of them, but that which eats dryest, without sticking either to the fingers or lips, is the best and pleasantest. The greatest part are of a slimy substance, and, as it were, a yellow pap covers the nuts, which lie in little holes. Some of the poorer people will boil or roast the nuts, and eat them, which have a kind of taste like our chestnuts, but are reckon'd hurtful to the lungs.

Taverniere tells a long story of the rare mice[18] that are in this country, of many sorts, yet I never was at a feast of any, and therefore am no competent judge of their daintiness; I know the *Portuguese* eat them physically in several distempers.

The next thing to be taken notice of, is a particular kind of birds-nests, which indeed are in great esteem amongst all *Indians*, and kept at a great price, being taken as great restoratives, and by some counted stimulaters to venery; but *Taverniere* saith, they are not to be found but in the four islands of *Cochin-china A.B.C.D.*[19] which I am sure is a great mistake, neither do I know those islands, or of any birds-nests to be found in *Cochin-china*: The birds which makes these nests are less than swallows. As to the form and figure of these birds-nests, they are much as he describes them, and the greatest quantities of them come from *Jehor* [Johore], *Reho* [Riau], *Pattany* [Patani], and other *Malayan* countries; but that they are, when boiled, of that exceeding fragrance and odoriferousness, as he pretends, is a fiction.[20] These nests are laid to soak in warm water two hours, then pulled out in strings, the smaller the better, and so stewed with hens, pigeons, or any other flesh, with a little water: In stewing they dissolve almost to jelly without either taste or smell.

---

[13] Vietnamese *na* is usually translated as custard-apple.

[14] The scientific name is Anona squamosa; see Crevost and Lemarie, *Catalogue des Produits de l'Indochine*, p. 193.

[15] Probably the French Pamplemousse, Vietnamese *bưởi*, similar to a grapefruit.

[16] From Malayalam *cakka*, called jak, jack, or jack-fruit in English.

[17] Vietnamese *mít*.

[18] Tavernier, "A New and Singular Relation of the Kingdom of Tunquin," pp. 8-9, describes bats (rere mice) "as big as a good Pullet, insomuch as their wings are above a foot and a half long" who roost hanging upside down in trees: "They are accounted a great dainty among the Portugals, who leave their Pullets to eat them." Tavernier says he ate them in the company of Portuguese and they tasted like chicken (pullets).

[19] This is a reference to Tavernier's map.

[20] Tavernier, "A New and Singular Relation of the Kingdom of Tunquin," p. 9: " ... All the Spices of the East put together do not give that effectual relish and savour as these nests do, to the meats and dishes wherein they are used. ... You would believe in eating those Meats which are seasoned therewith, that those Nests were composed of all the Spices in the Orient." Also pages 41-42: " ... they have those Birds-nests ... which give the Meat a tast of almost all sorts of Spices."

And as M. Taverniere is very erroneous in his map, so I do not know nor have I heard of those islands, 1, 2, 3, 4, and 5, that afford, as he says, such infinite numbers of tortoises. The goodness of the said tortoises is sufficiently known to our *English* seamen, in their homeward bound voyages; but that the *Tonqueenese* or *Cochin-chinese* do not believe that they have entertain'd their friends at banquet as they ought, 'till the tortoise is brought in, is altogether fabulous; for when we were at the island *Twon Bene*, or according to the *Dutch, Rovers Island,*[21] a tortoise of about twenty pounds weight was brought to the custom house, where I lodged, to be sold, and the *Tonqueenese* not caring to buy it, I had it for a small matter: Moreover, coming from *Siam* I touch'd at *Pulo Uby,*[22] where my mariners took five or six very large tortoises, and brought them on board, but the *Tonqueenese* seamen that were with me (who were compell'd to take up that imploy, because of great famine that ravaged their country) would not touch them; neither do I know, as he asserts, that any of those tortoises are wont to be pickled by either of these two nations, or that there is any commerce carry'd on therewith amongst them; therefore I wonder how Monsieur *Taverniere* could dream of a war between them, merely on account of catching them.[23]

Tonqueen affords no great store of *Ananas* or *Pine-apples.*[24] The Citrons he mentions are not altogether so large as those of *Europe,*[25] which look green before they are ripe, and being mature look yellow.

They make good store of silks in the kingdom of *Tonqueen*, of which both rich and poor make themselves garments, since they can purchase them as cheap almost as outlandish callicoes.

As for sweet-smelling flowers, tho' I do not profess myself a florist, yet I know above two sorts in *Tonqueen*; but what he calls the *Bague*[26] I cannot smell out: For, first, there is a beautiful rose, of a white colour mix'd with purple; and another of almost the same kind, red and yellow; it grows on a bush without prickles or thorns, but has no scent.

The flower that is nothing else but a bud, resembles a caper, but much lesser, smells as fragrant and odoriferous as any flower I know, and will retain the scent above a fortnight, tho' off the tree; the ladies of the court use it amongst their wearing apparel.

---

[21] See Chapter II.

[22] Island off the southern tip of the Camau Peninsula, called Poulo Obi on many colonial maps, today in Vietnamese called Hòn Khoai.

[23] Tavernier, "A New and Singular Relation of the Kingdom of Tunquin," pp. 9-10: "The Tunquineses and Cochinchineses do not believe they have entertained their friends at a banquet as they ought to do, till the Tortoises are brought in. Those two Nations pickle up great quantities of them, and send them abroad, which is a vast trade among them; and indeed the chiefest occasion of the Wars between them is, because the Cochinchineses do all they can to hinder the Tunquineses to fish for them, alledging that those seas and islands belong to them."

[24] Ibid., p. 10: "Tunquin also affords great store of Anana's ..."

[25] Ibid.: " ... Orange trees, of which there are of two sorts: the one that bears a fruit no bigger than an Abricot; the other bigger than those of Portugal."

[26] Ibid.: "As for sweet smelling Flow'rs, the Tunquineses have but one sort, which they call the Flow'r of Bague. It grows like a large Nosegay, and the Branches of the Shrub that bear it, spread themselves crawlingly upon the ground."

The *Indian* lilly [lily] grows here as in several other parts of *India;* the shape somewhat resembles the *European* lilly, but is a great deal less; it grows on a pretty tree, is of white colour, and yields a good scent, tho' a little faintish.

Here is a small flower, snow white, in scent like jessamine [jasmine], but more vigorous; it grows on a low tree, or rather shrub: in *Persia* there are such great quantities of it, that they load whole ships with the water distilled from it. These flowers being of no great esteem among the natives, I shall pass them by.

Here are plenty of sugar-canes, but they have no great skill to refine the sugar they make from them; however, they do it after their manner, and use it, but not after meals, as *Taverniere* saith, for concoction.[27]

Tigers and harts here are, but not many; apes in great plenty; of cows, hogs, hens, ducks, geese, *&c.* there is no want; their horses are small, but very mettlesome and lively, and were it not that they are so seldom rid, and kept too tender, they might be of good use, and fit for service.

Their elephants are all trained up for war, and are not of that prodigious bigness he would make one believe, for I have seen larger in *Siam*; neither are they nimbler than other elephants that are taught to lie down for the rider to mount.[28]

They have many cats,[29] but no great mousers, which defect is pretty well supplied by their dogs, which are fit for little else.

Birds here are not many, but wild fowl in abundance.

Near the sea-side and in the city they have a great many musketoes [mosquitos], but in the country they are not so much troubled with them: Those that will be free of them must either smoke their room, or lie in close curtains, made of thin silks for that purpose. The cold northern wind drives them away, and frees the country of those tormentors for a while.

What he saith of the white emmets is true.[30] This vermin is very mischievous; in *Siam* hardly any house is free from them, so that merchants are forced to make hearses, and to rub the feet thereof with oil of earth, (which scent they cannot endure) in order to secure their merchandize.

The way of pickling hen or duck eggs, as *Taverniere* describes, is true, but these eggs serve only for sauces, and not to be eaten otherwise.[31]

---

[27] Ibid.: "As they have great store of sugar, so they eat very much, while it is yet in the cane, not having the true art to refine it: and that which they do grosly refine, they make into little loaves weighing about half a pound. They eat very much, making use of it always after Meals to help digestion."

[28] Ibid., p. 11: "These elephants are of a prodigious bigness, neither are there any so tall nor so nimble in any part of Asia; for they will bow themselves, and stoop so low, that you may get on their backs without help."

[29] Ibid.: "They have no cats ... "

[30] Ibid.: " ... the infinite numbers of white Emmets, which though they are but little, have teeth so sharp, that they will eat down a wooden post in a short time."

[31] Ibid., p. 12, has a paragraph on pickling eggs.

CHAPTER IV

OF THE RICHES, TRADE, AND MONEY
OF THE KINGDOM OF TONQUEEN.[1]

The chief riches, and indeed the only staple commodity, is silk, raw and wrought; of the raw the *Portuguese* and *Castilians*, in former days; the *Hollanders* lately; and at present the *Chinese*, export good quantities to *Japan*, &c. Of their wrought silks, the *English* and *Dutch* expend the most.

This kingdom has no lignum aloes[2] at all, but what is imported by foreign traders.

Musk we have here brought from *Bowes* and *China* annually, sometimes the quantity of five or six *Peculls*,[3] sometimes less; neither have they any gold but what comes from *China*. Their silver is brought in by *English, Dutch,* and *Chinese* trading to *Japan*. They have iron and lead mines, which afford them just enough of those minerals to serve their occasions.

Their domestick trade consists in rice, salt fish, and other sustenance; little raw and wrought silk for their own wear. They likewise drive a commerce with *Bowes* and *Ai*, though with no great profit, by reason of high expenses and large presents to the *Eunuchs*, who command the avenues; nor do the *Chinese* that pass those ways fare better, being often exacted upon, and sometimes stripp'd of all they have, by the ravenous *Mandareens:* And since it is one of the policies of the court not to make the subjects rich, lest they should be proud and ambitious, and aspire to greater matters, the king connives at those disorders, and oppresses them with heavy taxes and impositions; and should he know that any persons were to exceed the ordinary mean of a private subject, they would incur the danger of losing all, on some pretence or other; which is a great discouragement to the industrious and necessitates them to bury their wealth, having no means to improve it.

As for foreign traders, a new-comer suffers, besides hard usage in his buying and selling, a thousand inconveniencies; and no certain rates on merchandizes imported or exported being imposed, the insatiable *Mandareens* cause the ships to be rummaged, and take what commodities may likely yield a price at their own rates, using the king's name to cloak their griping and villainous extortions; and for all this there is no remedy but patience.

Yet strangers that are experienced here are less subject to those irregularities and oppressions, escaping their clutches, tho' not without some trouble and cost; in a

---

[1] Jean-Baptiste Tavernier, "A New and Singular Relation of the Kingdom of Tunquin," Chapter IV: "Of the Riches, Trade, and Money of the Kingdom of Tunquin."

[2] Aromatic wood; Tavernier, "A New and Singular Relation of the Kingdom of Tunquin," p. 13, says that after silk it is the "chief riches of the country" and devotes a paragraph to it.

[3] Picul, from Malay *pikul*, meaning the weight an average man can lift.

word, the *Tonqueen* trade is at present the most fastidious[4] in all *India*, wherefore I wonder our author should say, it is a great pleasure to deal with them; for if you bargain for any thing, and are likely to lose thereby, you are sure to bear the loss: Nothing almost is sold but upon trust for three or four months time, and yet then you run the hazard to lose what is so sold, or at least to undergo a thousand troubles for the recovery of the debt, and at last are likely to suffer, either in bad coin or unmerchantable goods. This defect and disorder in trade, proceeds more from their indigency and poverty than from any thing else; for there is not a *Tonqueenese* merchant that has ever had the courage and ability to buy the value of two thousand dollars at once, and to pay it upon the nail. But after all, the *Tonqueenese* are not altogether so fradulent, and of that deceitful disposition as the *Chinese*; it may be, by reason they are inferior to them in craft or cunning.[5]

There is this further difference between these two nations; a *Tonqueenese* will beg incessantly, and torment your purse sufficiently, if you have business with him; whereas a *Chinese* is cruel and bloody, maliciously killing a man, or flinging him into the sea for small matters.

Another occasion of hindrance and stop to trade is, that they permit the greater part of what silver comes into the country (commonly a million dollars *per annum*) to be carried to *Bowes* and *China*, to be exchanged for copper cash, which rises and falls according as the *Choua* [*chúa*] finds it agree with his interest; besides, this cash will be defac'd in a few years, and consequently not current, which grand inconvenience causes considerable losses to merchants, and signal prejudice to the publick. Thus goes the silver out of the country, and no provision is made against it, which is very bad policy.

And tho' the *Choua* values foreign trade so little, yet he receives from it, embarass'd as it is, considerable annual incomes into his coffers; as taxes, head-money, impositions, customs, *&c.* But tho' these amount to vast sums, yet very little remains in the treasury, by reason of the great army he maintains, together with several other unnecessary expenses. In fine, 'tis pity so many conveniencies and opportunities to make the kingdom rich, and its trade flourishing, should be neglected; for if we consider how this kingdom borders on two of the richest provinces in *China*, it will appear, that with small difficulty most commodities of that vast empire might be drawn hither, and great store of *Indian* and *European* commodities, especially woolen manufactures, might be vended there; nay, would they permit strangers the freedom of this inland trade, 'twould be vastly advantageous to the kingdom; but the *Choua* (jealous that *Europeans* should discover too much of his frontiers, by which certainly he can receive no injury) has, and will probably in all time to come, impede this important affair.

They have no coin but copper cash, which comes from *China*, as aforesaid. Gold and silver they cash into bars about fourteen dollars weight, and they are current amongst them.

---

[4] The seventeenth-century sense of the word: irksome and disagreeable.

[5] Tavernier, "A New and Singular Relation of the Kingdom of Tunquin," p. 13: "It is so much the more pleasure and profit to trade with the People of Tunquin, by how much the more faithful and frank they are in their dealing than the Chinese, who will deceive you if they can; so that it is a hard thing to be too cunning for them, as I have often found by experience."

CHAPTER V.

OF THE STRENGTH OF THE KINGDOM OF TONQUEEN.[1]

The kingdom of *Tonqueen* might be reckon'd very formidable, were the strength wholly to consist in the number of men, for the standing force cannot be less than one hundred and forty thousand, all well trained up, and fit to handle their arms, after their mode; and they can raise twice that number on occasion. But since courage in the men is to be likewise attended to, we cannot esteem them very formidable, being of dejected spirits and base dispositions, and their leaders being for the most part capadoes [eunuchs], and want their manhood.

The general may muster up about eight or ten thousand horse, and between three and four hundred elephants; his sea force consists in two hundred and twenty gallies, great and small, more fit for the river than the sea, and rather for sport and exercise than war.[2] They have but one gun in the prow, which will carry a four pound shot; they have no masts, and are forc'd to do all by strength of oars; the men that row stand all exposed to great or small shot, and other engines of war. They have about five hundred other boats, called *Twinjaes*,[3] which are good and swift to sail, but too weak for war, being only sew'd together with rattans; however, they serve well enough for transportation of provisions and soldiers.

In one of these boats I was forc'd to go to *Siam*, the last year, with three other gentlemen in company with me, we being left by a *Chinese* (in whose junk we had taken passage) on an isle on the westmost part of the bay of *Tonqueen*, where we were forced to this shift; yet, thanks be to God, we got our passage in twenty-three days, to the admiration of all who knew of it.

---

[1] Jean-Baptiste Tavernier, "A New and Singular Relation of the Kingdom of Tunquin," Chapter V: "Of the Strenght of the Kingdom of Tunquin by Sea and Land."

[2] Ibid., p. 15, gives a description Tavernier attributes to his brother of the Tonkinese army " ... in the year 1649, when the King was preparing to make War against the King of Cochinchina ... " This year 1649 is an error for 1648, for the Tonkinese expedition against Cochinchina occurred in 1648 and Tavernier's brother died in Java in late 1648. The description: "The Army that was then prepared to march upon this Expedition was composed of 8000 Horse, 94 thousand Foot, and 722 Elephants; 130 for the War, and the rest to carry the Tents and Baggage of the King and the Nobility; and 318 Galleys and Barks, very long and narrow, with Oars and Sails; and this was that which my Brother saw."

[3] Perhaps this is Baron's transcription of *thuyền giã*, per the suggestion of Baron's French translator (*Revue Indochinoise* XXII,8 [August 1914]: 200), or, as seems more plausible and idiomatic to me, *thuyền chài*, "fishing boat"; *thuyền* means "boat" while the modifiers *giã* and *chài* each refer to a fishing net.

They are likewise provided with guns and cannons of all sorts, and also calibres, some of them of their own fabrick, but the greatest part bought of the *Portuguese, Dutch,* and *English,* and stored with other ammunition suitable to their occasions.

But to return to the condition of the soldiery of *Tonqueen;* It is a very toilsome and laborious situation, and of little advantage; once a soldier and always a soldier,[4] and hardly one in a thousand riseth to preferment, unless he be very dextrous in handling his weapons, or so fortunate as to obtain the friendship of some great *Mandareen,* to present him to the king: Money may likewise effect somewhat, but to think of advancement by mere valour, is a very fruitless expectation, since they rarely find occasion to meet an enemy in open field, and so have no opportunity to improve themselves, or display their prowess; not but that some few have, from mean beginnings, mounted to high preferment and great dignity, by some bold achievement; but this being extraordinary, is not to be generally reckon'd upon.

Their wars consist in much noise and great trains; so they go to *Cochin-china,* look on the walls, rivers, &c. and if any disease or sickness happens amongst their army, so as to carry off some few of their men, and they come within hearing of the shouts of the enemy, they begin to cry out, A cruel and bloody war, and turn head, running, *re infecta,* as fast as they can home. This is the game they have play'd against *Cochin-china* more than three times, and will do so, in all probability, as long as they are commanded by those emasculated captains called *Capons.*

They have had amongst themselves civil wars, wherein they contended for superiority, and he that has been the cunningest has prevailed always against him that has been valiant. But in former days, when they fought against the *Chinese,* they have shew'd themselves bold and courageous, but it was necessity that forced them to it. The general will sometimes take delight in seeing his soldiers exercise, either in his arsenal, or with his gallies on the river, and sometimes when he finds a soldier to exceed his companions, it may be, he gratifies him with the value of a dollar in cash.

The soldiers have very small pay, not above three dollars in a year, besides rice, except those of the life-guard, who have twice as much; they are free of all taxes, and are dispersed among the *Mandareens,* which *Mandareens* have certain *Aldeas* assign'd them, which pay an income to them for the maintenance of the soldiers.

Castles, forts, strong-holds, citadels, &c. they have none, nor do they understand the art of fortification, and make but small account of our skill therein; though they have so little reason to depend, like the *Lacedemonians,* on the bravery of their soldiers.[5]

---

[4] Tavernier, "A New and Singular Relation of the Kingdom of Tunquin," p. 15: "The condition of the souldiery is very toilsome and laborious, and of little advantage in the Kingdom of Tunquin. For they are all their life time so ti'd and engag'd to the service of the wars … "

[5] The reference here is to the ancient Spartans, famed for their formidable infantry.

CHAPTER VI.

OF THE MANNERS OF THE PEOPLE OF TONQUEEN.[1]

The people of *Tonqueen* are rather of a working and turbulent spirit, (tho' cowards) than naturally mild and peaceable,[2] since quiet and concord can hardly be maintain'd amongst them, without a heavy hand and severity; for they have often conspired and broke out in open rebellion. True it is, that superstition (to which the meaner sort are miserably addicted) did further the evil very much, and drove them headlong into the precipice, no less than ambition; but persons of great note, or *Mandareeens* of quality, are very seldom found to be embark'd in those dangerous attempts, and rarely aim to make themselves heads of publick factions, which, questionless, proceeds from the little credit they give to those fictions and fopperies of their blind fortunetellers, who delude and mislead the ignorant and superstitious vulgar, and from this their consciousness, that their folly and perfidiousness will hardly fail to meet with deserved destruction.

They are not given much to choler, yet are addicted to the far worse passions of envy and malice, even to an extreme degree. In former times they had in great esteem the manufactures of strange countries, but now that passion is almost worn out, and only a few *Japan* gold and silver pieces, and *European* broad cloth remain at present in request with them. They are not curious to visit other countries, believing they can see none so good as their own, and give no credit to those who have been abroad, when they can relate what they have seen.

They are of happy memory and quick apprehension, and might prove of eminent abilities by good and due instructions: Learning they love, not so much for its own sake, but because it conducts them to publick employs and dignities. Their tone in reading is much like to singing. Their language is full of monosyllables, and sometimes twelve or thirteen several things are meant by one word, and have no other distinction, but in their tone, either to pronounce it with a full mouth, heavy accent, pressing or retaining voice, &c. and therefore it is difficult for strangers to attain any perfection therein.

I do not find any difference between the court language and the vulgar, except in matter of ceremony and cases of law, where the *China* characters are used as the *Greek* and *Latin* sentences amongst our learned.

---

[1] Jean-Baptiste Tavernier, "A New and Singular Relation of the Kingdom of Tunquin," Chapter VI: "Of the Manners and Customs of the People of the Kingdom of Tunquin."

[2] Ibid., p. 16: "The people of Tunquin are naturally mild and peaceful, submitting easily to reason, and condemning the transports of choler."

Both sexes are well proportioned,[3] rather of small stature and weak constitutions, occasioned, perhaps by their intemperate eating and immoderate sleeping.

They are generally of brown complection, like the *Chinese* and *Japanese*, but the better sort, and women of quality, are almost as fair as the *Portuguese* and *Spaniards.*

Their noses and faces are not so flat as the *Chineses*, their hair black, and if long, 'tis reckon'd an ornament; both men and women, without distinction, wear it down as long as it will grow;[4] but soldiers, when they are in their exercises, and handicrafts-men about their trades, put it up under their caps, or tie it in a great roll on the top of their heads. Both boys and girls, when they are past sixteen or seventeen years of age, black their teeth as the *Japanese* do, and let their nails grow as the *Chinese*, the longest being accounted the finest, which has place amongst persons of quality and those of wealth only.

Their habit is long robes, very little differing from those of *China*, and not at all resembling the *Japan* garb, or the picture in *Taverniere's* description, where he makes them wear girdles, a mode these people are strangers to.[5]

They are forbidden by an old tradition the wear of hose or shooes, except the literadoes (*Literati*) and those that have taken the degree of *Tuncy*[6] (or *Doctor*); however, at present the custom is not observed so strictly as formerly.

The condition of the vulgar sort is miserable enough, since they are imposed on by heavy taxes, and undergo sore labour; for the males at eighteen, and in some countries and provinces twenty years of age, are liable to pay the value of three, four, five, six, and seven dollars *per annum*, according to the goodness and fertility of the soil of their *Aldea*, or village; and this money is gathered in two several terms, as *April* and *October*, being the harvest of the rice. From this tax are exempted the royal blood, the king's immediate servants, all publick ministers and officers of the kingdom, together with the Literadoes, or learned men, from a *Singdo*,[7] upwards, (for the latter are obliged to pay half tax), all soldiers and military persons, with a few others that have obtained this freedom, either *gratis*, or bought it for money, which exemption is granted only for life, and is purchas'd of the *Choua*, or General; yet those that desire the continuation of the said privilege, may have their patent renew'd for a moderate sum of money, by the succeeding prince, who seldom denies to grant them their redemption on such an account; but merchants, though they live in the city, are rated in the *Aldeas* or villages of their ancestors and parents, and are liable besides to the *Vecquan*,[8] or lord's service, of the city, at their own expenses, and are obliged to work and drudge themselves, or hire another in their room, to perform what the governor orders, whether it be to mend the broken walls, repair the banks and ways of the city, dragging timber for the king's palaces, and other publick buildings, *&c.*

---

[3] Ibid., p. 17: "The Tunquineses, as well as Men as Women, are for the most part well proportion'd . . ."

[4] Ibid.: "Their Hair is very black, which they usually wear as long as it will grow, being very careful in combing it."

[5] Ibid.: "Their Habit is grave and modest, being a long Robe that reaches down to their heels, much like that of the Japonneses, without any distinction of sex."

[6] Vietnamese *tiến sĩ*, the highest academic degree awarded in the examination system.

[7] Vietnamese *sinh đồ*, the lowest-level degree awarded in the examination system.

[8] Vietnamese *việc quan* (corvée).

The handicrafts-men, of what profession soever, are bound to this *Vecquan* six moons in the year, and receive nothing, nor dare they demand any thing for their labour in all that time; it depends on their Masters, the *Mandareens*, direction and bounty, to allow them the charges for their very victuals; the other half year they are allow'd to make use of for themselves and family, and it must be suppos'd to be hard enough with them, especially if they are burthen'd with many children.

As for the poor *Aldeans*, who inhabit barren soils, and therefore are unable to pay their taxes in rice or money, they are employ'd to cut grass for the general's elephants and horses, and though their stations and villages be often very remote from the place where they fetch the grass, they are obliged to bring it by turns the whole year, on their own expenses, to the city.

By what is said, it appears, with what politick maxims this prince keeps his subjects poor and needy; and in truth, it seems to be necessary enough, for if their proud turbulent spirits were not kept in the bounds of their duty and allegiance with a strong rein, they would often forget themselves; however, every one enjoys what he gets by his own industry, and may leave his estate to his heirs and successors; always provided that the rumour of his wealth sounds not so loud as to charm the general's ear.

The eldest son's portion is much larger than the rest of the children of the deceased; the daughters have some small matter allow'd them, yet can claim but little by law, if there be an heir male.

And as the *Tonqueenese* are ambitious of many dependents and opulent kindred, so they have a custom among them to adopt one another (both sexes indifferently) to be their children, and of their family; and those so adopted are obliged to the same duty as their own children, *viz.*

At festival times to sombey[9] and present them; to be ready on every occasion in their service; to bring them the first-fruits of the season, and the new rice at harvest; to contribute to the sacrifice made to some of the family, as the mother, brother, wife, *&c.* or near relations, of the *Patroon* [patron], that are dead, or shall die. To these and several other expenses they are obliged, several times in the year, at their own cost: And as this is the obligation of the adopted, so the *Patroon* takes care to advance or promote them, according as occasion and their power will permit, defending and protecting them as their own children, and when the *Patroon* dies, they have a legacy almost equal to the youngest children; and they mourn for the *Patroon* as for their own father and mother, though they both be alive.

The manner of adopting is thus: He that intends to be adopted, sends to acquaint the person of whom he requests that favour, with his intention, who, if content therewith, returns a satisfactory answer; upon which the suppliant comes and presents himself before him, with a hog and two jars of arrack, which the *Patroon* receives of the party, who having made four sombeys, and given satisfactory answers to some questions, he is adopted.

Strangers who reside here, or use the trade, have often taken this course, to free themselves from those vexations and extortions, which they usually meet with from some insolent courtiers. I myself was adopted by a prince, who then was presumptive, and now heir apparent to the general,[10] and had his *Chaop*, or *Chop*, which is his seal. I always gave him presents at my arrival from a voyage, which

---

[9] To bow in greeting.

[10] The "general" is Trịnh Căn; the "heir apparent" is mentioned again in Chapter XII.

chiefly consisted in foreign curiosities. This prince, tho' he be of a generous, noble mind, and had an extraordinary kindness for me, yet I was not the better for him in my troubles; for on the decease of his grandfather,[11] it pleased God to visit him, in the height of his prosperity with madness, which was the overthrow of my business, by incapacitating him to protect me in my greatest trouble and necessity; but lately I understand he is recover'd again.[12]

The *Aldeans* or Villagers, for the most part, are simple people, and subject to be misled by their over-much credulity and superstition. The character that is given of some other nations is applicable enough to them; that is, they are extraordinary good, or extreme bad.

'Tis a great mistake, that the people of *Tonqueen* live out of pleasure, or choice, in their boats upon the rivers,[13] when mere necessity and indigence drives them to that course of life; for to run from port to port, and from one village to another, with wife and children, to look out for a livelihood, in a small boat, cannot be very pleasant, although they do not know here what a crocodile means.

The largest of the *Tonqueen* rivers has, as I said before, its source in *China*, and the great rains there, in the months of *March, April,* and *May,* cause the waters to descend here with that incredible rapidity (this country being, without comparison, lower than *China*) as threatens banks and dams with destruction; sometimes the waters will rise so fast, and swell to that degree, as to over-top most barricadoes, all human industry notwithstanding, drowning thereby whole provinces, which causes lamentable disorders and great losses, both of men and beasts.

---

[11] Trịnh Tạc died in 1682.

[12] Temporary "insanity" was not an unusual method for Vietnamese princes to employ in order to avoid difficult or unwanted situations.

[13] Tavernier, "A New and Singular Relation of the Kingdom of Tunquin," p. 18: " . . . the Tunquineses take great delight to live upon the Rivers ... ."

CHAPTER VII.

OF THE MARRIAGES OF THE TONQUEENESE. [1]

The *Tonqueenese* cannot marry without the consent of their father and mother, or of the nearest kindred.[2] When a young man comes to the age of sixteen, eighteen, or twenty, his father and mother being resolved to get him a wife, make their application to the parents of the party they design for him, carrying with them an hundred dressed beetles,[3] in a decent box, one jar of arrack, or strong liquor, and a live hog; under favour of such a present only, this is to be proposed. The friends of the maid seeing the visitants thus prepar'd, and knowing by the custom of the country whereto it tends, give fitting answers to the question in hand, according to their inclinations; for if they are unwilling it should be a match, they find their subterfuges and excuses, by pretending their daughter's youth and inability to take upon her the burthen of a household, and that, however, they will consider of the matter further hereafter, and the like compliments, wherewith they and their presents are sent back again.

But in the case they are content to bestow their daughter on the young man, the presents are readily accepted of, with expressions of their approbation of the business; and then immediately, without any other formality, they consult and agree about the most auspicious time (in which they are guided by their blind superstition) for the solemnization of the wedding: In the mean time the parents of the bridegroom send often presents of victuals to the bride, and visit her now and then yet the young people are not permitted so much as to speak to each other.

At the prefix'd time the wedding is kept, with a feast agreeable to the condition and abilities of the parents of the young couple, which doth not last above a day. The ceremony of the marriage is barely this: In the afternoon of the day that precedes the wedding, the bridegroom comes to the bride, and brings with him, according to his quality, either gold, silver, or a quantity of cash (the more the greater honour), and victuals prepared, all which he leaves there, and retires to his own home. The next morning being the wedding day, the bride is dress'd in her finest robes, with bracelets of gold, pendants, &c. her parents, acquaintance, and servants are ready to conduct and wait on her to the bridegroom's, whither she goes about ten o'clock in the forenoon, with all this train attending her, whilst all her moveables, household-

---

[1] Jean-Baptiste Tavernier, "A New and Singular Relation of the Kingdom of Tunquin," Chapter VII: "Of the Marriages of the Tunquineses and their severity toward adulteresses."

[2] Compare with ibid., p. 18: "The Tunquineses cannot marry without the consent of the father and mother, or if they be dead, without the allowance of their nearest kindred."

[3] "Dressed beetles" means packets of areca nut and betel leaf smeared with a lime paste, ready to be chewed.

stuff, and whatever else her father and mother gave for her portion, together with what she had of the bridegroom, is carried in great state; and for a more glorious shew, it passes a long field before her and the whole company, all which enter the bridegroom's house, who receives her and them with kindness and courtesy, after their mode, and presents them with victuals prepared for the purpose, whilst musick and other expressions of joy, are not neglected: And this is the whole solemnity of the wedding, without any further formality of either magistrate or priest, as our author talks.[4]

Plate 4: "In this Manner goes the Bride to the Bridegroom." 1. The Bridegroom. 2. His Father and Kinsman. 3. The Bride Carried in her Hammock. 4. Her Brother and Kinsman. 5. Her Waiting Gentlewomen with her Slippers Box and Beetle. 6. A Chest with Gold, Silver, and Money.

Polygamy is here tolerated; however, that woman whose parents are of the greatest quality, is chief amongst them, and has the title of wife.

Rapes, and the like, are not known, much less practiced in this country. The law of the land permits the man to divorce his wife, but the woman has not the same privilege, and can hardly obtain a separation, against the good-liking of the husband,

---

[4] Tavernier, "A New and Singular Relation of the Kingdom of Tunquin," p. 18: "They must also have the permission of the Judge or Governour of the place where the Marriage is to be made … "

unless she be of a family that is able to compel him to it, by mere authority. When the husband designs to repudiate his wife, he gives her a note, declaring under his hand and seal, that he has no more pretensions to her person, and that she is free to dispose of herself, as she finds occasion, which liberty capacitates her to marry another; neither would any person dare to pretend to her, without being certain of the said note, for fear of the former husband, who in that case can claim her again, and thereby embroil such a one in the labyrinths of the law, and recover a good sum of money from him.

The woman so repudiated, when she departs from her husband, may take along with her the same quantity of gold, silver, cash, &c. as he brought to her house, at the time of his espousing her. The children born during the time of their mutual cohabitation, the husband keeps; but their *Mandareens* seldom, and only on urgent occasions, or for capital offences, will deal thus severely with their wives; yet their concubines are thus served, on every light occasion, when the humour takes them to make an exchange, or that they are satiated with their persons. Among the meaner sort, when a man and his wife disagree, and mutually desire a separation, they are divorced in the presence of some small judge and publick officers, by mutual discharges in writing; but the village husband, that cannot read nor write, breaks a copper cash, this country money, or a stick in the presence of his wife, as a testimony of his resolution to dismiss her; the one half he keeps himself, and the other he gives to her, which she carries to the heads and elders of the *Aldea*, or village, requesting them to bear witness, her husband hath discharged her of her duty, to be any longer his wife, and that he has nothing more to pretend to her, for ever; so she may either keep or throw away the piece of cash, or stick, and marry again as soon as she pleases.

As for adultery, if a man of quality surprises his wife in the fact, he may freely, if he pleases, kill her and her paramour, with his own hands; otherwise the woman is sent to be trampled to death by an elephant; the adulterer is delivered to the justice, who proceeds with him to execution without any further delay: But with the meaner sort of people it is not so; they must go to law, where the offenders will have severe punishment inflicted on them, if they are proved guilty of the crime.

The story that Monsieur *Taverniere* relates to have happened whilst his brother was in *Tonqueen* is not at all agreeable to the customs of this people, or congruous with their dispositions; wherefore, in all probability, 'tis only a fiction.[5]

---

[5] Ibid., pp. 19-21. Tavernier attributes a story to his brother about the case of a "prince" consorting with a "princess" who was a woman of a deceased "king"; this prince was reportedly punished with several years of imprisonment and then banishment to the frontiers as a common soldier, while the "princess" was executed by starvation and exposure to the sun.

CHAPTER VIII.

OF THE VISITS AND PASTIMES OF THE TONQUEENESE. [1]

Their visits are generally made in the afternoon.[2] It is uncivil to come to any great man's house before dinner, unless necessitated by urgent business, or expressly invited, because they then have the least time to spare; for in the morning very early they go to court, to attend the general; which attendance takes them up 'till eight o'clock: when they come home, they imploy themselves a while in ordering their domestick concerns, among their servants (if more important state-affairs will permit it); the little space that remains between that and dinner is reserved for their retirement and repose.

The princes, or great *Mandareens*, ride either on elephants, or carried in *hangmack* [hammock], and followed by most of their servants, soldiers, dependants, &c. that are not otherwise occupied in such a season, which is more or less numerous, according to the degree of the person's dignity; those of lesser rank ride on horseback, and are followed by as many as they are able to maintain, without limitation, which usually is not above ten persons, but to be sure all that can, must go, for they are very ambitious of many attendants.

If he that gives the visit is of greater quality than the person visited, he[3] dares not to offer him anything of meat or drink, no, not so much as a beetle, unless he calls for it: Their water and beetle is always carried with them by their servants.

In discoursing with them, especially if the person be of authority, care must be had not to move any mournful subject, either directly or indirectly; but things that are pleasant, in commendation of them, are best approved. But that which is most intolerable in those lords is, that they permit the men of their train (a rude brutish gang) to enter with them into the most private apartments of other people's houses, especially when they come to visit *Europeans*, where they behave themselves very apishly, and commit many absurdities and impertinencies in their talk and jestings; and moreover, often steal whatever they can lay hold on: In all which their stupify'd masters rather take delight, than check them for their sauciness and misdemeanours. But if they are invited by their inferiors or equals, then they entertain them as they find occasion, either with tea or meat, &c. not omitting beetle, which is always the first and last part of the regale. The boxes wherein the beetle is presented, are generally plain lacquered, either black, red, or some grave colour; yet the gentry, and the princes and princesses of the royal blood, have them of massy gold, sliver,

---

[1] Jean-Baptiste Tavernier, "A New and Singular Relation of the Kingdom of Tunquin," Chapter VIII: "Of the Visits, Feasts, and Pastimes of the Tunquineses."

[2] Ibid., p. 21: "Generally they make their visits about noon."

[3] The person visited.

tortoiseshell, or inlaid with mother of pearl; the painted and gaudy ones are only used at their sacrifices in their *Pagodas*. But such rich boxes as M. *Taverniere* avers to have seen, to the value of four or five hundred thousand livres,[4] at the *Great Mogul's* court, were certainly no *Tonqueen* ones; for diamonds, rubies, emeralds, and other jewels do not grow in this country, neither are they in request among the natives, nor could they have been brought there by any *Tonqueen* ambassador, since the king sends none thither, nor is there the least commerce between the two nations.[5]

They seldom visit sick persons, and they hardly care to admit any but their kindred and relations to put them in mind of death, how desperate soever their state may be, and the least admonition to settle their affairs and concerns, would be a heinous crime and unpardonable offence; so that those that die make no will, which defect often creates vexatious law-suits among the kindred, if the deceased leaves no children behind him, even to the ruin of their own estates, and the loss of what they contend for.

In the halls of great men's houses are several alcoves, where they sit cross-legg'd upon mats, according to their degree, the higher the more honorable; and these seats are all cover'd with mats, answerable in fineness to their stations; except in time of mourning, when they are oblig'd to use coarse ones. As for carpets, they have none, neither can they afford them; wherefore I wonder at our author's saying, that the mats are as dear as fine carpet, which at the cheapest, costs from thirty to fifty rupees, and upwards, in *Persia* and *Surat*; whereas the best and finest mat may be bought here for the value of three or four shillings at the most; neither do I believe that any *European*, besides himself, has ever seen a *Tonqueen* mat nine ells[6] square, and as soft as velvet: However, this is like the rest of his fables.[7] As for cushions, these people use none, either to sit or lie on; but they have a kind of bolster made of reeds or mats, to sleep or lean on.

As for their victuals they are curious enough therein,[8] though their diet doth not generally please strangers. The common sort must then be content with green trade,[9] rice, and salt fish, or the like; the great lords may, if they please, feed themselves with the best in the land.

I can make no comparison for neatness, between the *Europeans* and them, in their houses, wherein they have but little or no furniture more than usual in the meanest cots, sometimes tables and benches, seldom chairs. They use neither table-cloths nor napkins, nor do they want them, since they do not touch their meat with their

---

[4] An old French unit of value.

[5] Tavernier, "A New and Singular Relation of the Kingdom of Tunquin," pp. 21-22, about betel boxes, writes: " … I have seen some at the Apartments of some of the Princes that came to the Court of the Great Mogul, which were worth above 4 or 500000 Livres: One shall be cover'd with Diamonds, another with Rubies and Pearls, another with Emraulds and Pearls, or else with other Jewels."

[6] An ell is an old English unit of length equal to 45 inches.

[7] Tavernier, "A New and Singular Relation of the Kingdom of Tunquin," p. 22: "Being at Bantam I bought one of these mats of a Tunquinese, which was admired for its fineness. It was nine ells square, and as even and as soft as velvet. With these mats they cover the beds or couches, upon which the Mandarins, or Princes, and the Nobility which accompany them, seat themselves around the chamber, every one having one cushion under him, and another at his back."

[8] Ibid: "As for their diet the Tunquineses are not very curious."

[9] Green herbs and vegetables.

fingers, but use two sticks, as the *Chinese* and *Japanese* do. All their victuals is served in little plates and dishes, not made of wood, and then varnish'd or lacquer'd over, as Mr. *Taverniere* affirms,[10] but of *China* and *Japan* wares, which are in esteem here. Persons of quality or condition use a kind of formality and decency at their feasts; but as for the rest, as soon as they are at the *bandeses*,[11] which are small laquer'd tables, they do not so much as mind any discourses; and this not out of good manners or reverence to the aged and grave persons,[12] but a greedy desire to fill their guts, they being generally great eaters and true epicures; also they may be afraid to lose their share by prating, whilst others make all the silent haste they can, to empty the platters and dishes. I have often seen the followers and attendants of the *Mandareens* at the like sport, and used to admire their eating both for quantity and greediness, in which I believe no nation under the cope of heaven can match them.

As for drinking, though the clowns and meaner sort seldom fall under the excess and debauchery of strong drink, yet amongst the courtiers and soldiers drunkeness is no vice. A fellow that can drink smartly, is a brave blade. It is no custom of theirs to wash their hands when they go to table, only they rinse their mouths, because of the beetle; yet after meals, they often wash both; and having cleaned their teeth with a piece of bamboo, prepared for the purpose, they eat beetle. At a friend's house the entertained may freely, if he please, call for more boiled rice, or anything else, if he is not satisfied, which the host takes very kindly. They do not ask one another, how they do, but compliment them with a Where have you been thus long? and, What have you done all this while? And if they know or perceive by their countenance, that they have been sick or indisposed, then they ask, How many cups of rice they eat at a meal? (for they make three in a day, besides a collation in the afternoon, amongst the rich and wealthy) and, Whether he eats with appetite or no?

Of all the pastimes of the *Tonqueenese,* they affect most their balls, ballads, and singing, which are, for the most part, acted in the night, and last 'till morning, and are what Monsieur *Taverniere* calls comedies: A very improper name,[13] and resembling them in no respect, much less are they set out with beautiful decorations and machines, as he says, very pleasing to behold; and they are skillful to represent sea and river water, and marine combats thereon,[14] as they are able to describe the fight in 1588, between the *English* and the *Spaniards;*[15] neither have they in the city

---

[10] Tavernier, "A New and Singular Relation of the Kingdom of Tunquin," p. 22: "Whatever is set before them to eat, is served in little plates, not so big as our trenchers, being made of wood lackered with all sorts of flowers."

[11] Vietnamese *bàn* means "table"; it is unclear what term is being transcribed by *bandes(es)*.

[12] Tavernier, "A New and Singular Relation of the Kingdom of Tunquin," p. 23: "When there are several sitting at the table, either at their ordinary meals, or upon some festival, they account it a great piece of manners to be silent; or if they have a desire to discourse, they always allow the eldest the honour of beginning, bearing a great respect to them that are aged."

[13] Ibid.: "Among all the Pastimes of the Tunquineses there are none wherein they take so much delight as in Comedies … "

[14] Ibid.: " … they are set out with beautiful decorations and machines, very pleasing to behold. They are excellently well skilled in representing the Sea and Rivers, and a shew of seafights, and combats between galleys and barks … "

[15] Baron is ridiculing Tavernier's description of theatrical sea battles by saying it is as plausible to imagine as it would be to expect that Vietnamese would be able to reenact the famous battle of the English with the Spanish Armada in the English Channel which took place a century before.

any theatres to act upon, but every *Mandareen*'s hall, and the yards of other houses must serve turn: Yet in their *Aldeas* they have singing houses, erected at the expense of three, four or more *Aldeas* or villages, and in this they celebrate their festival times, singing and banqueting, after their mode. The actors of one house are sometimes three, four, or five persons; their fees are no more than a thousand cash, to the value of a dollar for a whole night's labour: But the liberal spectators give them presents, as often as they perform any thing dexterously. They are usually habited in country taffeties [taffeta], palongs,[16] satins, and the like. They have but few songs, and not above five different tunes, and those composed most in praise of their kings and generals, interspers'd with amorous interjections and poetical elegance. The women only dance, and she that dances must sing too, and will be, between whiles, interrupted by a man that plays the part of a jester, who is generally the wittiest mimick they can find, and such a one as is able to make the company laugh at his inventions and postures. Their musical instruments are drums, copper basons,[17] hautboys [oboes], guitars, with two or three sorts of violins *&c.* Besides this, they have another kind of dancing, with a bason filled or piled up with small lamps lighted, which a woman sets on her head, and then dances, turning, winding, and bowing her body in several shapes and figures, with great celerity, without spilling a drop of oil in the lamps, to the admiration of the spectators; this act will last about half an hour.

Dancing on ropes their women are also expert at, and some will perform it very gracefully.

Cock-fighting is a mighty game amongst them, so that it is become a princely sport, and much in fashion with courtiers. They lose much that lay[18] against the general, for right or wrong he must and will win, whereby he impoverishes his grandees, so they will not be able to undertake any thing.

They delight much in fishing, and have the conveniency of many rivers, and infinite ponds.

As for hunting, there is scarce a wood or forest proper for this exercise, in all the country, neither are they expert in that sport.

But their grand pastime is their new year's feast, which commonly happens about the 25th of *January,* and is kept by some thirty days; for then, besides dancing and the recreations aforesaid, all their other sorts of games, as playing at football, swinging on an engine erected of bamboos at most corners of the streets, tricks of bodily activity, and a kind of hocus-pocus, are brought on the stage, to increase merriment; neither are they behind-hand to prepare their feasts and banquets plentiful and large, striving to outdo each other therein, for the space of three or four days, according to their ability; and as this is indeed the time to gormandize and debauch to excess, so he is accounted the most miserable wretch that doth not provide to welcome his friends and acquaintance, tho' by so doing he is certain to beg the rest of that year for his livelihood.

---

[16] Perhaps paillon, meaning embroidered with decorative designs.

[17] Cymbals; bason is an old English variant of "basin."

[18] i.e., to lay bets.

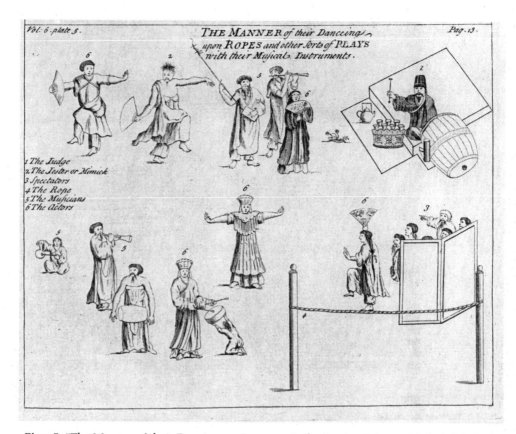

Plate 5: "The Manner of their Dancing on Ropes and other sorts of Plays with their Musical Instruments." 1. The Judge. 2. The Jester or Mimick. 3. Spectators. 4. The Rope. 5. The Musicians. 6. The Actors.

The first day of the year the ordinary sort do not stir abroad (unless they are dependants of some lords), but keep themselves close shut up in their houses, admitting none but their nearest relations and domesticks; to others they would deny, on that day, a draught of water, or a coal for fire, and be very angry too at any one's making such a request, superstitiously believing its consequence would be to subject them to infallible malediction, and that if they should give you any thing that day, it would be their bad destiny to give continually, and beggar themselves thereby at last. Their reason for not stirring abroad proceeds from the same cause, which is, fear to encounter with some ominous thing or other, that might presage evil to them, that day, which would make them unfortunate all the year; for they observe superstitiously many frivolous niceties as good and bad luck: But the second day of the new year, they go to visit each other, and acquit themselves of their duty and obligations to their superiors, to sombay them; as likewise do their soldiers and servants to them. But the *Mandareens* go the first day to the king and general, of which they are as careful observers as the others are sharp and precise exactors of this attendance.

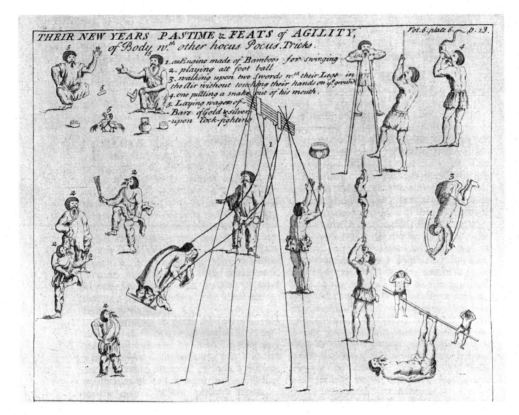

Plate 6: "Their New Years Pastime and Feats of Agility of Body with other Hocus Pocus
Tricks." 1. An Engine made of Bamboos for Swinging. 2. Playing at Foot Ball.
3. Walking upon Two Swords with their Legs in the Air without Touching their Hands on the
Ground. 4. One Pulling a Snake out of his Mouth.
5. Laying Wagers of Bars of Gold and Silver upon Cock-fighting

Some reckon their new year from the 25th of their last moon, but very
improperly; their ground for it is, because the *Sup Unn*,[19] implying as much as *the
great seal reversed*, is then put into a box, with the face downward, for a whole
month's time, and in that interval, the law is, as it were, laid asleep, and no acts
whatsoever pass under the said seal; all courts of judicature are shut up; debtors
cannot be seized on; small crimes, as petty larceny, fighting, beating one another, *&c.*
escape with impunity; only treason and murder the governors of the city and
province take account of, and keep the malefactors prisoners 'till the grand seal
comes to be active again, to bring them to their trial, *&c.* But their new year more
properly begins at the first of their new moon, which falls out usually about our 25th
of *January* as aforesaid, and lasts, according to the *China* custom, one whole month.

By what is related it appears how excessively our author has hyperboliz'd on
these passages, especially where he commends the *Tonqueenese* for laborious and

---

[19] Vietnamese *sụp ấn*, "to tumble the seal."

industrious people, prudently imploying their time to the most advantage,[20] which in some degree may be granted in the women, but the men are so lazy and idle generally, that were they not by mere necessity compell'd to work, I verily believe they would be glad to spend their time only in eating and sleeping; for many will surfeit themselves by over-gorging their stomachs, feeding as if they were born only to eat, and not to eat for the support of life chiefly.

It is also a mistake to say, the *Tonqueenese* deem it a disgrace to have their heads uncover'd;[21] for when an inferior comes to a *Mandareen*, either upon business or some errand from a *Mandareen*, he has always his black gown and cap on, and the *Mandareen* receives him bare; but if the messenger comes with an order from the king, either verbal or in writing, then they dare not hear the message, or peruse the note, without putting on their gown and cap. Of this more will be said when I come to speak of the court of *Tonqueen*.

As to criminals, they are shaved as soon as they are commended to die, because they may be known and apprehended if they should chance to out-run their keepers, which is a different thing from being uncover'd, which M. *Taverniere* talks of. So likewise to nail malefactors on crosses,[22] or to dismember them, by four small gallies that row several ways,[23] are torments unheard-of in this country.

---

[20] Tavernier, "A New and Singular Relation of the Kingdom of Tunquin," p. 24: " ... being better husbands of their time than we, not sparing any part of it from business."

[21] Ibid., p. 22: "The Tunquineses take it for a great dishonour to have their Heads bare, which is only for Criminals ... "

[22] As described in ibid., p. 22.

[23] As described in ibid., p. 21.

CHAPTER IX.

OF THE LEARNED MEN OF TONQUEEN.[1]

The *Tonqueenese* have a great inclination for learning, because it is the only step to acquire dignity and preferments, which encourageth them to a studious and diligent application to learning; which is often attended with good or ill success, as in other countries, according to their several talents, and as they are indued with vivacity, spirit, and more-especially as they are furnish'd with a good or bad memory; which is the chief requisite for mastering that sort of learning which is in repute in this country, which consists mostly of hieroglyphick characters, whereof they have as many as words or things, requires a very retentive memory. Hence it is, that some scholars are fit to take degrees upon them after twelve or fifteen years study, others in twenty-five or thirty, many not in their life-time.

They may, as soon as they think themselves able or capable, adventure their trial, without either obligation to continue longer a scholar, or limitation of years: Nor have they any publick schools, but every one chuses such a preceptor for his children as he fancies, at his own cost.

Their learning consists not in the knowledge of languages, as among us in *Europe*, much less are they acquainted with our philosophy: but they have one *Confucius*, a *Chinese*, (or, as the people call him, *Congtu*[2]) the founder of their arts and sciences, which are the same with those of the *Chinese*. This man composed but one book,[3] but he compiled four others[4] from the works of the ancient *Chinese* philosophers, containing morals and political precepts, with their rites and sacrifices, &c. Moreover, his disciples have out of his works extracted diverse rules, sentences, and similies, fit for the state in general, and every person in particular; all which is collected into one tome, divided into four parts, and entitled *The four Books*,[5] which, with the five before-mention'd make nine books, and are the ancientest they have, and of that reputation, that they will admit no contradiction whatsoever against them; and these are the sole foundation of the learning, not only of the *Chinese* and this nation, but also of the *Japanese*, some small differences excepted.

---

[1] Jean-Baptiste Tavernier, "A New and Singular Relation of the Kingdom of Tunquin," Chapter IX: "Of the learned men in the Kingdom of Tunquin."

[2] Vietnamese *Khổng Tử*.

[3] A reference to the *Lun Yu* (Analects).

[4] Baron apparently counts the *Lun Yu* as one of the "Five Classics," supposedly compiled by Confucius, which in fact do not include the *Lun Yu*.

[5] The "Four Books" traditionally include *Lun Yu*, *Mengzi* (Mencius), and two excerpts from *Liji* (Record of rituals), which is one of the "Five Books."

The said books comprehend likewise the greatest part of their hieroglyphical characters, the multitude of which none can easily affirm, yet they commonly reckon ninety or an hundred thousand; because their learned have a way of compounding and connecting them, to shrink that number; and as it is not necessary for the vulgar sort to know many, so very few do, and twelve or fourteen thousand is sufficient for usual writing.

They are wholly ignorant of natural philosophy, and not more skill'd in mathematics and astronomy; their poesy I do not understand, and their musick I do not find delightful or harmonious; and I cannot but wonder by what faculty Monsieur *Taverniere* has discover'd them to be the most excellent of all the oriental people in that art.[6]

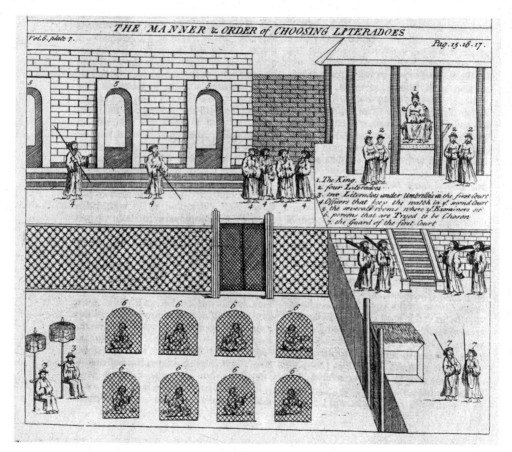

Plate 7: "The Manner and Order of Choosing Literadoes." 1. The King. 2. Four Literadoes. 3. Two Literadoes under Umbrellas in the First Court. 4. Officers that Keep the Watch in the Second Court. 5. The Several Rooms where the Examiners Sit. 6. Persons that are Tried to be Chosen. 7. The Guard of the First Court.

---

[6] Tavernier, "A New and Singular Relation of the Kingdom of Tunquin," p. 25: "... the musicians and actors of Tunquin are accounted the best in the whole Eastern part of the World."

Having thus confusedly mention'd a word or two, in general, of their learning, I return to the scholars: They must, in the acquisition of employ and dignity, (I do not say nobility for the custom is here, that all the honours die with the person, and descend not to his posterity) pass through three degrees; the first of a *Singdo* [*Sinh đồ*], something like the *Batchelors*, in *Europe*; the second a *Hung-cong* [*Hương cống*], resembling our *Licentiates*; the third degree is a *Tuncy* [*Tiến sĩ*], equal to the degree of *Doctor* with us.

Out of these doctors they choose the ablest, and elect him *Trangiveen* [*Trạng nguyên*], which is as much as to say, a president, or professor of learning.

And indeed, the election of these literadoes is manag'd with the most commendable policy and justice, that I know of, among them; for whereas in all other things they are sway'd by corruption, partiality, or private passions; in the distribution of these degrees they respect singularly the deserts of persons, since no man can obtain any of them, unless he is found worthy thereof, by a strict and most exact examination.

The order and method observed in the promotion of *Singdos*, or batchelors, is thus: Once in three years it is customary for the king and general to nominate two or three *Tuncies*, with some *Wene Quan* [*Văn quan*], or justice of the peace, who has the degree of *Hung-cong*, to be examiners of the design'd academy in that province where the election is to be made (for in this they proceed from one province to another, by turns) whither they repair immediately on receiving their commission. Great care is taken, that none speak with those to be examined on the way, or receive any bribes of them. Being arrived, they take up their lodgings in houses built of bamboos and straw; incompassed with a wall of the same materials, leaving a spacious empty place in the midst thereof for a theatre. The *Tuncies* are presently separated from the *Wene Quan* and the rest in distinct apartments, and are not to speak one with the other, during their function, strict guards being kept at the several doors, and all comers in or out are searched for papers, writings, &c. If any is found to have transgressed herein, he is rigorously punished, and loses his dignity.

In the morning of the day prescrib'd, for the commencing of the said examination, all the students resort to this place, where they find an officer, who exhibits to them five short sentences, written in capital letters, whereof every one, as many as there are, may take copies; which being done, they are all searched for papers or other writings, and then plac'd on the bare ground of the yard aforemention'd, at good and equal distance, and many watches are set, that none comes to speak with them.

Thus they sit to write their themes, which they must finish before evening, neither must the said answer contain more than twenty-four sides of paper. And as every one brings in his, he fastens to it, on a particular sheet, his name, the names of his parents and village, which the *Tuncies* tear off, and mark the answer and paper of names with the same number, which are put up severally, according to their province and aldeas.

All the papers being thus served, the *Tuncies* send them to the *Wene Quan*, (the names of their authors being kept in the custody of another officer) to be examined, who throws out all the bad, and sends the good ones to the *Tuncies* again. They, upon a strict review, put out a great many more, so that sometimes of four or five thousand pretenders, only one thousand are approved the first time; the second, perhaps no more than five hundred; and on the last proof only three hundred are to be graduated batchelors. Such as have behaved themselves well in the first trial, their names come out in publick within eight or ten days after, to be prepared for the second examination; and those whose names are thus thrown out, need not stay, for they cannot be admitted that sessions any more. In the same manner they continue in the second and third trial, only their task at the second trial is but of three sentences, and the answer twelve sides; the last of two sentences, and its reply eight sides, but more difficult than the former. Whosoever passes these trials is declared batchelor, and has his name register'd among those of the same rank, in the book of state, and from that time they pay but half the taxes which they were rated at before, and likewise enjoy some other petty immunities.

Now follows their manner of electing the *Hung-congs*, or licentiates. These are selected out of the batchelors, more or less, as the king pleases to order; they are examin'd by the same officers, and created alternately in the place aforesaid, where the batchelors were. If they can overcome but one proof more, which is the fourth, including the three preceding of the *Singdoes*, or batchelors, they become licentiates. The formality used in this proceeding is in a manner the same with the former, only they and their examiners are still more severely watched, and they are not permitted to see or speak with any of the competitors; they are separated, and distant enough from each other, when they write their meditations, *&c.* And all those *Hung-congs* of former creation, must leave, at that time, the province where the school is held, by repairing to the capital city, and abide there 'till the end of the act; many spies are set over them, and they are numbered every day. The like care is recommended to the governors of the other provinces about the said *Hung-congs*, during the solemnity, to prevent frauds and deceits in that behalf.

The examiners propound three sentences out of the book of their prince of philosophers, *Confucius*, and four more out of the volume of his disciples; the arguments of so many orations, which the candidate is to answer with so many themes in writing, which is to be in an elegant and sententious style, and adorned with the best of their rhetorick; the more concise the better.

The examiners then reject the worst, and present the best, who are to proceed to the *Tuncies*, or chief-examiners, and they chuse those that are to be admitted graduates, and expose their names with much ceremony. The privileges and immunities of the licentiates are far greater than the batchelors; besides, they have the honour to be presented to the king, who gives to each of them a thousand small pieces of coin, about the value of a dollar in money, and a piece of black callicoe for a gown, worth about three dollars more.

The last or third degree, called *Tuncy,* answerable to our doctors, is conferred every fourth year, at the capital city or court of the kingdom, in a particular palace with marble gates, formerly the best in the country, but now, through age, much decay'd. The choicest and learnedst of the *Hung-congs,* or licentiates, are only admitted to this trial; of many competitors few are successful. Their examiners are the king himself, the princes, and most eminent doctors of the realm, with other principal magistrates. This trial is in most circumstances like the two former, except in the questions propounded, which are both of greater number, and more intricate, grave, and specious, being commonly the most difficult part of their ethicks, politicks, and civil law, and something of poesy and rhetorick, all which they are to expound and resolve in writing, at four several times, in the space of twenty days, and he that doth it, is admitted doctor. This is no easy task, considering what a burthen it is to the memory, to retain all the characters of the four last of the nine books of *Confucius,* which necessarily they must have, word for word, by heart, to acquit themselves well therein.

They write their themes and meditations on the exhibited sentences, in a close cage made of bamboos for that purpose, and covered with callicoe, wherein they sit from the morning to night, being search'd, that they have nothing about them, but pen, ink, and clean paper; and to watch them the narrower, two doctors, or *Tuncies,* sit at a good distance from them, under umbrello's. Thus they are served at four different times, before they are made *Tuncies* or doctors. The king and general honour this solemnity with their presence the two first days, as the most important, and leave the compleating thereof to the ministers. Those thus graduated are congratulated by their friends, applauded by the spectators, and honour'd by their brother doctors, with many complimental expressions; the king presents each of them with a bar of silver, of the value of fourteen dollars, and a piece of silk, besides the revenue of some aldeas or villages for their maintenance, which is more or less, according to favour or desert, and they are feasted at the publick expense of their aldeas for some time. Out of these the principal magistrates of the kingdom are chosen, and they are sent Embassadors to *China,* and are permitted to wear *Chinese* boots and caps, with their proper vest.

The rejected licentiates may, if they please, continue their study, and try fortune again; if not, they are capable of some magistracy in the country, as justice of peace, head of an aldea, *&c.*

The batchelors have the same privilege; and those that are unwilling to make any further progress in learning, may find likewise imployment, if they have money, among the governors of provinces, in the courts of justice, or as clerks, stewards, secretaries, or sollicitors to the *Mandareens*; and in all this an eloquent tongue is not so requisite as a good pen.

Such fire-works as Monsieur *Taverniere* mentions these people to be exquisite in the making of, I have met none all the time I frequented this country, nor any other sorts, unless it be squibs, or the like. And as for those machines, or change of scenes in every act of their comedy, they may be long enough sought after, but will never be found here, where-ever he saw them.[7]

In astrology, geometry, and other mathematical sciences, they are but little skilled,[8] but they understand arithmetick reasonably well; their ethicks are confusedly deliver'd, not digested into formal method, as is their logick.

---

[7] Ibid., pp. 25-26: "Nor indeed is there any pastime more frequent then that of the theatre in this country; for there is never any solemn festival among them, which is not accompanied and set forth with artificial fireworks, in making whereof these people are exquisite; after which they have their comedies, with machines, and change of scenes in every act."

[8] Ibid., p. 25: " ... the Mathematicks, and particularly Astronomy, to which all the Orientals have a great inclination, as being great observers of the stars ... "; and p. 26: "They that will learn the Mathematicks, must make their own Instruments themselves, and spend five years in this study."

CHAPTER X.

OF THE PHYSICIANS AND DISEASES OF THE TONQUEENESE.[1]

Every one that pleases may be a physician in *Tonqueen,* and indeed every one almost is his own doctor, whereby this noble science is become the publick practice of the very dregs of the nation, to the disgrace of the publick in tolerating it.

Their principal study in this science consists only of an examination of some *Chinese* books, that direct them how to boil and compound their roots, herbs, and simples, with some obscure notions of their several qualities, nature, and virtue, but generally so confused, that they know little or nothing, until they add thereto their own experience. They understand hardly any thing of anatomy, or the nature of composition of mens bodies, with the divisions of the several parts thereof, which might lead them to form a judgment of the diseases incident to the human system; but attribute all to the blood, as the principal cause of all the disorders that befall the body, and therefore consider no further the constitution or temper in the application of their remedies; and with them it is enough to succeed well in three or four cures, though by mere chance (for they are hardly ever able to give a reason for what they do) to get the reputation of an excellent *Medicus,* which oftentimes, as it increases their practice, so gives them a greater power to kill their fellow-creatures. Their patients are generally very impatient under the hands of their doctors, who if he doth not afford them present ease and speedy cure, they send for other help, and so often go from bad to worse, 'till they are either well or kill'd, for want of patience on one side, and judgment on the other.

These people generally on visiting a patient, feel the pulse in two places, and that upon the wrist, as the *Europeans;* but they must be the *Chinese* physicians, whom Monsieur *Taverniere* extolls for their skill in the pulse;[2] and I own that some of that nation excell in it, but the far greater number are mere pretenders to this art, and affect to amuse the patient by ostentatious conjectures, and conceited and confused notions, to inspire a belief of their skill, in discovering thereby the cause of diseases, and so gull the credulous patients of their money, and oftentimes their health to boot.

These people have no apothecary among them, every one that professeth the art of the physick prepares the dose himself, which consists, as I mention'd, in the composition of herbs and roots, boiled in water.

---

[1] Jean-Baptiste Tavernier, "A New and Singular Relation of the Kingdom of Tunquin," Chapter X: "Of their Physicians, and the Diseases of the Tunquineses."

[2] Ibid., pp. 28-29, describes at length methods of feeling the pulse in different parts of the body.

The pestilence, gravel,[3] and the gout are hardly known in these countries: Fevers, agues, dysenteries, the jaundice, small pox, &c. reign here most; to all which they administer the said drugs for remedies, sometimes with desired success, wherein more is to be ascribed to the patient's own care, sparing diet and abstinence, (in which they are most singular, occasion'd perhaps by their more common fear of death) than the skill and judgment of the physician.

The grandees drink the herb tea, of *China* and *Japan*, but 'tis not much admired; they use most their native tea, called by them *Chia Bang*,[4] the leaf of a certain tree, and *Chiaway*,[5] the buds and flowers of another certain tree, which after they are dry'd and roasted, they boil and drink the liquor hot; the last is of a good pleasant taste. Besides these two sorts, they have many other sorts of liquor, made of beans, roots, &c.

I need not here describe the quality and virtue of the *China* and *Japan* tea, since they are so well known in *England*, and most other parts of *Europe;* only I will note how grosly M. *Taverniere* was mistaken, to prefer the *Japan* tea before that of *China*,[6] when in the choice of them there is above thirty *per cent* difference.

Phlebotomy, or blood-letting, is rarely practiced amongst this people, and when they do it, 'tis not after our way, in the arm, and with a lancet, but on the forehead, and with the bone of a fish tied to a small stick, in form like the horsefleams in *England*, which instrument is applied to the vein of the forehead; then they give thereon a fillip with a finger, and the blood gushes out. Their grand remedy is fire, in most distempers, which is used as they see cause, not regarding therein either the time of day or night precisely: The matter wherewith they burn is the leaf of a tree, well dry'd, and then beaten in a mortar until it grows almost like to our beaten hemp, and this they take and fix on every place to be burnt (for they do it in many places at the same time) so much as will lie on a farthing,[7] striking each parcel with ink of *China* at the bottom, that it may stick to the skin, then they fire it with a match of paper: Many account this a sovereign remedy, how true I cannot affirm: however, I am certain, that it puts the patient to great torment, and that our use of letting blood is but a flea-bite, in comparison of it.

But most common and frequently amongst them cupping is used, because cheap and easier. Their way here is much after the same manner as ours in *Europe*, only that they have calabashes instead of glasses.

Of anatomy they understand nothing, as I said before, and of surgery little, admiring much our *Europeans* art in that behalf. To broken bones they apply certain herbs, which, they say, will heal them in the space of twenty-four days, and cement them as strong as ever. They have another remedy, which is, to take the raw bones of hens, and beat them to powder, making thereof a paste, which applied to the part affected, is esteemed by them a sovereign medicine.

Their little children are much subject to dangerous obstructions, which deprive them of the benefit of nature, both by stool and urine, causing their bellies to swell

---

[3] Kidney and bladder stones.

[4] *Chè/trà bạng.*

[5] *Chè/trà hoa/huế.*

[6] Tavernier, "A New and Singular Relation of the Kingdom of Tunquin," p. 29: "They mightily admire the Herb tea, which comes from China and Japan; which latter country produces the best."

[7] A very small coin.

so, that often their lives are endangered thereby. Their remedy for this is, cock-roaches and onions roasted and beaten together; this they apply to the navel of the child, which is often attended with good success.

These people affirm, that crabs are turned into stones by the power of the sun, and use them as physick, but not in fevers and dysenteries: Moreover, they take up by the sea-side a kind of cockles, which being beaten to powder, they drink in the cholick [colic].

CHAPTER XI.

OF THE ORIGINAL GOVERNMENT, LAW, AND POLICY OF THE TONQUEENESE, WITH SOME CONSIDERATIONS THEREON.[1]

It is without all dispute that the *Tonqueenese* ever were a nation of themselves different from the *Chinese*, who call them *Manso*,[2] or *Barbarians*, and their country *Gannam*,[3] because situated far to the south, in reference to them, and the inhabitants bearing a great affinity with other *Indians*, in eating penang, coloring their teeth, going barefoot, and that their right great toe standeth athwart from their foot, as is to be seen yet by some of the *Tonqueen* cast. But how this country was govern'd before it was made a province of *China*, is hard to know, since they had in those days no characters; by consequence no history of that time can be extant among them: what was afterward compiled thereof may be suspected as fictions, invented at pleasure, and indeed, they are most of them so unaccountable, that they ought rather to be look'd upon as dreams and chimera's than historical narrations; neither is there much appearance of verity in those relations of theirs, which make this people so valiant, that they were not only able to contend with, but vanquish also the formidable armies of the prodigious empire of *China*, and maintain their liberty in spite thereof for many ages: but 'tis most likely that they have set the best face in their narrations, upon their actions, that they might not hand themselves down to posterity and to strangers in the base light, which it seems to me, their cowardice and ill conduct have deserved.

They pretend they have had the use of the *Chinese* characters amongst them before the reign of *Ding*,[4] one of their first kings, according to their best historians, which, by computation, cannot be less than two thousand years; if so, I infer, they were once before either conquer'd, or voluntary subjects to that empire, because the *China* laws, rites, customs, characters, &c. could have been neither of that antiquity, or so entirely and all at once introduced among them, as it was by their own testimony; besides, this agrees with the *China* chronicles, that mention, about the same time their empire was in great glory, calling it a triumphant one, whose limits

---

[1] Jean-Baptiste Tavernier, "A New and Singular Relation of the Kingdom of Tunquin," Chapter XI: "Of the Original Government and Policy of the Kingdom of Tunquin."

[2] Possibly *man rợ*.

[3] Baron's transcription of *An Nam*.

[4] Đinh Bộ Lĩnh (reigned c. 968-979), Đinh Tiến Hoàng (Đinh the First Emperor). The mention of "two thousand years" later in this sentence accords neither with real chronology nor with Baron's own calculations.

extended as far as *Siam*; therefore there is no reason to believe this neighboring kingdom could have remained unmolested, since it lies as a bar just in the way to hinder and obstruct their progress, but rather, that it was immediately incorporated with their empire.

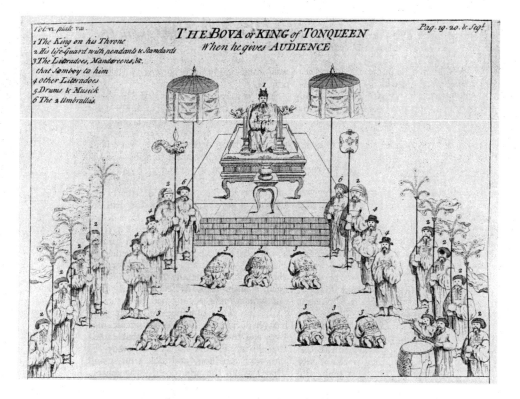

Plate 8: "The Boua or King of Tonqueen when He Gives Audience." 1. The King on his Throne. 2. His Life-guard with Pendants and Standards. 3. The Literadoes, Mandareens, etc. that Sombey to Him. 4. Other Literadoes. 5. Drums and Musick. 6. The 2 Umbrellas.

Yet, it may be, the *Chinese* did not keep the country the first time long under subjection, but left them on the invasion of the *Tartars*,[5] or on some other motives, so that after their departure *Ding* was king: Now, whether they made him so, or whether he usurped the regality, by the assistance of great numbers of vagabonds, and other scum of the nation, is differently deliver'd. They say, that king *Ding* had enjoy'd the scepter but a small time before the great ones murmured against him; the malcontents finding the common people disobedient, whose affections, whether he had lost by cruel and harsh usage, or that they disdained to be any longer subject to their country-man, as it commonly falls out with people accustomed to servitude, to be incapable of using well their new-recover'd liberty, (with other occult motives and malignant influences that caused the effects of those distractions,) they fell into open rebellion, and took arms against *Ding*, whom they murdered, whereon ensued

---

[5] It is unclear whether Baron has in mind the Mongols of the thirteenth century or some earlier invasion from the plains north of China; later he uses the term "Tartars" to refer to the Manchu Qing.

bloody civil wars for many years, 'till being weary, they chose, by general consent, a puissant prince of theirs, called *Leedayhang*,[6] for their king.

In his reign, they say, the *Chinese* invaded the country, not mentioning for what reason: Probably they were *Chinese* rebels, that fled thence, and that this people fought many battles against them with good success. Yet, in the height of this war *Leedayhang* dying, whether in battle or otherwise is uncertain, left to his successor *Libatvie*,[7] a politick and valiant prince, the prosecution thereof, which he carry'd on with no less valour than prosperity; for having encounter'd and routed the *Chinese* in six or seven battles, he restored peace and tranquillity to the whole kingdom, and built that large and magnificent palace of marble, which is now, through age, so decay'd, that nothing but the gates and some of the walls of that sumptuous structure remain.

They say, that after this king, his posterity possessed the crown to the fourth or sixth generation, successively, and ruled in great prosperity; but the last left the succession to a daughter, having no heir male, which princess coming to the crown, married a powerful lord of the family of *Tran*,[8] who ruled with her jointly but a few months; for another of their grandees, called *Hoe*,[9] rebelled against them, and having vanquish'd them in battle, put them to death, and ascended the throne himself.[10]

He govern'd not long, for the people conspired against him; for what cause I cannot find: it may be suspected, that he used bad means for the maintaining of his unjust possession; and having call'd the *Chinese* to their assistance, they kill'd the usurper, and withal lost their own freedom, for the *Chinese* shew'd themselves true auxiliaries, in seizing the whole kingdom for a reward of their labour and victory.

A *Chinese* viceroy or general was then ordered over this people, to govern them as formerly, which continued for the space of sixteen years,[11] when they began to be weary of the *Chinese* oppressions and insolence, and withal, commemorating their former condition, they resolved to endeavour to free themselves from the *Chinese* yoke, and accordingly took arms under the leading of a valiant captain, by name *Lee*,[12] and fought with the *Chinese*, and routed them in several battles, killing many of them, with their viceroy or general *Luetang*;[13] which disaster, with the charges of the war abroad and civil commotions at home, and the small profit this country yielded, were perhaps the motives why the *China* emperor *Humvew*[14] thought convenient to

---

[6] Lê Đại Hành (r. 980-1005).

[7] Probably Lý Bát Vị (The Eight Rulers of Lý, a reference to the eight kings of the Lý dynasty, 1009-1225), here used in reference to the first king of the Lý dynasty, Lý Công Uẩn (Lý Thái Tổ, r. 1009-1028).

[8] Trần dynasty (1226-1400).

[9] Reference to Hồ Qúy Ly, who came to power in the late fourteenth century and founded his own short-lived dynasty in 1400; in 1407 he was captured by the Ming Chinese when they gained control of the country.

[10] Baron's historical narrative from Đinh Bộ Lĩnh to Hồ Qúy Ly contains many curiosities, among which is the shortening of the Trần dynasty to "but a few months."

[11] The Ming occupation, from the initial invasion until final evacuation, was from 1407 to 1427.

[12] Lê Lợi.

[13] Liu Sheng, killed in the Battle of Chi Lăng, 1427.

[14] Appears to refer to the Hongwu Emperor (r. 1368-98); the Ming occupation of Vietnam was the policy of the Yongle Emperor (r. 1402-24), a policy that was abandoned by his successors.

quit it again, which is now about four hundred and fifty years ago.[15] Having therefore imposed on them certain conditions, and taken security for their faithful performance, (*viz.* to come every three years, once to the imperial city, *Pekin*, with several presents, which they call tribute, and to do homage to the emperor, in acknowledgment that they hold this their kingdom and liberty of his mere grace and bounty) he withdrew his troops from *Tonqueen*; and these conditions are punctually observed to this very day.

Among the presents, they are to carry images of gold and silver, made in the posture of criminals, denoting that they are such to the *China* empire, for the murder of *Luetang*, the 'foresaid general, and that they are to remain evermore supplicants to that court for the said offence. The kings of *Tonqueen* have likewise their *chaop*, or seal, from the *China* emperor as a mark of their dependency. And tho' this formality be a mere piece of *Chinese* vanity, they make no little ado about it. This year (1683) came here an embassador from the imperial court of *Pekin*, to bring a title for the *Boua*, that had been inaugurated above eight or nine years before;[16] he was received with all the pomp and magnificence that the general could devise, or was capable to put in practice, and that not out of love, but mere ostentation, to shew the *Tartars*[17] his grandeur and puissance. They had presented to their view a great number of soldiers, richly cloathed in *English* and *Dutch* manufactures; most of their elephants and cavalry in their best furniture, gilded gallies, *&c.* But for all this, the embassador did not deign to visit his highness; as indeed no embassadors of that empire ever do, making of him no other account than as of a plebian usurper, obscure in comparison of their emperors.

But to return: The *Chinese* having thus forsaken the country, *Lee* was proclaimed king, who reigned several years, and his family enjoy'd the scepter afterwards uninterrupted, for the space of above two hundred years,[18] and then *Mack*[19] usurped the crown. This man was of a low and vile original, born about *Batshaw*,[20] a fisher village, at the river's mouth where the *European* ships enter it; he was a wrestler by profession, and so dextrous therein, that he raised himself to the degree of a *Mandareen*, or lord: But his ambition, that aspired higher, could not be satisfied with any other condition but the sovereignty itself, and accordingly he conspired against the king, and effected his design, rather by crafty practices and stratagems than force.

---

[15] In fact about 250 years.

[16] The emperor Lê Hi Tông (r. 1676-1705).

[17] The Manchus of the Qing dynasty.

[18] The dynasty established by Lê Lợi in 1428 lasted about a hundred years, to the 1520s.

[19] Mạc Đăng Dung, b. 1483, r. 1527-1541.

[20] According to *Đại Việt Sử Ký Toàn Thư, Bản Kỷ Tục Biên* XV:69b (Hanoi: Nhà Xuất Bản Khoa Học Xã Hội, 1993), III:109, Mạc Đăng Dung was born in the coastal region south of the modern city of Hải Phòng, at Cổ Trai village in Nghi Dương district, names that appear on French colonial maps west of Đồ Sơn at the mouth of Văn Úc River, four to five miles north of the mouth of Thái Bình River, which was a major entry point for seventeenth-century ocean-going ships. *Batshaw* is unidentified, but I suspect *shaw* is Vietnamese *xã*, "village" (for such is how Baron transcribes this word later in this chapter), in which case *Bat* would transcribe the name of the village. An early fifteenth-century Chinese itinerary identifies a major water route into northern Vietnam as follows: "Entering from Đồ Sơn one arrives at the Cổ Trai route and then arrives at Nghi Dương district ... " Bửu Cầm et al., *Hồng Đức Bản Đồ* (Saigon: Bộ Quốc-Gia Giáo-Dục, 1962), p. 64.

Having thus usurped the crown, he fortified *Batshaw* and other places, because of his many enemies, especially one *Hoawing*,[21] a mighty and powerful prince, in the province of *Tingwa* [Thanh Hóa], of whom he most stood in fear, since he was in open defiance of the usurper. This *Hoawing* married his daughter to *Hoatrin*,[22] a man of singular strength and valour, who had been formerly a notorious robber, and made him general of his forces, and when he died, left him the guardianship and tuition of his only son, at that time about fourteen or fifteen years of age. *Hoatrin* having gotten the forces of his deceased father-in-law at his devotion, made open war against *Mack*, and after many petty encounters, with various success, at last overcame him. The usurper finding himself reduced to a nonplus, was necessitated to fly for his security to *Cabang* [Cao Bằng], a kingdom on the frontier of *China*, and subject to this king, formerly inhabited by a kind of wild people: But *Hoatrin* came immediately after the victory to *Cacho*,[23] the metropolis, and having first demolished the fortifications of *Mack*, he made proclamation, if there was any heir male of the house of *Lee*, he might freely discover himself, promising to place him on the throne of his ancestors, and protested he had taken arms for that end; and accordingly, when a youth of the house of *Lee* was brought to him, he expressed much joy, placed him on the throne with abundance of readiness, and owned him his sovereign, ordering every one to pay obedience to *Lee*, lawful king of *Tonqueen*, &c. and for himself he reserved the title of *Choua*, or general of all the forces. This was to the infinite discontentment of his pupil, the young *Hoawing*,[24] who did not dream that his brother-in-law would have converted all the effects of his father's forces and army, with the prosperous success thereof, to his particular use, greatness, and advancement, by excluding the orphan; but he was deceived in his account, for *Hoatrin* having previously made the requisite provision for the settlement of the government, he sent a peremptory letter to his brother-in-law, requiring his obedience to this prince of the house of *Lee*, or by default, to declare him a rebel, and open enemy to the state; This occasioned a civil war, and a rent in the kingdom of *Tonqueen*; for young *Hoawing*, altho' he was not against *Lee*, yet could he not endure to think that *Tring*[25] should make himself general, esteeming that place more justly to belong to him. But finding he was too weak to resist the power of *Tring*, and to remain so near as *Tingwa* is to the city of *Cacho*, he thought it the safest way to retire to *Cochin-china*, where he was joyfully received by those governors and soldiers, who immediately elected him *Choua*, or general to *Lee*, their rightful *Boua* [vua], or king, proclaiming *Tring* a traitor and rebel; so that ever since, now above two hundred and twenty years,[26] this kingdom has remain'd divided, under two lieutenant-generals, with royal authority; both own *Lee* as king and ruler, according to their ancient laws, customs, and rights, but are mortal enemies, and wage continual war against each other.

---

[21] Nguyễn Hoằng Kim (d. 1545).

[22] Trịnh Kiểm (d. 1570).

[23] The colloquial name for Hanoi, in Chapter II it is spelled with a hyphen: Ca-cho.

[24] Nguyễn Hoàng (1525-1613).

[25] Here Baron's transcription shifts from *Hoatrin* to *Tring*, perhaps in some way an indication of Trịnh Tùng (d. 1623), who became leader of the Trịnh after the death of his father, Trịnh Kiểm, in 1570.

[26] Here Baron expands less than a century into 220 years; perhaps the era of Trịnh-Nguyễn warfare, which began in the 1620s, seemed to have been that long.

I return now to *Tring*, and see why, as victor, he did not ascend the throne, and take upon him the name and title of a king. Certainly, it was not for want of ambition, or altogether out of modesty and sense of justice that he did not accept of any higher title, than that of general; but it was in consideration of two very specious reasons; for should he assume the crown and royal title to himself, he would be regarded as usurper, and expose himself to the general hate and envy of the natives, and more-specifically to the persecution of *Hoawing*, who would be able, under the most just and plausible pretexts, to work his ruin and extirpation: The other motive was his apprehension, that the *Chinese* emperor should be against him, as knowing he was a stranger to the royal race of the kings of *Tonqueen*, whereby *Tring* would involve himself in a torrent of troubles, and be, probably, the cause of his own perdition; therefore he thought it was the securest way to set up a prince of the house of *Lee*, with only the bare name of king, and reserve the royal power for himself; and indeed, all that belongs to the sovereign resides in the *Choua*, for he may make war or peace as he thinks fit, he makes and abrogates laws, pardons and condemns criminals, he creates and deposes magistrates and military officers, he imposes taxes and orders fines according to his pleasure, all strangers make their application to him, except the ambassadors of *China*; and, in a word, his authority is not only royal, but absolute and unlimited, wherefore the *Europeans* call him The king and the true king is called, for distinction sake, The emperor; whilst the *Boua* or king, is shut up in his palace, attended by none but spies of the *Choua*, neither is he permitted to stir abroad more than once a year, and that on the great solemnity of their annual sacrifices, &c. As for the rest, he serves only to cry *amen* to all that the general doth, and to confirm, for formality sake, with his *Chaop*, all the acts and decrees of the other; to contest with him the least matter would not be safe for him; and though the people respect the *Boua*, yet they fear the *Choua* much more, who is most flatter'd because of his power.

The general's place is like the king's, hereditary, the eldest son succeeds the father; yet often the ambition of the brothers has occasioned commotions and civil broils, aiming to supplant each other, therefore it is a common saying amongst them, that the death of a thousand *Boua's* doth not endanger the country in the least; but when the *Choua* dies, every one's mind is possessed with great tremors and heavy consternation, expecting fearful changes in state and government.

This kingdom is properly divided into six provinces, not reckoning the country of *Cubang*,[27] and a small part of *Bowes*,[28] which are maintain'd as conquer'd lands, that people being of a different language and manner from the *Tonqueenese*; and five of the six provinces are govern'd by their particular governors, which at present are all eunuchs, with ample power; but he that rules in *Giang*,[29] the frontiers of *Cochin-china*, the sixth province, is a kind of viceroy, or lieutenant-general, and the militia under him are not less in number than forty thousand soldiers. His authority is in a manner absolute, from whom there is no appeal, except in cases of high-treason, to the supream court of the kingdom. This viceroy is usually a person of great favour,

---

[27] Cao Bằng, transcribed as *Cabang* above.

[28] On *Bowes*, see above in Chapter II.

[29] The southernmost province of Tonkin was Nghệ An, just to the south of which was the Gianh River, which served as the border with Cochinchina. I suppose Baron's "Giang" is a transcription of the river's name, used by extension to indicate the adjacent border province. Today, the southern part of what then was Nghệ An is Hà Tĩnh province.

and much confided in by the general, who, to oblige him the more, marries either his daughter or sister to him; for it would be of ill consequence to the whole kingdom, especially for the general, if this man should revolt to *Cochin-china*.

In former times they had eunuchs to govern this province too; but since the trick the *Cochin-chinese* put on one of them, they have not placed there any more as governors in chief. The jest was thus: The *Cochin-chinese*, who hate these kind of creatures, and never imploy any of them in business of importance, especially in the militia, knowing the capon-viceroy of that province was appointed generalissimo for the expedition in hand against them, they sent him, in contempt, a breast-piece of silk, such as is worne by their women, for a present, desiring him to make use of it; giving thereby to understand, that such a dress and ornament better became him, than either to command soldiers or to govern provinces, &c. as approaching so near the female sex.

The governors of provinces have for their seconds a literado *Mandareen*, or lawyer, to assist them in the civil government and administration of their laws, who sit with the governors in publick courts of justice; besides this, each province has its several inferior courts of judicature, and one among the rest that is independent of the governor's authority, the judges whereof have their characters immediately of the sovereign court of the *Quan fo Lew*[30] at *Cacho*.

In small controversies of property of grounds, houses, debts, or the like, they proceed thus: A man that has an action against another gives his complaint into *Ongshaw*,[31] or the head of his aldea, who takes some cognizance of the matter, and brings it before the *Wean Quan*,[32] head of twenty, thirty, or forty aldeas, or villages, where the plaintiff and defendant are heard, and then sentence is given: But if one of the parties be not content to stand to this award, he appeals to the *Foe Quan*,[33] head of eighty, an hundred, or an hundred and fifty aldeas, where the matter is examin'd, with the sentence of the *Wean Quan*, who, as he finds cause, passes his sentence: And in case this does not satisfy them, the suit is brought before the provincial governor, where it receives its final determination, without further appealing, provided the matter be of no great importance, as I said before; but if the debt be considerable, or the pretensions ample, &c. they may appeal from the governor to *Inga Hean*, a court, as is noted above,[34] which the provincial governors have no jurisdiction over. In this tribunal a *Tuncy* of the class of the first literadoes always presides, and from thence

---

[30] What Baron transcribes in this chapter as *Quan fo Lew* he transcribes in the next chapter as *Quan-fo-lieu*, calling it the "supreme court." This is *Quan Phủ Liệu*; see Philippe Langlet, "La Tradition Vietnamienne: un état national au sein de la civilization Chinoise," *Bulletin de la Société des Etudes Indochinoises* XLV, 2 & 3 Trimestres (1970): 23, 305; also Dang Phuong Nghi, "Les Institutions Publiques du Viet-Nam au XVIII siècle," *Publications de l'Ecole Française d'Extrême-Orient* LXIV (1969): 70.

[31] Probably *ông xã*, "Mister Village," a plausible colloquial term for a village head.

[32] *Huyện quan*, "District Official."

[33] *Phủ quan*, "Prefecture Official."

[34] This is Baron's first and only mention of the *Inga Hean*, so his reference to noting it previously is a mystery. Perhaps *Inga Hean* is *Hình Khoa Hiến*; what is being referred to here is apparently the *Thanh Hình Hiến Sát Sứ Ty*, commonly shortened to *Hiến Ty*, an office related to the censorate that took appeals from the regular provincial administration. In Baron's terminology, there may be some conflation of this with the *Hình Khoa*, which was an office that exercised control over the regular judicial administration of the central government at the capital. See Langlet, "La Tradition Vietnamienne," p. 34, and Dang Phuong Nghi, "Les Institutions Publiques du Viet-Nam au XVIII siècle," p. 81.

the suit may be removed to the several courts of the city, if they are firmly resolved, by prosecuting the law, to ruin each other; and altho' the judges cannot hinder the parties appealing from one court to another, yet if two different courts give the like sentence on one and the same cause, then the courts from which the appeal is made, has the privilege to inflict some corporal punishment on the appellants, or fine them, as is ordained by law.

Criminal cases, as theft, or the like matters, belong wholly to the governors of the province, who punish immediately small offences; but such as deserve death, their sentences are sent to the general, to have his consent for the execution thereof.

The quarrels of the great ones come generally to the city of *Cacho*; but the names of all the courts, and the precise methods of process, I cannot exactly affirm. However, I think they begin with the courts called *Quan Key Dow*,[35] then an appeal lies to *Quan Gay Chue*,[36] and in case of great moment, petition being made to the general, he remits the cause at last for a revise to *Quan fo Lew*, who hold their assize in the general's palace. The persons who compose this college are most of them old literadoes, reputed wise, and such as have been presidents of the chief courts of judicature, and known, or at least supposed to be of great integrity and honesty, and exalted to be principal ministers and counsellors of state, on whose care and prudence reposes the whole weight of the civil government and laws of the kingdom.

Quarrels indifferent about ground, houses, &c. in and about the city, belong to the court called *Quan fu Douan*,[37] where all such differences are decided; but the party may appeal to *Quan gnue Sew*,[38] and thus successively to *Quan fo Lew*, by way of petition.

Rebellion and conspiracy against the general, &c. falls under the cognizance of the court of *Quan fo Lew*, and the governor of the city puts their sentences or decrees in execution, who are as much as presidents of life and death of the city and its jurisdiction: But more immediately appertain to them all causes of murther, theft, and other like crimes, both to judge and punish the offender without further appeal.

They are the rebels that come before the general with a whisp of straw in their mouths, after they have made their peace, and obtain'd pardon, to shew, that by their disorderly life, they have made themselves equal to the brute beasts; but not those guilty of murther, as *Taverniere* is pleas'd to assert.[39]

The *China* laws are in use amongst them, which indeed may be considered as their civil and written law; but the temporal edicts, statutes, and constitutions of their princes and chiefest doctors, intermix'd with their old customs, are of greatest force, and in a manner the whole directory of the government, and the rule of the peoples obedience; all which are committed to writing, and digested into several

---

[35] Unidentified; perhaps *Quan Kế Đô*, "Official to examine the capital."

[36] Unidentified.

[37] *Quan Phủ Doãn*, the main civil authority and court of justice in the capital city; see Langlet, "La Tradition Vietnamienne," p. 36 and Dang Phuong Nghi, "Les Institutions Publiques du Viet-Nam au XVIII siècle," pp. 44, 81, 97.

[38] *Quan Ngự Sử*, officials of the censorate.

[39] Tavernier, "A New and Singular Relation of the Kingdom of Tunquin," p. 37: "As for Murder, they are very exact in punishing that crime. For they carry the Person apprehended before the Judge; and then he must hold to his Mouth a little wisp of Grass, to shew, that by his disorderly life he had made himself a Beast."

books that make at present their body of law: and to give this people their due, they shew much more good nature and honesty than the *Chinese*, or *Aristotle* himself in that respect, where both their laws tolerate, nay, command the exposing of all maimed, deformed, and female children, which are maxims that these people abhor as unnatural and brutish.

With no less disdain they reject that law of their neighbours which encourageth the most execrable and abominable vice not fit to be nam'd:[40] Questionless their primitive legislators were wise and good-intentioned politicians; but how commendable soever those institutions were, yet the misery of human imperfections, degeneracy by length of time, multiplicity of lawyers, together with the daily increase of other petty officers, has brought justice now to that corruption, that for money most crimes will be absolved, since there are few of their judges but what are subject to bribes.

Justice thus betray'd and perverted even by its officers, has brought the country into much disorders, and the people under great oppressions, so as to be involv'd in a thousand miseries; and woe be to a stranger that falls into the labyrinths of their laws, especially into the clutches of their capon *Mandareens* to be judges of his particular affairs; for to them it commonly happens in the like cases that matters are referred, and he must look for nothing less than the ruin of his purse, and be glad if he escapes without being bereav'd of his senses too; whereof I could alledge many examples of my own knowledge, to my woeful experience, were it to the purpose.

Having thus amply spoken of their Laws and their manner of proceeding therein, it remains now to consider the other state column as it stands at present, their Policy, in which is very remarkable, their great veneration for the family of their lawful kings, whose title, tho' an empty one, is used in all their writings. The *Choua's* are exceedingly to be commended for their religiously observing their promises to maintain both the royal stock, and the laws and constitutions of the land, and to innovate nothing therein, tho' repugnant to the interest of their usurped power.

To this is owing chiefly that we see the heir of the crown permitted to live after he is stripped of his rights and royal authority; a thing, I believe, that has no where an example, and is not to be found in the histories of any other nation, and may sound like a strange paradox in the ears of the politicians of other countries. Nor is it altogether the fear of *China* that ties the general's hands so as not to be able to instigate him against the king, nor ignorance of the power of those temptations which generally the lustre of a diadem inspires in the minds even of such as have no reason to pretend to it; nor are they strangers to the practices of other oriental monarchs, who retain their possessions by what means soever they acquire them, tho' it be by the subversion and violation of all laws human and divine.

But in truth, we may say, these generals were moderate, and that of those qualities proper to tyrants, as ambition, covetousness and cruelty, this last was never found predominant in them; whereof their brothers, who are often intrusted with important employs, as governors of provinces, the conduct of armies, &c. are both convincing proofs and manifest arguments. They are, in short, too generous to follow the maxim of killing them for their own imaginary security.

---

[40] Unclear what Baron refers to here.

One prince indeed, I knew, who was poison'd by order of his brother the general; but the necessity (if one may so say) was so urgent, that there was no other way in that exigency, to preserve his own life, as will be noted in the next chapter.[41]

Their method of promoting scholars to their several degrees, which I have already mention'd, is both regular and just, and a great encouragement to learning, and the well-deserving therein.

The often removing their *Mandareens* from their government, is good prudence to prevent plots and conspiracies; but as there is no government but what has its defect as well as its perfection, so this is not wanting in both qualities; and it is certainly a great weakness in their politicks, as it is a needless charge to the publick, to maintain such a great army idle, as they do in time of peace, and must needs be a mighty burthen to the commonalty, who feel the weight most.

The general is likewise short, in not making timely provision for the great numbers of his people, since their daily encrease will make them too numerous and incapable of living together; therefore it would be a good expedient to find some outlet for those superfluous humours, for fear they might in time cause some violent convulsion in the state, which perhaps might irretrievably overturn it. The last famine, in particular, swept away two-thirds of the inhabitants, who, if they had been imploy'd against the *Cochin-chinese*, or some other hostile Countries, they might have destroy'd it with their very hands and teeth.

The over-great confidence the general reposes in the capons, as it is a mean thing, so it is contrary to good policy to tolerate so much evil as they occasion in the state, for the small and unjust benefits which he receives by their means.

The custom of selling most offices indifferently to such as will pay most for them, not regarding condition or capacity of persons, is certainly a foul merchandize, and a baseness unbecoming the publick, especially as to the offices of judicature; for if they buy their places dear, 'tis likely they will make the most advantage thereof, at the expence of right and justice.

Their militia, as it is also much more numerous than is required in a defensive war (which is a conduct, that for several years they have thought it their interest to observe) or befitting peaceable times, so it may prove of dangerous consequence, if they should be troublesome. Some years ago these soldiers mutined;[42] and had they then found one to head them, it would have gone very hard with the general, who perhaps might have experienc'd from them some such insolences and devastations as several *Roman* emperors met with from their pretorians, and the *Turks* from their janizaries. He doth well to shift them from place to place, and change often their commanders, and to keep them in continual labour or action. But the worst of all is, that the captains of his militia are eunuchs, who, generally, are cowardly fellows; and, it is thought, their baseness has been the grand cause of the many overthrows this nation has received of the *Cochin-chinese*, and will be (as long as they are thus employ'd) always a hindrance in the conquest of that spot of ground, which in comparison of them, contains but a handful of men.

They trust more to their infantry, than to their cavalry or elephants, by reason the country is low, swampy, and full of rivers and brooks, which renders them of small service.

---

[41] Reference to an event in 1674 narrated in Chapter XII.

[42] Baron refers to an event in 1674 that he narrates in the next chapter.

Their soldiers are good marksmen, and in that, I believe, inferior to few; and surpassing most nations in dexterity of handling and quickness of firing their muskets.

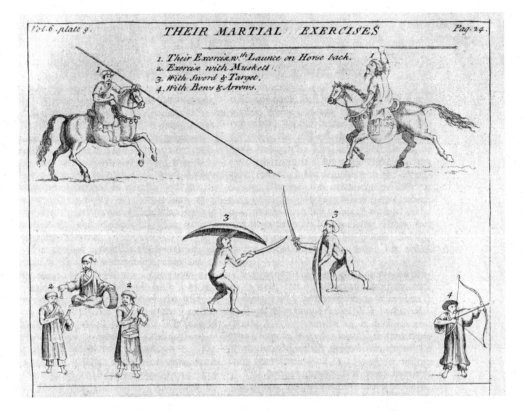

Plate 9: "Their Martial Exercises." 1. Their Exercise with Launce on Horseback. 2. Exercise with Muskets. 3. With Sword and Target. 4. With Bows and Arrows.

Firelocks are not in use amongst them,[43] but the bow is mightily in fashion in which they are expert to admiration.

In fine, they soon learn their exercise of arms, and are good proficients therein. But to mount the great horse, is no more with them, than the getting astride on a common beast; which this country produces for the most part small, yet very lively.

Their elephants are trained up for war, and imboldened against some sort of fireworks and the noise of guns, as far as the nature of the creature is capable of: as for artificial fire-works, they are rather ignorant than skilful therein.

Their finances, or invention to bring in money to the general's coffers, over and above his usual revenue, are, by the sale of most offices in the kingdom; by the fines imposed on *Mandareens*, and transgressors; the tenths of all contrabands;

---

[43] By "firelock" Baron apparently means "flintlock," the ignition device for muskets developed in the sixteenth century. The muskets mentioned in the previous paragraph were likely ignited by "matchlocks" or "wheel locks," earlier devices for igniting the powder.

considerable shares out of the estates of deceased *Mandareens*; but he is heir-general of the eunuchs or capons, and has in a manner all they leave; add to this, his accidental revenue, which comes in by strangers, merchants, *&c.* (which is more or less according as ships and vessels come to trade in this port); the poll or head-money; excises on provisions, and impositions on inland merchants commodities, *&c.* so that the general's revenues must needs amount to a very considerable sum. But since this money, for the most part, is taken from one to feed the other, the publick wealth is nothing better'd thereby, but rather the worse; forasmuch as it is the sweat and blood of the industrious, which the lazy and idle often spend most prodigally and profusely; also for that the oppressive taxes do not surcease thereby: which (together with their proceedings in matters of commerce, which they hold in scorn, as much as they despise the traders, neglecting the great convenience they have thereby to render their country rich and flourishing, which is the study of all well-govern'd nations throughout the world) renders them, in the main, but a mean and miserable people.

I have noted this more particularly in the chapter treating about the trade, *&c.* of the kingdom; so referring thereto, I shall proceed next to give some account of the general and his grandees and court.

CHAPTER XII.

OF THE GENERAL OF TONQUEEN, *HIS FAMILY, OFFICERS, AND COURT.*[1]

By what hath been said in the foregoing chapter, it may easily be understood how far the authority of the *Boua* of *Tonqueen* extends, and that the general has really the helm in hand; let us then consider him as the spirit and life of this state. His power is, like that of most *Eastern* kings, monarchical in excess, yet not so tyrannical as many of them, since they ever had their laws and old customs in great veneration, and comported their actions agreeable thereto.

The present general is the fourth of the house of *Tring*,[2] in a direct line, that has, as one may say, sway'd the scepter over this people; his family was establish'd in the government as soon as *Mack* the usurper was suppressed,[3] and then laid the foundation of their present greatness. He is aged fifty-three years, and is a sharp subtile politician, but of an infirm constitution. He succeeded his father in the year 1682, with whom he reigned jointly several years.[4] He had three sons, and as many daughters, by sundry concubines; but his eldest and youngest sons dying, the second, just on his grandfather's decease, fell mad or distracted, but is now recovered,[5] and has the title of *Chu-ta*,[6] that is, young general (the usual title of the eldest surviving son) who keeps his court separate, and almost as magnificent as his father, has his *Mandareens*, servants, and offices of the same denomination, only that in precedency they give place to those of the father; but as soon as the prince succeeds the general, then his servants take place of the others, very few excepted, who often for their wisdom and experience keep their former stations.

If the general marries (which seldom happens but in their latter years, when there are but little hopes of issue by the person), this lady, as wife, is chief of all his women, and has the name and title of Mother of the Land, because of her extraction, which is always royal; but concubines he takes early, and sometimes before eighteen, the number not limited, sometimes three hundred, often five hundred, and more, if he pleases, for it is an honour to excel therein: and in the choice of them, their beauty is not so much regarded as their art and skill in singing and dancing, and playing on

---

[1] Jean-Baptiste Tavernier, "A New and Singular Relation of the Kingdom of Tunquin," Chapter XII: "Of the Court of the Kings of Tunquin," is relatively short (pp. 38-41) and concentrates on discussion of the Lê emperors (*Boua/Vua*).

[2] Trịnh Căn (d. 1709)

[3] Trịnh Căn's great-grandfather Trịnh Tùng expelled the Mạc from Hanoi in 1592.

[4] Trịnh Căn's father Trịnh Tạc gave him the titles of authority in 1674 as a result of the mutiny described later in this chapter.

[5] This prince is mentioned in Chapter VI as having "adopted" Baron.

[6] Probably *chủ tá*, "assistant master/ruler," apparently a colloquial sobriquet, for it does not to my knowledge appear in historical texts of this time.

a musical instrument, and to have the wit to divert the general with diversity of pleasing sports. Of these, she that proves mother of the first son, is honoured as soon as her son is declared heir apparent, with the name and title of True and Legitimate Wife, and tho' not quite so much respected, yet far better beloved than the former;[7] the rest of the concubines, that have children by him, are called *Ducba* [Đức bà], or excellent women; his male-children, the eldest excepted, are saluted with the appellation, *Duc-ong* [Đức ông], i.e. excellent person, or man; the daughters are called *Batua* [Bà chúa], which is as much as to say princess with us; the like titles have his brothers and sisters, but not their children, nor his grand-children, except those descending from his eldest son.

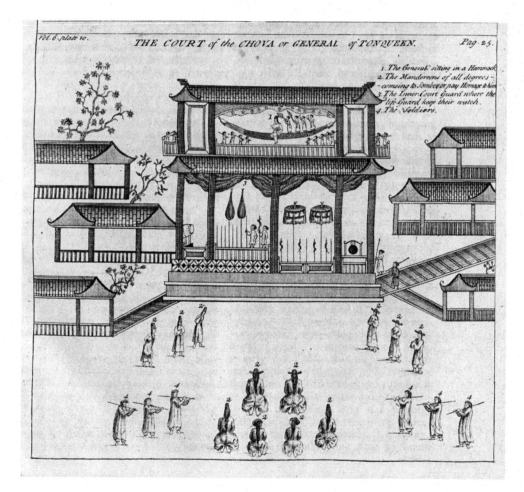

Plate 10: "The Court of the Choua or General of Tonqueen." 1. The General Sitting in a Hammock. 2. The Mandareens of all Degrees Coming to Sombey or Pay Homage to Him. 3. The Inner Court Guard where the Life-guard Keep their Watch. 4. The Soldiers.

---

[7] The "former" being a reference to "Mother of the Land."

For his own children, questionless, he provides well, but his sisters and brothers must be content with such revenues as he is pleas'd to allow them out of the publick, which decreases in their family as it declines and grows remote from his blood, so that those of the fourth or fifth descent can expect no such provision.

The present general has many brothers and sisters, but he is not over kind to them, which I take to proceed from his suspicious temper and weakly constitution. Most of his predecessors were otherwise inclined; they admitted their brothers to publick affairs, and conferred on them the titles and power of generals, field-marshals, and provincial governors, with the trust of numbers of soldiers, always imploying them in honourable charges, and such as became the general's brothers.

As I said before, I never could hear of more than one example amongst them, of killing a brother in cool blood, and is, that of the late deceased general against prince *Chechening*;[8] which, all circumstances considered, can hardly be termed cruelty. The history runs thus.

This *Chechening* was second brother to the deceased general, a prince imbued with many heroick virtues; his liberality, generosity, and courteous disposition, made him popular and so beloved among the soldiers, that they would call him their father. A prudent captain he was, and no less eminent in valour, for having given the *Cochin-chinese* several overthrows, he was so extremely redoubted, that they called him the Lightning of *Tonqueen*. His fame thus daily increasing both abroad and at home, it at length drove him on the rocks and precipices of his brother's envy and jealousy, which the good prince perceiving, endeavoured to remove; humbly telling him he would do nothing but what he should order; and that the good success he had in arms, proceeded wholly from his wise and prudent direction, protesting, and solemnly swearing, he never did, nor would undertake any thing that might in the least be prejudicial to him; and, that if the soldiers or rabble should dare to offer him his place, he would not only refuse and abhor it, but punish also most severely the movers of such propositions.

This declaration gave, for the present, some seeming content and satisfaction to the general, but few years after, whether the ground was the envy and jealousy aforesaid, or that he had done somewhat that could be misconstrued or suspected, or was falsely accused, or whatsoever else the matter was, for it is indifferently reported, the general sent for him and part of his army from the frontiers of *Cochin-china*. In obedience to this command, he came to court, where, by order of the general, he was immediately clap'd in irons, and confin'd to a certain close prison near the palace.

In this condition he continued several years, by which it seems his faults were not capital, or at least nothing could be proved against him to take away his life; but in the interim, as fate would have it, about the year 1672,[9] the soldiers that were in

---

[8] This appears to be a transcription of *Tiết chế Ning*. The prince being referred to here was a younger brother of Trịnh Tạc who, because of his popularity among the soldiers, was imprisoned in 1657 upon the death of their father. His end came in 1674 as Baron narrates. His name was Trịnh Toàn; his title was Duke of Ning; *Tiết chế*, "to be in control of," was an expression often used to designate official assignments or those who received such assignments. Here Baron seems to combine this expression with the title of this prince.

[9] Vietnamese annals date these events in 1674. Baron's knowledge of these events, if not from firsthand, apparently came from William Gyfford or others who accompanied Gyfford to Tonkin in 1672 and resided there with him during the next four years. Baron's mention of 1672 probably comes from that being the year when Gyfford arrived in Tonkin to establish a presence there for the English East India Company. For more on this, see the Introduction.

the city of *Chacho*, a great number, no less than forty thousand meeting all at once, and filling every corner thereof with fear and tumultuous noises, and driving out thereby its vulgar to their several aldea's, came with sad exclamations to the palace gate, yet had so much reverence as not to enter; they brought no arms but their hands and tongues, rudely bawling forth their random thoughts against the general in opprobrious language, reproaching his ungratefulness towards them, and prodigality to his women, whom he permitted to squander and waste the treasure of the land, while they were ready to perish in want and misery, as if he purposely design'd their destruction and confusion by the most uneasy and insupportable methods of famine and nakedness; magnifying their own deserts in his service, threatning to take some severe course, if he did not enlarge their pay, and distribute some money among them, committing the mean while a thousand insolent enormities, hovering round the palace, and encamping at the several avenues thereof, as if they intended to besiege the general therein; and in effect, none could go out or in without their commission.[10]

In this extremity and streight, the general consulted with the *Quan fo Lew*, and other privy-counsellors, what to do. One of them, a great literado, was of the opinion, 'twas best to grant the soldiers their desires; which being moderate, they might easily be appeased, alledging, that to quell the country people, when rebellious, 'twas customary to use the soldiers, but to quiet the mutinous soldiers, money was the only expedient; but another literado, by name *Ong Trangdame*,[11] of great fame for his wisdom, and in high respect for his dignity, of a violent resolute nature, opposed the first opinion, saying, it was imprudent, and of pernicious consequence to indulge a company of mutinous fellows too far; adding, that it was much the better remedy to seize some of the ring-leaders, and put them to death, which would amaze and astonish the rest so, as to make them shift for their safety and security. The general, inclin'd most to this last advice, for love of his money, yet was doubtful in his resolution. The soldiers having their spies in the palace (as he had among them) had presently notice of what passed, which so incensed them against *Trangdame*, that watching the time of his coming forth the palace to go home, they immediately seized him, and treated him in the most cruel and barbarous manner an enraged multitude could invent; for having inhumanely bruised and beaten him with their fists, knees, elbows, knobs of their fans, *&c.* they trampled the breath out of his body with their feet, and then, dead as he was, they drew him ignominiously thro' the street to the sandy island near the arsenal, where they tore and cut his body into small pieces. This audacious cruelty, together with other notorious affronts put on several *Mandareens* at the same time, plunged the general and his courtiers in divers deep perplexities, and filled them with mortal fears, insomuch, that most began to creep in holes and corners to avoid the rage of this terrible tempest, leaving their master in a manner desolate.

The discreetest among the soldiers finding that they had passed the *Rubicon*, thought there was no retiring, and therefore advised their companions to provide themselves with a head who might guide and order their irregular and tumultuous

---

[10] For the context of these events see K. W. Taylor, "Literati Revival in Seventeenth-Century Vietnam," *Journal of Southeast Asian Studies* 18,1 (March 1987): 18-21.

[11] Nguyễn Quốc Trinh (1625-1674). *Ong Trang* of *Ong Trangdame* is Vietnamese Ông Trạng, "Mister Great Man"; *dame* is uncertain, but is apparently a transcription of the name by which he was popularly known, as many prominent literati were known popularly by the expression *Trạng* (Great Man), followed by a personalized sobriquet.

proceedings, proposing prince *Chechening* as fit for the purpose; to which they unanimously consented, and would have fetch'd him out of prison that instant, and proclaimed him general, but that the night, which was already come on, hinder'd the enterprize, and caus'd them to defer it to next morning; but the general having item of their intentions, prepared with his own hands a dose for prince *Chechening*, and sent it him in the dead of the night, by a trusty eunuch, with order that he should drink all the potion. The capon, as soon as he came to the prince, after he had made four sombeys, deliver'd his errand, and the general's present, which the prince presently guess'd to be what it was; but what he said is not well known, only, that he made four sombeys toward the general's palace, and then took off the draught, and in few hours after dy'd. This was the end of prince *Chechening*, whose vertue was his greatest crime, the soldiers unseasonable love causing his untimely death. The next morning he[12] ordered a great quantity of silver and copper cash to be given to the mutineers, quenching thereby in an instant the fire of this popular insurrection; but several of them perish'd afterwards, few knew how.

It is time now to return from our digression, to take a view of the lords of the blood, *Mandareens, &c.* either civil magistrates or military officers, who at the time of their abode in the city, go every morning early to court to wait on the *Choua* and prince. The *Boua* is complimented on the first and fifteenth of every moon, by them, in their violet or blue garb, with caps of their own callicoe manufactures, in which they are obliged to cloath their retinue. The *Choua* receives them in great state, sitting at a great distance uncovered, for the more pomp (unless on some solemnity) his numerous life-guard in arms in the palace-yard, surrounded by many capon servants, who carry his order and commissions to the *Mandareens*, and bring their answers, or, according to their method of speaking, supplications, which they deliver to him on their knees. In fine, at this time, most state-matters are here handled and dispatch'd; the acts and resolutions of the *Quan-fo-liew*,[13] or supream court (whose Sessions is in this palace) is presented to him, to have his approbation thereon. The prince likewise has his solicitors near the general (for he himself comes hardly once in a moon to court) who gives him notice of all that passes, that he may regulate his proceedings accordingly. No business of requests or petitions slide in this court, except it be greased with presents and gifts answerable to the import of affairs.

It is a goodly sight to see such a crowd of lords, and how every thing is carry'd here with that decency and decorum, that strikes an awe in every beholder, and would have really much majesty in it, if they would dispense with, or abrogate that slavish custom of going barefoot. The general indulges his *Mandareens* much, treating them with respect and tenderness as to their lives, which are seldom in danger, but for treason; for other offences they are fined or disgraced, by being turned out of employ, or banish'd the court.

When any *Mandareen* interceeds for their friends or kindred that have offended, they come covered before the general, then putting off their caps, they sombey four times, a way of reverence, or rather adoration, which consists in falling first on their knees, then touching the ground with their bodies, after the *Chinese* mode, they request his highness to pardon the crime, and impute the fault to the intercessor, who is ready by the sign of standing bare, which on such-like occasions, intimates

[12] Trịnh Tạc.

[13] Previously spelled *Quan-fo-lew*.

the condition of a criminal, to undergo such punishment as the prince shall please to inflict on him.

About eight o'clock the general withdraws from the audience place, and the lords, *&c.* retire from court, all but the captain of the guard, with some that have offices at court who are capons, of which a great number begin young, are menial servants, who, with the domestick maids, are only permitted to enter his privy apartments and seraglio of women and concubines.

Of these capons, a pest of mankind, the parasites, sycophants, and perverters of these princes, there are no less than four or five hundred belonging to the court, who are usually so proud, imperious and unreasonable, as makes them not less hateful and abhorred, than feared by the whole nation; however, the prince confides most in them, both for domestick and state matters; for, after they have served seven or eight years in the inner court, they are raised gradually to publick administrations and dignities, so as to be graced with the most honourable titles of provincial governors, and military prefects, while several of the more deserving, both of the military officers, and the classes of the literadoes are neglected, and suffer for want: But it is certain, the general respects his own present profit (whatsoever the consequence may be) in the advancing them; for when they die, the riches they have accumulated by foul practices, rapine and extortion, fall, in a manner, all to the general, as next heir; and tho' their parents are living, yet in regard they contributed nothing to their well-being in the world but to geld them, to which they were prompted by great indigence, and hopes of court preferment, therefore they can pretend to no more than a few houses and small spots of ground; which also they cannot enjoy but with the good-liking and pleasure of the general.

However, not to detract from truth, some of these capons have been of extraordinary merit, and among them more especially these three by name, *Ong-Ja-Tu-Lea, Ong-Ja-Ta-Foe-Bay,* and *Ong-Ja-How-Foe-Tack;*[14] these were indeed the delight of *Tonqueen;* but they were such as lost their genitals by chance, having them bit off either by a hog or dog. These sort of capons are, by the superstitious *Tonqueenese,* believed to be destined to great preferments and eminence.

The last of these is yet living, and at present governour of *Hein,*[15] and the largest province in the country, admiral of all the sea forces, and principal minister for the affairs of strangers; a prudent captain, a wise governour, and an uncorrupted judge, which renders him admirable to these heathens, and a shame to many christians, who, tho' they are blest with the light of the gospel, rarely arrive at that heighth of excellence, as to know how to be great, good and poor at once.

Remarkable is what they relate of *Ong-Ja-Tu-Lea,* famous for his sharp brain, and prodigious parts, and no less for his sudden rise, as strange and tragical fall; whose history take as follows.

In the minority of the house of *Tring* (that is to say, before it was firmly establish'd in the government) the then reigning general having great necessity for some able statesman (on whom he might disburden some part of his weighty affairs) and being afflicted with continual perplexities on this head, he chanced to dream that he should meet a man the next morning, whom he could trust and employ; and,

---

[14] *Ong-ja* is almost certainly *ông già,* "mister old" or "venerable sir," a respectful form of address. The other syllables are apparently transcriptions of personal names.

[15] Apparently refers to Phố Hiến, the trading center located on the Red River between Hanoi and the sea where foreign merchants were allowed to reside.

as it happened, the first man that came to the court in the morning, was this *Tu-Lea*, who agreeing exactly with the imaginary picture of his dream, both in proportion, stature and physiognomy, the general conferred with him; and, after some discourse, found him of great ability, and exactly acquainted with their *arcana imperii*; whereupon he raised him immediately, and, in a little while, augmented his authority so greatly, that there was hardly any difference between the master and the servant, but, if any, *Tu-Lea* was more respected, courted and feared than the general himself. Whether this was the cause of his displeasure against him, or that this mushroom (raised in a night) forgetting his obligation, prompted by his overmuch prosperity, did conspire really to destroy his master, and to assume the place himself (as the common bruit was) or that this was merely a pretence to colour the general's jealousy of his over-grown greatness, I will not determine; but, to be brief, he was, by the general's order, torn in pieces by four horses, his body and dismembred limbs cut in pieces, and then burnt, and the ashes thrown into the river.

Every year about the latter end of our *January*, which falls out about their last moon, all the mandareens, officers and military men are sworn to be faithful to the king and general, and that they shall not conceal treasonable machinations against their persons, on forfeiture of their lives. The mandareens take the like oath of their wives, servants and domesticks. He that reveals high treason, has at most but thirty dollars, and a small employ for a reward, which is far short of our author's multiplication.[16]

They have annual musters for the levy of soldiers through the whole kingdom; in which choice they greatly respect the tallness of persons: Those of extraordinary heighth are allotted to be the general's life-guard, the others are disposed of according to occasions. All those that have any degree in learning and handicrafts men are exempt from this muster. How they proceed with deserters I cannot affirm; but am certain, the *Tonqueense* know not what hanging means: their way is to behead them; only those of the royal blood are strangled. I must need say, they are neither cruel nor exquisite in these inventions.

As for strangers, they employ none; thinking none so wise as themselves: however, when I came from *Siam*, I was examined about the affairs of that kingdom and *Cochin-china*, and concerning my voyage in the *Tonqueen* Sing Ja,[17] and whether those boats might be able to transport soldiers through the high seas; to which I answered as I thought fit. Then I was questioned how, if the general should give me the command of two or three hundred soldiers to be employed against *Cochin-china?* to which I replied, I was, by profession, a merchant, consequently ignorant of martial affairs, and therefore incapable of serving his highness in that respect. Which excuse and refusal, tho it served for that time, yet it operated against me when I was accused by the *Chinese*.[18]

[16] Tavernier, "A New and Singular Relation of the Kingdom of Tunquin," p. 39: "They that discover any Treason never fail of any reward; only with this distinction, in reference to the quality of the Persons that reveal it. For as for the Mandarins and Gentlemen, the King rewards them according to his own pleasure: But as for the meaner sort, whether Men or Women, they are ennobl'd, and gratified with a reward of 50 Pains of Gold, and 500 Bars of Silver, which in all amounts to 53000 Livres."

[17] Apparently another rendering of the earlier transcription *Twinjae, thuyền chài*, "fishing boat," in which, according to Chapter V, he traveled to Siam.

[18] What is being alluded to here is unknown, but it may have been related to Baron's "troubles" obscurely referred to in Chapter 6.

With the nobility of this country, as I have hinted elsewhere, and acquainted you, that nobility only descends to the posterity of the king and general, and that only to the third degree; but the rest, as they obtained it by arms, learning, or money, so it is but *durante vita*. By the first means few are raised, by the second some, but the third is the true loadstone which attracts most favour.

The general's court stands in *Ca-cho*, almost in the midst of the city; it is very spacious, and walled about; within and without built full of low small houses for the conveniency of the soldiers: Within they are two stories high, most open for air. The gates are large and stately, all of iron-wood, as indeed the greatest part of the palace is. His own and womens apartments are stately and costly edifices, set forth with carved, gilded, and lacquer work. In the first plain of the court are the stables for his biggest elephants and best horses; on the hinder part are many parks, groves, walks, arbours, fish-ponds, and whatsoever else the country can afford for his pleasure or recreation, since he seldom stirs out.

CHAPTER XIII.

THAT THERE IS NO SUCH MANNER OF CORONATION AND INTHRONIZATION OF THEIR KINGS, AS IS RELATED BY M. TAVERNIERE.[1]

As our author is most erroneous throughout his book, so this his thirteenth chapter is, in a manner, one intire error; for, how diligent soever I was to enquire of their learned men, and other persons of quality, I could not find, that they used the solemnity of inthroning or coronation of their kings with such pomp and magnificence, or any thing like it, as he relates; nay, scarce that they observe any ceremony at all.

They told me, that such external gallantries, and all ostentations were contrary to their customs and practice; for when their king or general dies, all publick shews whatsoever that express mirth, or demonstrate any magnificence, or have any sign of glory, so much as the wearing gold, silver, or gaudy cloaths, are not only forbidden throughout the whole kingdom, but reckoned very scandalous to be used. Neither must a courtier, during the time of his mourning for his prince, appear in rich furniture himself, or in his horse, elephants, palankeens, hammocks, &c. but the worst, coarsest, and meanest habiliments they can invent, are accounted the properest, especially for the highest dignified, and nearest of blood, with many other nice observations, whereof more amply in due place.

All the ceremony they use on these occasions, consists only to sombey, and present the prince so succeeding, who entertains the complimenters of note with meat, yet not with the usual court-splendor or merriment, by reason of his mourning for his predecessor. But was it usual with them to advance their king (who at present has no interest in the state) with so much grandeur and state to the throne, questionless they would have some degrees of honour likewise for the general when he assumes his dignity, since his power and authority, tho' intruded, controls all, and that on all occasions he is most respected and observed.

In 1682, when I arrived here from *Siam*, the old general was newly deceased: his heir made no noise at all when he succeeded; nay, he carried himself so private therein, that none abroad heard of court matters, or perceived the least alteration of government whatsoever; neither would he receive the usual honours from his own *Mandareens*, or admit strangers to audience, either to condole his sorrow, or to congratulate his advancement; only their presents were received. Thus, without any

---

[1] Jean-Baptiste Tavernier, "A New and Singular Relation of the Kingdom of Tunquin," Chapter XIII: "Of the ceremonies observed when the Kings of Tunquin are advanced to the Throne."

other formality, the general took possession of his office; and undoubtedly he would never condescend the king should exceed him in that kind, not only because he is to bear all such charges and expences, but also for fear the other should increase too much in reputation thereby.

Our author then is to be admired for relating things both unknown, and contrary to the customs of this people; confidently affirming, his brother was an eye-witness of that ingenious invented romance, on this occasion: For what are they else than fables, to say, that, in this solemnity, all the artillery of the court walls were fired? when there is not so much as a great gun upon the walls, nor ever was, by relation; that all the soldiers were drawn thither from the frontiers; which is to open the gates of the kingdom to the *Cochin-chinese*, who are always upon the watch for such an opportunity, to incorporate with their dominion, the two adjoyning provinces, which were once ruled by the predecessors of their *Choua*: That they swear fidelity to the king, and that they will defend him and the country against the *Chinese* their inveterate enemies; when, as we have recounted, they are tributary to the *China* empire, now in possession of the *Tartars*, whom they endeavour by all means imaginable not to offend, for fear of losing their country and freedom: That the king's liberality extends that day to one million of *Panes* of gold; which, in silver, amounts at least to one hundred and fifty millions of crowns; a sum, I am sure, the whole kingdom can hardly muster up both in gold and silver, tho' he aims to perswade the world, that the king of *Tonqueen* possesses the riches of *Croesus*: That the king makes presents of money to officers of unknown names, and offices never heard of in the country: That he bestows so many *Panes* of gold and silver on the constable, meaning thereby the general, from whom he receives all he has: That the sacrifices should be so large, as to contain that prodigious number of beasts, whereby necessarily the plow must stand still, and the people be content to fast the whole year, as to flesh.

After this *Epicurean* banquet, together with what he mentions of the bonzes, fire-works, birds nests, colts flesh &c. impertinent contradictions and absurdities, not worthy [of] regard; I must confess he notes some things and passages here proper to *Siam*, and agreeable to the manners and constitutions of that people, so that he is only mistaken in the application. What is to be said of the king's going out, I will note in the next chapter.

The ladies of quality, when they go abroad, are carried according to their several degrees, either in close sedans, or hammocks upon the shoulders of men. Neither doth this nation keep their women so strict from the sight of others, as the *Moors* and *Chinese* do.

The celebration of their nativity they observe very punctually, from the prince to the meanest, each to his ability and power, with feasting, musick, and other pastimes, fire-works excepted; in which they are very deficient, as I hinted before. They are also presented, on the said occasions, by their kindred, friends and dependents, who attend them to honour the solemnity.

As to the king's liberality, who sent his son and successor a donative of a thousand *Panes* of gold, intrinsick value, an hundred and fifty thousand dollars, and five hundred bars of silver, above seven thousand dollars, at once, it is altogether impossible; because the yearly revenue allowed him, comes to no more than eight thousand dollars. He errs likewise in his multiplication, making those *Panes* of gold and bars of silver to be only an hundred and twenty thousand livres.

As to the king's successor, he himself is often ignorant which of his sons is to succeed him, if he has more than one; and, if but one, it is not certain that he shall be king after him, since it lies in the general's breast, to name such an one as he likes best, provided he be of the royal stock; tho' he seldom puts by the next heir, unless it be for great reasons, and urgent political motives, *&c.*

CHAPTER XIV.

OF THE CEREMONY OF THE KING'S BLESSING THE COUNTRY,[1] VULGARLY AMONGST THEM, CALLED BOUA-DEE-YAW,[2] OR, ACCORDING TO THEIR CHARACTERS, CAN-JA[3]

The king seldom or never goes out to take his pleasure, but once a year he shews himself in publick (not reckoning when he is carried by the general on particular occasions) on the solemnization of their grand ceremony, at the beginning of their new year, on a particular chosen day; for they believe some to be good, others better, some indifferent, others bad; whereof they are so superstitiously observant, as to undertake nothing of importance, without consulting first most seriously, both their *China* almanacks, and blind country diviners.

The king, general and prince, with most of the *Mandareens* of the court, on this solemn occasion, go, before break of day, severally to a place at the south end of the city, purposely built for this occasion, with three gates different from their other pagodas; neither are there any images in the house. Here they stay without in sundry apartments till day-light; the king, in the mean time, is to wash his body, and put on new cloaths, never worn before.

About eight of the clock a piece of ordnance is fired; on which signal the general, prince and *Mandareens* repair to the king to do homage, tho' it extends, as to the general and prince, no further than a bare point of formality. This compliment passes in silence, yet with much state and gravity on both sides: Then immediately the second signal of a gun is heard; whereupon the king is accompanied to the gates of the said house, which are all shut, whereat he knocks, and is, by the door-keepers, asked who he is. He answers, The king, and they let him in; but none may enter with him, that being contrary to their superstition. Thus he does three several times, till he comes into the house, where he falls to his devotion with prayers and supplications, having kept a strict fast to the gods, after their mode; which done he seats himself in a gilt chair placed in the yard of the said house; and, having paused a little, a plow, with a buffalo tied to it in the same manner as they use them for tilling the ground, is presented him, who holding it by the place usually taken hold of when they work it,

---

[1] In this and the next chapter, Baron diverges from Tavernier's chapter scheme to discuss two ceremonies that interest him. He returns to Tavernier's plan in his last three chapters, although spending two chapters on the topic of funerals rather than only one, as Tavernier does.

[2] *Vua đi Giao*, "The king goes to make sacrifice to heaven and earth" (a vernacular expression).

[3] *Càn gìa*, "Heaven's family" (a classical expression).

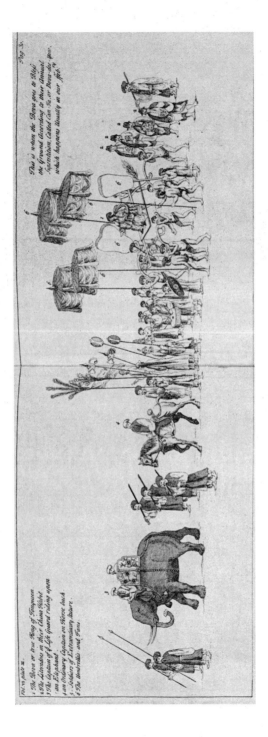

Plate 11. "This is When the Boua Goes to Bless the Ground according to their Annual
Superstition called Can-Ja or Boua-dee-yaw, which Happens usually in our February.
1. The Boua or True King of Tonqueen. 2. The Literadoes in their China Habit. 3. The Captain
of the Life-guard Riding upon an Elephant. 4. An Ordinary Captain on Horse back.
5. Soldiers of Extraordinary Stature. 6. The Umbrellas and Fans.

he blesses the country, and teaches the people by this emblem, that none should be ashamed to be a husbandman, and that the diligent, industrious and provident, especially in the culture of the ground, may certainly expect the enjoyment of their labour and pains.

I am informed by some, that, at the same time, the ceremony of the cups is used; others again contradict that, and affirm it to be on the day of installing the new king.

Be it when it will, the manner is thus: on a *bandesia*,[4] or lacquer'd table, stand several cups with prepared victuals in them; and among the rest there is one with boiled white rice, another with yellow rice, one with water, and one with herbs or greens: All these cups are neatly covered with fine paper, and with starch fasten'd thereon, so that one cannot be known from another. One of these the king takes at adventure, which is immediately opened; and if he lights on the yellow rice, there is great rejoycing, because it portends (as they believe) plenty in the land; if on the white rice, a good harvest; if water, an indifferent year; but the herbs or greens is extreme bad, denoting great mortality, famine and desolation; and so the rest of the cups, every one hath its particular signification and augury, according to what their idolatry and superstition dictates.

With this ends this grand cermony; and the third gun being fired, the king mounts his open chair, covered with many umbrelloes, and is carried on the shoulders of eight soldiers, as it were in procession, thro' several streets, to his palace, accompanied by many literadoes in their *China* vests, all on foot. He is likewise attended by a handsome guard of the general's soldiers, some elephants and horses under the noise of drums, timbrels, scalmay,[5] copper basons [cymbals] and hautboys, &c. standards and colours flying.

As he passes along he demonstrates his liberality to the poor spectators and aldea people, by throwing cash or copper coin amongst them. A while after the king, the general follows, riding on a stately elephant, waited on by many princes of his own and royal family, with most of the military officers and civil magistrates of the kingdom, richly attired, and guarded by a detachment of three or four thousand horse, and about an hundred, or an hundred and fifty elephants with sumptuous furniture, and an infantry of no less than ten thousand men, all fine and gallantly cloathed, with coats and caps made of *European* manufactures, so that he far exceeds the king in pomp and magnificence. He comes a great part of the same way the king did, till he arrives at the street that leads directly to his palace, where turning, he leaves the other on his march. The prince brings up the rear of this cavalcade; he has half the train of his father, comes the same way, but takes the nearest cut to his own palace.

---

[4] Mentioned in Chapter 8 as *bandeses* in the plural.

[5] A straight-bodied woodwind musical instrument; *scalmay* is from Middle English *schalme*, variously spelled *schalmei* or *schalmey*, which in modern English is rendered as *shawm* or *shalm*.

CHAPTER XV.

OF THE THECKYDAW,[1] OR PURGING THE COUNTRY FROM ALL MALEVOLENT SPIRITS.

The *Theckydaw* is observed commonly once every year, especially if there be a great mortality amongst the men, elephants, or horses of the general's stables, or the cattle of the country. The cause of which they attribute to the malicious spirits of such men as have been put to death for treason, rebellion, and conspiring the death of the king, general or princes, and that in revenge of the punishment they have suffer'd, they are bent to destroy every thing, and commit horrible violence. To prevent which, their superstition has suggested to them the institution of this *Theckydaw*, as a proper mean to drive the devil away, and purge the country of evil spirits. For the performance of which the general consults and elects a fit day, which commonly happens about the twenty-fifth of our *February*. Just on the *Chaop*'s re-assuming new life and vigour. When the needful orders are given for preparation, and that every thing is got in readiness, then the general, with most of the princes and other qualified persons of the land, repairs to the arsenal about eight o'clock in the morning of the day appointed; he either rides on an elephant or horse, or else in a palankeen upon wheels, which is push'd forward by lusty fellows kept for that purpose, and shadowed by many umbrelloes. The guard that follows him is very numerous, not less than sixteen or eighteen thousand men, besides elephants and horses, all set forth to the best advantage. The streets thro' which he passes, are adorn'd with standards, pendants, and armed soldiers, to hinder the people from opening either doors or windows, for fear of sinister designs and machinations, tho' strangers are sometimes permitted to see this stately procession, if they will request it.

Being arrived at the arsenal, the *Mandareens* go to their several posts (which have been kept for them by their soldiers) on the sandy island near the said arsenal, which is heaped up and increased yearly by the descending waters from *China*, whose rapid and violent courses do not only eat away much of the land in some places, and cast it up again in others, but spoil the river too: Here, I say, they build many slight houses with bamboos, and raise infinite tents to shelter them from the injuries of rain and

---

[1] *Tế kỳ đạo*; see Adriano di St. Thecla, *Opusculum de Sectis apud Sinenses et Tunkinenses: A Small Treatise on the Sects among the Chinese and Tonkinese: A Study of Religion in China and North Vietnam in the Eighteenth Century*, ed. and trans. Olga Dror (Ithaca, NY: Cornell Southeast Asia Program, 2002), pp. 129-131. H. Deseille, Baron's French translator, relying on a comment by Father Cadière about popular religious practices in the twentieth century, surmises that the term here is *tế khí đau*, "sacrifice to bad air." See S. Baron, "Description du royaume de Tonquin," trans. H. Deseille, *Revue Indochinoise* XXIII, No. 3-4 (March-April 1915): 296. However, Adriano di St. Thecla (page 32 of the Latin manuscript) clearly writes it as *tế kỳ đạo* (sacrifice of the leader's banner).

sun, and place their soldiers, foot, horse, and elephants, as it were in battle array, with flying colours, standards and pendants, their ordnance placed on advantage, the boats of war along the bank, in good postures, and every thing else in the method of an exact formidable army, noble and glorious to behold; and is indeed a shew that would, above all others, sufficiently express the power of the kingdom, were but their courage proportionable to their conveniences, and their leaders, men instead of capons; for the number of infantry present on that occasion, cannot be less than eighty thousand soldiers well disciplined, expert either for sword, pike, musket, aigenats,[2] &c. and the cavalry about five thousand, with rich furniture, armed with bows, arrows, swords and guns; then there are about two hundred and fifty elephants trained up for war, many of them fearless of fire and the noise of guns, having on their backs a box or chair richly gilded and lacquer'd, and two men in them, with a kind of carabines and lances; and there are no less than three hundred pieces of artillery ranged in proper order: nor do the lords, *Mandareens*, commanders, &c. in their best garb of fine scarlet, with gold buckles on the breast, in manner as we wear our loops, and a cap of the said cloth on their heads, make the least part of this glorious shew. The soldiers of the general's life-guard are stout lusty fellows, some of prodigious heighth, with caps and coats of the same fashion and fabrick as those of the *Mandareens*, the gold loops excepted, and the cloth not altogether so fine. The general's ten horses and six elephants of state far outshine the rest in splendor, their furniture being massy gold and scarlet, with an infinite number of standards, flags, pendants, hautboys, drums, copper basons, and all other sorts of warlike musick and gallantry ranged promiscuously; and the whole being attended with a vast concourse of people, makes the island very glorious and pleasant for that time.

Every thing being thus ready, three blows on a large drum are heard, keeping good time between every stroak, which sounds almost like the discharge of a small piece of ordnance: on this signal the general comes from the arsenal to the place (where the soldiers stand in order) and enters the house prepared for him. In a while after, three other stroaks are given on a great copper bason or gong, in the same manner as on the drum for distance of time; the general beginneth then to offer meat-offerings to the criminal devils and malevolent spirits (for it is usual and customary likewise amongst them, to feast the condemned before their execution) inviting them to eat and drink, when presently he accuses them in a strange language, by characters and figures, &c. of many offences and crimes committed by them, as to their having disquieted the land, killed his elephants and horses, &c. for all which they justly deserve to be chastised, and banished the country. Whereupon three great guns are fired, as the last signal; upon which all the artillery and muskets are discharg'd, that by their most terrible noise, the devils may be driven away; and they are so blind, as to believe for certain, that they really and effectually put them to flight.

At noon every one may feast himself at his own cost; but the soldiers are fed with the offered meat.

In the evening the general retires to his palace in the same state with which he went forth, much glorying that he has vanquished his enemies on so easy terms.

---

[2] Unidentified; Baron's French translator, H. Deseille, conveniently ignores this word. See S. Baron, "Description du royaume de Tonquin," trans. H. Deseille, *Revue Indochinoise* XXIII, No. 3-4 (March-April 1915): 297.

The *Boua* or king never appeareth in this solemnity; perhaps the general suspects that the soldiers, if they should be dissatisfy'd with him, might take the opportunity to revolt, and confer on the king the real and essential power which at present resides in him, and therefore finds it unsafe that the king should be then present: but on journeys in the country be they but for two or three days (if he makes any), and when he goes to war, he never omits to carry the king along with him, not only to cloke all his designs with the royal name, but also to prevent any plots which in his absence the king might give into to his utter ruin, or by condescension, permit others to seize his royal person, whereby they would authorize their pretentions, and gain so much reputation as might subvert and confound both the general's greatness and government.

They imagine our way of firing great guns to compliment friends, or the saluting therewith each other's health, very strange and barbarous, because contrary to their customs, since they entertain only their enemies, and the malicious devils with such a noise, as is related.

CHAPTER XVI.

OF THE FUNERALS IN GENERAL. [1]

The *Tonqueenese*, as they have a great horror at death, so the conceit they have thereof, is not less superstitious; for they believe that only the spirits of young children are transmigrated into the bodies of other infants who are yet in the mother's womb; but all others come to be devils, or at least spirits that can do either good or harm; and that they would wander up and down as poor vagabonds ready to perish for want and indigence, if they were not assisted by their living kindred, or if they did not steal and commit violence to subsist; so that death, in their estimation, is the ultimate and greatest misery that can befall human nature. They note, with incredible care and exactness, the time, hour, and day, (all which are distinguish'd by several particular names, as apes, dogs, cats, mice, &c.) wherein a party dies; which if it happen at the like time in which his father, mother, or near relations were born, it is reckon'd very ominous, and bad for his heirs and successors, who therefore permit not the corpse to be interr'd till their conjurers and diviners advise them of a good and auspicious time, for which they wait sometimes two or three years, sometimes less, as their critical rites and blind doctors shall direct them. The body is coffin'd the mean while, and kept in a particular place, and must stand no other ways than on four stakes erected for that purpose.

This nicety is only observed among the rich, but others who do not die in this scruple, are bury'd within ten or fifteen days; but the longer the corpse is kept, the more expensive it is, not only to the wife and children (who present him daily three times with victuals, and keep always lamps and candles burning in the room, besides the offering of incense, perfumes, and a quantity of gold and silver paper, some made in the shape of gold and silver bars, others in the likeness of horses, elephants, tygers, &c.) but the rest of the kindred and relations are also obliged to contribute their several shares to the funeral feast, but most liberally at this time; besides, it is very toilsome and a great deal of trouble both to the children and all that are of kin, to resort so often to the corpse to salute and adore it, by prostrating themselves four times on the ground, and lamenting him three times a day, at the hours of repast, with endless other ceremonies, too tedious here to relate.

All that have means are very careful to provide their own coffin, when they are well advanced in years, in which they are extraordinary choice, both as to the thickness and goodness of the wood, as well as the workmanship, and regard no expences to have it to their fancies.

They observe this distinction in the sexes. If a male die, he is cloathed with seven of his best coats; if a female, with nine. In the mouth of those of quality are put small

---

[1] Jean-Baptiste Tavernier, "A New and Singular Relation of the Kingdom of Tunquin," Chapter XIV: "Of the Funeral Pomp of the Kings of Tunquin, and of the manner of burying their dead." Baron spends two chapters, this one and the next, on the topic of funerals.

pieces of gold and silver, with some seed pearl. This they fancy will not only render him honourable in the other world, but prevent also want and indigence; yet the poorer sort use the scrapings of their fingers and toes, believing that the mouth of the deceased being filled with this filth, he cannot plague and torment his living relations. Likewise some will place on the coffin a cup of rice, which is shifted every meal, and at last bury'd with the corpse.

They use no nails to fasten the lid to its coffin, but cement it with lacker [lacquer], so tight, as is really admirable, esteeming it a great injury to nail up the body of the deceased.

When the sons accompany the corpse, they are clad, for that day, in very coarse robes, made of the refuse of silk, and caps of the same stuff, which are ty'd with cords on their heads; they have staves in their hands to lean on, for fear grief should cause them to faint.

The wives and daughters of fashion have a curtain, very large, held over their heads, that they may not be seen; yet they are easily heard by their moans and lamentations, which are made *viva voce,* and very loud. As the corpse is carry'd through the streets, the eldest son will lie down now and then on the ground, for the corpse to pass over him (which, in their opinion, is the greatest mark of filial duty); then rising again, he pushes the coffin back with both his hands, as 'twere to stop it from going further on, which is continued till they come to the grave.

Painted and gilded images, in the shapes of men and beasts, all of paper-work, follow the hearse in great numbers, with some fryers,[2] with the noise of drums, timbrels, hautboys, copper basons, &c. much in the nature of a popish procession; which paper finery is to be burnt immediately after the Interrment.

More or less sumptuous is the funeral, according to the condition or quality of the person; for those of account are not only carried by many men, but have also double coffins, one in another, and over it a canopy of state, richly set forth, attended by soldiers, and honoured with the presence of great *Mandareens.*

Their manner is to cut their hair to the shoulders, and to wear ash-coloured cloaths, and a particular sort of straw hats, for the space of three years, for either father or mother, yet the eldest son must add thereunto three months more; for other relations less.

Their way of reckoning is very strange, for if one should die, or a child be born, in *January,* be it the last day of the moon, *February* following being the first moon of their new year, they count him to have been dead two years, or the child to be two years old, when, in effect, it is no more than one day.

During the time of their mourning, they seldom use their wonted lodgings; they lie on straw mats on the bare ground; their diet is not only mean and sparing, but the very bandesia[3] and cups the victuals are served in, are coarse, and of the worst sort. They forbear wine, and go to no feasts or banquets; they must lend no ear to musick, nor eye to dancing, nor contract matrimony; for on the complaint of their kindred on this head, the law will disinherit them. They have a great care not to appear in publick anywise fine, but rather austerely abstain from all merriment and finery whatsoever: but as the three years grow near an end, they gradually decline too in the severity of this discipline.

---

[2] That is, "friars," i.e., Buddhist monks.

[3] "Table"; see above chapters 8 and 14.

Their sepulchres are in the several *Aldeas* of their parents nativity, and unhappy is he deem'd whose body or bones are not brought home, as they term it; but how to chuse the best place to inter the dead, is the grand mystery, and held to be of that consequence that they verily believe, that infallibly thereon depends the happiness or misery of their successors; wherefore they usually consult many years with *Tay-de-lee*,[4] before they come to a conclusion in that affair.

During these times of mourning, they feast the dead four times a year, in the months of *May, June, July,* and *September,* spending in each of them two, three, or four days; but the sacrifice which is made at the expiration of the three years is the greatest and most magnificent of all, tho' they are in the rest prodigal enough, and will spend not only their whole substance therein, but run themselves in debt too, and yet are for so doing both highly respected and commended of friends and acquaintance. After this they keep their anniversary offering on the day of the party's decease, which is punctually observed from generation to generation, to perpetuity. I have, in jesting, told some of them, I should not like to die a *Tonqueneese*, were it only because the custom of the country, whilst living, allowed me three meals a day, but when dead they would feed me but once a year; a severity more than sufficient to starve the dead, had they need of food.

It cannot fail of being entertaining to our readers, to add to our author in this place,[5] what the learned father *Calmet*[6] has collected, in relation to the practice of setting food upon the tombs of the dead; and of repasts made at their funerals: whereby it will be perceived, that this custom is not confin'd to *Tonqueen*, or even to *China*; but that it had obtained almost universally in the darker ages of the world. What he says, will be found under the head of REPAS, and is so curious, that we shall give the translation of it entire.

> REPAST, or food, *says he*, that was set upon the tombs of the dead. *Cœna mortui. Baruch* mentions it in these words. *Rugiunt autem clamantes contra deos suos, sicut in cœna mortui.* {Baruch vi. 31} The pagans howl in the presence of their gods, as in the repast which is made for the dead. He speaks of certain solemnities, wherein the idolaters us'd to make great lamentations: for example, in the feasts of *Adonis*. As to the repasts for the dead, they are distinguish'd into two kinds: One was made in the house of the defunct, at the return of the mourners from the grave. To this were invited the kindred and friends of the deceased; where they did not fail to express their grief by cries and lamentations. The other kind was made upon the tomb itself of the dead person, where they provided a repast for the wandering souls, and believed that the goddess *Trivia*, who presides over the streets and

---

[4] *Thầy địa lý*, i.e., geomancer.

[5] The rest of this chapter was added by Baron's eighteenth-century publisher, who considered the topic of particular interest to his readers.

[6] Dom Augustin Calmet (1672-1757); the excerpt that follows is from his *Dictionnaire historique, critique, chronologique, geographique et litteral de la Bible,* first published in Paris in 1720, with a new revised edition in 1730. An English translation by Samuel D'Oyley and John Colson was published in the same year as Baron's account with the title *An Historical, Critical, Geographical, Chronological, and Etymological Dictionary of the Holy Bible* (London: J. J. & P. Knapton, 1732).

highways, repair'd thither in the night-time. But in truth they were beggars and poor people, who came thither in the darkness of the night, and carry'd away what was left upon the tomb.

> *Est honor & tumulis animas placare paternas,*
> *Parvaque in extructas munera ferre pyras.* {Ovid. Fast.}

Sometimes, however, the relations made a small repast upon the tomb of the deceased. *Ad sepulchrum antiquo more silicernium confecimus, id est,* [Greek letters are printed here] *quo pransi discedentes dicimus alius alii Vale.* {Nonnius Marcell. ex Varrone.}

The custom of setting food upon the sepulchres of the dead, was common among the *Hebrews. Tobit* thus advises his son: *Pour out thy bread on the burial of the just, but give nothing to the wicked.* {Tob. iv. 17.} That is to say, not to partake in the repast with the relations, who performed the same ceremony. And *Jesus* the son of *Sirach* affirms, that *delicates poured upon a mouth shut up, are as messes of meat set upon a grave.* {Ecclus. xxx. 18.} What is thus set upon a tomb, is utterly lost as to the dead person; he can have no benefit from it. And elsewhere; *A gift hath grace in the sight of every man living, and for the dead detain it not.* {Ecclus. vii. 33.}

This custom was almost universal. We find it among the *Greeks,* the *Romans,* and almost all the people of the east. It still obtains in *Syria,* in *Babylonia,* and in *China.* St. *Austin* observes, that in his time, in *Africa,* they laid victuals upon the tombs of the martyrs, and in church-yards. {Aug. Ep. 22. 29. nov. edit.} The thing at first was done very innocently, but afterwards it degenerated into an abuse; and the greatest saints, and most zealous bishops, as St. *Austin* and St. *Ambrose,* had much difficulty to suppress it. {Aug. Confess. 1. 6. c. 2.} St. *Monica* being at *Milan,* had a mind, according to custom, to offer bread and wine to the memory of the martyrs; but the porter would not open the door to her, because St. *Ambrose* had forbid him; she therefore submitted with an humble obedience.

The repast that was made in the house of the deceased among the *Jews,* was also of two kinds. One was during the time that the mourning continu'd, and these repasts were look'd upon as unclean, because those that partook of them were unclean, as having assisted at the obsequies of the dead person. *Hosea* says: *Their sacrifices shall be unto them as the bread of mourners; all that eat thereof shall be polluted.* {Hos. ix. 4.} And in the form that the *Israelites* made use of when they offer'd their first-fruits, they address'd themselves thus to the Lord; *O Lord, I have not neglected thy ordinances; I have not used these things while I was in mourning; I have made no use of them at the funerals of the dead.* God would not permit *Ezekiel* to mourn for his wife. *Cover not thy lips, and eat not the bread of men.* {Eze. xxiv. 17.} And *Jeremiah; Neither shall men give them the cup of consolation, to drink for their father, or for their mother.* {Jer. xvi. 7.}

The other repasts made in the time of mourning, are those which were given after the funeral. *Josephus* relates, that *Archelaus* treated the whole people in a magnificent manner, after he had compleated the seven days mourning for the king his father. {Joseph. de bello, 1. 2. c. 1.} He there adds, that it was the custom of his nation to make great feasts for the relations, which could not be done without an injury to many families, which were not in a condition to support such large expences. Saint *Pauline* commends *Pammachius*, for having made a great feast for the poor, in the basilicon of St. *Peter*, on the day of the funeral of his wife *Paulina*. {Paulin. illustrat. p. 29, 30.}

CHAPTER XVII.

OF THE FUNERAL POMP OF THE CHOUA OR GENERAL OF TONQUEEN.[1]

The funeral obsequies of the choua, or general of *Tonqueen*, are performed with the same pomp and magnificence as were usually observed at the burial of their former kings, and in many respects exceed that of their present kings. As soon then as the general dies, his successors and courtiers endeavour, with all imaginable art, to conceal his death, for the space of three or four days; for should it presently be known abroad, it would unavoidably put the country, especially the chief city of *Cacho*, in great terror and consternation, because it has constantly happened at the decease of every one of them (this last excepted); that the state was disturbed with broils, contentions and civil wars, amongst the surviving sons and brethren, who strive for superiority; wherefore it is no marvel, if in this case the people are affected with their contention.

The first thing they do to their dead general is, to wash his body, and to put him on seven of his best coats, and to present him with victuals, with which he is served in the best manner possible. Then his successor, and all the princes and princesses of the blood come to lament his departure, prostrating themselves five times before him, weeping aloud, asking him Why he would leave them, and what he wanted, &c. After them the *Mandareens*, most in favour, are permitted to perform their duty, but their ceremony of condolence is to be returned them again, by the prince successor and eldest son, tho' they dare not to receive it. Except those persons, none are permitted to have a sight of the defunct; nay, those related afar off cannot have this honour. After which ceremony they put into his mouth small pieces of gold, silver, and seed pearl. The corpse is laid in a stately coffin, lacker'd over very thick, and of excellent wood; at the bottom of which they strew powder of rice and carvances [caraway], to prevent any noisome smell, over which they spread fine quilts and carpets. The corpse thus served, is placed in another room, where lamps and candles are continually kept burning; thither all his children, wives, and nearest kindred, repair three times a day, when the deceased is presented with victuals, *viz.* in the morning between five and six o'clock, twelve at noon, and five in the evening, and they pay their adoration to him. This continues all the time he is above ground.

There is no such thing as embalming the body to lie in state sixty-five days, and liberty for the people to come and see him, as our author pretends; neither do the bonzes and poor partake of the victuals set before him; nor does the provincial governor receive any order from court how long the country is to mourn, since their

---

[1] This chapter is based upon events related to the death of Trịnh Tạc in 1682-83, when, as indicated in Chapter 13, Baron was in Tonkin.

custom directs them therein sufficiently, without such particular provisions.[2] The whole country is oblig'd to mourn, as well for the general as king, the space of twenty-four days; the prince successor three years and three months, his other children and wives three years; the other near relations one year; and those further off, some five and others but three months; but all the great mandareens three years, equal with the children.

I cannot imagine in what part of the palace those towers, he speaks of, stood, or what became of those bells that never left tolling, from the general's expiring to the bringing of the corpse into the galley,[3] since they were silent at the last funeral pomp of the general in 1683.

When the needful preparations are ready, then the gallies appointed to transport and accompany the body, wait near the arsenal, which is not distant two days journey, as he says,[4] from the palace, but only something less than half an hour, whither the corpse is conducted in the following manner.

Several companies of soldiers, all in black, with their arms, being led by their respective captains, or mandareens, bring up the van of this funeral pomp, marching on gravely and silently; then follow two fellows of gigantick stature, carrying a kind of partisans,[5] with targets in their hands, and a mask or vizard [visor] on their face, to scare the devil, and open the way for the hearse to pass; next come the musicians with their drums, hautboys, copper basons, &c. playing their mournful tunes, which really are very doleful. Next is carried the funeral elogium and titles, which are more illustrious than what he had in his life time; and he is stiled, The incomparable greatness, most precious, and noble father of his country, of most splendid fame, and the like; all which is embroider'd in golden characters, on a piece of fine scarlet, or crimson damask, which is fix'd on a frame of two or three fathom high, and almost one fathom wide, and erected on a pedestal, and carried on the shoulders of twenty or thirty soldiers of the life-guard.

After this their idol, or pagoda, takes place, carried in a small gilded house, but with great reverence; then the two pennants, follow'd by the mausoleum or state cabbin, richly gilded, and curiously carved, wherein is the general's corpse. The said mausoleum doth not stand in a chariot, nor is it drawn by eight stags, trained to that

---

[2] Jean-Baptiste Tavernier, "A New and Singular Relation of the Kingdom of Tunquin," p. 46: "When the King of Tunquin dies, he is presently Embalm'd and laid in a Bed of State, where for sixty five days the People have liberty to come and see him. All that time he is serv'd as he was when he was alive; and when the Meat is taken from before the Body, one half is given to the Bonzes, and the other half to the Poor. So soon as the King has breath'd his last gasp, the Constable gives notice thereof to the Governours of Provinces, and orders them how long they should Mourn."

[3] Ibid.: "Three Bells which hang in one of the Towers of the Palace never leave tolling from the King's expiring till the Corps be put into the Galley."

[4] Ibid.: "From the Palace to the place where the Galleys wait for the body, it is about two days Journey ... "

[5] A partisan was a weapon of the sixteenth and seventeenth centuries with a long shaft and a blade resembling both a spear and a halberd.

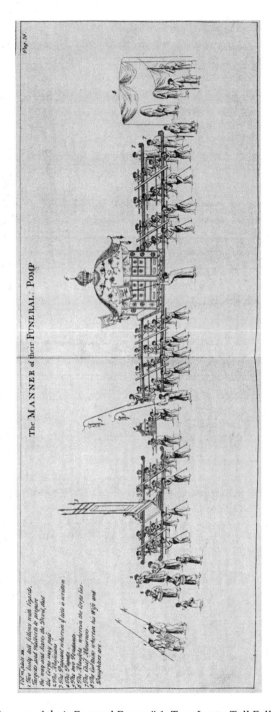

Plate 12: "The Manner of their Funeral Pomp." 1. Two Lusty Tall Fellows with Vizards, Targetts, and Halberts to Prepare the Way and Scare the Devil that the Corps May Pass. 2. The Musicians. 3. The Pageant wherein the Title is Written. 4. The Pagoda. 5. The Two Pendants. 6. The Mausola wherein the Corps Lies. 7. The Chief Mourners. 8. The Curtain wherein his Wife and Daughters Are.

service, and led by so many captains of the life-guard, as related by our author[6] (for it is a rare thing to see either deer or stag in this country); but it is carried on the shoulders of a hundred, or a hundred and fifty soldiers, in good order and great silence, with many fans and umbrelloes round about it, as well to shade it, as for state.

Just behind the hearse comes the eldest son and successor, with his brothers, all clad with coats made of refuse silk, not unlike our sackcloth, of a brown colour, tied with cords to their bodies; their caps are of the same, and fastened in like manner; they all have sticks in their hands, and only the eldest has straw shoes. These are immediately follow'd by the deceased's wives, concubines, and daughters, under a curtain, or pavillion, of white callicoe, very coarse, their garb of the same stuff, howling and lamenting. Behind these come the servants of the inner court, both damsels and young capadoes; as the front, so the rear and flanks are guarded by armed soldiers, under their several commanders, so that in this funeral pomp neither elephants, horses, nor chariots, appear, as he relates, unless those of paper and painted wood, whereof great quantities accompany the interrment, to be burnt at the grave.

Being arrived at the gallies, in one of them, which is all black, lacker'd plain, and without any ornament of carv'd and gilded work, the corpse is placed; the rest of the gallies that attend the solemnity are but ordinary, fifty or sixty in number: Thus they set forth from *Cacho* for *Tingeva* [Thanh Hóa], the aldea and birth-place of his ancestors, a journey of five or six days at least, as they make it; for the galley the corpse is in, is towed leisurely, by five or six others, and must use neither oars, nor make the least noise by drums or musick, for fear of disturbing the dead. The other gallies are also to keep as much silence as may be. By the way they stop at certain places, in each province, appropriated by the said governors to sacrifice; for which service they prepare large provisions of cows, buffaloes, hogs, &c. The new general, however, very often stays at home, and seldom permits any of his brothers to go, for fear of plots and innovation, but his sisters are commanded to attend the funeral. The ordering of the whole solemnity is intrusted to the care and conduct of some great favourite.

When they arrive at the intended aldea, there is more than a little to do with their obsequies and ceremonies, according to their rites: the particular place where he is buried few know precisely, and those are sworn to secrecy; and this not for fear of losing the treasure that is interred with him, as M. *Taverniere* fancies,[7] (for there is none but what is put into their mouths, as I mention'd before) but out of

---

[6] Ibid., item 5 of the key for the illustration entitled, "The Order observ'd in the March of the Funeral Pomp at the Interment of the Kings of Tunquin," that follows page 40: "The Chariot which bears the Mausolee, wherein is the King's Corps, is dragged by Eight Stags trained to this Service. Each of these Stags is led by a Captain of the Life Guard." The illustration indeed shows eight stags, which may have been an exuberance of the artist, for in the text (p. 47), Tavernier says: " ... eight Horses, every one of them led by a Captain of the Guard, who draw the Herse."

[7] See ibid., the explanation for the illustration entitled, "A Continuation of the Order observed at the Funeral Pomp of the King of Tunquin setting out from the City of Bodlego," preceding page 41: " ... for six onely of the chief Eunuchs of the Court are to know where the King hath been buried. An Oath is tendered to them never to reveal the place. And this is done perhaps on some Religious Motive, and likewise through Fear, that the Treasures which are buried by him should be digged up. These Riches are ordinarily some Massy Bars of Gold and Silver, as likewise some Pieces of Cloth of Gold and Silver, and such kinds of other rich Furnitures."

superstitious motives, as well as state-jealousy; for, as they believe, they shall be happy and great if they meet with a good favourable sepulchre for their relations; so the general is always fearful that the place where his predecessor rests being known to their enemies, it would depend on their malicious power to ruin his family, only by taking out his ancestor's bones, and interring those of their own family in their place. Indeed we have many examples in this country of such fools, as thought to make way for their exaltation, by thus transplacing the bones of the dead men; but as many as have attempted it have suffer'd for their foolish presumption.

As to those lords and ladies that, according to him, will needs be buried alive with the king or general;[8] it is a thing so contrary to their customs, as well as repugnant to their natures, that I verily believe, if they thought we had such an opinion of them, they would treat us as brutes and savages. Nor do I know of any city and its far castle, in the whole kingdom of *Tonqueene*, that is called *Bodligo*; but indeed those banks of the river, opposite to the city of *Cacho*, are call'd *Bode*;[9] but, however, there is neither king's house, palace, or castle, on or near the same.[10]

But it remains to speak something of their third annual sacrifices and feast, for the defunct general, which happens about three months before the mourning expires. The celebration whereof extends not only to his family, but all the mandareens that hold any office must appear at this grand solemnity, to pay their offering, in token of their gratitude to their deceased benefactor and common father.

The manner is thus: Just before the arsenal, on the sandy island, there are built of bamboos and slight timber, many large and spacious houses, after the manner of their palaces, with wide yards and open courts, wrought most curiously with basket work, &c. The apartments thereof, especially that where the altar stands, are richly hanged with gold and silver cloth; the posts and stands are either covered with the same, or with fine scarlet or other European manufactures; the roof is canopy'd with silk damask, and the floor is covered with mats and carpets. The altar itself is most curiously carved, lacker'd, and splendidly daub'd with gold, to profusion of cost, labour, and diligence. And as this is the general and his families share, so the mandareens of quality, according to their abilities, strive to out-do each other in their funeral piles, as I may call them, which are placed round about the former work, in good order, and at an equal distance and height, and of a like fashion, either four, six, or eight feet square, about fifteen or twenty feet diameter, resembling much our large lanterns, open on all sides, with shutters within the banisters and rails, very neatly set forth with rich, painted, carved, and lacker'd work; and hangings of costly silks and good pieces of broad cloth; the structure itself of slight timber and boards: The great mandareens each build two of these; the others one apiece; so that this barren place is covered in less than the space of fifteen days, with all this finery, which makes it resemble another city, or an Antiochian-like camp:[11] in which interim the whole country flocks thither to see this goodly and pompous erection; and many

---

[8] Ibid.: "Many lords and Lords and Ladies of the Court will needs be buried Alive with him, for to serve him in the places where he is to go."

[9] *Bồ Đề*, the ferry landing just across the river from Hanoi.

[10] Baron is commenting upon the illustration in Tavernier before page 41, entitled "A Continuation of the Order observed at the Funeral Pomp for the Interment of the Kings of Tunquin setting out from the City of Bodlego," which shows European-style castles and palaces.

[11] The allusion here is unclear, whether to the city of Antioch or to the Seleucid kings of Syria named Antiochus.

strange beasts, as tygers, bears, baboons, monkeys, and what other wild creatures they can get, are brought thither from far places; for which they have been sometimes diligently seeking, perhaps days and years. From all which the people (who gather together in such prodigious crowds, as give a great idea of the populousness of the country) take occasion to admire the general's grandeur and love to his deceased father. But for about three days before the time prefix'd for this sacrifice, no spectators are so much as to approach this place, because then they are busy'd in setting the image of the defunct before the altar, richly habited with many coats; and to serve it with victuals; and to present him with amber, pearl, and coral necklaces, gold and silver tankards, cups, basons, tables, and in short, with all the finery and toys that he delighted in, and made use of in his life-time; and at the same instant they erect, in a court-yard, where this altar stands, a machine; in the making whereof they had before employ'd five or six months, under the direction and oversight of three or four great mandareens, resembling somewhat the mausoleum, which M. *Taverniere* describes;[12] which they call *Anja Tangh*.[13] It is about three or four stories, or forty feet high, and about thirty feet long, and twenty broad, made of thin boards and slight timber, to be light and portable; and the different parts of it are so contriv'd as to take off and on; the undermost part stands on four wheels, whereon the rest are placed, one by one, by means and help of such instruments and engines as our carpenters use to mount their heavy timber. The pageant, or fabrick itself, is mighty neat, handsome, and glorious, adorn'd with carved, gilded, painted, and lacker'd work, as rich and costly as possible can be made of that kind, with many pretty little inventions of galleries, balconies, windows, doors, porches, &c. to adorn it the more. On this magnificent throne is placed another image of the dead general, in rich cloaths, which is afterwards burnt with the rest.

Matters being brought to this order, the general and his family repair thither early in the morning of the last three fore-mentioned days, the ways being lin'd with soldiers, and he attended by his life-guard, follow'd by *Mandareens* and grandees, where most of the day is spent in tears, mourning and lamentations, sombeys, sacrifices and offerings for his father; but, in the evening, the offered viands and other victims are divided amongst the assistants and soldiers.

Of the wild and savage creatures, some are drowned, to send their ghosts to the deceased prince, to be at his devotion in the other world, and others are given away. About ten o'clock, an infinite number of images of all sorts of fowls, horses, and elephants in paper-work, &c. are burnt in the open court, just before the machine or mausoleum, where likewise the general, with his relations and *Mandareens*, sombeys to the image of his predecessor therein; their magicians, *Thay*,[14] *Phou*,[15] *Thwee*,[16] all the while singing, reading, jumping, and playing so many antick tricks, and making

---

[12] This is a reference to the illustration in entitled, "The Order observ'd in the March of the Funeral Pomp at the Interment of the Kings of Tunquin," in Tavernier, "A New and Singular Relation of the Kingdom of Tunquin," following page 40, which shows a two-storey tower-like conveyance containing the royal corpse, identified as "the Mausolee."

[13] *Tangh* is probably Vietnamese *tang*, "mourning, death, burial ceremony." *Anja* is unclear.

[14] *Thầy*, "teacher/master."

[15] *Phụ*, "father/venerable."

[16] Baron's French translator, H. Deseille, thinks this should be read as *thủy* and that it means "magician." See S. Baron, "Description du royaume de Tonquin," trans. H. Deseille, *Revue Indochinoise* XXIII, No. 5-6 (May-June 1915): 448.

such terrible postures, as would scare some, and perswade others, they were either really demoniacal, or at least possessed with madness. About three hours after midnight fire is set to all this finery, the general, *&c.* retiring, taking along with him the pearls, amber, gold and silver that was on the altar (which are reserved for the service of the defunct, in a peculiar place of his palace). The *Mandareens* also send to their houses again whatsoever gold, silver, *&c.* they brought thither, leaving the rest to be consumed by the flames; and its ashes the wind scatters where it pleases, so that but very little, if any, comes where it was designed.

CHAPTER XVIII.

OF THE SECTS, IDOLS, WORSHIP, SUPERSTITION, AND PAGODAS OR TEMPLES OF THE TONQUEENESE.[1]

Tho' there are many sects amongst this people, yet only two are chiefly followed. The first is that of Congfutu, as the *Chinese* call him, (the *Tonqueenese, Ong-Congtu,*[2] and the *Europeans, Confucius*) the ancientest of the *Chinese* philosophers. This man they esteemed holy; and, for wisdom, he is reputed not only amongst them and the *Chinese,* but the *Japanese* too, the *Solomon* of all mortals: Without some proficiency in whose learning, none can attain any degree in their civil government, or be anyways allow'd to know matters of importance; tho' the truth thereof, and very quintessence of his doctrine, is nothing else but what we call moral philosophy, and consists in the following position,

> "That every one ought to know and perfect himself, and then, by his good and virtuous example, bring others to the same degree of goodness, so as they jointly may attain the supreme good; that it is therefore necessary to apply themselves to the study of philosophy, without which none can have a proper insight or inspection of things, and be able to know what is to be followed or avoided, nor rectify their desires according to reason;"[3]

with other the like precepts, wherein consists the *Chinese* doctrine and wisdom.

But his disciples, building on his principles, have extracted therefrom many rules and precepts, which soon after became the main subject of their superstition and religion. They acknowledge one supreme deity, and that all terrestrial things are directed, governed and preserved by him: that the world was eternal, without either beginning or creator. They reject the worship of images; they venerate and pay a kind of adoration to spirits. They expect reward for good deeds, and punishment for evil. They believe, in a manner, the immortality of the soul, and pray for the deceased. Some of them also believe, that the souls of the just live after separation from the body; and that the souls of the wicked perish as soon as they leave the body. They teach, that the air is full of malignant spirits, which is their dwelling place; and that those spirits are continually at variance with the living. They particularly recommend to their pupils, to honour their deceased friends and

---

[1] Jean-Baptiste Tavernier, "A New and Singular Relation of the Kingdom of Tunquin," Chapter XV: "Of the Religion and Superstition of the Tunquineses.

[2] Ông Khổng Tử, "Mr. Confucius."

[3] I am unable to identify this quotation.

parents; and do much concern themselves in performing certain ceremonies thereunto belonging, as I have mentioned already; and hold several other things very rational, and, in my opinion, in many things nothing at all inferior to either the ancient *Greeks* or *Romans*. Neither must we think, that the wiser and better sort amongst them are so shallow-brained, as to believe the dead stand in need of victuals, and that therefore they are so served, as I have mentioned in its due place; no, they know better, and tell us, they do it for no other reason, than to demonstrate their love and respect to the deceased parents; and withal to teach their own children and friends thereby, how to honour them when they shall be no more.

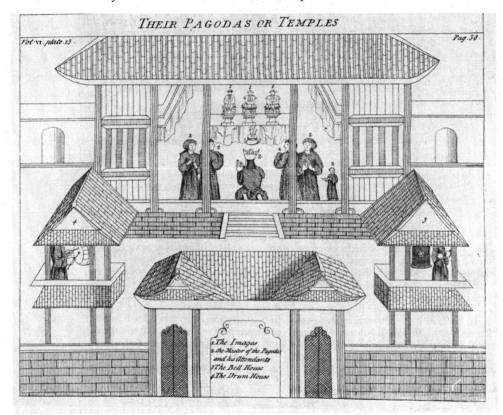

Plate 13: "Their Pagodas or Temples." 1. The Images. 2. The Master of the Pagoda and his Attendants. 3. The Bell House. 4. The Drum House.

However, the vulgar sort, and those that carry their judgment in their eyes, credit that as well as many other impertinent impossibilities of their superstition. In fine, tho' this sect hath no pagodas erected, nor particular place appointed to worship the king of heaven in, or priests to preach and propagate the said doctrine, nor a due form commanded or observed, but it is left to every one's discretion to do as he pleases in these respects, so as he gives thereby no scandal, yet it has their kings, princes, grandees, and the learned men of the kingdom for its followers.

In former days, the king of the land might only sacrifice to the king of heaven; but, since the general has usurped the royal power, he has assumed this sovereign prerogative, and performs the said ceremony in his palace himself, in case of publick calamity, as want of rain, famine, great mortality, &c. befalling the kingdom, which no other may do, on peril of their lives.

The second sect is called *Boot*,[4] which signifies the worship of idols or images, and is generally followed by the ignorant, vulgar and simple sort of people, and more especially the women and capadoes, the most constant adherents thereunto. Their tenets are, to worship images devoutly, to believe transmigration. They offer to the devil, that he may not hurt them. They believe a certain deity coming from three united gods.[5] They impose a cloister and retired life, and think their works can be meritorious, and that the wicked suffer torments together; with many foolish superstitious niceties, too idle to repeat: however, they have no priest, any more than the former sect, to preach and propagate their doctrine; all they have, are their Sayes, or Bonzes, as M. *Taverniere* calls them (which, by mistake, he terms priests) which are a kind of friers or monks.[6] They have some nuns also, whose dwellings are about, and sometimes in their pagodas, who most commonly are invited to celebrate their funerals with their drums, trumpets, and other musick: they subsist for the most part by alms, and the charity of the people. In brief, this is that sect that has spread its fopperies and impertinences very far; and, in effect, with its schism and imposture, has overspread, in part or whole, most of the eastern countries, as this of *Tonqueen, China, Japan, Correa* [Korea], *Formosa, Cambodia, Siam,* the *Gentues*[7] of coast *Cormandel*[8] and *Bengal, Ceylon, Indosthan,*[9] &c. From one of these two last places it was first brought into *China,* on the following occasion.

One of the *Chinese* emperors coming to the knowledge of a famous law that was taught in the west, which was very efficacious for instructing and conducting mankind to wisdom and virtue, and that the doctors and expounders thereof were persons extremely celebrated for their exemplary lives, and stupendous and miraculous actions, &c. he therefore dispatched several sages to find out this law, and bring it to *China.* These ambassadors, after they had travelled, or rather erred, to and fro the space of almost three years, arrived either in *Indosthan* or *Mallabar;*[10] where finding this sects of *Boots* very rife, and of mighty veneration, and being deceived by the devil, and weary of travelling any further, they thought they had found what they sought for; and so, without more ado, they got seventy-two books of those false tales, of the natives, with some able interpreters, and returned to *China,* where the emperor received them most kindly and joyfully; and ordered directly, that the said sect should be publickly taught throughout all his dominions. In which miserable blindness they have ever since continued.

---

[4] *Bụt,* Vernacular Vietnamese for Buddha/Buddhism.

[5] Possibly a reference to the Buddhas of "past," "present," and "future."

[6] See note 16 in Chapter 1. Baron's French translator, H. Deseille, proposes to read "Sayes" as *thầy,* "teacher," a form of address often used for Buddhist monks (S. Baron, "Description du royaume de Tonquin," trans. H. Deseille, *Revue Indochinoise* XXIII, No. 5-6 [May-June 1915]: 451), but since later in this chapter we see that Baron transcribes *thầy* as "thay," here he must be referring to *sãi,* on which see Chapter One, note 8.

[7] Gentes, i.e., clans/lineage groups.

[8] Coromandel, the southeastern coast of India.

[9] Hindustan, the basin of the five Punjab rivers and the upper Gangetic Plain in northern India.

[10] Malabar, the southwest coast of India.

I cannot help making an observation in this place, for the honour of the Christian religion; and that is, that, in all appearance, this new law which the *Chinese* emperor at that time had heard of, could be no other than the first promulgation of the gospel in and about *Judea*; and its being then preached to *Jews* as well as gentiles, by the holy apostles, which was attended with so many miracles, that it was no wonder the fame thereof should extend to the remotest regions, and reach the ears of the *Chinese* emperor: and this is still the more probable, because, by the nearest calculation that can be made, the time which the emperor of *China* is recorded to have heard of the publication of this new doctrine, agrees punctually with that of the appearance of our Saviour, and the preaching of the apostles. And had the sages sent by that emperor, proceeded as they ought, not only the great empire of *China*, but all the vast territories adjacent, that now lie immers'd in paganism, and the dregs of superstition, might have been converted, and brought to the glorious light of Christianity.[11]

Some other sects, as that of *Lanzo*,[12] are but slenderly followed, as is said before, tho' their magicians and necromancers, as *Thay-Boo*,[13] *Thay-Boo-Twe*,[14] *Thay-de-Lie*,[15] are the proselytes and followers thereof, and in great esteem with the princes, and respected by the vulgar, so that they are consulted by both in their most weighty occasions; and they receive their opinions and false predictions as very oracles, believing they speak by divine inspiration, and have the fore-knowledge of future events: wherefore it is not probable, that they were of this sort that were sent to the frontiers for soldiers, as M. *Taverniere* has it.[16]

I know indeed, that the general rummages[17] sometimes a certain sort of vagabonds that haunt every corner of the kingdom, pretending to be conjurers and fortune-tellers, cheating and misleading thereby the simple and ignorant people, and infecting them with notions contrary to the belief of the sects publickly tolerated. But as the *Tonqueenese* are really very credulous, and ready to embrace almost every new opinion they meet withal, so are they not less tenacious in retaining any notions which they are in possession of, and observe carefully times and seasons, as good and bad; in which they will not undertake any voyages or journey, nor build houses, cultivate grounds, nor bargain for any thing considerable; nor even will they attempt, on ominous days, to cure their sick, bury their dead, nor in a manner,

---

[11] This refers to an event attributed to the reign of Emperor Han Mingdi (CE 58-75) used to account for the introduction of Buddhism into China. The idea that the emperor had in fact heard about Christianity, but that his envoys returned with reports of Buddhism instead, was common among Europeans in the seventeenth and eighteenth centuries. See Adriano di St. Thecla, *Opusculum de Sectis apud Sinenses et Tunkinenses: A Small Treatise on the Sects among the Chinese and Tonkinese*, ed. and trans. Olga Dror, pp. 186-189.

[12] Apparently a garbled transcription of Laozi, Vietnamese Lão Tử.

[13] *Thầy Bói*, "prognosticator."

[14] *Thầy Bói Tuy*, "sorcerer."

[15] *Thầy Địa Lý*, "geomancer."

[16] Tavernier, "A New and Singular Relation of the Kingdom of Tunquin," p. 50, introduces Laozi as "one of the greatest Magicians in the East" who "taught much of [Buddhist] Doctrine" and advocated building hospitals where "several of the Nobility" and "a great number of the Bonzes" went "to look after the Sick." He then writes: "While my brother was there, the Choua [*chúa*], a great Enemy to these Vagabonds, sent for a great number of Bonzes and Says, or idle Fellows, and picking out the strongest and best proportion'd, sent them away to the Frontiers for Souldiers."

[17] The sense of "to rummage" here is "to search out" with the intent to eradicate.

transact any thing without the advice of their soothsayers and blind wizards, who are principally divided into three classes, that is, those who are followers of *Thay-Boo*, or *Thay-Boo-Twe*, or *Thay-de-Lie*, and have not the least sense of their being most grossly cheated and deluded by the fallacious pretensions of those impudent fellows, who live wholly by selling their directions to them, at excessive rates, as the most desirable and current merchandize. And, since these pretended conjurers are so much observed and venerated by the deluded people, I will descend to the particular functions of every one of them, and speak first of *Thay-Boo*, and his class.

These pretend to declare all such future events as concern marriages, building of houses, and, in general, pretend to foretell the success of any business of consequence. All that come to him, or those of his class, are kindly used for their money, and receive, for answers, what is suppos'd will satisfy them best, but always so ambiguous, as will bear a double and doubtful interpretation. The magicians of this tribe are generally blind, either born so, or come to be so by some accident or other. Before they pronounce their sentence on the proposed question, they take three pieces of copper coin, inscribed with characters, which they throw on the ground several times, and feel what side of it falls uppermost; then prating and mumbling some strange kind of words to themselves, they deliver the result of the conjuration.

Secondly, Thay-Boo-Twe, to whom they resort in all distempers. This class of pretended magicians have their books, by which they pretend to find out the cause and result of all sickness; and never miss to tell the sick party, that his distemper proceeds from the devil, or some water gods; and pretend to cure it by the noise of drums, basons and trumpets. The conjurer of this tribe is habited very antickly, and sings very loud, and makes hideous noises, pronouncing many execrations and blasphemous words, sounding continually a small bell, which he holds in his hand, jumping and skipping as if the devil were really in him; and all this while there is store of victuals prepared for an offering to the devil, but it is eaten by himself: and he will continue this sport sometimes for several days, till the patient be either dead or recovered, and then he can give an answer with some certainty.

It belongs to them to dispossess such as are possess'd by the devil, which is the ultimate of their conjuration, and is commonly effected after this manner. They curse, and most impiously invoke I do not know what demon; and they paint the pictures of devils, with horrible faces, on yellow paper, which is fixed to the wall of the house; then they fall to bauling so terribly, and scream so loud, dancing and skipping, as is most ridiculous, sometimes fearful to see and hear. They also bless and consecrate new houses; and if they be suspected to be haunted, they drive the devil out of them by their conjuration, and the firing of muskets.

Thay-de-Lie's business is, to be consulted, which are the fittest places for burial of the dead; so that the living relations and kindred may, by this means, be happy and fortunate; and the like follies.

I will speak nothing of *Ba-Cote*,[18] because they are only the pretended witches amongst the baser sort.

As for temples and pagodas, since the *Tonqueenese* are not very devout, there are neither so many, nor those so sumptuous, as I have seen in some of the neighbouring countries; and the preceding plate [plate 13: "Their Pagodas or Temples"] will give you a sufficient idea of them.

---

[18] *Bà Cốt*, "female medium."

BIBLIOGRAPHY

Andrade, A. A. de. "Antes de Vernei nascer ... O. P. Critovão Borri lança, nas escolas a primeira grande reforma cientifica (Before Vernei was born ... Father Cristoforo Borri Launhes the First Major Scientific Reform in the schools). *Brotéria* XL, 4 (1945): 369-379.

Argelati, Filippo. *Bibliotheca scriptorum mediolanensium*. Mediolani: In Aedibus Palatinis, 1745.

Backer, Augustin de, with Alois de Backer and Carlos Sommervogel. *Bibliothèque des écrivains de la Compagnie de Jésus*. Liége: A. de Backer; Paris: C. Sommervogel, 1869.

Baldini, Ugo. *Saggi sulla cultura della Compagnia di Gesù* (secoli XVI-XVIII) (Essays on the Culture of the Society of Jesus [XVI-XVII centuries]). Padova, Italy: CLEUP Edifice, 2000.

Baldinotti, P. "La relation sur le Tonkin du P. Baldinotti," Italian text with French translation by Dr. Mario Carli. *Bulletin de l'Ecole Française d'Extrême-Orient* 3 (1903): 71-78.

Baron, Samuel. "A Description of the Kingdom of Tonqueen." *A Collection of Voyages and Travels*, eds. Awnsham and John Churchill, vol. 6. London, 1732, 1-40, reprinted in the 1744 edition, vol. 6, 117-160

———. "Description du Tonquin." *Histoire Generale des Voyages*, vol. IX. Paris: Didot, 1751, 91-123.

——— . "Description du royaume de Tonquin," trans. H. Deseille. *Revue Indochinoise* XXII, no. 7 (July 1914): 59-75; no. 8 (August 1914): 197-208; no. 9-10 (September-October 1914): 331-343; no. 11-12 (November-December 1914): 429-454; *Revue Indochinoise* XXIII, no. 3-4 (March April 1915): 291-301; No. 5-6 (May-June 1915): 443-454.

Bartoli, Daniello. *Dell'Historia della Compagnia di Giesu, La Cina, terza parte, dell'Asia.* Rome: Nella Stamperia del Varese, 1663.

Bellarmine, Robert. Lecture, "Whether by Its Nature the Sky Is Corruptible." In *The Lovain Lectures (Lectiones Lovanienses) of Bellarmine and the Autograph Copy of his 1616 Declaration of Galileo*, ed. Ugo Baldini and George V. Coyne, S. J. Vatican: Specola Vaticana, 1984.

Biển Niên Lịch Sử Cổ Trung Đại Việt Nam (Annals of Ancient, Medieval, and Modern History of Vietnam. Hanoi: Nhà Xuất Bản Khoa Học, 1987.

Bonifacy, A. *Les débuts du Christianisme en Annam des origines au commencement du 18e siècle*. Hanoi: Imprimerie Tonkinoise, 192-?.

Borri, Christoforo. *Relatione della nuova missione delli PP. della Compagnia de Giesu, al Regno della Cocincina, scritta dal Padre Christoforo Borri milanese della mede sima compagnia, che fu uno de primi ch'entrarono in detto regno. Alla Santita di N. Sig. Urbano PP. ottavo.* Rome: F. Catanio, 1631.

Translations and editions of Borri's *Relatione* (arranged chronologically):

Relation de la nouvelle mission au royaume de la Cochinchine, trans. Father Ant. de la Croix, S. J. Lille: Pierre de Rache, 1631.

Relatio de Cocincina R. P. Christophori Borri e Societate Jesu, trans. Father J. Bucelleni. Vienna: Domo Professa Societatis Jesu, 1632.

Historie van eene nieuvve seyndinghe door de paters der Societeyt Iesv in't ryck van Cocincina, trans. Father Jacobus Susius, S. J. Louvain: By de weduwe van H. Haestens, 1632.

Relation vod dem newen Königreich Cochin China, trans. Michel Riekhes. Wein, 1633.

Cochinchina: Containing Many Admirable Rarities and Singularities of that Countrey. Extracted out of an Italian Relation, lately presented to the Pope, by Christophoro Borri, that lived certaine yeeres there, trans. Robert Ashley. London: Printed by Robert Raworth, 1633.

"An Account of Cochin-China." *A Collection of Voyages and Travels, some now first printed from original manuscripts, others now first published in English*, eds. Awnsham and John Churchill, vol. 2. London, 1704, pp. 787-838, reprinted in the 1732 edition of the same Collection (vol. 2, pp. 721-765), as well as in the 1744 edition (vol. 2, pp. 699-743).

"Relation de la nouvelle mission au royaume de Cochinchine," transl. A. Bonifacy. *Bulletin des Amis du Vieux Hué* 18, 3-4 (July-December 1931): 279-402.

Xứ Đàng Trong Năm 1621 (Cochinchina in 1621), translated and annotated by Hồng Nhuệ, Nguyễn Khắc Xuyên, & Nguyễn Nghị, Hochiminh City: Nhà Xuất Bản Thành Phố Hồ Chí Minh, 1997.

Boxer, C. R. *The Christian Century in Japan 1549-1650*. Berkeley, CA: University of California Press, 1967.

Bucelleni, J. *Relatio de Cocincina R. P. Christophori Borri e Societate Jesu*. Vienna: Domo Professa Societatis Jesu, 1632.

Buch, W. J. M. Buch. "La Companie des Indes Néerlandaises et l'Indochine." *Bulletin de l'Ecole Française d'Extrême-Orient* 36 (1936) and 37 (1937).

Bửu Cầm et al. *Hồng Đức Bản Đồ*. Saigon: Bộ Quốc-Gia Giáo-Dục, 1962.

Cadière, L. "Le culte des arbres." *Bulletin de l'Ecole Française d'Extrême-Orient* 7,18 (1918).

———. "Le mur de Đồng Hới." *Bulletin de l'Ecole Française d'Extrême-Orient* 6 (1906).

Caillaud, Romanet du. *Essais sur les origines du Christianisme au Tonking and dans les autres pays annamites*. Paris: Augustin Challamel, 1915.

Campanella, Thommaso. *Philosophiae rationalis partes quinque: videlicet, grammatical, dialectica, rhetorica, poetica, historiographia, iuxta propria principia*. Paris: Apud Ioannem Du Bray, 1637-8.

Carvalho, Joaquim de. "Galileu e a cultura porgutuesa." *Biblos* XIX (1943): 438-465.

Chappoulie, Henri. *Rome et les missions d'Indochine au XVIIe siècle*, 2 vols. Paris: Bloud et Gay, 1943.

————. *Aux origins d'une église: Rome et les missions d'Indochine au XVII siècle,* vol. I. Paris: Bloud et Gay, 1943.

Chapuis, A. "Les noms annamites." *Bulletin des Amis du Vieux Hué* XXIX, 1 (January-March 1942).

Charlevoix, *Le Christianisme au Japon 1542-1660.* Lille: L. Lefort, 1853.

Chavannes, E., trans. and annot. *Les memoires historiques de Se-Ma Tsien.* Leiden: E. J. Brill, 1967.

Clavius, Christopher. *In sphaeram Iohannis de Sacro Bosco commentaries.* Rome: Victorium Halianum, 1570.

Coedes, G. *The Making of South East Asia.* Berkeley, CA: University of California Press, 1967.

Cordara, Julio. *Historiae societatis Jesu.* Rome: Ex Typographia Antonii de Rubeis, 1750.

Cortesão, Armando, trans. *The Suma Oriental of Tomé Pires: An Account of the East, from the Red Sea to Japan, Written in Malacca and India in 1512-1515.* London: The Hakluyt Society, 1944.

Corvo, João Andrade. "Linhas isogónicas no século XVI" (Isogone Lines in the Sixteenth Century). In João Andrade Corvo, *Roteiro de Lisboa a Goa* (Pilgrim from Lisboa to Goa) (Lisbon, 1882).

Costa, M. G. da. "Inéditos de filosofia em Portugal." *Revista Portuguesa de Filosofia,* 5, 1 (1949): 37-77.

Crevost, Ch. and Ch. Lemarié. *Catalogues des produits de l'Indochine,* vol. I. Hanoi: Gouvernement Général de l'Indochine, 1917.

Croix, Ant. de la, S. J. *Relation de la nouvelle mission au royaume de la Cochinchine.* Lille: Pierre de Rache, 1631.

Crooke, William, ed. *Travels in India by Jean-Baptiste Tavernier, Baron of Aubonne, Translated from the original French Edition of 1676 with a biographical sketch of the Author, Notes, Appendices, etc.,* 2 vols. London: Oxford University Press, 1925.

Đại Nam Thực Lục (Chronicle of the Nguyễn Dynasty), vol. I. Tokyo: Keio Institute of Linguistic Studies, 1961.

Đại Việt Sử Ký Toàn Thư (Complete history of great Viet). Hanoi: Nhà Xuất Bản Khoa Học Xã Hội, 1993.

Dampier, William. "Mr. Dampier's Voyages, Vol. II, Part I: His Voyage from Achin in Sumatra, to Tunquin, and Other Places in the East-Indies." In *A Collection of Voyages, in Four Volumes.* London: James and John Knapton, 1729.

Đặng Chấn Liêu, et al., *Từ Điển Việt Anh* (Vietnamese-English Dictionary). Hochiminh City: Nhà Xuất Bản Thành Phố Ho Chí Minh, 1999.

Dang Phuong Nghi, "Les institutions publiques du Viet-Nam au XVIII siècle." *Publications de l'Ecole Française d'Extrême-Orient* LXIV (1969).

————. *The Catholic Missions in China.* Shanghai: The Commercial Press, Ltd., 1954.

Dun, J. Li, ed. *China in Transition, 1517-1911.* New York, NY: Van Nostrand Reinhold, 1969.

Elia, Pasquale M. de, S. J. *Galileo in China,* trans. Rufus Suter and Matthew Sciascia. Cambridge, MA: Harvard University Press, 1960.

Elliot, J. H. *The Count-Duke of Olivares: The Statesman in an Age of Decline.* New Haven, CT and London: Yale University Press, 1986.

"Les Européens qui ont vu le vieux Hue: Cristoforo Borri." *Bulletin des Amis du Vieux Hué* 18,3-4 (July-December 1931).
> "Preface," by L. Cadière, pp. 261-65.
> "Notice," by C. Maybon, pp. 269-75.
> "Introduction," by A. Bonifacy, pp. 279-283.
> "Annotated Translation," by A. Bonifacy, pp. 285-402.
> "Postscript," by A. Bonifacy, pp. 403-05.
> "1621 letter of Gaspard Luis," with annotations, by L. Cadière, pp. 407-432.

Gauchat, Patritius, O. M. *Hierarchia catholica medii aevi* (Catholic Hierarchy through Times). Monasterii: Sumptibus et Typis Librariae Regensbergianae, 1935.

Geerts, M. A. C. J. "Voyage du yacht hollandais *Grol* du Japan au Tonquin." *Excursions et reconnaissances* 13 (Saigon) 1882.

Ghisalberti, Alberto M. *Dizionario biografico degli italiani.* Rome: Istituto della Enciclopedia Italiana, 1971.

Gil, Luis. "The Embassy of Don Garcia de Silva y Figueroa to Shah Abbas (1614-1624)." Abstract of the paper presented at the Conference of the Iranian Heritage Foundation, London, "Iran and the World in the Safavid Age" (September 2002). http://www.iranheritage.com/safavidconference/soas/abstract24.htm.

Gorman, Michael John. "The Angel and the Compass: Athanasius Kircher's Geographical Project." In *Athanasius Kircher: The Last Man Who Knew Everything,* ed. Paula Findlen. New York, NY: Routledge, 2004.

Grant, Edward. *Planets, Stars, and Orbs: The Medieval Cosmos, 1200-1687.* Cambridge: Cambridge University Press, 1994.

——— . "Celestial Orbs in the Latin Middle Ages." *Isis* 78, 2 (1987): 152-173.

Hartig, Otto. "Borrus (Borri, Burrus), Christopher." In Charles G. Herbermann, et al., *The Catholic Encyclopedia,* vol. 2. New York: Robert Appleton Company, 1907.

Herrera, Antonij de. "Indiae Occidentalis descriptio," *Descriptio Indiae Occidentalis.* Amsterdam: Apud Michaelem Colinium bibliopolam, 1622.

Innes, Robert L. "The Door Ajar: Japan's Foreign Trade in the Seventeenth Century." PhD dissertation, University of Michigan, Ann Arbor, 1980.

Jacques, Roland. *Portuguese Pioneers of Vietnamese Linguistics Prior to 1650.* Bangkok: Orchid Press, 2002.

Jardine, Lisa. *The Curious Life of Robert Hooke, The Man Who Measured London.* New York: Harper Collins, 2004.

Kammerer, Albert. *La découverte de Madagascar par les portugais et la cartographie de l'île.* Lisbon, 1950.

——— . *La découverte de la Chine par les portugais au XVIème siècle et la cartographie des portulans.* Leiden: E. J. Brill, 1944.

Kircher, Athanasius. *China monumentis.* Amsterdam: Apud Joannem Janssonium à Waesberge & Elizeum Weyerstraet, 1667.

——— . [Kircheri, Athanasii.] *Magnes; sive, De arte magnetica.* Rome: L. Grignani, 1641.

Koffler, Jean. "Description historique de la Cochinchine." *Revue Indochinoise* XVI,12 (December 1911).

Langlet, Philippe. "La tradition vietnamienne: Un état national au sein de la civilization chinoise." *Bulletin de la Société des Etudes Indochinoises* XLV, 2 & 3 Trimestres (1970).

Lattis, James. *Between Copernicus and Galileo: Christoph Clavius and the Collapse of Ptolemaic Cosmology.* Chicago, IL and London: The University of Chicago Press, 1994.

Launay, Adrien. *Histoire de la mission du Thibet.* Lille-Paris: Desclée de Brouwer, n.d.

Li Tana. *Nguyễn Cochinchina.* Ithaca, NY: Cornell Southeast Asia Program Publications, 1998.

Lord, Henry. "A Discussion of Two Foreign Company Sects in the East-Indies; viz. The Sect of the Banians, the Antient [*sic*] Natives of India and the Sect of the Persees, the Ancient Inhabitants of Persia." In *A Collection of Voyages and Travels,* ed. Awnsham Churchill. London: John Walthoe et al., 1732.

Louvet, L.–E. *La Cochinchine religieuse.* Paris: Challamel Ainé, 1855.

Malleret, Louis. "Une source de la relation du voyageur Tavernier sur le Tonkin." *Bulletin de la Société des Etudes Indo-Chinoises de Saigon,* nouvelle serie 7,1 (Janvier-Mars 1932).

Manguin, Pierre-Yves. *Les Portugais sur les côtes du Viêt-Nam et du Campa: Etude sur les routes maritimes et les relations commerciales, d'après les sources portugaises: XVI, XVII, XVIII siècles.* Paris: Ecole Française d'Extrême-Orient, 1972.

Marini, Gio. Filippo de. *Relation nouvelle et curieuse des royaumes de Tunquin et de Lao,* tr. L.P.L.C.C. Paris: Gervais Clouzier, 1666.

Maybon, Charles B. *Histoire moderne du pays d'Annam.* Paris: Librarie Plon, 1920.

——— . "Une Factorerie Anglaise au Tonkin au XVIIe Siècle (1672-1697)." *Bulletin de l'Ecole Française d'Extrême-Orient* 10 (1910).

Mercati, Angelo. "Notizie sul gesuita Cristoforo Borri e su sue "inventioni" da carte finora sconosciute di Pietro della Valle, il pellegrino" (Note on the Jesuit Cristoforo Borri and on His "Inventions" from the Until Now Unknown Letters of Pietro della Valle, a Traveler). *Acta,* 15, 3 (1953): 25-46.

Montézon, F. de and Ed. Estève, eds. *Mission de la Cochinchine et du Tonkin.* Paris: Charles Dounoil, 1858.

Morley, Joe. "Feature: First Priest to the Great South Lands." *The Catholic Weekly.* Sydney, April 14, 2002.

Mungello, D. E., ed. *The Chinese Rites Controversy: Its History and Meaning.* San Francisco, CA: Institute Monumenta Serica, 1994.

Needham, Joseph. *Chinese Astronomy and the Jesuit Mission: An Encounter of Cultures.* London: The China Society, 1958.

Nguyễn Đức Diệu et al. *Vương Triều Mạc* (Kings of the Mac Dynasty). Hanoi: Nhà Xuất Bản Khoa Hoc Xã Hội, 1996.

——— . *Văn Bia Thời Mạc* (Inscriptions of the Mac Period). Hanoi: Nhà Xuất Bản Khoa Hoc Xã Hội, 1996.

Nguyễn Khoa Chiêm. *Viêt Nam Khai Quốc Chi Truyện* (Story of the Foundation of the Vietnamese State), trans. and annot. Ngô Đức Thọ and Nguyễn Thúy Nga. Hanoi: Nhà xuất bản Hội Nhà Văn, 1994.

Nguyễn Văn Tố and L. Cadière. *Lịch Sử Đạo Thiên Chúa ở Việt Nam.* Hue: Đại Việt Thiên Bản, 1944.

Norindr, Panivong. *Phantasmatic Indochina: French Colonial Ideology in Architecture, Film, and Literature.* Durham, NC and London: Duke University Press, 1996.

Nyström, Johan Fredrik. *Geografiens och de geografiska upptäckternas historia* (The History of the Geography and Its Discoverers). Stockholm: C. E. Fritzes Kongl. Hofbokhandel, 1899.

Oyley, Samuel de and John Colson, trans. *An Historical, Critical, Geographical, Chronological, and Etymological Dictionary of the Holy Bible.* London: J. J. & P. Knapton, 1732).

Pastor, Ludwig Freiher von. *The History of the Popes From the Close of the Middle Ages,* trans. Dom Ernest Graf, O. S. B., 2nd edition. London: Routledge & Kegan Paul Ltd., 1955.

Peri, N. "Essai sur les relations du Japon et de l'Indochine aux XVIe et XVIIe siecles." *Bulletin de l'Ecole Française d'Extrême Orient* XXIII (1923): 1-136.

Petech, L. "Borri, Cristoforo." In Alberto M. Ghisalberti, *Dizionario biografico degli italiani,* vol. 13. Rome: Istituto della Enciclopedia Italiana, 1971.

Pollen, J. H. "Society of Jesus." *The Catholic Encyclopedia* vol. XIV. New York: Robert Appleton Company, 1912, 81-110.

Poncet, C. "La princess Marie d'Ordonez de Cevallos." *Bulletin des Amis du vieux Hué* 4 (1941).

Ramusio, Giovanni Battista. *Delle navigationi et viaggi.* Venetia: Giunti, 1554.

Rhodes, Alexandre de. *Histoire du royaume de Tunquin et des grands progrez que la predication de l'evangile y a faits en la conversion des infidèlles, depuis l'année 1627 jusques à l'année 1646,* translated from Latin by R. P. Henry Albi. Lyon: Jean Baptiste Devenet, 1651.

———. *Dictionarium Annnamiticum, Lusitanum, et Latinum.* Rome: Sacr. Congreg, 1651, col. 671.

———. *Histoire du royaume du Tonkin,* annot. J.-P. Duteuil. Paris: Éditions Kimé, 1999.

———. *Từ Điển Annam-Lusitan-Latinh* (Annamite-Portuguese-Latin Dictionary), ed. and trans. Thanh Lãng et al. Hochiminh City: Nhà Xuất Bản Khoa Học Xã Hội, 1991.

———. *Rhodes of Vietnam,* trans. Solange Hertz. Westminster, MD: The Newman Press, 1966.

Ribadeneira, Pietro, Philippo Alegambe, and Nathanaele Sotvello. *Bibliotheca scriptorum societatis Iesu.* London: Gregg International Publishers, 1969; first edition, Rome, 1676.

Richard (Abbe). *Histoire naturelle, civile, et politique du Tonquin.* Paris: Chez Moutard, 1778.

Robinson, Henry W. and Walter Adams, eds. *The Diary of Robert Hooke (1672-1680).* London: Taylor & Francis, 1935).

Santos, D. Mauricio Gomes dos. "Vicissitudes da obra do P. Cristóvão Borri." *Anáis* (Academia Portuguese da História) 3 (1951): 119-150.

Santos, Ribeiro dos. "Memórias históricas sóbre alguns metemáticos portugueses e estrangeiros domicilidrios em Portugal ou nas Conquistas." *Memórias de literature portuguesa publicadas pela Academia Real das Ciências de Lisboa*, vol. VIII, part I. Lisboa, 1812.

Schmidlin, Joseph. "Die ersten Madagascarmissionen im Lichte der Propagandamaterialien (The First Madagascar Missions in the Light of Propaganda Material). *Zeitschrift für Missionswissenschaft und Religionswissenschaft* vol. XII (1922): 193-205.

Schütte, Joseph Franz, S. J. *Monumenta historica japoniae I, Textus Catalogorum Japoniae, 1549-1654*. Rome: Monumenta Historica Soc. Iesu, 1975.

Shea, William R. "Galileo, Sunspots, and Inconstant Heavens." In *Galileo's Intellectual Revolution: Middle Period, 1610-1632*. New York, NY: Science History Publications, 1972, pp. 49–74.

Sommervogel, Carlos, S. J. *Bibliothèque de la Compagnie de Jésu*. Paris: Alphonae Picard; Bruxelles: Oscar Schepens, 1890.

Sprengel, M. C. and G. Forster. *Neue Beiträge zur Volkerund Länderkunde*. Leipzig: P. G. Kummer, 1793.

St. Thecla, Adriano di. *Opusculum de Sectis apud Sinenses et Tunkinenses: A Small Treatise on the Sects among the Chinese and Tonkinese: A Study of Religion in China and North Vietnam in the Eighteenth Century*, ed. and trans. Olga Dror. Ithaca, NY: Cornell Southeast Asia Program, 2002.

Susius, F. Jacobus, S. J. *Historie van eene nieuvve seyndinghe door de paters der Societeyt Iesv in't ryck van Cocincina*. Louvain: By de weduwe van H. Haestens, 1632.

Tabert, A. J. L. *Dictionarium Anamitico-Latinum*. Serampore: J. Marshnam, 1838.

Tavernier, Jean-Baptiste. "A New and Singular Relation of the Kingdom of Tunquin." In *A Collection of Several Relations and Treatises Singular and Curious*. London: A. Godbid & J. Playford, for Moses Pitt at the Angel in St. Paul's Churchyard, 1680.

Taylor, K. W. "Literati Revival in Seventeenth-Century Vietnam." *Journal of Southeast Asian Studies* 18,1 (March 1987).

———. "Nguyen Hoang and the Beginning of Viet Nam's Southward Expansion." In *Southeast Asia in the Early Modern Era*, ed. Anthony Reid. Ithaca, NY: Cornell University Press, 1993, 42-65.

Thoren, Victor E. "The Comet of 1577 and Tycho Brahe's System of the World." *Archives Internationales d'Histoire des Sciences* 29 (1979): 53-67.

Thorndike, Lynn. *A History of Magic and Experimental Science*, vol. VII. New York, NY: Columbia University Press, 1958.

Tissanier, Joseph. *Relation du voyage du P. Joseph Tissanier de la Compagnie de Jesus, depuis la France jusqu'au royaume de Tonkin, avec ce qui s'est passé de plus memorable dans cette mission durant les années 1658, 1659, et 1660*. Paris: Edm. Martin, 1663.

Trần Trọng Kim, *Việt Nam Sử Lược* (Short History of Vietnam). Nhà Xuất Bản Văn Hóa Thông Tin, 1999.

Venturi, Tacchi. *Opere storiche del P. Matteo Ricci*. Macerata, 1913.

Visch, R. D. Caroli de. *Bibliotheca scriptorum sacri ordinis cisterciensis.* Coloniae Agrippinae: Apud, 1656.

Vossius, Gerhard Johann. *Opera* (Works). Amsterdam: P. & J. Blaev, 1699.

Vu Khanh Tuong. "Les missions jesuites avant les missions étrangères au Vietnam (1515-1665)." PhD dissertation, Institute Catholique de Paris, 1956.

SOUTHEAST ASIA PROGRAM PUBLICATIONS

Cornell University

Studies on Southeast Asia

Number 41   *Two Views of Seventeenth-Century Vietnam: Christoforo Borri on Cochinchina and Samuel Baron on Tonkin*, ed. Olga Dror and K. W. Taylor. 2006. 290 pp. ISBN 0-8772-7741-9 (pb).

Number 40   *Laskar Jihad: Islam, Militancy, and the Quest for Identity in Post-New Order Indonesia*, Noorhaidi Hasan. 2006. 266 pp. ISBN 0-877277-40-0 (pb).

Number 39   *The Indonesian Supreme Court: A Study of Institutional Collapse*, Sebastiaan Pompe. 2005. 494 pp. ISBN 0-877277-38-9 (pb).

Number 38   *Spirited Politics: Religion and Public Life in Contemporary Southeast Asia*, ed. Andrew C. Willford and Kenneth M. George. 2005. 210 pp. ISBN 0-87727-737-0.

Number 37   *Sumatran Sultanate and Colonial State: Jambi and the Rise of Dutch Imperialism, 1830-1907*, Elsbeth Locher-Scholten, trans. Beverley Jackson. 2004. 332 pp. ISBN 0-87727-736-2.

Number 36   *Southeast Asia over Three Generations: Essays Presented to Benedict R. O'G. Anderson*, ed. James T. Siegel and Audrey R. Kahin. 2003. 398 pp. ISBN 0-87727-735-4.

Number 35   *Nationalism and Revolution in Indonesia*, George McTurnan Kahin, intro. Benedict R. O'G. Anderson (reprinted from 1952 edition, Cornell University Press, with permission). 2003. 530 pp. ISBN 0-87727-734-6.

Number 34   *Golddiggers, Farmers, and Traders in the "Chinese Districts" of West Kalimantan, Indonesia*, Mary Somers Heidhues. 2003. 316 pp. ISBN 0-87727-733-8.

Number 33   *Opusculum de Sectis apud Sinenses et Tunkinenses (A Small Treatise on the Sects among the Chinese and Tonkinese): A Study of Religion in China and North Vietnam in the Eighteenth Century*, Father Adriano de St. Thecla, trans. Olga Dror, with Mariya Berezovska. 2002. 363 pp. ISBN 0-87727-732-X.

Number 32   *Fear and Sanctuary: Burmese Refugees in Thailand*, Hazel J. Lang. 2002. 204 pp. ISBN 0-87727-731-1.

Number 31   *Modern Dreams: An Inquiry into Power, Cultural Production, and the Cityscape in Contemporary Urban Penang, Malaysia*, Beng-Lan Goh. 2002. 225 pp. ISBN 0-87727-730-3.

Number 30   *Violence and the State in Suharto's Indonesia*, ed. Benedict R. O'G. Anderson. 2001. Second printing, 2002. 247 pp. ISBN 0-87727-729-X.

Number 29   *Studies in Southeast Asian Art: Essays in Honor of Stanley J. O'Connor*, ed. Nora A. Taylor. 2000. 243 pp. Illustrations. ISBN 0-87727-728-1.

Number 28   *The Hadrami Awakening: Community and Identity in the Netherlands East Indies, 1900-1942*, Natalie Mobini-Kesheh. 1999. 174 pp. ISBN 0-87727-727-3.

Number 27   *Tales from Djakarta: Caricatures of Circumstances and their Human Beings*, Pramoedya Ananta Toer. 1999. 145 pp. ISBN 0-87727-726-5.

Number 26   *History, Culture, and Region in Southeast Asian Perspectives*, rev. ed., O. W. Wolters. 1999. Second printing, 2004. 275 pp. ISBN 0-87727-725-7.

Number 25   *Figures of Criminality in Indonesia, the Philippines, and Colonial Vietnam,* ed. Vicente L. Rafael. 1999. 259 pp. ISBN 0-87727-724-9.

Number 24   *Paths to Conflagration: Fifty Years of Diplomacy and Warfare in Laos, Thailand, and Vietnam, 1778-1828,* Mayoury Ngaosyvathn and Pheuiphanh Ngaosyvathn. 1998. 268 pp. ISBN 0-87727-723-0.

Number 23   *Nguyễn Cochinchina: Southern Vietnam in the Seventeenth and Eighteenth Centuries,* Li Tana. 1998. Second printing, 2002. 194 pp. ISBN 0-87727-722-2.

Number 22   *Young Heroes: The Indonesian Family in Politics,* Saya S. Shiraishi. 1997. 183 pp. ISBN 0-87727-721-4.

Number 21   *Interpreting Development: Capitalism, Democracy, and the Middle Class in Thailand,* John Girling. 1996. 95 pp. ISBN 0-87727-720-6.

Number 20   *Making Indonesia,* ed. Daniel S. Lev, Ruth McVey. 1996. 201 pp. ISBN 0-87727-719-2.

Number 19   *Essays into Vietnamese Pasts,* ed. K. W. Taylor, John K. Whitmore. 1995. 288 pp. ISBN 0-87727-718-4.

Number 18   *In the Land of Lady White Blood: Southern Thailand and the Meaning of History,* Lorraine M. Gesick. 1995. 106 pp. ISBN 0-87727-717-6.

Number 17   *The Vernacular Press and the Emergence of Modern Indonesian Consciousness,* Ahmat Adam. 1995. 220 pp. ISBN 0-87727-716-8.

Number 16   *The Nan Chronicle,* trans., ed. David K. Wyatt. 1994. 158 pp. ISBN 0-87727-715-X.

Number 15   *Selective Judicial Competence: The Cirebon-Priangan Legal Administration, 1680–1792,* Mason C. Hoadley. 1994. 185 pp. ISBN 0-87727-714-1.

Number 14   *Sjahrir: Politics and Exile in Indonesia,* Rudolf Mrázek. 1994. 536 pp. ISBN 0-87727-713-3.

Number 13   *Fair Land Sarawak: Some Recollections of an Expatriate Officer,* Alastair Morrison. 1993. 196 pp. ISBN 0-87727-712-5.

Number 12   *Fields from the Sea: Chinese Junk Trade with Siam during the Late Eighteenth and Early Nineteenth Centuries,* Jennifer Cushman. 1993. 206 pp. ISBN 0-87727-711-7.

Number 11   *Money, Markets, and Trade in Early Southeast Asia: The Development of Indigenous Monetary Systems to AD 1400,* Robert S. Wicks. 1992. 2nd printing 1996. 354 pp., 78 tables, illus., maps. ISBN 0-87727-710-9.

Number 10   *Tai Ahoms and the Stars: Three Ritual Texts to Ward Off Danger,* trans., ed. B. J. Terwiel, Ranoo Wichasin. 1992. 170 pp. ISBN 0-87727-709-5.

Number 9   *Southeast Asian Capitalists,* ed. Ruth McVey. 1992. 2nd printing 1993. 220 pp. ISBN 0-87727-708-7.

Number 8   *The Politics of Colonial Exploitation: Java, the Dutch, and the Cultivation System,* Cornelis Fasseur, ed. R. E. Elson, trans. R. E. Elson, Ary Kraal. 1992. 2nd printing 1994. 266 pp. ISBN 0-87727-707-9.

Number 7   *A Malay Frontier: Unity and Duality in a Sumatran Kingdom,* Jane Drakard. 1990. 2nd printing 2003. 215 pp. ISBN 0-87727-706-0.

Number 6   *Trends in Khmer Art,* Jean Boisselier, ed. Natasha Eilenberg, trans. Natasha Eilenberg, Melvin Elliott. 1989. 124 pp., 24 plates. ISBN 0-87727-705-2.

Number 5	*Southeast Asian Ephemeris: Solar and Planetary Positions, A.D. 638–2000*, J. C. Eade. 1989. 175 pp. ISBN 0-87727-704-4.
Number 3	*Thai Radical Discourse: The Real Face of Thai Feudalism Today*, Craig J. Reynolds. 1987. 2nd printing 1994. 186 pp. ISBN 0-87727-702-8.
Number 1	*The Symbolism of the Stupa*, Adrian Snodgrass. 1985. Revised with index, 1988. 3rd printing 1998. 469 pp. ISBN 0-87727-700-1.

SEAP Series

Number 23	*Possessed by the Spirits: Mediumship in Contemporary Vietnamese Communities*. 2006. 186 pp. ISBN 0-877271-41-0 (pb).
Number 22	*The Industry of Marrying Europeans*, Vũ Trọng Phụng, trans. Thúy Tranviet. 2006. 66 pp. ISBN 0-877271-40-2 (pb).
Number 21	*Securing a Place: Small-Scale Artisans in Modern Indonesia*, Elizabeth Morrell. 2005. 220 pp. ISBN 0-877271-39-9.
Number 20	*Southern Vietnam under the Reign of Minh Mạng (1820-1841): Central Policies and Local Response*, Choi Byung Wook. 2004. 226pp. ISBN 0-0-877271-40-2.
Number 19	*Gender, Household, State: Đổi Mới in Việt Nam*, ed. Jayne Werner and Danièle Bélanger. 2002. 151 pp. ISBN 0-87727-137-2.
Number 18	*Culture and Power in Traditional Siamese Government*, Neil A. Englehart. 2001. 130 pp. ISBN 0-87727-135-6.
Number 17	*Gangsters, Democracy, and the State*, ed. Carl A. Trocki. 1998. Second printing, 2002. 94 pp. ISBN 0-87727-134-8.
Number 16	*Cutting across the Lands: An Annotated Bibliography on Natural Resource Management and Community Development in Indonesia, the Philippines, and Malaysia*, ed. Eveline Ferretti. 1997. 329 pp. ISBN 0-87727-133-X.
Number 15	*The Revolution Falters: The Left in Philippine Politics after 1986*, ed. Patricio N. Abinales. 1996. Second printing, 2002. 182 pp. ISBN 0-87727-132-1.
Number 14	*Being Kammu: My Village, My Life*, Damrong Tayanin. 1994. 138 pp., 22 tables, illus., maps. ISBN 0-87727-130-5.
Number 13	*The American War in Vietnam*, ed. Jayne Werner, David Hunt. 1993. 132 pp. ISBN 0-87727-131-3.
Number 12	*The Voice of Young Burma*, Aye Kyaw. 1993. 92 pp. ISBN 0-87727-129-1.
Number 11	*The Political Legacy of Aung San*, ed. Josef Silverstein. Revised edition 1993. 169 pp. ISBN 0-87727-128-3.
Number 10	*Studies on Vietnamese Language and Literature: A Preliminary Bibliography*, Nguyen Dinh Tham. 1992. 227 pp. ISBN 0-87727-127-5.
Number 8	*From PKI to the Comintern, 1924–1941: The Apprenticeship of the Malayan Communist Party*, Cheah Boon Kheng. 1992. 147 pp. ISBN 0-87727-125-9.
Number 7	*Intellectual Property and US Relations with Indonesia, Malaysia, Singapore, and Thailand*, Elisabeth Uphoff. 1991. 67 pp. ISBN 0-87727-124-0.
Number 6	*The Rise and Fall of the Communist Party of Burma (CPB)*, Bertil Lintner. 1990. 124 pp. 26 illus., 14 maps. ISBN 0-87727-123-2.

Number 5	*Japanese Relations with Vietnam: 1951–1987*, Masaya Shiraishi. 1990. 174 pp. ISBN 0-87727-122-4.
Number 3	*Postwar Vietnam: Dilemmas in Socialist Development*, ed. Christine White, David Marr. 1988. 2nd printing 1993. 260 pp. ISBN 0-87727-120-8.
Number 2	*The Dobama Movement in Burma (1930–1938)*, Khin Yi. 1988. 160 pp. ISBN 0-87727-118-6.

Cornell Modern Indonesia Project Publications

Number 75	*A Tour of Duty: Changing Patterns of Military Politics in Indonesia in the 1990s*. Douglas Kammen and Siddharth Chandra. 1999. 99 pp. ISBN 0-87763-049-6.
Number 74	*The Roots of Acehnese Rebellion 1989–1992*, Tim Kell. 1995. 103 pp. ISBN 0-87763-040-2.
Number 73	*"White Book" on the 1992 General Election in Indonesia*, trans. Dwight King. 1994. 72 pp. ISBN 0-87763-039-9.
Number 72	*Popular Indonesian Literature of the Qur'an*, Howard M. Federspiel. 1994. 170 pp. ISBN 0-87763-038-0.
Number 71	*A Javanese Memoir of Sumatra, 1945–1946: Love and Hatred in the Liberation War*, Takao Fusayama. 1993. 150 pp. ISBN 0-87763-037-2.
Number 70	*East Kalimantan: The Decline of a Commercial Aristocracy*, Burhan Magenda. 1991. 120 pp. ISBN 0-87763-036-4.
Number 69	*The Road to Madiun: The Indonesian Communist Uprising of 1948*, Elizabeth Ann Swift. 1989. 120 pp. ISBN 0-87763-035-6.
Number 68	*Intellectuals and Nationalism in Indonesia: A Study of the Following Recruited by Sutan Sjahrir in Occupation Jakarta*, J. D. Legge. 1988. 159 pp. ISBN 0-87763-034-8.
Number 67	*Indonesia Free: A Biography of Mohammad Hatta*, Mavis Rose. 1987. 252 pp. ISBN 0-87763-033-X.
Number 66	*Prisoners at Kota Cane*, Leon Salim, trans. Audrey Kahin. 1986. 112 pp. ISBN 0-87763-032-1.
Number 65	*The Kenpeitai in Java and Sumatra*, trans. Barbara G. Shimer, Guy Hobbs, intro. Theodore Friend. 1986. 80 pp. ISBN 0-87763-031-3.
Number 64	*Suharto and His Generals: Indonesia's Military Politics, 1975–1983*, David Jenkins. 1984. 4th printing 1997. 300 pp. ISBN 0-87763-030-5.
Number 62	*Interpreting Indonesian Politics: Thirteen Contributions to the Debate, 1964–1981*, ed. Benedict Anderson, Audrey Kahin, intro. Daniel S. Lev. 1982. 3rd printing 1991. 172 pp. ISBN 0-87763-028-3.
Number 60	*The Minangkabau Response to Dutch Colonial Rule in the Nineteenth Century*, Elizabeth E. Graves. 1981. 157 pp. ISBN 0-87763-000-3.
Number 59	*Breaking the Chains of Oppression of the Indonesian People: Defense Statement at His Trial on Charges of Insulting the Head of State, Bandung, June 7–10, 1979*, Heri Akhmadi. 1981. 201 pp. ISBN 0-87763-001-1.
Number 57	*Permesta: Half a Rebellion*, Barbara S. Harvey. 1977. 174 pp. ISBN 0-87763-003-8.

Number 55 *Report from Banaran: The Story of the Experiences of a Soldier during the War of Independence*, Maj. Gen. T. B. Simatupang. 1972. 186 pp. ISBN 0-87763-005-4.

Number 52 *A Preliminary Analysis of the October 1 1965, Coup in Indonesia (Prepared in January 1966)*, Benedict R. Anderson, Ruth T. McVey, assist. Frederick P. Bunnell. 1971. 3rd printing 1990. 174 pp. ISBN 0-87763-008-9.

Number 51 *The Putera Reports: Problems in Indonesian-Japanese War-Time Cooperation*, Mohammad Hatta, trans., intro. William H. Frederick. 1971. 114 pp. ISBN 0-87763-009-7.

Number 50 *Schools and Politics: The Kaum Muda Movement in West Sumatra (1927–1933)*, Taufik Abdullah. 1971. 257 pp. ISBN 0-87763-010-0.

Number 49 *The Foundation of the Partai Muslimin Indonesia*, K. E. Ward. 1970. 75 pp. ISBN 0-87763-011-9.

Number 48 *Nationalism, Islam and Marxism*, Soekarno, intro. Ruth T. McVey. 1970. 2nd printing 1984. 62 pp. ISBN 0-87763-012-7.

Number 43 *State and Statecraft in Old Java: A Study of the Later Mataram Period, 16th to 19th Century*, Soemarsaid Moertono. Revised edition 1981. 180 pp. ISBN 0-87763-017-8.

Number 39 Preliminary Checklist of Indonesian Imprints (1945-1949), John M. Echols. 186 pp. ISBN 0-87763-025-9.

Number 37 *Mythology and the Tolerance of the Javanese*, Benedict R. O'G. Anderson. 2nd edition, 1996. Reprinted 2004. 104 pp., 65 illus. ISBN 0-87763-041-0.

Number 25 *The Communist Uprisings of 1926–1927 in Indonesia: Key Documents*, ed., intro. Harry J. Benda, Ruth T. McVey. 1960. 2nd printing 1969. 177 pp. ISBN 0-87763-024-0.

Number 7 *The Soviet View of the Indonesian Revolution*, Ruth T. McVey. 1957. 3rd printing 1969. 90 pp. ISBN 0-87763-018-6.

Number 6 *The Indonesian Elections of 1955*, Herbert Feith. 1957. 2nd printing 1971. 91 pp. ISBN 0-87763-020-8.

Translation Series

Volume 4 *Approaching Suharto's Indonesia from the Margins*, ed. Takashi Shiraishi. 1994. 153 pp. ISBN 0-87727-403-7.

Volume 3 *The Japanese in Colonial Southeast Asia*, ed. Saya Shiraishi, Takashi Shiraishi. 1993. 172 pp. ISBN 0-87727-402-9.

Volume 2 *Indochina in the 1940s and 1950s*, ed. Takashi Shiraishi, Motoo Furuta. 1992. 196 pp. ISBN 0-87727-401-0.

Volume 1 *Reading Southeast Asia*, ed. Takashi Shiraishi. 1990. 188 pp. ISBN 0-87727-400-2.

Language Texts

INDONESIAN

Beginning Indonesian through Self-Instruction, John U. Wolff, Dédé Oetomo, Daniel Fietkiewicz. 3rd revised edition 1992. Vol. 1. 115 pp. ISBN 0-87727-529-7. Vol. 2. 434 pp. ISBN 0-87727-530-0. Vol. 3. 473 pp. ISBN 0-87727-531-9.

Indonesian Readings, John U. Wolff. 1978. 4th printing 1992. 480 pp. ISBN 0-87727-517-3

Indonesian Conversations, John U. Wolff. 1978. 3rd printing 1991. 297 pp. ISBN 0-87727-516-5

Formal Indonesian, John U. Wolff. 2nd revised edition 1986. 446 pp. ISBN 0-87727-515-7

TAGALOG

Pilipino through Self-Instruction, John U. Wolff, Maria Theresa C. Centeno, Der-Hwa V. Rau. 1991. Vol. 1. 342 pp. ISBN 0-87727—525-4. Vol. 2., revised 2005, 378 pp. ISBN 0-87727-526-2. Vol 3., revised 2005, 431 pp. ISBN 0-87727-527-0. Vol. 4. 306 pp. ISBN 0-87727-528-9.

THAI

A. U. A. Language Center Thai Course, J. Marvin Brown. Originally published by the American University Alumni Association Language Center, 1974. Reissued by Cornell Southeast Asia Program, 1991, 1992. Book 1. 267 pp. ISBN 0-87727-506-8. Book 2. 288 pp. ISBN 0-87727-507-6. Book 3. 247 pp. ISBN 0-87727-508-4.

A. U. A. Language Center Thai Course, Reading and Writing Text (mostly reading), 1979. Reissued 1997. 164 pp. ISBN 0-87727-511-4.

A. U. A. Language Center Thai Course, Reading and Writing Workbook (mostly writing), 1979. Reissued 1997. 99 pp. ISBN 0-87727-512-2.

KHMER

Cambodian System of Writing and Beginning Reader, Franklin E. Huffman. Originally published by Yale University Press, 1970. Reissued by Cornell Southeast Asia Program, 4th printing 2002. 365 pp. ISBN 0-300-01314-0.

Modern Spoken Cambodian, Franklin E. Huffman, assist. Charan Promchan, Chhom-Rak Thong Lambert. Originally published by Yale University Press, 1970. Reissued by Cornell Southeast Asia Program, 3rd printing 1991. 451 pp. ISBN 0-300-01316-7.

Intermediate Cambodian Reader, ed. Franklin E. Huffman, assist. Im Proum. Originally published by Yale University Press, 1972. Reissued by Cornell Southeast Asia Program, 1988. 499 pp. ISBN 0-300-01552-6.

Cambodian Literary Reader and Glossary, Franklin E. Huffman, Im Proum. Originally published by Yale University Press, 1977. Reissued by Cornell Southeast Asia Program, 1988. 494 pp. ISBN 0-300-02069-4.

HMONG

White Hmong-English Dictionary, Ernest E. Heimbach. 1969. 8th printing, 2002. 523 pp. ISBN 0-87727-075-9.

VIETNAMESE

Intermediate Spoken Vietnamese, Franklin E. Huffman, Tran Trong Hai. 1980. 3rd printing 1994. ISBN 0-87727-500-9.

* * *

Southeast Asian Studies: Reorientations. Craig J. Reynolds and Ruth McVey. Frank H. Golay Lectures 2 & 3. 70 pp. ISBN 0-87727-301-4.

Javanese Literature in Surakarta Manuscripts, Nancy K. Florida. Vol. 1, *Introduction and Manuscripts of the Karaton Surakarta.* 1993. 410 pp. Frontispiece, illustrations. Hard cover, ISBN 0-87727-602-1, Paperback, ISBN 0-87727-603-X. Vol. 2, *Manuscripts of the Mangkunagaran Palace.* 2000. 576 pp. Frontispiece, illustrations. Paperback, ISBN 0-87727-604-8.

Sbek Thom: Khmer Shadow Theater. Pech Tum Kravel, trans. Sos Kem, ed. Thavro Phim, Sos Kem, Martin Hatch. 1996. 363 pp., 153 photographs. ISBN 0-87727-620-X.

In the Mirror: Literature and Politics in Siam in the American Era, ed. Benedict R. O'G. Anderson, trans. Benedict R. O'G. Anderson, Ruchira Mendiones. 1985. 2nd printing 1991. 303 pp. Paperback. ISBN 974-210-380-1.

To order, please contact:

Cornell University
Southeast Asia Program Publications
95 Brown Road
Box 1004
Ithaca NY 14850

Online: http://www.einaudi.cornell.edu/southeastasia/publications/
Tel: 1-877-865-2432 (Toll free – U.S.)
Fax: (607) 255-7534

E-mail: SEAP-Pubs@cornell.edu
Orders must be prepaid by check or credit card (VISA, MasterCard, Discover).